Managing Sustainable Tourism

Managing Sustainable Tourism tackles the tough issues of tourism, such as impacts on the natural and built environment and concerns for the heritage and culture of local communities, to provide answers that produce positive economic growth for the industry. It offers practical plans for fostering harmonious relationships among local communities, the private sector, not-for-profit organizations, academic institutions, and governments at all levels, as well as developing management practices and philosophies that protect natural, built, and cultural environments while reinforcing positive and orderly economic growth. It also confronts and explains the challenges on the tourism industry with respect to climate change and global warming.

Since the first edition, there have been many important developments in the field, and this second edition has been revised and updated in the following ways:

- Updated content to reflect issues and trends, including: impact of the internet and new directions in cultural tourism, ecotourism, responsible tourism, geotourism, and pro-poor tourism;
- New and updated international case studies of successes and failures to reflect current challenges and practices;
- A complete history of sustainable tourism from ancient times to the present;
- New lecturer and student online resources including PowerPoint slides and practical scenarios.

This volume provides a wealth of information and guidance on managing sustainable tourism now and in the future and will be invaluable to educators, students, developers, entrepreneurs, investors, tourism strategists, planners and policymakers.

David L. Edgell, Sr. is a Professor of trade, tourism, and economic development and Senior Professor of Graduate Studies in sustainable tourism at East Carolina University, located in Greenville, North Carolina. In his past career he has served as consulting Vice President for Strategic Marketing at MMG Worldwide. Dr. Edgell has specialized in most of his education and work in trade, tourism, and economic development. He has authored ten books and over a hundred articles, has served as the Under Secretary of Commerce for Travel and Tourism (the U.S. Government's highest position in tourism), was the first Commissioner of Tourism for the U.S. Virgin Islands, and is a founding member of the International Academy for the Study of Tourism.

Managing Sustainable Tourism

A legacy for the future

Second Edition

David L. Edgell, Sr.

Routledge
Taylor & Francis Group

LONDON AND NEW YORK

Second edition published 2016
by Routledge
2 Park Square, Milton Park, Abingdon, Oxon OX14 4RN

and by Routledge
711 Third Avenue, New York, NY 10017

Routledge is an imprint of the Taylor & Francis Group, an informa business

First edition published by The Haworth Press 2006

British Library Cataloguing in Publication Data
A catalogue record for this book is available from the British Library

Library of Congress Cataloging in Publication Data
Names: Edgell, David L., Sr. (David Lee), 1938-
Title: Managing sustainable tourism: a legacy for the future/David L. Edgell, Sr.
Description: Second edition. | New York: Routledge, 2016. | Includes bibliographical references and index.
Identifiers: LCCN 2015033279| ISBN 9781138918634 (hbk) | ISBN 9781138918641 (pbk) | ISBN 9781315688343 (ebk)
Subjects: LCSH: Ecotourism–Management. | Heritage tourism–Management.
Classification: LCC G156.5.E26 E38 2016 | DDC 910.68/4–dc23
LC record available at http://lccn.loc.gov/2015033279

ISBN: 978-1-138-91863-4 (hbk)
ISBN: 978-1-138-91864-1 (pbk)
ISBN: 978-1-315-68834-3 (ebk)

Typeset in Frutiger
by Sunrise Setting Ltd, Brixham, UK

Dedication

This book is dedicated to the men and women of the world who strive, through their efforts in sustainable tourism, to establish a legacy of protecting our planet for future generations to enjoy;

and,

to Sarah Jane Gust, my best friend and lovely wife who supported and assisted me in writing this book about sustainable tourism.

Contents

List of illustrations   viii
List of case studies   ix
Preface   x
Acknowledgements   xii

1   A philosophic approach to sustainable tourism   1

2   The worldly travelers and a sense of sustainability   33

3   Sustainable tourism milestones: twentieth and
    twenty-first centuries   60

4   Sustainable tourism and the United Nations Millennium
    Development Goals   94

5   Rural tourism and sustainability   115

6   Sustainable tourism and the prospects for peace   137

7   Strategic planning for sustainable tourism   157

8   Marketing the sustainable tourism product   179

9   Managing sustainable tourism in the new millennium   196

10 Future world issues that will impact on managing
    sustainable tourism   215

Index   234

Illustrations

Figures

1.1	Panoramic view of the Ecotourism Lodge in Dominica	13
1.2	The relationship of ecotourism, geotourism, responsible tourism and cultural tourism to sustainable tourism	19
1.3	Map of Dominica and its major cities	21
1.4	View of the ecotourism lodge in the Kalinago Territory of Dominica	28
4.1	Prepare for globalization in sustainable tourism through partnerships at all levels	104
5.1	A mother and baby black bear in Pocosin Lakes National Wildlife Refuge	125
7.1	Tree diagram: goal-oriented tourism planning	164
8.1	Strategic marketing plan development flow chart	184
9.1	Coopetition strategy for managing sustainable tourism	202

Table

1.1	Selected sectors of the tourism industry	3

Case studies

1   The Commonwealth of Dominica as a sustainable tourism destination
    and the development of an ecotourism project within the
    Kalinago Territory   19
2   John Lawson: Father of sustainable tourism in the New World   46
3   Climate change, sustainability, and impacts on tourism – the Outer
    Banks of North Carolina   79
4   Cuban tourism at the crossroads of the modern era of sustainability 104
5   Experiential tourism – the Flint Hills and the Kansas Tallgrass Prairie
    National Preserve   127
6   Travel, the language of peace and sustainability   148
7   Peru: the Condor Lodge Ecotourism Project   170
8   Sustainable tourism and Ambergris Caye, Belize   188
9   The managerial and educational aspects in the context of
    sustainable tourism – Contentnea Creek   206
10 Sustainable tourism as a development strategy along coastlines   227

Preface

This second edition of *Managing Sustainable Tourism: A Legacy for the Future* provides the student, professional, and businessperson with the philosophy, concepts, principles, practices, and management tools to fully understand the field of sustainable tourism from a knowledge perspective and as a profession. The author of this book has extensive experience working with businesses, governments, organizations, local communities and students throughout the world on sustainable tourism issues and projects. The book is a compilation of sustainable tourism research, of experience in teaching sustainable tourism in the classroom, and based on practical consulting work in the field of sustainable tourism at the local, national and international levels.

We have a finite earth that must be conserved, protected and nurtured in order that tomorrow's generations have opportunities to enjoy the enigmatic nature of our beautiful planet. We, the current caretakers of the earth, must live and work always with the view that we have a limited natural and built environment that needs our positive attention to sustain it for the future. Those of us in the travel and tourism industry have a moral and ethical obligation to seek ways and means to communicate best practices for sustaining travel and tourism throughout the world.

Holistically, sustainable tourism is a concern for the conservation of the natural environment and of an understanding of the history, heritage and culture of humankind. We need to be conscious of conserving the earth's resources and in protecting the contributions made by the inhabitants to the world's history, heritage, and culture. As travelers journey throughout the world, they seek to visit the unique structures left behind by their ancestors and to understand the differing cultures that have developed in differing parts of the globe. Taken together, the natural environment and the history, heritage, and culture of the local community, are the ingredients that contribute to our interest in managing sustainable tourism. The question is how to best manage these resources sustainably for the next generations to enjoy.

Sustainable tourism is a part of an overall shift that recognizes that orderly economic growth, combined with concerns for the environment and quality-of-life social values, will be the driving force for long-term progress in tourism development and policies. *Managing Sustainable Tourism: A Legacy for the Future* (second edition) presents some policy prescriptions for orderly growth and development that adhere to an important set of criteria for improving the quality of life through sustainable tourism. If we do not define clear-cut directions for sustainable tourism at this juncture in the growth of tourism, there may never be another chance. This book provides new information, concepts and management principles to help map a favorable course of action for the future of sustainable tourism. Well-managed sustainable tourism links the policy guidelines and planning functions, with the social goals of tourism into a concrete set of principles to give us direction as we move ahead. With the information and precepts presented in this book, students, business people, government represen- tatives, travelers and professionals will have a complete set of conceptual tools for understanding the issues in sustainable tourism.

David L. Edgell, Sr. has a lifetime career of more than 35 years' involvement at all levels, global, national and local, in the tourism policy, planning and management arena. He had a distinguished tourism leadership and policy career in the U.S. Government, serving at one point as the Acting Under Secretary of Commerce for Travel and Tourism, the highest policy position in travel and tourism. He also held several executive positions in the U.S. Travel and Tourism Administration representing the U.S. Government as head of delegation to the World Tourism Organization, the Caribbean Tourism Organization, and tourism committees of the Organisation for Economic Co-operation and Development, the Organization of American States, and the Asia-Pacific Economic Cooperation. He was also the Executive Director for World Fairs and Expositions and led efforts to bring WorldCupUSA94 to the U.S. Later, he served in the capacity as the first Commissioner of Tourism for the U.S. Virgin Islands during which he provided leadership, management and administration for tourism development, marketing, policy, planning, budgeting, legislative relations, and invest- ment. He also worked in senior executive positions within private-sector companies involved in travel and tourism and as a private consultant. Currently, Dr. Edgell is a full time professor of tourism, trade and economic development in the School of Hospitality Leadership, College of Business, East Carolina University. He has written ten books and over 100 articles on tourism, trade, and economic development, consults on a wide variety of tourism projects, and is a frequent speaker at conferences.

You may note in this book numerous references to the book *Tourism: Principles, Practices, Philosophies* (twelfth edition) by Charles R. Goeldner and J. R. Brent Ritchie. The reason for the many citations to this book is because it is the single best textbook written about fundamental tourism issues, practical guidelines for tourism develop- ment and well-researched tourism concepts. It is used by many in the tourism industry as a key reference document in order to better understand the broad trends in travel and tourism.

Reference is often made to the book *Tourism Policy and Planning: Yesterday, Today, and Tomorrow* (second edition) by David L. Edgell, Sr., and Jason R. Swanson because it gives an overall view of sustainable tourism policy and planning. It also contains valuable background information on important tourism issues not found elsewhere in the tourism research literature. In addition, there is reference made to some infor- mation contained in the first edition of *Managing Sustainable Tourism: A Legacy for the Future.*

It is not possible to write about global issues in the travel and tourism industry without mentioning the World Tourism Organization. This organization, along with the World Travel and Tourism Council are referenced frequently in this book. Another fre- quent reference in the book is to "peace through tourism." It is absolutely clear that the opportunities for mobilizing the international community toward sustainable tourism is dependent on a more peaceful world. The old adage "When peace prevails, tourism flourishes" has a strong truthful ring to it. In that respect, the book includes a segment on the International Institute for Peace through Tourism. The book mentions a favorite quote that the present author mentions frequently: "We have not inherited the earth from our ancestors; we have only borrowed if from our children" (author unknown).

Acknowledgements

This book would not have been possible without the help, encouragement, and advice of numerous individuals over a long period of years, too many to mention herein; and the author's concern of possibly missing a special contribution from someone in the past who shared knowledge and wisdom about the tourism industry with him. However, over the past two years, when the idea for this book was being contemplated, and then, finally written, there were certain people instrumental in providing content and direction for the book. In that respect, I wish to include a special thanks to a few of the following individuals.

This book could not have been written without the support and efforts of my wife, Sarah Jane Gust. When I needed to be inspired and nudged to keep at my work, she was there for me. She read every page of the book and provided key content and edits on a continuous basis.

I wish to especially thank Ms. Philippa Mullins of Routledge for supporting my efforts to write the book and for giving me a gentle nudge to keep me on track for the completion of the book on time. Her help was greatly appreciated in every way.

In addition, I am grateful to Ms. Emma Travis of Routledge for helping me to embark on the adventure of writing this book. Her initial remarks, advice, and support were instrumental in moving the idea for writing the book. Finally, I wish to thank Mr. Daniel Bourner, editor of this book, for his patience, understanding, and efforts to improve the writing of the book.

I wish to thank Dr. Taleb Rifal, Secretary-General of the World Tourism Organization, Mr. David Scowsill, President and CEO of the World Travel and Tourism Council, and Mr. Louis D'Amore, President and Founder of the International Institute for Peace through Tourism for providing me with special important quotes on sustainable tourism that I could include in the book.

A special thanks to Mr. Louis Hill, the developer of the Ecotourism Lodge in the Commonwealth of Dominica, for information for one of the case studies and in providing me with photos I could display in the book.

I want to recognize Mr. Fred Goss, Director of the Flint Hills Discovery Center for his comments and help in work on one of the chapters and one of the case studies in the book.

I wish to thank Ms. Elaine Barr, biologist assigned to the Pocosin Lakes National Wildlife Refuge (Refuge) for her excellent comments on the flora and fauna in the Refuge. She was also nice enough to take me on a tour to see black bears in the Refuge and to provide me with photos of the black bears for use in the book.

Of special note, when I needed information, technology support and a student's viewpoint, I received all from a former student and friend Mr. Merric Jackson.

Chapter 1

A philosophic approach to sustainable tourism

"We have not inherited the earth from our ancestors; we have only borrowed it from our children."

Anonymous

The tourism stage in the twenty-first century presents profound challenges to all actors involved in the tourism industry. Consumers of tourism in the new millennium are demanding greater quality in their tourism products. They want new and different destinations, greater variety, and more flexibility in their travels. Increasingly tourists are expressing a desire for a clean environment, nature tourism experiences, adventure travel activities, and tourism products that include culture, heritage, and history. In response, more destinations have become interested in developing higher-quality tourism products and have placed greater emphasis on the natural environment and the built environment, which includes historic, heritage, and cultural sites. Furthermore, businesses, government, academia, not-for-profit, and local tourism leaders are now more likely to focus their attention on the need to develop and promote sustainability based on preserving the resources on which tourism's success depends. They want to manage sustainable tourism as a legacy to ensure that their children and grandchildren can enjoy a wide variety of quality tourism products. The result is that today's tourism destinations and products are now more concerned with being compatible with the environment, both natural and constructed.

The first chapter will present a general understanding about the travel and tourism industry and explain some of the basic principles of the tourism industry, its powerful economic impact, and a discussion of international organizations that contribute to the overall concerns for quality tourism programs. It introduces the topic of sustainable tourism and describes such subsets of sustainable tourism as ecotourism, geotourism, responsible tourism and cultural tourism to form the basis for better understanding the concept of sustainable tourism. Later chapters will introduce approaches to the management of sustainable tourism. Another important aspect of understanding sustainable tourism is to look at its origins from a historical perspective.

Chapter 2 will take on the task of introducing the reader to a historical perspective of elements of sustainable tourism through the eyes of a few selected worldly travelers. Ancient travelers were just as mesmerized by edifices and stories about the history and culture in the countries they visited as we are today. Later travelers, many of them explorers and naturalists, noted the beauty of the natural environment, the amazing differing unique species of flora and fauna, and a general interest in protecting such resources for future generations to enjoy. Fortunately many of the worldly travelers authored books and publications that allow us to see the world as they saw it and to follow the transformation of changes into our world.

Understanding tourism

In this book, the term "tourism" is used synonymously with all aspects of travel and tourism, unless otherwise specified. With respect to international tourism, this text uses the following definitions, as recommended by the World Tourism Organization (UNWTO), which is described later in this chapter.

- **Visitor:** Any person visiting a country (or community) other than that in which the person usually resides, for any reason other than following an occupation remunerated from within the country visited. This definition covers two classes of visitors: *tourist* and *excursionist*.

  o **Tourist:** A temporary visitor staying at least 24 hours in the country (or community) visited, the purpose of whose journey can be classified under one of the following headings: (a) leisure, recreation, holiday, health, study, religion, or sport; or (b) business, family, mission, or meeting.
  o **Excursionist:** A temporary visitor staying less than 24 hours in the country (or community) visited (including travelers on cruises).

- **Tourism:** In terms of balance-of-trade accounting, tourism is defined as travel and transportation and is determined as a *business service* export *from* the tourism recipient *to* the tourism generating economy.

Tourism is an inherently complex field of inquiry. It is a multifaceted industry of many sometimes unrelated parts, resisting comparability within itself and with other industries. It is an industry that cuts across many different constituent components, as indicated in Table 1.1 below.

The study of tourism incorporates such human science topics as anthropology, archeology, geography, demography, economics, history, sociology, and natural philosophy. Despite the complexities of the tourism industry, tourism in and of itself is basically the practice of traveling for business and pleasure.

The tourism industry is composed of businesses that provide various products, services, and facilities associated with tourist travel. Tourism is not a single industry but instead an amalgam of industry sectors – a demand force and a supply market, a personal experience, and a complicated international phenomenon. Tourism incorporates social, cultural, and environmental concerns beyond physical development and marketing.

Table 1.1 Selected sectors of the tourism industry

Hotels, motels and resorts
Bed and breakfast establishments and inns
Vacation rental homes and condos
Restaurants
Taverns and bars
Airlines
Cruise ships
Trains
Buses
Taxis
Automobile rentals
Attractions
Theme parks and entertainment venues
Gaming
Shopping
Boating
Skiing
Museums
Special services: spas, hair salons, etc.
Museums
Art galleries
Travel agencies
Tour operators
Tour guides
Sports events
Outdoor and recreation activities
Hiking
Camping
Fishing
Hunting
Bird-watching

It encompasses both supply and demand, more than the sum of marketing and economic development. As the world's most dynamic industry it demands a constant reassessment of its quality, variety, and sustainability for the future. Because tourism is such a fast-growing industry it must be mindful of potential issues and directions that could lead to disastrous impacts on the industry. For this reason, it is necessary to understand its powerful impact on the natural and built environment so that well-constructed polices, plans, and management practices can be put in place to ensure its future quality growth.

The popular textbook *Tourism: Principles, Practices, Philosophies* (twelfth edition, 2012) defines tourism as "the processes, activities, and outcomes arising from the relationships and the interactions among tourists, tourism suppliers, host governments, host communities, and surrounding environments that are involved in the attracting and hosting of visitors."[1]

Describing the sustainability elements in the study of tourism

Tourism has strong links to cultural and social pursuits, foreign-policy initiatives, economic development, the history and heritage of an area, environmental goals, and sustainable planning. Tourism includes the buying, selling, and management of services and products (to tourists), which might range from buying hotel rooms to selling souvenirs or managing an airline. To accomplish these complex activities, tourism demands the most creative and innovative managers, partly because tourism represents collections of perishable products. For example, if hotel rooms, airline seats, cruise-ship cabins, or restaurant tables are not filled daily and repeatedly, the point-of-sale moments to generate revenues from these products are gone forever. There is no opportunity to put such unsold products on sale at a later time, in storage, or in inventory. This immediate perishability distinguishes tourism from consumer goods, such as automobiles, sunglasses, or food sales in retail markets.[2]

Demographic changes, increasing disposable income levels, heightened emphasis on sustainability, greater availability of leisure time, new communication tools and technology, higher levels of education, emerging tourism markets, greater variety of tourism products, more flexibility in planning trips, growth in the supply of facilities and destinations, and other supplementary factors are having an impact on demand for tourism. Tourism has become one of the most dynamic industries throughout the globe as it adapts to technological change, product innovations and new markets. Tourism embraces technology in its widespread use of e-commerce tools, its application to new products such as space and undersea tourism, and in developing new methods of marketing, managing, planning, and promotion. Managing sustainable tourism in today's world adds an important dimension to the growth of tourism.

The concept of sustainability as a resource development and management philosophy is permeating all levels of policy and practice relating to tourism, from local to global. Sustainable tourism management of the natural and physical environment must, more than ever before, coexist with the economic, socio-cultural, health, safety, and security objectives of localities and nations. Finding a balance between economic growth and the protection of natural and built resources is challenging governments and businesses alike to cooperate. The tourism community faces the additional broad challenge of cooperation to support sustainable tourism – in particular, cooperation is necessary among small businesses and local communities who compete at the local level but who wish to attract a broader segment of the market from greater distances. An attempt to further explain the dynamic relationship involving "*cooperation*" at the local level to meet the "*competition*" in the broader tourism market led to the concept of "*coopetition*" (Edgell and Haenisch, 1995).[3] Coopetition has numerous applications in managing sustainable tourism resources which will be described later in this book.

This book also emphasizes strategic planning as a major management tool to achieve the goal of tourism sustainability in an ever-changing environment. By managing the development, marketing, and promotion of sustainable tourism through a strategic sustainable tourism plan, the community is able to project itself as a very special place that tourists will want to visit, return to, and possibly move to. In the final analysis, responsibly managed tourism enhances and enriches natural, heritage, and cultural values and embraces the need to preserve them so that the community and visitor have a quality tourism experience now and in the future.[4]

The importance of tourism in a global context

The twenty-first century is seeing increases in leisure time and income for millions of people. Shorter working hours in some cases, greater individual prosperity, faster and cheaper travel relative to the past, more destinations to choose from, and the impact of advanced technology have all helped to make tourism one of the fastest growing economic sectors in the world. The significance of tourism as a viable source of income and employment, and as a major factor in the balance of payments for many countries, has been attracting increasing attention on the part of government, regional and local authorities, and others with an interest in economic development. Furthermore, sustainable tourism, concerns for the environment, social conditions, and other concepts have entered the decision-making process and will forever change the way tourism grows throughout the world.

The latest research reports with respect to the growth of global travel and tourism over the past 40 years clearly demonstrate that it is growing much faster than the world economy in general and that it is likely to continue to grow rapidly in the future. The travel and tourism industry is one of the largest contributors to the world economy and it will continue to dominate the job market for the foreseeable future. Both the World Travel and Tourism Council (WTTC) and the UNWTO have been tracking tourism data over a long period of time, and with very few exceptions the trend lines of growth have been positive. With new and better data sources and improved forecasting tools, it is now possible to prepare strategic tourism plans well into the future.

According to research conducted by Oxford Economics (an arm of the Oxford University Business School) for the WTTC, travel and tourism is among the world's largest industries, at $7.6 trillion in 2014, accounting for 9.8 percent of Global Development Product and generating more than 277 million jobs in 2014 (1 in 11 of the world's total jobs). By 2025, the number of global jobs in tourism is expected to reach 356 million.[5] WTTC also produces travel and tourism economic data for individual countries and includes a comprehensive analysis with respect to the travel trends of the future.

The UNWTO reported that international tourist arrivals in 2014 grew by 4.7 percent over 2013, reaching 1.138 billion.[6] International tourism receipts reached a new record of US$1,245 billion.[7] Data provided by the UNWTO over a period of years show enormous growth trends for tourism arrivals and tourist expenditures. Of equal importance is the fact that tourism, as an export, is of critical importance to both industrialized and developing nations. As an economic factor, tourism is growing faster than the rest of the world economy in terms of export, output, value added, capital investment, and employment.

Tourism from an international perspective

Because tourism is the world's largest industry, concerns for preserving and managing the natural and built environments becomes the most important strategy for the future growth and development of the tourism industry. If international tourism is not properly planned for, implemented, and managed well we have the potential to destroy not only the natural environment, but the built environment. We have already seen many destinations fraught with overcrowding, pollution, overbuilding and other developmental nightmares that have the potential to destroy the very places we want to visit. If we don't meet these concerns now, there may not be a pleasant future for tourism development. We must act locally, nationally, and internationally to sustain our tourism-dependent resources for future generations to enjoy. We want to see quality growth for the tourism industry and this means that governments and organizations at all levels must act in unison to support sustainable tourism principles and practices, as described later in this book.

For many years, even though tourism as an economic sector was growing rapidly, it was relatively neglected as an important international economic policy issue. Much has changed today as international organizations are recognizing the broad ramifications of the tourism industry. International organizations will play a crucial role in providing the plans and policies needed for the tourism industry's quality growth in the future.

As part of the overall growth of services, tourism's recognition as an important sector in the global economy is now more frequently accepted. Key multilateral governmental policy organizations such as the United Nations (New York), the World Tourism Organization (Madrid), the Organisation for Economic Co-operation and Development (Paris), the Organization of American States (Washington, D.C.), the Asia-Pacific Economic Cooperation (Singapore), the Caribbean Tourism Organization (Barbados), and other international bodies provide important research reports and data to country governments and to a broad range of members of the tourism industry. One of their shared goals is to link tourism to other sectors of the international economy. With respect to the above mentioned organizations the present author was, for many years, the U.S. representative to these organizations and some of the following information is based on his notes.

The European Community, North American Free Trade Agreement, and other regional economic instruments are seeking to break down traditional barriers to providing and assessing tourism services across borders, which will ultimately aid international tourism. The World Travel and Tourism Council (London), the Pacific Asia Travel Association (Bangkok), and other groups representing mainly private interests and some public concerns are already establishing a higher level of cooperation and coalition building to tackle broad tourism policy issues. These changes indicate increasing recognition of the impact of tourism in the twenty-first century. The most important intergovernmental global body with respect to all aspects of tourism is the World Tourism Organization, headquartered in Madrid, Spain.

The World Tourism Organization

The World Tourism Organization (as a specialized unit of the United Nations, it is abbreviated as UNWTO) is the United Nations agency responsible for the promotion of responsible, sustainable and universally accessible tourism. It evolved through many different regional iterations, beginning with the International Congress of Official Tourist Travel Associations that was formed at The Hague, Netherlands in 1925. It became operational as the World Tourism Organization (WTO) on November 1, 1974, held its first WTO General Assembly meeting in Madrid, Spain in 1975 and established its headquarters in Madrid in the same year. In 2003, at the WTO Fifteenth General Assembly meeting, the Assembly approved the transformation of the WTO into a United Nations specialized body, which was then ratified at the United Nations General Assembly, hence the abbreviation UNWTO.

As the leading international governmental organization in the field of tourism, UNWTO promotes tourism as a driver of economic growth, inclusive of developmental and environmental sustainability, and offers leadership and support to the sector in advancing knowledge and tourism policies worldwide. The organization works in six main areas – competitiveness, sustainability, poverty reduction, capacity building, partnerships and mainstreaming – to achieve responsible, sustainable and universally accessible tourism. It encourages the implementation of the *Global Code of Ethics for Tourism*, to maximize tourism's socioeconomic contribution while minimizing its possible negative impacts, and is committed to promoting tourism as an instrument in achieving the *United Nations Millennium Development Goals*, geared towards reducing poverty and fostering sustainable development. UNWTO is also a proponent of utilizing the tourism sector as an important mechanism toward sustainable tourism, cultural exchanges and other programs aimed toward a more peaceful world.

UNWTO generates market knowledge reports, promotes competitive and sustainable tourism policies and instruments, fosters tourism education and training, and works to make tourism an effective tool for development through technical assistance projects in over 100 countries around the world. UNWTO's membership includes 156 countries, 6 Associate Members and over 400 affiliate members representing the private sector, educational institutions, tourism associations and local tourism authorities. The UNWTO General Assembly is the principal gathering of the World Tourism Organization members. It meets every two years to approve the budget and program of work and to debate topics of vital importance to the tourism sector. Every four years UNWTO members elect a Secretary-General. The Secretariat of UNWTO is led by a Secretary-General who supervises about 110 full-time staff at UNWTO's Madrid headquarters. The official languages of UNWTO are Arabic, English, French, Chinese, Russian and Spanish. The UNWTO is not only supported by governments throughout the world but also by private-sector groups, an important partner being the World Travel and Tourism Council.[7]

World Travel and Tourism Council

The World Travel and Tourism Council (WTTC), founded in 1990 and headquartered in London, UK is a global non-profit, non-governmental organization dedicated to providing important data, communications, and information with respect to the world travel and tourism industry. Its composition of members includes approximately 150 chief executive officers, presidents and chairs of companies from all the industry sectors that make up the travel and tourism industry – airlines, airports, hotels, cruise lines, travel agencies, tourism operators, travel technology suppliers and others. The WTTC works to raise awareness of travel and tourism's huge capacity to have a positive influence on the world, including not only with respect to providing economic growth, but as a driver of peace, creating a wider understanding of cultures and communities, and supporting efforts toward managing sustainable tourism.

The WTTC is renowned for conducting in-depth research. For the last 25 years WTTC has spearheaded global analysis of the economic importance of the travel and tourism industry. WTTC's research programs, in partnership with Oxford Economics (a quality economic forecasting entity within the Business College of Oxford University), produce world tourism statistics and research accepted throughout the global travel and tourism industry.[8]

WTTC is also concerned with social issues and is a strong advocate and supporter of global sustainable tourism efforts and world programs aimed toward peace initiatives through tourism. Both WTTC and UNWTO have worked on peace-through-tourism issues, a topic discussed elsewhere in this book. There are also regional organizations that, in essence, support many of the same objectives of WTTC and UNWTO in furthering socioeconomic goals of the travel and tourism industry. The following are brief notes regarding tourism activities with respect to such regional organizations as the Organisation for Economic Co-operation and Development, the Organization of American States, the Asia-Pacific Economic Cooperation, the Caribbean Tourism Organization and the International Institute for Peace through Tourism.

Tourism Committee of the Organisation for Economic Co-operation and Development

The Organisation for Economic Co-operation and Development (OECD) initially included 18 European countries and the United States and Canada. OECD (headquartered in Paris, France) now includes 34 member countries, spanning the world from North and South America to Europe and the Asia-Pacific region. The "Tourism Committee" of the OECD, created in 1948, acts as the forum to provide an in-depth analysis of tourism trends and policy developments and for monitoring tourism policies and structural changes affecting the development of domestic and international tourism in the member countries. The OECD concentrates on economic cooperation and development, but also is a strong proponent of sustainable tourism.[9]

While the OECD actively promotes the sustainable economic growth of tourism it also provides valuable reports on non-economic issues. For example, the Tourism Committee cooperates on a broad range of tourism policy issues, including sustainable tourism, climate change and tourism, and many other important tourism concerns. OECD tourism efforts often supplement information provided by the UNWTO, the United Nations Environmental Program, the International Labour Organization, the Asia-Pacific Economic Cooperation and the European Commission.

The Inter-American Travel Congress of the Organization of American States

Of the tourism related organizations described herein, the Organization of American States (OAS) is the world's oldest regional organization, dating back to the First International Conference of American States, held in Washington, D.C., on April 14, 1890. The OAS currently has 35 member states and is headquartered in Washington, D.C. Within the OAS, matters pertaining to travel and tourism are delegated to the Inter-American Travel Congress (IATC). The IATC is the instrument of the OAS responsible for ensuring and enhancing the important role played by travel and tourism in the economic, social, cultural and educational sectors within the member states.[10]

On January 31, 1997 the IATC issued an important report titled "Sustaining Tourism by Managing Its Natural and Heritage Resources." The essence of the report stated that "sustainable tourism development is dependent on policies which seek to include a harmonious relationship among local communities, the private sector, and governments in developmental practices that protect natural, built and cultural environments compatible with economic growth . . . Sustainable tourism management of the natural and physical environment, more than ever before, must coexist with economic, socio-cultural, and health and safety objectives of localities and nations." This philosophy on sustainable tourism continues to be an important goal of the IATC.[11]

The Asia-Pacific Economic Cooperation Tourism Working Group

The Asia-Pacific Economic Cooperation (APEC), headquartered in Singapore, consists of 21 Pacific Rim countries and seeks to promote free trade and economic coopera-tion throughout the Asia-Pacific region. Within the structure of APEC is a Tourism Working Group (TWG), which was formed in 1991 to foster economic development in the Asia-Pacific region through sustainable tourism. Sustainable tourism is a key eco-nomic driver for the Asia-Pacific region, creating jobs and promoting investment and development.

TWG's objective is to foster economic development in the Asia-Pacific region through sustainable tourism, recognizing that tourism is one of the region's fastest growing industries and is of significant importance to the economic development of APEC economies. The APEC Tourism Charter has as its objectives:

● Removal of impediments in tourism business and investment
● Increase mobility of visitors and demand for tourism goods and services
● Sustainable management of tourism outcomes and impacts
● Enhance recognition and understanding of tourism as a vehicle for economic and social development

APEC has been an early leader in sustainable tourism. In 2001 APEC and the Pacific Asia Travel Association issued a "Code for Sustainable Tourism" (there is more information about this code later in this book). In 2002 APEC's Tourism Working Group issued one of the most important sustainable tourism documents, titled "Public/Private Partnerships for Sustainable Tourism: Delivering a Sustainability Strategy for Tourism Destinations." This report set the tone for managing sustainable tourism in the APEC region.[12]

The Caribbean Tourism Organization

No other region in the world is more dependent on tourism as an economic develop-ment strategy than the Caribbean nations (where collectively tourism accounts for almost three quarters of their economies). The Caribbean Tourism Organization (CTO), with headquarters in Barbados, comprises 32 member countries. The primary objective of the CTO is to provide to and through its members the services and information nec-essary for the development of sustainable tourism for the economic and social benefit of the Caribbean people. The CTO's vision and purpose is "to position the Caribbean as the most desirable, year round, warm weather destination by 2017 and our purpose is Leading Sustainable Tourism – One Sea, One Voice, One Caribbean." [13]

In 2006 the Secretary General of CTO, along with the Secretary General of the World Tourism Organization and high level participants of the Organization of American States, The Bahamas Ministry of Tourism, the United Nations Environmental Program, and the faculty of the University of the West Indies, and other knowledgeable tourism authorities (including the author of this book), met in Nassau, The Bahamas to discuss "Maximizing Economic Benefits & Sustaining Tourism in Development." This conference set the stage for numerous new initiatives for managing sustainable tourism in the Caribbean.[14] Later, in 2014, a more comprehensive conference was organized by UNWTO, Ministry of Tourism of The Bahamas and the Inter-American Bank and held in Nassau, Bahamas, to share knowledge and new concepts that had been learned from more recent information on sustainable tourism development in Island States.

The International Institute for Peace through Tourism

While the International Institute for Peace through Tourism (IIPT) has as its basic philosophy the goal of fostering tourism initiatives aimed toward a more peaceful world, it sees sustainable tourism as a potential driving force toward global peace. Its mission statement includes the following words: "The IIPT is a not for profit organization dedicated to fostering and facilitating tourism initiatives which contribute to international understanding and cooperation, an improved quality of environment, the preservation of heritage, and through these initiatives, helping to bring about a peaceful and sustainable world." Later, in a separate chapter on peace through tourism, additional attributes of IIPT's sustainable tourism policy approach will be presented.

A summary with respect to international organizations and sustainable tourism

A common theme in all of the organizations described above is their interest in sustainable tourism policies. There are many additional international organizations engaged in sustainable tourism programs, some of which will be mentioned later in this book. However, the just-described organizations have been leaders and strong proponents for sustainable tourism policies and programs over a long period of time.

Educational institutions for the study of travel, tourism, and hospitality

As the travel and tourism industry has grown, there has been a greater demand for well-educated and well-trained professionals and managers. For example, new technology being introduced in the tourism industry is demanding managers who understand the need to provide tourist information through a variety of internet and social media sources, as well as navigation systems. A second example on the horizon will be employment opportunities in the tourism industry related to new advances in space tourism. In addition, sustainable tourism is beginning to take a front-row seat in the future of worldwide tourism programs, changing the way some tourism destinations operate and presenting new sustainable tourism type positions never dreamed of in the past. The success of the travel and tourism industry in the global environment will ultimately depend on the professionalism of its workforce. Much progress needs to be made in fostering policies to improve tourism education and training.

Economic and non-economic benefits

Tourism is an economic activity that provides local destinations, states, provinces, and/or countries with opportunities for new sources of economic growth and for additional foreign-currency exchange earnings. In effect, tourism helps local communities increase their economic development, realize increased revenues, create new jobs, benefit from a diverse economy, add new products, generate additional income, spawn new businesses, and contribute to overall economic integration while enriching the public and private partnerships and improving the quality of life of the local citizenry. The impacts tourism has on non-economic benefits include stimulating cultural exchanges, providing a better understanding of the local history, heritage and culture, and broadening the visitors' knowledge about a destination's natural environment, all of which are essential to sustainable tourism growth. Gradually, destinations throughout today's world are recognizing that for their destination to succeed, it must adhere to sustainable tourism principles and practices. In this regard it is important for destinations, communities, governments, and travelers to understand just what connotes the field of study of sustainable tourism.

Understanding sustainable tourism

The author of this book first became interested in what would become the study of sustainable tourism in 1990, when he published the book *International Tourism Policy* (Edgell, 1990). He stated in the opening paragraph of that book:

> International tourism in the twenty-first century will be a major vehicle for fulfilling people's aspirations for a higher quality of life, a part of which will be through facilitating more authentic social relationships between individuals and, it is hoped, laying the groundwork for a peaceful society through global touristic contacts. International tourism also has the potential to be one of the most important stimulants for global improvement in the social, cultural, economic, political, and ecological dimensions of future lifestyles. Finally, tourism will be a principal factor for creating greater international understanding and goodwill and a primary ingredient for peace on earth. This supports the author's view that the highest purpose of tourism policy is to integrate the economic, political, cultural, intellectual, and environmental benefits of tourism cohesively with people, destinations, and countries in order to improve the global quality of life and provide a foundation for peace and prosperity.[15]

In essence this paragraph provides the foundation for the author's philosophic approach to sustainable tourism.

The challenges of managing the dimensions of sustainable tourism inclusive of the natural environment and the built environment – history, heritage, and culture – and balancing those concerns with economic development is critical at this stage in the tourism industry. Understanding responsible tourism, community-based tourism, the impact of the tourism industry on poverty alleviation, rural tourism development and sustainability, and climate change issues presents a unique set of questions that need to be answered. This book will assess policy and planning concepts for sustainable tourism and suggest strategies crucial to sustainable tourism development.

The first edition of *Managing Sustainable Tourism* provided an uncomplicated, straightforward and insightful view of the interfacing of sustainability and tourism. It attempted to tackle tough issues like negative environmental impact and cultural degradation and provide commonsense answers that don't sacrifice positive economic growth. It noted that sustainable tourism is a part of an overall shift that recognizes that orderly economic growth, combined with concerns for the environment and quality-of-life social values, will be the driving force for long-term progress in tourism development and policies. In other words, sustainable tourism management of the natural and physical environment must, more than ever before, coexist with the economic, socio-cultural, health, safety, and security objectives of localities and nations. The book emphasized that strategic planning is the principal management tool to achieve the goal of tourism sustainability in an ever-changing world.[16]

The most popular tourism textbook, *Tourism: Principles, Practices, Philosophies* (twelfth edition, Goeldner and Brent Ritchie, 2012), suggests the following challenges as very important to sustainable tourism:

1 Managing the dynamic growth of tourism while maintaining sustainability
2 Poverty alleviation: Meeting tourism's commitment to contribute to the UN's foremost millennium goal of halving world poverty by 2015
3 Maintaining support for conservation
4 Ensuring the health, safety, and security of tourists
5 Addressing the effects of climate change

The book also discusses the difficult sustainable tourism issue of "carrying capacity," defining it as "the maximum amount of development, use, growth or change that a site or destination can endure without an unacceptable alteration in the physical environment, the community's social fabric, and/or the local economy, and without an unacceptable decline in the quality of experience gained by the visitor."[17]

Defining sustainable tourism

The concept of sustainable tourism is a part of an overall shift that recognizes that orderly economic growth, combined with concerns for the environment and quality-of-life social values, will be the driving force for long-term progress in tourism development and policies. In practice, sustainable tourism links the planning functions of tourism development with the social goals of tourism into a concrete set of guidelines to give us direction as we move ahead into the future. This book stresses that positive sustainable tourism development is dependent on forward-looking policies and new management philosophies that seek harmonious relations between local communities, the private sector, not-for-profit organizations, academic institutions, and governments at all levels to develop practices that protect natural, built, and cultural environments in a way compatible with economic growth.

In the first edition of *Managing Sustainable Tourism: A Legacy for the Future* (Edgell, 2006) the author stated that "Sustainable tourism, properly managed, can become a major vehicle for the realization of humankind's highest aspirations in the quest to achieve economic prosperity while maintaining social, cultural, and environmental integrity."[18] Some aspects of sustainable tourism have remained the same over the past few years, but new precepts have also come forward that need to be discussed.

Figure 1.1 Panoramic view of the Ecotourism Lodge in Dominica
(Photo: Louis Hill)

Components of sustainable tourism such as ecotourism, geotourism, responsible tourism and cultural tourism are elements of tourism that have largely evolved from the mid-1980s. To better understand sustainable tourism (defined later in this book) it is helpful to know something about ecotourism, geotourism, responsible tourism and cultural tourism.

Ecotourism today

In today's world the etymology for the term "ecotourism" gives credit to the Mexican architect Héctor Ceballos-Lascuráin, who coined the word in 1983. His original description of the term was:

> Ecotourism is tourism that involves traveling to relatively undisturbed natural areas with the specific object of studying, admiring, and enjoying the scenery and its wild plants and animals, as well as any existing cultural aspects found in these areas. Ecotourism implies a scientific, esthetic, or philosophical approach, although the 'ecotourist' is not required to be a professional scientist, artist, or philosopher. The main point is that the person who practices ecotourism has the opportunity of immersing him or herself in nature in a way that most people cannot enjoy in their routine, urban existences. This person will eventually acquire a consciousness and knowledge of the natural environment together with its cultural aspects that will convert him into somebody keenly involved in conservation issues.[19]

Many different organizations, countries, and so-called experts in ecotourism have provided differing definitions of ecotourism. However, most of us who have labored in the field of ecotourism and sustainable tourism for many years generally accept the definition of ecotourism as set forth in 1990 by The International Ecotourism Society (TIES), which defines ecotourism as "Responsible travel to natural areas that conserves the environment and improves the well-being of local people." In addition to defining ecotourism, TIES ecotourism principles include:

- Minimize impact
- Build environmental and cultural awareness and respect
- Provide positive experiences for both visitors and hosts
- Provide direct financial benefits for conservation
- Provide financial benefits and empowerment for local people
- Raise sensitivity to host countries' political, environmental, and social climate[20]

TIES' definition and principles provide wide latitude for expressing differing and expanding views on the practices of ecotourism. For example, one of the foremost experts on ecotourism, Martha Honey, expands on TIES' principles and adds practical guidelines for ecotourism:

- Involves travel to natural destinations
- Minimizes impact
- Builds environmental awareness
- Provides direct financial benefits for conservation
- Provides financial benefits and empowerment for local people
- Respects local culture
- Supports human rights and democratic movements[21]

The case study at the end of this chapter, "The Commonwealth of Dominica as a sustainable tourism destination and the development of an ecotourism project within the Kalinago Territory," will expand on some of the practicalities of ecotourism and its interrelationship with sustainable tourism.

Geotourism

Geotourism, like ecotourism, is a subset of the more encompassing term "sustainable tourism." In 1995, geologist Thomas Hose developed the early definition of geotourism as follows:

> The provision of interpretive and service facilities to enable tourists to acquire knowledge and understanding of the geology and geomorphology of a site including its contribution to the development of the Earth sciences beyond the level of mere aesthetic appreciation.[22]

This definition is heavily entrenched in "geological" tourism and is used extensively throughout the world. However, in this book a quite different definition of geotourism is utilized that is more closely associated with sustainable tourism as later defined.

Largely promoted and used in the United States of America, there is a geotourism concept unlike that devised by geologist Thomas Hose; instead of the focus on "geological" tourism it focuses on "geographical" tourism. In this sense geotourism is defined by *National Geographic's Center for Sustainable Destinations* as ". . . tourism that sustains or enhances the geographical character of a place – its environment, culture, aesthetics, heritage, and the well-being of its residents." This idea was first coined in

1997 by Jonathan Tourtellot, Senior Editor of *National Geographic Traveler*, and his wife Sally Bensusen.

In 2002 the *Travel Industry Association of America* (renamed in 2009 as the *U.S. Travel Association*) in conjunction with *National Geographic Traveler* magazine produced a major study titled *Geotourism: The New Trend in Travel*, which in Phase I studied travelers' environmental and cultural attitudes and behaviors. It found that 55 million American travelers are inclined to exhibit geotourism attitudes and behaviors. In Phase II it was noted that one in every three U.S. travelers said they were influenced by the actions of travel companies with respect to protecting the environment and/or sustaining the local culture.[23]

The National Geographic Society has developed a "National Geographic Geotourism Charter," based on 13 principles that can be utilized by destinations and countries:

Integrity of place: Enhance geographical character by developing and improving it in ways distinctive to the locale, reflective of its natural and cultural heritage, so as to encourage market differentiation and cultural pride.

International codes: Adhere to the principles embodied in the World Tourism Organization's Global Code of Ethics for Tourism and the Principles of the Cultural Tourism Charter established by the International Council on Monuments and Sites.

Market selectivity: Encourage growth in tourism market segments most likely to appreciate, respect, and disseminate information about the distinctive assets of the locale.

Market diversity: Encourage a full range of appropriate food and lodging facilities, so as to appeal to the entire demographic spectrum of the geotourism market and so maximize economic resiliency over both the short and long term.

Tourist satisfaction: Ensure that satisfied, excited geotourists bring new vacation stories home and send friends off to experience the same thing, thus providing continuing demand for the destination.

Community involvement: Base tourism on community resources to the extent possible, encouraging local small businesses and civic groups to build partnerships to promote and provide a distinctive, honest visitor experience and market their locales effectively. Help businesses develop approaches to tourism that build on the area's history and culture, including food and drink, artisanry, performance arts, and so on.

Community benefit: Encourage micro- to medium-size enterprises and tourism business strategies that emphasize economic and social benefits to involved communities, especially poverty alleviation, with clear communication of the destination stewardship policies required to maintain those benefits.

Protection and enhancement of destination appeal: Encourage businesses to sustain natural habitats, heritage sites, aesthetic appeal, and local culture. Prevent degradation by keeping volumes of tourists within maximum acceptable limits. Seek business models that can operate profitably within those limits. Use persuasion, incentives, and legal enforcement as needed.

Land use: Anticipate development pressures and apply techniques to prevent undesired overdevelopment and degradation. Contain resort and vacation-home sprawl, especially on coasts and islands, so as to retain a diversity of natural and scenic environments and ensure continued resident access to waterfronts. Encourage major self-contained tourism attractions, such as large-scale theme parks and convention centers unrelated to character of place, to be sited in needier locations with no significant ecological, scenic, or cultural assets.

Conservation of resources: Encourage businesses to minimize water pollution, solid waste, energy consumption, water usage, landscaping chemicals, and overly bright night-time lighting. Advertise these measures in a way that attracts the large, environmentally sympathetic tourist market.

Planning: Recognize and respect immediate economic needs without sacrificing long-term character and the geotourism potential of the destination. Where tourism attracts in-migration of workers, develop new communities that themselves constitute a destination enhancement. Strive to diversify the economy and limit population influx to sustainable levels. Adopt public strategies for mitigating practices that are incompatible with geotourism and damaging to the image of the destination.

Interactive interpretation: Engage both visitors and hosts in learning about the place. Encourage residents to show off the natural and cultural heritage of their communities, so that tourists gain a richer experience and residents develop pride in their locales.

Evaluation: Establish an evaluation process to be conducted on a regular basis by an independent panel representing all stakeholder interests, and publicize evaluation results.[24]

Responsible tourism

A third main component in supporting the concept of sustainable tourism as dealt with in this book is a relatively new term referred to as "responsible tourism." The fundament for the term responsible tourism was educed from an initial "White Paper on the Development and Promotion of Tourism in South Africa" (May, 1996). After numerous meetings, discussions, reviews, suggestions by international tourism specialists and others, a "responsible tourism" policy evolved. In this paper, responsible tourism was described as "tourism that promotes responsibility to the environment through its sustainable use; responsibility to involve local communities in the tourism industry; responsibility for the safety and security of visitors and responsible government, employees, employers, unions and local communities."[25]

In 2002, Cape Town, South Africa hosted the first conference on "Responsible Tourism in Destinations," just prior to the Johannesburg, South Africa "World Summit on Sustainable Development." The Cape Town conference had 280 delegates from 20 countries and amongst other policy statements included in the "Cape Town Declaration" a reference to "work with others to take responsibility for achieving the economic, social and environmental components of responsible and sustainable tourism." This Declaration set the planning strategy for the future development of policy guidelines for responsible tourism.

In 2009, the City of Cape Town's Responsible Tourism Policy provided a framework for the management of tourism within the municipal area of the city, which has now been generally adopted as a description of responsible tourism:

- Minimizes negative economic, environmental and social impacts
- Generates greater economic benefits for local people and enhances the well-being of host communities
- Improves working conditions and access to the industry
- Involves local people in decisions that affect their lives and life chances

- Makes positive contributions to the conservation of natural and cultural heritage, embracing diversity
- Provides more enjoyable experiences for tourists through more meaningful connections with local people, and a greater understanding of local cultural, social and environmental issues
- Provides access for physically challenged people, and
- Is culturally sensitive, encourages respect between tourists and hosts, and builds local pride and confidence[26]

While responsible tourism is not yet universally accepted, it continues to gain adherents as more information becomes available. Certainly there are strong proponents of the concept, especially through such organizations as the International Centre for Responsible Tourism, headquartered in the United Kingdom with many sub offices throughout the world, and in the United States through the Center for Responsible Travel, located in Washington, D.C. and at Stanford University in Stanford, California.

Cultural tourism

The last of the four subsets of sustainable tourism described herein is cultural tourism. In this segment on cultural tourism the term will be used inclusive of the history, heritage, and culture of a destination. In most respects cultural tourism has been practiced since ancient times. Chapter 2 of this book will take the reader back to visit one of the earliest recorded cultural travelers, the historian and travel writer Herodotus. *Newgrange*, one of the oldest surviving buildings in the world, predating the trilithons at Stonehenge by 700 years and older than any pyramid in Egypt, was an early cultural structure depicting the ancient culture of Ireland. In addition, there are living cultural cities like the old walled city of Dubrovnik, Croatia, which received the United Nations Educational, Scientific and Cultural Organization's (UNESCO) designation as a World Heritage Site.

UNESCO became an operating arm of the United Nations in 1946 with the purpose "to contribute to peace and security by promoting collaboration among nations through education, science and culture in order to further universal respect for justice, for the rule of law and for the human rights and fundamental freedoms which are affirmed for the peoples of the world, without distinction of race, sex, language or religion, by the Charter of the United Nations." From a cultural tourism perspective, the designation of World Heritage Site status by UNESCO automatically bestows on a site a recognition that it is a special place for cultural tourism. In addition, most countries have their individual cultural tourism programs.[27]

For the United States, the most recognized program of cultural heritage tourism is the one developed by the National Trust for Historic Preservation (NTHP). In 1993 NTHP outlined "five principles" and "four steps" for a local community to begin a cultural heritage tourism program. NTHP's definition of cultural heritage tourism is "traveling to experience the places and activities that authentically represent the stories and people of the past and present. It includes historic, cultural and natural resources."[28]

There are many individuals and organizations that continue to separate cultural tourism into two parts: "cultural tourism" and "heritage tourism." If it suits their purposes to do so then they should do it. In 1995, then President of the United States Bill Clinton held a special *White House Conference on Travel and Tourism* (this author participated in that conference) and among other tourism principles a practical defini-tion for U.S. cultural and heritage tourism was developed as follows: "travel directed toward experiencing the arts, heritage, and special character of a place." The more universal definition for cultural tourism mentioned earlier in this section, with the inclusion of the word (and concept) "heritage" within cultural tourism, will suffice for describing sustainable tourism later in this book. From a broad tourism perspective, history, heritage, and culture inclusive as cultural tourism is pervasive when a commu-nity is marketing its tourism product.

A foundation for sustainable tourism

Sustainable tourism is a very positive response in an industry that sometimes ignores any venture that does not have immediate dollar signs to invigorate its development. Many communities are beginning to realize that if they manage tourism well, they can reap the economic rewards, conserve the environment, and improve social conditions. This paradigm shift toward careful management of sustainable tourism resources needs to be well understood if we are to leave a positive tourism legacy for future generations.

It is clear that properly managed sustainable tourism can lead not only to economic and environmental (built and natural) benefits, but also to the peace of mind that sites of historical significance, traditional culture, and native species will be available for this and future generations to appreciate. Some of the success in managing sus-tainability in the right way will come from good training, education, and public awareness. The training of students, employees and professionals will help develop leaders and managers qualified to tackle the sustainable tourism challenges in this millennium. If local, state/province, and national governments, working in tandem with private-sector companies, can devise good sustainable tourism policies and prac-tices, set strategic planning guidelines that emphasize positive goals and objectives for the environment, and manage resources conservatively, the world will benefit from quality tourism practices and programs.

Tourist destinations that encompass sustainability in their tourism products add a special dimension to economic growth and quality-of-life benefits for the community. Unspoiled natural ecosystems, well-maintained historic sites, and cultural heritage sites lead to satisfied visitors. To make this happen, there must be efforts to inspire busi-nesses and people to accept good practices, whether they choose to enhance the natu-ral scenic beauty of a destination as it intermingles with flora and fauna or enrich the built environment. In that respect, a major challenge is to provide best practices to help guide the management process and provide future generations with the opportunity to enjoy and benefit from sustainable tourism. That is what this book is all about.

For the time being, however, Figure 1.2 depicts the relationships between ecotour-ism, geotourism, responsible tourism, and cultural tourism, as discussed in this chapter. These four pillars of the foundation of sustainable tourism will resurface in later chap-ters of this book.

In Chapter 2 of this book a brief description of the early beginnings of what has become known today as sustainable tourism will be presented through the eyes of a few worldly travelers. The interest in cultural travel can be found in many of the early ancient civilizations. Fortunately, a few of the early worldly travelers provided written documents of what they saw, learned, and experienced regarding the places they visited.

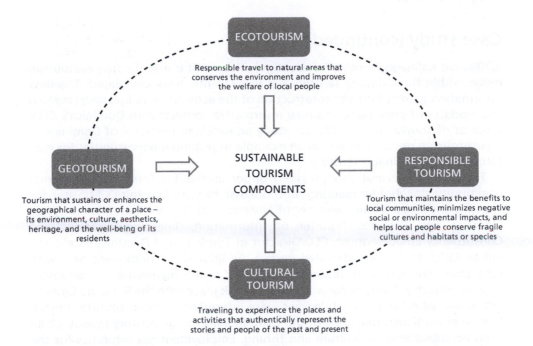

Figure 1.2 The relationship of ecotourism, geotourism, responsible tourism and cultural tourism to sustainable tourism

Case study 1: The Commonwealth of Dominica as a sustainable tourism destination and the development of an ecotourism project within the Kalinago Territory

"When we show our respect for other living things, they respond with respect for us."

Arapaho Proverb

Background

This case study was written by the present author and is based largely on information, data, and research collected as a result of two separate trips taken by him to the Commonwealth of Dominica and on updated information on the Commonwealth of Dominica from Edgell and Swanson's book *Tourism Policy and Planning: Yesterday, Today, and Tomorrow* (2013). The present author's second trip to Dominica in 2012 was taken as a knowledgeable volunteer expert on ecotourism oriented toward the needs of the 3,000 Kalinago natives in Dominica. Along with two other individuals, he provided advice on the feasibility and direction of the ecotourism project that has taken place within the confines of the

(Continued)

Case study (continued)

3,700-acre Kalinago Territory (reservation). The result is that the first ecotourism lodge within the Kalinago Territory has just recently been completed. The new information gained from the construction of the ecotourism lodge, new research and updates of prior facts, and new informative contacts with Dominica's CEO/Director of Tourism makes this case study an excellent portrayal of Dominica as an ecotourism destination and as an example of potential opportunities for ecotourism in the Kalinago Territory.

The author's second visit provided opportunities for formal and informal community stakeholder meetings and discussions with Dominica's Minister for Tourism and Legal Affairs; Minister of Environment, Natural Resources, Physical Planning and Fisheries; Minister of Information, Telecommunications and Constituency Empowerment; CEO/Director of Tourism; and Dominica's Kalinago Indian Chief and other interested parties. Additional meetings were held with ecotourism entrepreneurs, business people and others involved with Dominica's tourism industry. A very important meeting took place with the Kalinago Chief to determine whether the Carib Indians were interested in an ecotourism project. The Chief explained that most of the Carib Indians in the territory (about 3,000) lived on subsistence agriculture and fishing. Employment opportunities for the Kalinago Indians were very limited. Thus, an opportunity to become part of Dominica's tourism industry through the building of an ecotourism lodge had great appeal for most of the tribal members.[29]

By 2013 the stakeholders were on board with respect to the Kalinago Ecotourism Project. Initial financing was arranged to build the first ecotourism lodge. An ideal site was located; the necessary clearances, permissions, and permits were in order and work on the project began. As work on the project proceeded, extreme care was taken to protect and maintain the natural environment where the lodge was being developed. The initial ecotourism lodge has been completed and will likely be the springboard for other such initiatives in the Kalinago Territory. This unique case study discusses some of the background information for the ecotourism project, which is ultimately aimed toward utilizing ecotourism to contribute to the socioeconomic well-being of the Kalinago society in Dominica.

Introduction: the beautiful island of the Commonwealth of Dominica

In Megan Eileen McDonough's article "Discovering Dominica" in the November 2014 issue of *US Airways Magazine*, she described and introduced Dominica in this way: "If you've ever dreamed of a real-life Never-land, Dominica is as close as it gets. Here in this bubble of beauty, where rainbows dominate the skies and pirate-like ships glide along the deep blue waters, nature reigns supreme." She described the beauty of the island, its many unique hiking trails, and the bountiful flora that could be seen throughout. Her comments make it very clear that Dominica is an exceptional "nature island" with a population yielding a distinctive culture and heritage that offers the traveler memory-making adventures available nowhere else in the world.[30]

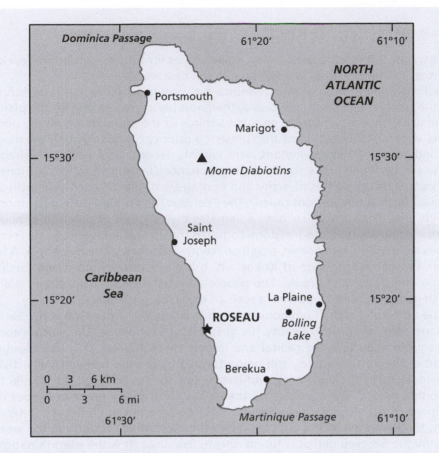

Figure 1.3 Map of Dominica and its major cities (Image: CIA)

Dominica, the nature island of the Caribbean

Dominica is truly the "Garden of Eden" for naturalists, nature enthusiasts, and adventurous travelers. Dominica's biodiversity and ecosystems yield flora so different and unique from that which exists in other countries of the world. The island is located midway along the Eastern Caribbean archipelago in the tranquil Caribbean Sea between the two lovely French overseas region islands of Guadeloupe and Martinique. As noted from the map in Figure 1.3, it is a small island. Yet it contains majestic mountains, serene coastlines, clear fast-flowing rivers, geothermal springs, unbelievable greenery throughout the island, lush forests, and magnificent water-falls. Mother Nature certainly left the island with bountiful amounts of different types of birds and butterflies, flowers of every variety. In most parts of the island the soil is rich in nutrients conducive to good agriculture production, the mainstay industry of the island. In addition, the waters along the coastline are teeming with fish, the other main sector of the economy. While Dominica's tourism industry is small in comparison with some other Caribbean islands, it is an important growth

(Continued)

Case study (continued)

industry for the country, with many opportunities for future ecotourism development, as will be described in detail later in this case study.

A little-known destination, Dominica has preserved more national forests,
marine reserves and parks, per capita, than possibly anywhere else on the planet.
Dominica's tropical rainforests cover two thirds of the island. It is sparsely populated, with 72,150 inhabitants that present a distinct culture through the mix of
the indigenous Kalinago Indians, and English, French, and African heritages.
These can be found in the food, arts, music, dances, languages, and traditions of
the people. Much of this diversity and heritage is displayed each year with the
carnival-festival celebrations called "The Real Mas" celebrated during the month
of February. The Catholic religion dominates the religious population although
there is complete religious freedom. English is the official language. Some French
is spoken and Antillean Creole, based on French, is spoken by many people. A few
speak the native language of Kokoy which is a mix of Leeward Island English-
Creole and Dominican Creole. The people are very friendly, helpful and polite,
which makes the visit to Dominica such an enjoyable experience.

The "motto" for the Commonwealth of Dominica is "After God is the Earth"
and the anthem is "Isle of Beauty, Isle of Splendor." Land-wise, Dominica is about
290 square miles and the capital and largest city is Roseau. It is the youngest
island in the Lesser Antilles, still being formed by geothermal-volcanic activity,
as evidenced by the world's second-largest hot spring, Boiling Lake. While the
Calibishie area in the country's northeast has some sandy beaches it does not
compare to the degree of beaches found elsewhere in the Caribbean. Interestingly, the island has 365 rivers, considered the most of any country in the world.
The unique Sisserou parrot is found only in Dominica. It is the island's national
bird and is featured on the national flag. The waters off the coast of Dominica
are rich in fish life and are home to several species of whales and dolphins. Like
most of the Caribbean islands, Dominica is vulnerable to hurricanes but generally
the weather is relatively mild, with bountiful amounts of rain.

The Commonwealth of Dominica as one of "the world's best islands"

From 2004 to 2010, the *National Geographic's Center for Sustainable Tourism Initiative* in conjunction with a team from Leeds Metropolitan University in England
conducted a series of complex global surveys. Over this time period, several
thousand destinations were rated, with the results being published by *National
Geographic Traveler*. The ratings were based on the use of six criteria: (1) environmental conditions; (2) social/cultural integrity; (3) condition of historic structures; (4) aesthetics; (5) tourism management; and (6) outlook. For the 2007
survey, a panel of 522 experts in sustainable tourism and destination stewardship
(this author being one of the experts) donated time to review conditions in 111
selected islands and archipelagos. Their report, containing the ratings on the
sustainability of the islands, appeared in the November/December 2007 issue of
National Geographic Traveler magazine.

The categories listed in *National Geographic Traveler* were "Best-Rated Islands," "Islands Doing Well," "Islands in the Balance," and "Islands in Trouble." The "Best-Rated Islands" were described as "In excellent shape, relatively unspoiled, and likely to remain so." Dominica's rating fell into the "Best-Rated Islands," with comments from the experts who made the ratings as: "Rugged, green, friendly . . . offers an authentic, unspoiled experience, with natural and cultural amenities." The only other Caribbean island with this high a rating was the Grenadines.

Tourism statistics for the Commonwealth of Dominica

With respect to other small islands in the Caribbean, Dominica is very competitive in the numbers of visitors to the island. The Caribbean Tourism Organization (CTO), which Dominica and the Caribbean countries are members of, produces most of the accepted tourism statistics for the region. The CTO's report, titled "Tourist (Stop-over) Arrivals and Cruise Passenger Visits in 2014," dated January 13, 2015, lists tourist arrivals to Dominica at 68,791. Comparable island numbers of visitors would include Anguilla with 62,353, St. Kitts and Nevis with 65,872 and Saint Vincent and the Grenadines with 56,581. Regarding cruise passenger visits, the CTO report shows that Dominica had 191,809. Those numbers are higher than the 153,064 cruise passenger visits for Grenada and the 142,270 cruise passenger visits for Martinique.[31]

A key question is: Can a nature island like Dominica maintain its image as a nature island and at the same time increase the numbers of visitors it receives? This is an important question and the answers are many and varied. Certainly a small island with a limited population and low marketing budget is not likely to be able to compete, from a marketing standpoint, with some of the larger Caribbean islands. In addition, Dominica, in comparison with most of the Caribbean countries, has not been marketing the island as a tourism destination for as long as others and Dominica's tourism programs are not as fully developed. While Dominica's tourism office is well organized and managed, it has few resources and has little opportunity to partner with many businesses. Furthermore, to keep the island as a special place for nature tourism it must not try to lure hotel chains to the island. Therefore most of the marketing effort depends on participating in trade shows, producing and distributing tourism brochures and building and utilizing an effective website. Possibly one of the best current marketing tools for Dominica is "word-of-mouth" advertising by satisfied visitors.

Another difficulty for Dominica is the number and size of airplanes flying to the island. While there are two airports, the major airlines do not fly their large airplanes to Dominica. A decision by the airlines to increase the size of the aircraft or the number of flights is usually based on the simple question of demand. Currently Dominica does not yet have a large enough market to warrant an expansion in air service. In addition, because Dominica does not have any world-famous chains of hotels, it does not benefit from a worldwide hotel network. This situation presents a dichotomy in that, on the one hand, as an ecotourism

(Continued)

Case study (continued)

destination, large hotels would take away the special ambiance of the islands, and yet, on the other hand, highly recognized international hotel properties would likely increase the number of visitors to Dominica.

The history and heritage of Dominica with a special focus on the Kalinagos

Exactly when the first human beings came to the shores of the island of Dominica continues to be an open question, as it is for the most part with respect to the continents of North and South America. For many years, archeologists, anthropologists and other scientists have debated the subject of just when the Americas became populated. The current understanding of human migration to the Americas is largely based on advances in four main areas: linguistics, archeology, physical anthropology, and DNA analysis (and maybe a fifth one: guesswork). The best guesstimate is that human migration coming across Beringia (a loosely defined region surrounding the Bering Strait, the Chukchi Sea, and the Bering Sea that lies partly in Russia and partly in the United States) probably happened around 15,000 years ago and reached the tip of South America 11,000 years ago.

In researching information for this case study, it appears that Dominica was likely populated about 5,000–7,000 years ago. There is some research that suggests that maybe a small group of hunter-gathers called the Ciboney or "stone people" left the South American coast or other Caribbean islands and canoed to Dominica. Other than a few stone relics, there is not much evidence to support this conjecture and, if it is true, questions remain as to how this tribe might have existed or what happened to them. What seems more likely to have happened is that a native group, the Arawaks, arrived from islands of the Greater Antilles, and settled in Dominica. They were skilled at agriculture and were also good sailors, fishermen, canoe makers, and navigators. They lived and adjusted very comfortably and peacefully in Dominica for possibly a thousand years.

By about 1200–1300 CE (Common Era) the more primitive but ferocious Caribs (Caribs was a Spanish name for the Indians but the natives referred to themselves as the Kalinago People; this case study will usually use Kalinago) arrived in Dominica, likely from the Orinoco region of Venezuela or from islands of the Greater Antilles. They raided the Arawak settlements to obtain slaves (especially female ones) and supposedly to get bodies for the completion of their rites of cannibalism. History does tell us that Christopher Columbus encountered the Kalinagos in Cuba in 1493 and recorded the Spanish word *Canibalis* from the Arawak term *Caniba*, as a variant corruption name by the Spanish for the *Caribs*, which was translated into English as cannibal. Interestingly enough, the name for the Caribbean Sea comes from the word Carib.

The first written history of Dominica exists from a few notes in Christopher Columbus's ship logs during his second voyage to the "New World." For his initial voyage in 1492 he had only three poorly constructed ships; by his second voyage in 1493 he had 27 vessels, which allowed him to explore more extensively as he cruised the Caribbean Sea. He frequently made island stops along the way so that his crew could obtain fresh water and food supplies from the natives. It is not clear whether his boat actually landed in Dominica on Sunday, November 3, 1493 or simply passed close to the island. Columbus called the island Dominica, Domingo being the Latin word for Sunday, and the name stuck with the Europeans who would later dominate the island. The Kalinago name for the island was *Waitikubuli* or "tall is her body."

The Spanish first attempted to subjugate the Kalinagos on Dominica but later learned it was easier and more convenient to simply trade with the natives, mainly for foodstuffs. With respect to the "discovery" of the "New World" the Spanish explorers such as Christopher Columbus and others were simply interested in finding gold, silver, or precious stones. Columbus thought his ships had discovered islands near China and India where they believed large amounts of valuable riches existed. The Spanish who followed after Columbus searched the island of Dominica for gold and when they found none, they lost interest in the island. They were not interested in developing a settlement in such an isolated territory (from Europe) and in fighting with the fierce island Kalinago warriors that inhabited the island at the time. The Spanish explorers simply collected their belongings and sailed away and no other Spaniards came after them and Dominica was left to the Kalinagos.

With the Spanish abandonment of Dominica, and European powers constantly seeking islands they could obtain for their benefactors, France decided to lay claim to Dominica in 1632 without actually occupying the island. Between 1642 and 1650 a French missionary, Raymond Breton, became the first regular European visitor to the island. In the meantime, the French and English trying to keep peace with respect to their island interests agreed that both Dominica and Saint Vincent should not be settled, but instead left to the Kalinago as neutral territory. That arrangement seemed to work for a while until both countries began needing more timber to build their ships. The European forests were fast disappearing as a result of ship building and many of the countries saw the New World as a good place to obtain lumber.

By 1690 the French already had colonies in the two surrounding islands of Dominica, Martinique and Guadeloupe, and as a result decided to found a settlement in Dominica where they could obtain wood needed for ships, as well as agricultural products, especially bananas, sugar and coffee. Thus by 1715 the French made an effort to colonize the island and in 1727 Dominica formerly became a colony of France. For French settlers to produce agriculture products, they needed workers and quickly learned that trying to enslave the Kalinago Indians as farm laborers was not going to work very well. The Kalinagos strongly resisted the French and were willing to fight to keep from being enslaved. The French then imported African slaves to work on their plantations.

In 1761, during the Seven Years' War, a British expedition went against the French on Dominica and was successful. When the French lost the war to the British, Dominica was one of the islands ceded to the victorious British in 1763. The French, who had already invested heavily in Dominica, mounted a successful invasion in 1778. However, in 1783 with the Treaty of Paris which ended the Seven Years' War, Dominica was returned to Britain. Additional French invasions

(Continued)

Case study (continued)

in 1795 and 1805 were unsuccessful. The British were slow to see much value in colonizing the island but finally in 1805 decided to establish a colony on Dominica. Like the French before them, they brought African slaves to the island to work on producing agriculture products.

Britain emancipated slaves throughout the British Empire in 1834. This move changed the way that Dominica was to govern itself. By 1838 Dominica became the first British Caribbean colony to have a legislative body controlled by an ethnic African majority. In 1896, the United Kingdom took over executive government control of the island and it became a Crown colony. It was not until 1978 that the independent nation of the Commonwealth of Dominica came into existence. In the short term an interim government ruled the island until general elections took place in 1980 and the people elected Eugenia Charles as the first Prime Minister of Dominica, and also the first female prime minister in the Caribbean region. Dominica is a parliamentary democracy, following a partial British model that was adopted by many of its former territories. The president is the head of state but the power rests with a cabinet headed by a prime minister.[32]

The Commonwealth of Dominica as an ecotourism destination

Dominica is an excellent island for ecotourism development. Generally speaking, an ecotourism destination is described as being connected to the natural environment and local culture and implies that visitors should have an opportunity for a pleasant experience but in such a way that the destination is sustained for future generations to also enjoy. Ecotourism is a growing market for those destinations with the right qualities and which are willing to follow sustainable tourism management. Earlier in Chapter 1 of this book there was a section discussing ecotourism, some of which is repeated in this case study because the Commonwealth of Dominica represents what ecotourism is all about.

The International Ecotourism Society (TIES) defines ecotourism as "Responsible travel to natural areas that conserves the environment and improves the well-being of local people." TIES have developed specific Principles of Ecotourism: "Ecotourism is about uniting conservation, communities, and sustainable travel. This means that those who implement and participate in ecotourism activities should utilize the following ecotourism principles:

- Minimize impact
- Build environmental and cultural awareness and respect
- Provide positive experiences for both visitors and hosts
- Provide direct financial benefits for conservation
- Provide financial benefits and empowerment for local people
- Raise sensitivity to host countries' political, environmental, and social climate."[33]

Dominica is a good example of the attempt to implement these principles. It is one of the finest ecotourism destinations anywhere in the world, with exciting adventure travel, hiking, bicycling, trekking, kayaking, fishing, diving, river tubing, aerial tram riding, horseback riding, snorkeling, sailing, and whale watching. A visit to the Caribbean's only United Nations Educational, Scientific and Cultural Organization's World Heritage Site, the magnificent Morne Trois Pitons National Park, is a must. The tourism opportunities of Dominica epitomize the best in terms of sustainable tourism products, outdoor recreation, and leisure activities.

The government of Dominica both welcomes the opportunity to expand its tourism market and at the same time wants to protect its natural environment and its history, heritage, and culture. *Sustainable tourism* is the watchword for this beautiful island. Currently the best option to increase the number of visitors interested in sustainability and nature and adventure tourism is through ecotourism.

The ecotourism project in the Kalinago Territory

As mentioned earlier, Dominica is a land of many different cultures, influenced by its interesting and fascinating history and heritage. A special part of that history, heritage, and culture belongs to the Kalinago people. Also mentioned earlier, most of the Kalinagos live on a 3,700-acre Kalinago Territory on Dominica's east coast, set aside for them in 1903. They number approximately 3,000 and elect their own chief, who holds the position for five years. Recently the first ecotourism lodge was constructed within the Kalinago Territory by a local Kalinago entrepreneur. Other such possible lodges are now under consideration. Since one of the goals of ecotourism development in the Kalinago Territory is to preserve and protect the Kalinago way of life through integrated sustainable economic development, he has used the Kalinago word "Aywasi" in the name for his project.

This ecotourism project has the support of the Kalinago Chief, and encouragement from other local Kalinagos of the Territory as well as the government of Dominica. If this project is successful and others like it are built, it will eventually provide an economic stream within the Territory and an incentive to preserve the best features of the area. It will also improve and perpetuate the small authentic craft businesses currently taking place, whereby tourists watch Kalinago artisans at work and purchase art items from roadside stands. The Kalinago handicraft production, which includes uniquely weaved baskets, has been handed down for many generations prior to the time of Columbus's visit to the island. Each one is different, in effect an original work of art, making such an item far more special than a simple souvenir of the island. Ultimately, if the initial ecotourism project is successful, then tourism can be counted on to help increase economic development, add additional income, create jobs, spawn new small businesses, and contribute to overall economic integration while enriching and improving the quality of life of the local Kalinagos and others in Dominica.

Dominica's tourism minister (political) and tourism director (operating officer) are fully supportive of an ecotourism strategy for the Kalinago Territory, as are other governmental leaders. If ecotourism in the Territory expands beyond the

(Continued)

Case study (continued)

Figure 1.4 View of the ecotourism lodge in the Kalinago Territory of Dominica
(Photo: Louis Hill)

initial project as planned, it can be marketed as a very special experience within the overall marketing mix of Dominica's tourism products. Fortunately, Dominica already has considerable experience with ecotourism projects so there is a wealth of information to draw from at this stage.

One question considered in the development, construction, and marketing of an ecotourism project in the Kalinago Territory is whether there is a precedent elsewhere for this kind of a project. A very limited review of the literature on ecotourism-type projects on native lands did not produce many examples. There are not many models to draw from that lend examples appropriate to the unique landscape of Dominica. The Kuna Indians of the San Blas Islands of the Republic of Panama have had some success in presenting to visitors their unique culture, language, customs, and locally-made products without undue corruption of their heritage and lifestyle. Also, in Panama there are the Embera indigenous communities that live within the Chagres National Park, who have developed, through a sustainable tourism approach, a plan to preserve their traditional way of life, protect the Chagres National Park, and improve their economic status. Visitors who wish to travel the river or explore the park must use native guides and canoeists for their trip. The Embera Indians also have a small gift shop of native-made products. There are other examples but none that quite fit the unique ecotourism project in the Kalinago Territory of Dominica.

As the first ecotourism lodge is completed and others are under construction, it will be useful to carefully monitor their progress. The marketing of the ecotourism lodges will become a major focal point as websites must be developed, target marketing must take place and the application of the new social-media marketing tools must be in place. However, if successful, ecotourism in the Kalinago Territory might just be the transforming initiative to help stimulate the economy, alleviate poverty in some parts of the Territory and bring greater prosperity and quality of life to the local population.

Ecotourism/sustainable tourism, key to future economic development in Dominica

Dominica is a special case for sustainable development because of its unique characteristics with respect to keeping the island as a pristine nature island and the gradual growth of ecotourism properties throughout the island. Sustainable tourism, possibly more than agriculture and fishing, is an essential source of foreign currency, job opportunities, livelihood, and quality growth in Dominica. It could also be a positive instrument towards the eradication of some pockets of poverty, continue Dominica's strong protection of the environment and the improvement of the quality of life for the local population.

Like many of the other small islands in the Caribbean, Dominica needs to promote policies that allow the economy and communities to gain the maximum benefits from tourism. The competition by countries for visitors to Caribbean destinations is fierce. Many islands promote white sandy beaches and the Caribbean Sea. Dominica must continue and intensify its marketing strategies and efforts to focus on the niche markets of nature and adventurer tourism. With new social-media marketing and a strong website, Dominica can reach an increased global market interested in nature and adventure travel.

A key for future success will include developing and maintaining sound governmental tourism policies and preparing a carefully designed strategic plan. The engagement with a wide range of stakeholders in the development of sustainable tourism strategies and action plans will help in the long term. Dominica should maintain a strategy to increase inter-island transport as well as longer-haul transportation. Dominica must also be mindful of strengthening the resilience to the consequences of natural disasters and other incidents that may affect their safety, security and attractiveness for tourists.

In summary, Dominica needs to continue diversifying its ecotourism development, the Kalinago Territory being one special example. Ecotourism continues to be one of the fastest-growing niche markets in the travel industry and is generally viewed as representing sustainable tourism. Dominica has the potential to be the premier ecotourism destination with respect to small islands throughout the world. With the right policies and strategic plans, Dominica can expand its ecotourism segment and offer experiences that enable visitors to enjoy natural areas and preserve the integrity of the environment.

Chapter summary

This first chapter presented a general understanding of the travel and tourism industry. It noted some of the basic concepts of sustainable tourism and the economic importance of tourism. The various international tourism organizations were introduced, with a description of their structures and locations. A common theme of the international organizations cited in Chapter 1 is their interest in sustainable tourism.

The chapter explained that consumers of tourism in the new millennium are demanding greater quality in their tourism products. The UNWTO definition of an international visitor was described. Also included in the chapter was a textbook definition of tourism and a description of the elements of sustainability with respect to sustainable tourism.

Through the introduction of key research data from the UNWTO and the WTTC it is clear that tourism is the world's largest industry. Other international organizations involved with the tourism industry were introduced. Most of the key international tourism organizations were described in detail. The basic ingredients in the definition of sustainability were explained. Ecotourism, geotourism, responsible tourism and cultural tourism, as components of sustainable tourism, were fully outlined in a special diagram.

The case study for Chapter 1 introduced one of the best country examples of sustainable tourism: the Commonwealth of Dominica. The background, history and heritage of Dominica was presented. There was a particular emphasis on the background of the Kalinago Indians who live in Dominica. The case study described an experimental ecotourism project located in the Kalinago Indian Territory.

Chapter review questions

1   What is tourism?
2   Describe a few of the sectors of the tourism industry.
3   How would you define the word "coopetition" as far as its use with respect to the tourism industry?
4   What is the name of the most important international tourism organization for governmental tourism in the world, and where is it located?
5   What is the name of the most important international tourism organization representing private-sector tourism, and where is it located?
6   In a few words, describe ecotourism, geotourism, responsible tourism and cultural tourism.
7   Explain the economic importance of the tourism industry.
8   Has the tourism industry been growing? Will it likely grow in the future?
9   What is the difference between a tourist and an excursionist?
10 What do UNWTO and WTTC stand for?
11 How many tourism-related jobs existed in 2014?
12 How many international tourism arrivals took place in 2014?

Notes

1   Goeldner, C. R. and Brent Ritchie, J. R. (2012) *Tourism: Principles, Practices, Philosophies* (12th edition), Hoboken, New Jersey: John Wiley & Sons, Inc., p. 4.

2 Edgell, Sr., D. L. and Swanson, J. R. (2013) *Tourism Policy and Planning: Yesterday, Today, and Tomorrow* (2nd edition), London: Routledge, pp. 1–2.

3 Edgell, Sr., D. L. and Haenisch, R. T. (1995) *Coopetition: Global Tourism beyond the Millennium*, Kansas City, Missouri: International Policy Publishing.

4 Edgell, Sr., D. L. (2006) *Managing Sustainable Tourism: A Legacy for the Future*, New York: The Haworth Hospitality Press, p. 123.

5 World Travel and Tourism Council (2014), www.wttc.org.

6 World Tourism Organization (UNWTO) (2015) press release, January 15, 2015.

7 World Tourism Organization (UNWTO) (2015) press release, April 15, 2015.

8 World Travel and Tourism Council (2015), "Economic Impact Analysis," www.wttc.org.

9 Organisation for Economic Co-operation and Development (2014), www.oecd.org.

10 Edgell, Sr., D. L. (1994) "An Assessment of the Organization of American States Inter-American Travel Congresses," General Secretariat of the Organization of American States, Washington, D.C., August 10, 1994.

11 Organization of American States Inter-American Travel Congress's Permanent Secretariat (1997): "Sustaining Tourism by Managing Its Natural and Heritage Resources," San Jose, Costa Rica, January 31, 1997.

12 Asia-Pacific Economic Cooperation (2002): "Public/Private Partnerships for Sustainable Tourism: Delivering a Sustainability Strategy for Tourism Destinations."

13 Caribbean Tourism Organization (2014), www.onecaribbean.org.

14 Small Island Developing States (2006): "Maximizing Economic Benefits & Sustaining Tourism in Development," Nassau, The Bahamas, June, 2006, pp. 7–9.

15 Edgell, Sr., D. L. (1990) *International Tourism Policy*, New York: Van Nostrand Reinhold, p. 1.

16 Edgell (2006), Preface.

17 Goeldner and Brent Ritchie (2012), pp. 372–382.

18 Edgell (2006), p. 1.

19 Retrieved from http://goodnature.nathab.com/spotlight-on-sustainability-origins-of-ecotourism/, January 10, 2015.

20 The International Ecotourism Society (2015), www.ecotourism.org.

21 Honey, M. (2008) *Ecotourism and Sustainable Development: Who Owns Paradise?* (2nd edition), Washington, D.C.: Island Press, pp. 29–33.

22 Hose, T. (1996) "Geotourism, or Can Tourists Become Casual Rock Hounds?" In M. Bennett, P. Doyle, J. Larwood, and C. Prosser (eds.) *Geology on Your Doorstep*, Bath, England: Geological Society, pp. 207–228.

23 Travel Industry Association of America (2002) *Geotourism: The New Trend in Travel*, Washington D.C.: Travel Industry Association of America.

24 *National Geographic* (2014) "The Geotourism Charter," retrieved from www.nationalgeographic.com/travel/sustainable/.

25 Government of South Africa, Department of Environmental Affairs and Tourism (1996) "White Paper on the Development and Promotion of Tourism in South Africa."

26 International Centre for Responsible Tourism (2009) "City of Cape Town Responsible Tourism Framework and Campaign Plan," Cape Town, South Africa.

27 United Nations Educational, Scientific and Cultural Organization (2015), retrieved from www.unesco.org.

28 National Trust for Historic Preservation (2015), retrieved from www.preservationnation.org.

29   Edgell and Swanson (2013), pp. 273–274.
30   McDonough, M. E. (2014) "Discovering Dominica," *US Airways Magazine*, November 2014.
31   The Caribbean Tourism Organization (2015) "Table 1 – Tourist (Stop-over) Arrivals and Cruise Passenger Visits in 2014," released on January 13, 2015.
32   U.S. Department of State (2008) "Background Note: Dominica."
33   The International Ecotourism Society (2015), www.ecotourism.org.

Chapter 2

The worldly travelers and a sense of sustainability

"Traveling is almost like talking with those of other centuries."

René Descartes, *Discourse on the Method*, 1637 CE

To better understand the four components of sustainable tourism described in Chapter 1 – "cultural tourism, geotourism, ecotourism and responsible tourism" – it is helpful to note that certain worldly travelers in the history of travel were practicing some of the attributes of sustainable tourism long before it became a popular topic in the new millennium. The prehistoric period covering the time before recorded history is understandably vague with respect to travel. Archeologists, paleontologists, and anthropologists have provided evidence that our ancestral species *Homo erectus*, about two million years ago, was the pre-human long-legged man that walked upright with long strides much as we do today. *Homo erectus* stood erect and had the ability to walk or run long distances. While *Homo erectus* had very small brains, the species was capable of building fires, organizing hunts for food, and fashioning crude tools. A next step in human evolution and in the history of travel is when *Homo erectus* began to journey beyond their normal home territory to new environments.[1]

By 400,000–500,000 years ago *Homo erectus* had evolved into our more advanced ancestors, *Homo sapiens*. With larger skulls, more brain capacity and greater curiosity, *Homo sapiens* traveled much greater distances than their predecessors. Likewise, another early species, about 300,000 years ago, *Homo neanderthalensis* were, like *Homo sapiens*, traveling further and migrating to such areas beyond East Africa as Eurasia, Western Europe, the Middle East and Northern Asia. The normal travel habits by both these species were largely dictated by movements from place to place in search of food, shelter, and safety from wild beasts and hostile tribes.[2] However, a few such early ancestors were more curious and began to venture beyond their normal surroundings just to explore new regions and to enjoy the beauty of the land.

While there is sparse information from tribal legends verbally handed down from generation to generation it is clear that many native populations throughout the world had a basic concept of sustainability. For example, Native American cultures understood their relationship with the environment and the need to sustain it for future generations to survive. In the book *Native American Wisdom* (edited by Kristen Cleary, 1996) the first chapter is titled "At One with Nature" and provides examples of Native Americans' respect for nature [environment] and kinship [culture]. Most Native American cultures noted that Mother Earth was the sustainer of life and therefore the earth was sacred. The Choctaw native tribe had a "Hunter's Prayer" which included the words, "Deer, I am sorry to hurt you, but the people are hungry." The Iroquois tribe had a belief that "[we] . . . shall offer thanks to the earth where men dwell, to the streams of water, the pools and lakes, to the maize and the fruits." The Hopi tribes had a creed that said, "Our land, our religion, and our life are one. It is upon this land that we have hunted deer, elk, antelope, buffalo, rabbit, [and] turkey. It is from this land we obtained the timbers and stone for our homes and kivas." Two Arapaho proverbs included (1) "When we show our respect for other living things, they respond with respect for us," and (2) "Before eating, always take a little time to thank the food . . . All plants are our brothers and sisters. They talk to us and if we listen, we can hear them."[3] Most such Native American tribes felt it was important to conserve and protect natural resources for future generations to survive and enjoy.

Possibly at about the same time that native populations of North America and in Africa understood the basic need to sustain the environment, there were newer progressive societies being formed in the Middle East region that were contributing to innovations in travel. A visit to the early civilization of the Sumerians, while not adding much clarification about sustainability, does provide information on new changes taking place in the way society would travel in the future. They, more than any other early society, would revolutionize the way people would travel.

Travel in antiquity

The period of antiquity spans from 4,000 BCE (Before the Common Era) to the fourth century CE (Common Era). After thousands of years and many evolutionary changes, antediluvian man migrated from the Rift Valley in East Africa, eventually into the Middle East and Asia. By about 4,000 BCE, the *Fertile Crescent,* sometimes referred to as *The Cradle of Civilization*, part of the present-day Middle East region (roughly including segments or all of the countries of Iraq, Iran, Kuwait, Turkey, Syria, Jordan, Israel, Lebanon, Palestine, and Egypt), is the area from which modern travel evolved. It was the intelligent and progressive Sumerians of this region and time period that would transform the ability for people to travel more easily and further. Their society invented the plow, the wheel, money, cuneiform writing, and the concept of a tour guide. Partially as a result of the plow, agricultural production expanded, which led to increased travel to nearby societies to trade food for goods. The invention of the wheel was of major significance as crude wagons using wheels were developed for the transport of agriculture products and other goods, as well as for other kinds of commercial travel. Having money allowed travelers a choice to either barter or pay for their travel and trade needs. Cuneiform writing made it easier to produce travel directions, rough maps, and to develop a travel itinerary. These inventions led to greater business relations with such distant countries as India, caused an increased desire to visit new destinations, and produced a need for a travel guide that could more efficiently and effectively impact on where and when they would travel.[4]

By 3,000 BCE the Egyptian society was building wooden boats as long as 75 feet for trade and military purposes, and for use in traveling the beautiful 4,000 miles of the Nile River to celebrate the changing of the seasons, as well as good harvests, and to thank the gods for their rich life. Thanks to the famous Greek historian, worldly traveler and travel writer Herodotus, we know a great deal about the early Egyptians. He was fascinated by the history, culture, and travel of the ancient Egyptians. In his renowned book on history titled *The Histories*, he reported in "Book II: Egypt: Geography, Customs, History, Tales" considerable details about the Egyptian culture and its natural and built environment, as described later in this chapter.

Shortly after 2,000 BCE, the Egyptians were taking what we would today call cultural-heritage trips, to visit pyramids, the Sphinx and other artistic and architectural edifices. Of the great wonders of the world in Egypt, none was greater than the pyramid at Giza, built as the resting place for the pharaoh Khufu. As noted by Justin Pollard in *Wonders of the Ancient World* (2008), "Virtually everything about Khufu's pyramid is a superlative . . . The largest of some 60 pyramids built by ancient Egyptians on the wet bank of the Nile, the Great Pyramid of Khufu remains a truly imposing sight 4,500 years after its construction."[5] The Greek historian Herodotus claimed that it took 100,000 laborers 20 years to build, but modern estimates vary from 50,000 men to over 300,000 taking anything from 10 to 20 years – all of whom would have had to be housed and fed.[6]

The walls of the temple of Deir el-Bahri in Luxor, Egypt hold bas-reliefs and text describing Egyptian Queen Hatshepsut's journey to the land of Punt in 1480 BCE. The Egyptians created many interesting structures that became popular tourist sites in ancient times and continue to this day to attract visitors from distant countries.[7] In his book *The Origins of Hospitality and Tourism* (2010), Kevin D. O'Gorman suggests that early visitors to the Sphinx and the three great pyramids probably slept in the open and garnered whatever food and hospitality they could from the local population. "However, priests or those on government assignment had everything provided for them. As they travelled they would be cared for at temples and government depots along the way; this was standard procedure in Egypt for all who were travelling on official business."[8]

Sometime around 2,000 BCE the master shipwrights and bold navigators, the Phoenicians, developed impressive seagoing vessels and traveled and mapped trade routes throughout the Mediterranean region. These highly intelligent peoples fabricated sophisticated seaworthy merchant vessels, state-of-the-art warships, and pleasure cruise ships that could sail the open seas safely and for long distances. Their mapped trade routes increased the knowledge of waterways and coastlines. They developed travel patterns that were made easier to follow by using stars to navigate (the North Star – so named by the Greeks – was originally known as the "Phoenician Star"). They also established trading centers along the coasts of North Africa, Sicily and Spain, spreading their culture and knowledge among less-advanced peoples. There are even theories that the Phoenicians were the first to travel to America, and accounts written by the Greek historian Herodotus imply that they circumnavigated Africa. In addition to seamanship, the Phoenicians excelled in literature, arts, architecture and engineering. They invented an alphabet (still in use today), teaching it to the Greeks and Mediterranean communities. Certainly their travels added important information about the history, heritage, and culture of Mediterranean destinations.[9]

The Greek society was the first to understand and write about cultural tourism as we know it today. Homer, writing in *The Odyssey* towards the end of the ninth century BCE, said, "A guest never forgets the host who had treated him kindly." This quotation is a precursor to the modern definition of the need for quality service in the travel industry.

The Greeks were also the first to organize, promote, and accommodate large numbers of visitors for sporting events. The early Greek society revered the body, especially with respect to performances in sporting events. As outlets for their athletic prowess and cultural interest, and to appease the gods, they developed a series of athletic-cultural events and contests. The more popular ones became known as the Olympic Games, Pythian Games, Isthmian Games, and Nemean Games. The oldest and most famous of the four great Games were the Olympic Games (Games), held every four years in honor of the Greek king of the gods, Zeus of Olympus. The Games, first held in 776 BCE, included, in addition to athletic events, contests of dance and choral poetry. During the Games, there was also much attention to art, music, sculpture, plays, story-telling, public speaking, food, drink, and other cultural activities.[10]

Because of the difficulty and danger of traveling very far from home, few of the ancient Greek pleasure travelers traveled great distances. Certainly there were military personnel, diplomatic persons, and international traders who traveled great distances but the pleasure traveler was more likely to just visit friends at country estates or at coastal homes, or possibly to travel for sporting and cultural events such as the Olympics. The exception to this pattern of travel was the great worldly traveler, historian, and travel writer Herodotus. He was intent on learning about the history and culture of Egypt and other lands. His interest in knowing about the world overrode the discomfiture, fatigue, and physical pain that would result from his travels. He was intelligent, inquisitive, strong, healthy, and wealthy enough to be interested in traveling and to endure the hardships of travel. Thus, Herodotus, with his unbridled imagination and genius, his innate ability to interact with peoples of other countries, his unusual, melodious and entrancing story-telling voice that attracted listeners, and his written accounts of what he saw and heard, would change the world. We can attribute our understanding of cultural tourism as an integral part of sustainable tourism to this fascinating individual.

Herodotus: the cultural traveler in the ancient world

In Chapter 1 a short definition of cultural tourism was presented as "Traveling to experience the places and activities that authentically represent the stories and people of the past and present." No one in the history of early travel better fits that definition of cultural tourism than the great worldly traveler Herodotus (484–425 BCE). In the fifth century BCE, he toured Phoenicia (Lebanon), Egypt, Cyrenaica (Libya), Greece, and areas around the Black Sea and recorded the history (particularly in traveling to experience the battle sites of the Greco-Persian wars), culture, customs, traditions, religions, geography, and practices of the people living in those areas. Up until Herodotus wrote his book *The Histories* about the countries he visited, Greek society knew very little about the larger world outside of the Greek city-states. Because of the difficulty of obtaining his book, most of the intellectual community learned of his travels through his oral presentations at major events throughout much of Greece. Political leaders and military strategists made important decisions based on his writings and oral presentations.

Herodotus (in ancient Greece only one identity name was in use) was a unique traveler, the first travel writer – he is also known today as the "Father of History" – and certainly the greatest traveler of his era. He was what we might refer to today as a special news reporter of events and people he encountered in his travels, and he repeated and noted historical facts and anecdotes told to him in the countries he visited. In many circumstances he commented on stories and legends told to him by individuals he met, not really knowing whether they were actual facts or fictitious myths that had been passed down verbally from generation to generation. In the 440s BCE Herodotus wrote an enormous and detailed tome titled *The Histories* which was the first early attempt to discuss the history of the ancient world. The book covered all the countries he had visited and included information about other places, as reported to him by people he met in his travels.

Born in 484 BCE, Herodotus came from a well-educated and wealthy family. He grew up in Halicarnassus in Caria (now Bodrum, Turkey). Herodotus lived in an era when Persia was the dominant world power. The Persian King Cambyses had conquered the great civilization of Egypt in 525 BCE, making it a province of Persia. Through a series of wars in the fifth and sixth centuries (Herodotus writes about these wars extensively in his book) Persia ruled most of the Middle East and areas beyond. Some of the Greek colonies bordering Persia, over time, were paying homage and taxes to a series of Persian kings in an effort to keep the Persian civilization and military at bay. Halicarnassus was one of these Greek colonies under the subjugation of the Persian Empire. It was a substantial travel distance from the well-known ancient Greek city-states of Athens and Sparta and thereby not readily defended by the Greek military, and it therefore had to pay homage to Persia as one of its satrapies.[11]

Herodotus's first major trip was traveling to the cultural center of Greece, the magnificent city of Athens. Athens was a stark contrast to Herodotus's birthplace, the city of Halicarnassus. Not only did the superb Athenian architecture surpass anything he had seen as a child in that distant Persian colony of Halicarnassus, but the political life and social milieu was radically different.

It was this fateful visit to Athens that set Herodotus's traveling itinerary in motion. He learned as much as he could about distant civilizations and became particularly enamored with reading about the mysterious culture of Egypt. He knew in advance that a journey to Egypt would be a serious challenge because of the formidable hardships of traveling such a long distance. After arriving in Egypt, Herodotus would have an onerous and long overland trek if he was to see and learn about the culture of Egypt. But he was not daunted by such potential difficulties and left Greece to sail across the Mediterranean Sea for Egypt as soon as he could make the arrangements. Travel from ancient Greece to Egypt in the fifth century BCE was a major feat of stamina, patience, and luck. The traveler prayed for good weather and hoped the pirates on the high seas did not attack. The trip was so perilous that many travelers, including this traveler, made sacrifices or said prayers to their favorite Gods before embarking on the journey. Herodotus's burning desire to visit and learn about the magnificence of the Egyptian culture and its celebrated antiquities and structures trumped the enormous burdens for a traveler to overcome during this early age of travel. He was fascinated by the marvelous architectural structures in Egypt and like most visitors then and today he was amazed and enamored with seeing the pyramids, and he described them in great detail in his book. Travel on the great Nile River was another aspect of Egyptian culture that captured his imagination. He noted that the Egyptians met to celebrate festivals and religious gatherings not once a year but a number of times. The biggest and most popular was at the city of Bubastis in honor of Artemis, the virgin goddess of the hunt and the moon, and twin sister of Apollo. Herodotus describes this event:

> Now, when they are coming to the city of Bubastis they do as follows: – men and women sail together, and a great multitude of each sex in every boat; and some of the women have rattles [castanets] and rattle with them, while some of the men play the flute during the whole time of the voyage, and the rest, both women and men, sing and clap their hands; and when as they sail they come opposite to any city on the way they bring the boat to land, and some of the women continue to do as I have said, others cry aloud and jeer at the women in that city, some dance, and some stand up and pull up their skirts. This they do by every city along the river-bank; and when they come to Bubastis they hold a festival celebrating great sacrifices, and more wine is consumed upon that festival than during the rest of the year.[12]

In his book, Herodotus writes many passages about the Nile. He writes about the many cruises that people took to celebrate various festivals and events. He describes in great detail the use of the river for trade purposes, and for obtaining goods and food items, and for transporting wood products and merchandise. He notes that, "When the Nile comes over the land [floods], the cities alone are seen rising above the water, resembling more nearly than anything else the islands in the Egean Sea; for the rest of Egypt becomes a sea and the cities alone rise above the water. Accordingly, whenever this happens, they ferry about not now on the channels of the river but over the midst of the plain."[13] He further explains that people use boats right in the middle of land during the flood, and in so doing sail near the pyramids. Herodotus also describes the many different kinds of plants and animals along the river basin, most of which were unknown to Greek society.

If good fortune prevailed, Herodotus would find succor when he arrived at his destination, or at temporary stopovers along the way in areas unknown to him. He also had to interact with local populations speaking unfamiliar languages and adapt to different social mores and customs. Because of his accumulated family wealth, he was able to have a servant to assist him on his difficult journey. Having a servant or slave help on such journeys was not uncommon for early Greek travelers. On segments of his trip, if he was lucky, he sought opportunities to join a caravan that included officials on government business and traders who had been to the destination before. Traveling in groups helped ward off thieves and highwaymen. It also provided companionship and information. His travel by boat was most difficult in that there were no "cabins" for sleeping, the deck was often crowded with people, and obtaining decent food and drink was always a challenge. The boats were often poorly constructed, making it very dangerous to be on the water during a storm.

Much of Herodotus's book *The Histories* is about the Persian and Greek societies and the many wars each was involved in. Herodotus's writings made major battles and the events leading to such conflicts come alive. His accounts of King Leonidas of Sparta and his 300 Spartans fighting thousands of Persians is aptly described in his book and has become the basis for many historic publications, movies, and television accounts. Most of his sources were oral conversations he had with individuals and groups such as descendants of the Spartans who died at Thermopylae. Thus, Herodotus as a unique cultural traveler, and his unbridled imagination and genius, his innate ability to interact with peoples of other countries, his entrancing story-telling ability to attract listeners, and his written accounts of what he saw and heard, give us a glimpse of "cultural tourism" of the ancient world.

Herodotus, by all known accounts, was a very passionate traveler. Everything about travel excited him and he could not wait to discover new destinations and to converse with local populations about culture, religion, and history. He was truly enigmatic. On the one hand he wrote of history and travels very carefully and accurately based on the facts available. But on the other hand, he frequently would repeat rumors or add mists of myth and legend, even though he knew that they were not necessarily true. Herodotus felt that the story of a historical incident must be told even if the facts of the story were not always clear or available. He noted that "Very few things happen at the right time, and the rest do not happen at all: the conscientious historian will connect these dots." Part of the problem in this regard was that Herodotus relied heavily on translators and received most of his knowledge third hand, which made him vulnerable to innuendos and subterfuges by local falsifiers of history, and possibly by individuals deliberately misleading him for their own aggrandizement. Still, with all these difficulties, his interesting descriptions made history come alive. From his picturesque descriptions of local customs, humor, heroes, tragedies and historical events, the world gained much knowledge about some of the early societies outside Greece. Herodotus was certainly a well-traveled, knowledgeable, and curious traveler who wanted to know as much as possible about the cultures of the places he visited. In his travels and country reports he covered many different areas of human activity (politics, economics, anthropology, religion, ecology, geography and the humanities).[14] Hence, as a result of his travels and the writing of his book *The Histories*, cultural travel or cultural tourism as we know it today was born.

Marco Polo: The cultural/geotourism worldly traveler of the Medieval Period

The Medieval Period or Middle Ages of Europe covers the fifth century to the fifteenth century, a time period that saw many changes in society and political structures, as well as producing many worldly travelers making new discoveries throughout the world. Within this period were the Renaissance and the Age of Discovery. One of the most interesting worldly travelers of this era, and a person that would change the future of travel, was none other than the famed Marco Polo.

As noted earlier in Chapter 1, "cultural tourism" is defined as "Traveling to experience the places and activities that authentically represent the stories and people of the past and present" and "geotourism" is described as "tourism that sustains or enhances the geographical character of a place – its environment, culture, aesthetics, heritage, and the well-being of its residents." No one in early history better fits both of these definitions and descriptions of cultural tourism and geotourism than Marco Polo.

Marco Polo (1254–1324) was one of the earliest Europeans known to have traveled from Europe (Republic of Venice) to China. The city-state Republic of Venice was a major maritime power, the epicenter of commerce and a trade leader with the Byzantine Empire and the Islamic world. Marco Polo began his travel to China at the age of 17, accompanying his father and uncle, both of whom were highly experienced merchants and travelers. Their travels from Venice to China and their return to Venice would take 24 years. They battled bouts of sickness with limited medical care. They crossed into territories where wars were taking place and sometimes had to retreat and wait until it was safe to travel again. They escaped from robbers at one point and almost died during snow storms in crossing certain mountainous terrains. For protection, they often joined a caravan of traveling merchants. However, in one situation, and under the cover of a sandstorm, the caravan they were a part of was attacked by bandits. The Polos and others had to fight for their lives. Many from the caravan were killed but the Polos escaped and were able to continue their travels toward China. Marco made notes of such adventures which would make for interesting reading at a later time. Fortunately, shortly after their return from China, Marco Polo wrote vivid accounts of the details of their travel during this period in his book *The Travels of Marco Polo* (1300). The book is replete with stories about the customs, culture, and geography of the places the Polos visited.

From Marco Polo's book and accounts of the experiences of other travelers, we have a good idea of the difficulties of traveling during the thirteenth century. A traveler to foreign countries was beset with strange customs, chaotic travel conditions due to the many conflicts and wars taking place, and, depending on the chosen destination and culture, varying degrees of hospitality. To pursue the wonders of the world at that particular time period, Marco Polo was willing to travel by foot, horseback, camel, donkey, carriage, and boat under some of the most difficult circumstances imaginable. However, he brought back with him copious amounts of information, revealing new inventions, different customs, interesting products, geographical descriptions, and nuances of other cultures. His interactions with the great Mongol ruler and founder of the Yan dynasty, Kublai Khan of China, and his ability to learn and to transfer knowledge are aptly chronicled in his travel book. *The Travels of Marco Polo*, a bestseller throughout Europe, was accepted as the *bible* for describing the social, cultural, economic, and environmental conditions of the places he had visited – Central Asia, Mongolia, China, Tibet, Burma, Siam, Ceylon, Java, India, and other destinations largely unknown in Europe. His book inspired other travelers and explorers, such as Christopher Columbus and Ferdinand Magellan.[15] The book also influenced European cartography, leading to the introduction of the Fra Mauro map.

Marco Polo's descriptions of certain places and events make for interesting reading. He describes in his travels considerable details of the mountains, rivers, valleys, open plains and even deserts in most fascinating prose. For example, in his book he mentions the particular difficulty of crossing deserts. He notes that some travelers become delirious and see mirages – images of trees and water, of people and places. His detailed explanations about desert travel make for enchanting reading. In one passage, Marco Polo describes crossing the great Gobi Desert:

> The truth is this. When a man is riding by night through this desert and something happens to make him loiter and lose touch with his companions, by dropping asleep or for some other reason, and afterwards he wants to rejoin them, then he hears spirits talking in such a way that they seem to be his companions. Sometimes, indeed, they even hail him by name. Often these voices make him stray from the path, so that he never finds it again. And in this way many travelers have been lost and have perished. And sometimes in the night they are conscious of a noise like the clatter of a great cavalcade of riders away from the road; and, believing that these are some of their own company, they go where they hear the noise and, when day breaks, find they are victims of an illusion and in an awkward plight. And there are some who, in crossing this desert, have seen a host of men coming towards

them and, suspecting that they were robbers, have taken flight; so having left the beaten track and not knowing how to return to it, they have gone hopelessly astray. Yes, and even by daylight men hear these spirit voices, and often you fancy you are listening to the strains of many instruments, especially drums, and the clash of arms. For this reason bands of travelers make a point of keeping very close together. Before they go to sleep they set up a sign pointing in the direction in which they have to travel. And round the necks of all their beasts they fasten little bells, so that by listening to the sound they may prevent them from straying off the path.[16]

Marco Polo was enamored with learning about the life and characteristics of Kublai Khan, the grandson of the famous warlord Genghis Khan. Kublai Khan is considered one of the most effective rulers and administrators in history and ruled the biggest empire to ever exist. Marco Polo endeared himself to the great ruler through his conversations about the Christian religion, of great interest to Kublai Khan, his ability to master several different languages, and his fascinating tales of travel. This friendship allowed Marco to become very close to the emperor and to gain his permission and support for special visits to many parts of his empire. In his book, Marco Polo describes each detail of Kublai Khan's life, how he commands his armies, how he rules his empire and how he accumulated his great wealth. Marco Polo particularly enjoys describing Kublai Khan's palaces. In the following segment he portrays certain attributes of one of Kublai Khan's palaces in such a way that it would appear to be an example of a "sustainable environment."

> Between the inner and the outer walls [of the palace], of which I have told you, are stretches of park-land with stately trees. The grass grows here in abundance, because all the paths are paved and built up fully two cubits above the level of the ground, so that no mud forms on them and no rain-water collects in puddles, but the moisture trickles over the lawns, enriching the soil and promoting a lush growth of herbage. In these parks there is a great variety of game, such as white harts [a male deer], musk-deer [hornless male deer], roebuck [a small Eurasian male deer], stags, squirrels, and many other beautiful animals. All the area within the walls is full of these graceful creatures, except the paths that people walk on.[17]

Marco Polo's book contains dozens and dozens of examples of the different cultures and customs of the cities and provinces he visited in his travels to China and his extensive travels within China's great empire. In one of the provinces in China called Manzi, he describes a special custom of the people in the community:

> You must know that all the people of Manzi have a usage such as I will describe. The truth is that as soon as a child is born the father or the mother has a record made of the day and the minute and the hour at which he was born, and under what constellation and planet, so that everyone knows his horoscope. Whenever anyone intends to make a journey into another district or a business deal, he consults an astrologer and tells him his horoscope; and the astrologer tells him whether it is good to undertake it or not. And often they are deterred from the venture. For you must know that their astrologers are skilled in their art and in diabolic enchantment, so that many of their predictions prove true and the people

repose great faith in them. When a marriage is planned, the astrologers first investigate whether the bridegroom and bride are born under concordant planets. If so, it is put into effect [they are married]; if not, it is called off.[18]

When Marco Polo returned home to Venice, after 24 years of continuous travel, he wrote his book *The Travels of Marco Polo*. The book made Marco Polo an instant celebrity throughout Europe. It was translated into all the major languages of Europe at the time. The book was a bestseller in Europe and it continues to be a bestseller today. Marco Polo, more than any other worldly traveler of his day, best meets the criteria for describing cultural tourism and geotourism.

Ecotourism and Charles Darwin

Marco Polo's travel book set the stage for a better understanding of some of the fundamentals of sustainable travel. By the eighteenth and nineteenth centuries there were many worldly travelers who understood the broad underpinnings of cultural travel and aspects of geotourism in traveling to other lands. There were naturalists at universities teaching the principles and practices of travel to natural areas and the need to conserve the environment. This era of travel, noting special attributes of nature and the natural and built environment, would set the stage for understanding the foundation of ecotourism. In Chapter 1 ecotourism was defined as "Responsible travel to natural areas that conserves the environment and improves the welfare of local people." Also mentioned in Chapter 1 was the first definition of ecotourism, offered up by the Mexican architect Héctor Ceballos-Lascuráin, who coined the word "ecotourism" in 1983:

> Ecotourism is tourism that involves traveling to relatively undisturbed natural areas with the specific object of studying, admiring, and enjoying the scenery and its wild plants and animals, as well as any existing cultural aspects found in these areas. Ecotourism implies a scientific, esthetic, or philosophical approach ... The main point is that the person who practices ecotourism has the opportunity of immersing him or herself in nature in a way that most people cannot enjoy in their routine, urban existences. This person will eventually acquire a consciousness and knowledge of the natural environment together with its cultural aspects that will convert him into somebody keenly involved in conservation issues.[19]

This comprehensive definition of ecotourism was echoed by many "naturalists" traveling in the eighteenth and nineteenth centuries.

One such giant in the field of natural history, who might qualify as an ecotourist in the eighteenth and nineteenth centuries is the famous naturalist Baron Friedrich Wilhelm Heinrich Alexander von Humboldt (generally referred to as Baron Alexander von Humboldt). This well-known German explorer, geographer, worldly traveler and writer, amongst his many travels and explorations throughout different parts of the world, spent considerable time studying the flora and fauna, and other natural phenomena, in Venezuela, Columbia, Ecuador, Peru, Mexico and Cuba. Based on his detailed environmental studies in these countries he wrote the book *Personal Narrative of a Journey to the Equinoctial Regions of the New Continent* (English translation), which became a classic in the study of plants and animals in the areas he visited. The book was published in six volumes, released each year from 1799 until 1804. Later he wrote many other books, but his work in South America set the foundation and guidelines for many future naturalists such as Charles Darwin.[20]

The young Charles Darwin, fresh from university – he had studied natural science and geology at Christ's College, Cambridge – was chosen by the British Navy as a crewman with the title of "naturalist" for a circumnavigation of the globe on the ship *HMS Beagle*, which began sailing on December 27, 1831. The trip was planned as a two-year voyage to map the east and west coasts of South America and to note the natural history of the places visited. However, due to storms and other delays, the voyage was extended into a five-year odyssey with many adventures along the way. Initially, Darwin felt useless – he had no sailing experience, he was frequently seasick, and he only had basic research knowledge, with no real experience relevant to his position as a naturalist. However, once he had settled into the journey he studied and read about natural history every day. Darwin read and reread the work of Baron Alexander von Humboldt. In fact, he read von Humboldt's book *Personal Narrative of a Journey to the Equinoctial Regions of the New Continent* so many times it was coming apart at the seams. Humboldt's book became Darwin's principal handbook on naturalism, and, later in life, he would reference it many times in his own publication *The Voyage of the Beagle*. As far as Darwin was concerned, Humboldt was his role model – he noted this in a letter, describing him as "the greatest scientific traveler who ever lived . . . I have always admired him; now I worship him."[21]

Darwin came from a wealthy and intellectual family that included his well-known medical doctor father and his uncle, a researcher in certain aspects of natural history. While his father wanted him to study for a medical career, Darwin had very little passion for medicine and became enamored with the study of nature and geology. What changed his life and set his career in motion as a naturalist was his voyage on the *Beagle*. His responsibility on this voyage was to study the natural attributes of plant and animal life and observe the culture and heritage of the inhabitants of the areas visited when opportunities arose to go ashore. Darwin's travel and explorations during the five-year voyage to such places as Brazil, Uruguay, Argentina, Chile, Ecuador, El Salvador, the Falkland Islands, Peru, and Tahiti excited him no end. As often as was possible, he sent to England samples of various plants, animals, and fossil specimens he had collected from these countries. He took copious notes and communicated such research and writings with his favorite professor, as well as with a very close sister who was interested in his research.

The most famous area that Charles Darwin visited in South America was the Galapágos Islands, a territory of Ecuador over 600 miles from the mainland. He found that each one of the islands was unique, with different but limited plant life, birds and reptiles – and especially numerous land iguanas. It was Darwin's study of bird life, in particular finches, which eventually led him to his theory of evolution and his famous and controversial book *On the Origin of Species*.

Three years after his voyage on the *Beagle*, Darwin wrote an account of his travels, based on his abundant notes, titled *The Voyage of the Beagle*. This book made him a very popular author and impacted heavily on his later work *On the Origin of Species*. Over the years, his first book became one of the most widely known and discussed books on travel (in reality, sustainable travel). It made Darwin famous at the age of 29. Later in life he wrote that "The voyage on the *Beagle* has been by far the most important event of my life and has determined my whole career. . ."[22]

A review of Darwin's travels, research, and writings would strongly suggest that he is the father of "ecotourism" within the context of Mexican architect Héctor

Ceballos-Lascuráin's definition of ecotourism. Charles Darwin certainly traveled to "relatively undisturbed natural areas with the specific object of studying, admiring, and enjoying the scenery and its wild plants and animals." Following the definition of ecotourism in more detail, it is clear that Darwin's travel also included careful study of the cultures he visited. Héctor Ceballos-Lascuráin's statement that "Ecotourism implies a scientific, esthetic, or philosophical approach" also applies to Darwin's travels. In addition, the statement that an ecotourist "will eventually acquire a consciousness and knowledge of the natural environment together with its cultural aspects that will convert him into somebody keenly involved in conservations issues" fits Charles Darwin's life, travels, and career as a naturalist.

Charles Lindbergh and responsible tourism

The last of the four components of sustainable tourism described in Chapter 1 is "responsible tourism," defined as "tourism that maintains the benefits to local communities, minimizes negative social or environmental impacts, and helps local people conserve fragile cultures and habitats or species." A special worldly traveler, who later in his life understood and practiced "responsible tourism," was the world famous aviator Charles Lindbergh. His story is an important one in terms of promoting "responsible tourism" before there was such a term.

Charles Augustus Lindbergh II, born on February 4, 1902 in Detroit, Michigan, is known the world over as the first aviator to fly across the Atlantic Ocean. By the time Lindbergh was ready to attempt a solo flight across the ocean in 1927, six well-known pilots had already died in similar attempts. However, the news about other pilots losing their lives attempting to fly across the ocean did not diminish Lindbergh's desire to do so. It seemed to inspire him and renew his spirit, courage, and daring, knowing the severe challenges he faced for such a flight.

At 7:52 a.m. on May 20, 1927 Lindbergh took off for Paris, France from a rain-soaked, muddy Roosevelt Field, Long Island, New York in his plane the *Spirit of St. Louis* (named in honor of his financial backers from St. Louis, Missouri). His flight from New York to Le Bourget Aerodrome in Paris was replete with many difficulties. He faced severe weather conditions, sleep deprivation, and other problems but finally arrived in Paris at 10:22 p.m. on May 21, after having flown 3,614 miles nonstop in thirty-three hours and thirty minutes. He was immediately mobbed by a crowd of 150,000 spectators. Thus began his life as the world's most popular superstar.[23]

During his stay in Paris, Lindbergh made several short flights to other European cities. In every city he visited, thousands of people admired him and his historic flight. Presidents and kings honored him with special dinners, awards, and distinguished medals. The U.S. Government sent the navy vessel *USS Memphis* to bring Lindbergh and his plane back to the United States. U.S. President Coolidge invited him to the White House and New York City honored him with their biggest parade of the century. Two months after his special tour of America he wrote the popular book *We*, a book about his transatlantic flight. Interestingly, his book was published by George P. Putnam, who would later marry the most famous female pilot, Amelia Earhart. The book was an instant bestseller.[24]

Lindbergh flew honorary flights throughout North and South America, continuing to receive honors wherever he went. He was given the rank of colonel in the U.S. Army-Air Force. While initially he opposed the U.S. entering World War II, once the attack on Pearl Harbor in Hawaii took place he did all that he could to aid the U.S. war effort, helping to design better airplanes, training navy pilots in new aviation techniques, and even flying combat missions. As a military officer, he received the highest medal awarded, the *Medal of Honor*, and Congress gave him their highest civilian medal, the *Congressional Gold Medal*. The author of seven books, he received the 1954 Pulitzer Prize for *The Spirit of St. Louis*, published in 1953. He probably received more medals from the U.S. and foreign governments than any other single person in history.

Lindbergh foresaw the day when ordinary passengers would fly throughout the world. While generally a shy person, he effectively utilized his celebrity status to advocate the development of U.S. commercial aviation and promote the U.S. airmail service. He joined with others of a like mind to begin to develop concepts for new aircraft that could fly further, faster, and with more passengers, including the concept of a supersonic passenger jet plane.

Then, almost overnight, during the early 1960s, Charles Lindbergh's whole attitude towards the advances that were being made in aviation changed. He began to regret the impact of aviation on the environment. He noted that "The primitive was at the mercy of the civilized in our twentieth-century times . . . and nothing had made it more so than the airplane I had helped develop. I had helped to [negatively] change the environment of our lives."[25] This troubled him a great deal. Ironically, it caused him, the person who all his life had supported technological improvements in civilian aircraft, to oppose the supersonic passenger jets being developed by the airlines. In fact, he noted that civilization often destroyed birds and other species. He went on to say, "I realized that if I had to choose, I would rather have birds than airplanes." Much of his travels from then on were related to nature and a concern for the welfare of people in primitive surroundings. He reread Henry David Thoreau's book *Walden* and noted one phrase in particular: "In wildness is the preservation of the World."[26]

A chance meeting between Charles Lindbergh and an African delegate, Jilin ole "John" Konchellah of the Masai tribe in Kenya, at the international conference "Moral Re-Armament" in Caux-sur-Montreux, Switzerland would have a major impact on Lindbergh. In a private meeting between the two men, Lindbergh became fascinated by the tribal customs of the Masai tribe. "Konchellah told Lindbergh that the Masai prayed to their own god (which did not have human form), worshiped the mountains, and sang to the sun and moon. Warriors rose at dawn to thank God for the light . . . He [Konchellah] invited 'the great white flyer' to visit him in Kenya, where Lindbergh had never been."[27] In 1962 Lindbergh went to visit Konchellah and spent several days living with the tribe. He was fascinated by the tribal customs of the Masai and fell in love with the place and its people. Within a couple of years of this visit he traveled two more times to Africa and by then had become a staunch environmentalist.

In 1962 Lindbergh became connected with the World Wildlife Fund and its parent organization the International Union for Conservation of Nature and Natural Resources (IUCN). Increasingly, he found that the views of the IUCN in terms of nature and the environment matched his own. He became deeply involved in most of the issues on the environment and in trying to save animals such as the great blue whales and other species. Because Lindbergh was so well known the world over, he used his popularity to proselytize for the causes that he supported to heads of governments in many different countries. His efforts in this regard helped to gain stronger policies to protect the wildlife in their countries.

In 1968 Lindbergh was made aware of state legislation in Alaska to protect the Arctic wolves. In an effort to help get this legislation passed, he flew to Alaska, met with then Governor Walter J. Hickel and addressed state legislators. The legislation passed. Lindbergh was also an advocate of the need to preserve the polar bears in Alaska.

Lindbergh also became intimately involved with the Nature Conservancy and with other conservation groups. When Governor Walter Hickel of Alaska became the Secretary of the Interior, he invited Lindbergh to help develop ideas and programs for the U.S. National Park Service. In addition, Lindbergh accepted the President's invitation to serve on The Citizens' Advisory Committee on Environmental Quality.[28] Lindbergh's travels in the 1960s and 1970s became opportunities for him to work on conservation projects in many different parts of the world, from Fiji to the Philippines, to Brazil and elsewhere around the world.

Lindbergh was especially concerned for the primitive people living in outlying islands of the Philippines. While visiting the Philippines on several occasions he learned there were some sixty tribal groups that still inhabited its islands, many subsisting at prehistoric cultural levels. He spent considerable time studying a few of these aboriginal societies, their environment and flora and fauna, and their needs for survival. In a rare circumstance, he allowed a reporter from the *New York Times* to accompany and interview him regarding his concerns for the Philippine natural areas, their tribal populations and his support of conservation issues.[29]

In light of Lindbergh's contributions in promoting the benefits of positive social and environmental impacts on local people and in the conservation of fragile cultures and species, he was certainly a major proponent of "responsible travel." Because of his celebrity status he was able to cause international political leaders and others to be more conscious of protecting the environment and understanding the needs of tribal populations. He worked on conservation issues right up until he died in 1974.

Case study 2: John Lawson: Father of sustainable tourism in the New World

> "Alexander von Humboldt was the greatest scientific traveler who ever lived."
>
> Charles Darwin

Background

As mentioned above, Alexander von Humboldt was one of the greatest scientific travelers, naturalists, explorers, geographers, and writers with respect to the study of nature and sustainability in much of Latin America. His findings, voluminous writings and understanding of nature provided such future travelers and naturalists as Charles Darwin and others with a roadmap for their studies of sustainability and nature. However, early in the eighteenth century, prior to the impressive sustainability discoveries of von Humboldt and Darwin, there was a little-known traveler, explorer, naturalist, surveyor and writer from England by the name of John Lawson who made major contributions to the understanding of nature, native cultures, and sustainability in a "New World" English colony called *Carolina*. Had he not been killed at the young age of 37, it is likely that

John Lawson would have left an even greater legacy of accomplishments in sustainability than what was reported in his book titled (in archaic English) "*A New Voyage to Carolina; Containing the Exact Description and Natural History of That Country* [Carolina]*: Together with the Present State Thereof. And a Journal of a Thousand Miles, Travel'd Thro' Several Nations of Indians. Giving a Particular Account of Their Customs, Manners, &c.* (*New Voyage to Carolina*) by John Lawson, Gent. Surveyor General of *North Carolina* London: Printed in the Year 1709." Lawson's book was one of the first written documents introducing North Carolina as a separate colony from the larger region *Carolina*.

John Lawson was born in London in 1674, the son of Dr. John Lawson, a prosperous medical doctor, and his wife Isabella. The family was wealthy, partially due to family inheritances, as well as monies from Dr. Lawson's successful medical practices. The family owned, among other possessions, estates in Kingston-on-Hull, Yorkshire. John Lawson attended the nearby Gresham College, which provided lectures in astronomy, geometry, physics, law, divinity, and other subjects of interest to him. His special interests included natural sciences, mathematics, inventions, travel, and scientific lectures given by scientists of the Royal Society. The Royal Society was relatively new during Lawson's college days and met frequently at Gresham College. It is likely that some of the lectures given by the Royal Society had an impact on John Lawson's interest in naturalism, travel, and exploration. In addition, his father had numerous social connections among leading scientists, ships' physicians, and explorers, people that he often invited to his home, and whose stories and knowledge influenced the young John Lawson. An interesting commentary about certain aspects of John Lawson's life is in the *Dictionary of North Carolina Biography*.

Through John Lawson's family connections and university surroundings he met many interesting people, including an Englishman he befriended, Mr. James Moore, from England's colonial community of Charles Town, Carolina (later called Charleston). At the time, North Carolina and South Carolina were just one designated colony known as *Carolina*, which was part of England's properties in the New World. Mr. Moore owned a ship that was getting ready to leave Cowes, England on May 1, 1700 for Charles Town. He had already told Lawson many stories about *Carolina*, its beauty, its mysterious native Indian [Native American] populations, and its opportunities for exploration. He offered Lawson free passage on the ship. Lawson, then 25 years old and interested in an adventure that might prove to be exciting and profitable, accepted the invitation. Mr. Moore was a resident and community leader of Charles Town. He was also familiar with the Indian tribes in the area. After their arrival, he willingly guided Lawson to the nearby countryside and introduced him to the community leaders and to his many acquaintances in Charles Town.[30]

The *Province of Carolina* (*Carolina*) was established by King Charles II of England to reward eight military and political supporters who had helped him defeat Oliver Cromwell. These individuals became the *Lord Proprietors of Carolina* under the Charter of *Carolina* on March 24, 1663. The Lord Proprietors had the authority to make land grants and otherwise oversee the development of Carolina as they

(Continued)

Case study (continued)

saw fit. Thus, when John Lawson arrived in Charles Town and first explored the area, it was not yet divided into North and South Carolina. It was not until 1712 that Carolina was split into two colonies, North Carolina and South Carolina. It is likely that John Lawson's explorations, surveys, and book, which covered mostly North Carolina, and which noted differing geographies, added to information suggesting the split into the two separate colonies.[31]

John Lawson, the explorer, nature-based traveler, and geographer-surveyor

Once John Lawson landed in Charles Town, he immediately took advantage of James Moore's knowledge of the area and invitations to meet the leaders of the local community and to explore the nearby environment. He quickly put together a small band of adventurers consisting of five Englishmen from Yorkshire and, through Mr. Moore's contacts, convinced a group of Indians to become guides for exploratory travels throughout Carolina. Because of Lawson's education and interests, he organized preparations for the group to explore and study the geography, flora and fauna, and the culture and customs of the Indian populations during their travels. Trained in mathematics and having some surveying skills, Lawson also decided to explore possibilities for commercial real-estate ventures beyond Charles Town.

On December 28, 1700, the 26-year-old John Lawson and the small band of English adventurers and Indian guides departed Charles Town, traveling along the Santee and Wateree Rivers (South Carolina) by canoe, and then on foot, to explore the wilderness of *Carolina*. Lawson kept a careful journal during this first expedition and made notes and observed the differences of the geography of the land, the flora and fauna, and the different Indian cultures he encountered (including the Santee, Congaree, Wateree, Waxhaw, Sugaree, Catawba and Tuscarora Indians). They came across large numbers of Tuscarora Indians living along Contentnea Creek near present-day Grifton, North Carolina and then they crossed the Tar River, entering what is now Greenville, North Carolina. From here his party split up, with some of the members traveling on to Virginia. Through Indian interpreters, Lawson recorded the verbal history of the customs and cultures of the different tribes as told to him, and he drew rough maps and pictures of animals and plants along the journey. On this first trip, he traveled some 550 miles in 59 days, through rough forests and across numerous streams, ending his trip on February 24, 1701 at the plantation of a man named Richard Smith near the mouth of the Pamlico River (North Carolina). He settled and built a small home near a creek (Lawson Creek) in an area later to be called New Bern, which is near the two present-day communities known as Washington, North Carolina and Bath, North Carolina. He further explored territory that would become known as Eastern North Carolina. He became friends with the nearby native tribes, including the powerful Tuscarora Indians.

Over the next several years John Lawson explored the entire region, including much of what is now North Carolina and South Carolina, and parts of Virginia and Georgia as well. He kept detailed notes of his travels and explorations.

He met and befriended the few settlers in the area as well as becoming close to many of the Indian tribal leaders of the places he visited. He became an unofficial historian for Carolina, the best known naturalist in the New World, and developed a good reputation as a surveyor. John Lawson began surveying the areas near the Pamlico River Basin and in 1705 he was appointed deputy surveyor for the *Lords Proprietor of Carolina*. By 1708 he was appointed the "surveyor-general" of *Lords Proprietor of Carolina*, a lucrative position for someone interested in land speculation and increasing the number of settlers to the area. In addition, he was the first person to draw an accurate map of *Carolina*.[32]

John Lawson, the Founder of Bath

Earlier, in 1696, the "County of Bath" had been founded and there were already landowners established in the general area that became Bath, North Carolina. Lawson purchased some land from the group of landowners, and also received additional plots of land through grants connected with his work as a surveyor. This land was near the Pamlico region along the banks of Old Town Creek (now known as Bath Creek). With Lawson's surveying skills, and based on interest by people in Virginia and elsewhere in the New World looking for a new area to settle, Lawson and other local landowners platted streets and laid out 71 lots for a new community to be called The Town of Bath, named in honor of Englishman John Granville, Earl of Bath (County of Bath). In the meantime, Lawson moved to Bath and built a new home in the town. On March 8, 1705, the General Assembly of Carolina incorporated Bath as the first town in what later would become the state of North Carolina.[33] John Lawson became one of the first town commissioners and later the clerk of court and public register for Bath County. Today, Bath, North Carolina is a beautiful small community along Bath Creek that flows into Pamlico Sound. The community meets most of the current criteria for being considered a sustainable tourism destination.

John Lawson's book describes flora and fauna and native cultures of North Carolina

John Lawson the well-educated traveler, naturalist, historian, and explorer had taken detailed notes of the flora, fauna and native cultures during his 550-mile trek, mostly through the wilderness of what is now the state of North Carolina. John Lawson the surveyor, land owner and businessman noted during his journey opportunities to entice new investors and settlers to the region. These interests led to his return to England early in 1709 to convert his notes into a book describing Carolina. The publisher, John Stevens, initially agreed to publish Lawson's notes as a serial contribution to a larger work titled *A New Collection of Voyages and Travels. With Historical Accounts of Discoveries and Conquest In all Parts of the World*. However, in learning that John Lawson would be leaving England shortly for Carolina, he decided to publish Lawson's journal as a separate book. Lawson's book added greatly to the travel literature of the time, but more importantly it

(Continued)

Case study (continued)

became an important document for understanding Carolina as a unique and beautiful area. He dedicated the book in the name of the "Lords-Proprietors of the Province of *Carolina* in *America*." Most of the rest of this section is predicated on notes from John Lawson's book (258 pages in length).

In one section of the Preface of the book, Lawson has this to say:

> Having spent most of my Time, during my eight Years Abode in Carolina, in travelling; I not only survey'd the Sea-Coast and those Parts which are already inhabited by the Christians, but likewise view'd a spacious Tract of Land, lying betwixt the Inhabitants [Indians] and the Ledges of Mountains, from whence our noblest Rivers have their Rise, running towards the Ocean, where they water as pleasant a Country [Carolina] as any in Europe; the Discovery of which being never yet made publick[.]

In the Introduction to the book he describes his voyage to the "New World" and the history of Charles Town. He discusses some of the military encounters between the English and their enemies, the French and Spanish. He suggests in one section that the French and Spanish did not treat the Indians well but that the English had a good relationship with the native inhabitants. The last sentence of the *Introduction* notes that "I shall now proceed to relate my Journey thro' [through] the Country, from this Settlement to the other, and then treat of the natural History of *Carolina*, with other remarkable Circumstances which I have met with, during my eight Years Abode in that Country."

The main body of the book gives numerous examples of fascinating customs and cultures of the different Indian tribes. He notes: "As we went up the River, we heard a great Noise, as if two Parties were engag'd against each other, seeming exactly like small Shot. When we approach'd nearer the Place, we found it to be some *Sewee Indians* firing [burning] the Cane Swamps, which drives out the Game, then taking their particular Stands, kill great Quantities of both Bear, Deer, Turkies, and what wild Creatures the Parts afford." He mentions that the *Sewee Indians* were a very large "nation" until the Europeans came and passed along many of their diseases, including small pox, which the Indians had no remedies for, and which killed off most of the tribe. In addition, he describes the terrible impact that liquor has on the Indians, causing not only drunkenness but resulting in many injuries as some natives would fall into a fire or off a cliff.

Lawson goes into considerable detail in the section of the book called "The Natural History," describing the plants and trees and geographical attributes of the areas he encountered during his trek through Carolina. In one section of the book he notes:

> And indeed, most of the Plantations in *Carolina* naturally enjoy a noble Prospect of large and spacious Rivers, pleasant Savanna's and fine Meadows, with their green Liveries, interwoven with beautiful Flowers, of most glorious Colours, which the several Seasons afford; hedg'd in pleasant Groves of the ever-famous Tulip-tree, the stately Laurel, and Bays, equalizing the Oak

in Bigness and Growth; Myrtles, Jessamines, Wood-bines, Honysuckles and several other fragrant Vines and Ever-greens, whose aspiring Branches shadow and interweave themselves with the loftiest Timbers, yielding a pleasant Prospect, Shade and Smell, proper Habitations for the Sweet-singing Birds, that melodiously entertain such as travel thro' the Woods of *Carolina*.

He mentions the numerous quantities of different wild edible plants, berries, and fruits, and, in addition, he describes dozens of the different herbs in the area: "Angelica, Balm, Bugloss . . ."

Lawson's book also includes a major section on "The Beasts of *Carolina*": *Buffelo, Bear, Panther, Cat-a-mount, Wild Cat, Wolf, Tyger, Polcat, Otter, Bever, Musk-Rat, Possum, Raccoon, Minx, Water-Rat, Rabbet, Elks, Stags, Fallow-Deer, Squirrel, Fox, Weasel, etc.* In addition, in this section of the book, he has drawn rough sketches of what some of the animals looked like. He noted that it was rare to see *Buffelo* but that he has "known some kill'd on the Hilly Part of *Cape-Fair-River*, they passing the Ledges of vast Mountains." He also noted that the "*Indians* cut the Skins . . . and make Beds to lie on." He includes a long commentary about the bears of North Carolina, how common they are, their habitat and many other characteristics. He describes the different wild cats of the area which at that time included Bob-cats and *Tygers* [Cougars] which "I once saw one . . . seem'd to be very bold Creature. The *Indians* that hunt in those Quarters, say, they are seldom met withal [seen]. It seems to differ from the Tyger of *Asia* and *Africa*."

After the discussion of the "The Beasts of *Carolina*" Lawson includes a major section on what he called the "Insects of *Carolina*." Interestingly, under this category he has some of the following entries: *Allegators, Rattle-Snakes, Horn-Snakes, Water-Snakes, Swamp-Snakes . . . Scorpion-Lizard, Green Lizard, Frogs, Tortois, &c.*" In his descriptions of the various categories of "Insects of *Carolina*" he notes this: "The Rattle-Snakes are accounted the peaceablest in the World; for they never attack any one, or injure them, unless they are trod upon or molested."

In addition, there is a very long section of the book on "The Birds of *Carolina*" because of the tremendous numbers of birds in the Carolinas. Likewise, a long section on "The Fish in the salt and fresh Waters of *Carolina*." He goes into considerable detail about the weather of the Carolinas, describing a "happy Climate, visited with so mild winters," probably compared to the weather in England. In this section he also promotes his business interests, noting that "Land being sold at a much cheaper Rate there [North Carolina], than in any other Place in *America*. . ."[34]

Explaining the confusion with respect to the name *Carolina* in John Lawson's book

The longest (70-page) chapter in John Lawson's book is titled "An Account of the Indians of North Carolina" and will be described in detail in the next section.

(Continued)

Case study (continued)

However, it is important at this juncture to explain the confusion surrounding the transition from the colony of Carolina to the two states of North and South Carolina. John Lawson, living in what is now known as North Carolina, included in his writings the division of Carolina into the two states of North Carolina and South Carolina before that division was made official by the political leaders. An explanation is in order. On October 30, 1629, King Charles I granted a patent [charter] to Sir Robert Heath for the lands south of 36 degrees and north of 31 degrees, "under the name, in honor of that king, of Carolina." *Carolus* is Latin for "Charles." These lands became the *"Province of Carolina"* including all or parts of the modern states of North Carolina, South Carolina, Georgia, Alabama, Tennessee, Mississippi, Florida, and Louisiana. However, in 1649 King Charles I was executed and Heath fled to France, where he died. Cromwell became the head of England until 1660, when the monarchy was restored with Charles II as king. On March 24, 1663, Charles II issued a new charter, granting the Carolina lands to eight noblemen who had supported his efforts to gain the throne. The eight were called *Lords Proprietors*. This charter allowed for the Lords Proprietors to make changes and set up the territory of Carolina (mostly just North and South Carolina) with "Charles Towne" (Charleston) as the capital. Until 1708, Carolina had just one government, ruled by the Lords Proprietors. By 1708 John Lawson and others increasingly began to refer to a "North" and a "South" Carolina. Between 1708 and 1710 religious disputes and disagreements between governmental representatives, together with the Tuscarora War and the Yamasee War, caused a split of Carolina into two units: North Carolina and South Carolina. To add to the confusion, the *Province of Carolina* was a colony under England from 1629 to 1707 and under Great Britain from 1707 to 1712. The division yielding the separate governments and colonies of North Carolina and South Carolina became complete in 1712, but both colonies remained under the rule of the Lords Proprietors until 1720, at which time a royal governor for South Carolina was appointed, and in 1729 a royal governor was appointed for North Carolina.[35]

During the time period of 1708–1709 John Lawson was putting his notes together based on his travels throughout North and South Carolina. His journeys had taken place while Carolina was the official name of the areas he traveled in. However, his major treks were more in what is now North Carolina than South Carolina. Thus, part of his book refers to the colony of Carolina and in other parts of the book a reference is made to only North Carolina. When his book was published in 1709 there was still only one territory: Carolina. The book has become a classic in understanding the nature, the customs and culture of Native Americans and as a foundation for understanding the history of North Carolina. It contains an excellent description of the flora and fauna in North Carolina during the early eighteenth century. As a naturalist, explorer, and traveler, John Lawson made important inroads to understanding America at that time. Europe was curious about the "New World" and thus Lawson's book became not only popular in England but elsewhere in Europe as well.

John Lawson and "An Account of the Indians of North Carolina"

As mentioned earlier, the longest chapter of John Lawson's book was devoted to his passionate interest in the culture and customs of the Indians of North Carolina. Lawson's initial description of the Indians is in great detail, including the following:

> The *Indians* of North-*Carolina* are a well-shap'd clean-made People, of different Statures, as the *Europeans* are, yet chiefly inclin'd to be tall ... As for their Legs and Feet, they are generally the handsomest in the World ... Their Eyes are black, or of a dark Hazle; The White is marbled with red Streaks ... Their Colour is of a tawny ... They are never bald on their Heads ... They are dexterous and steady both as to their Hands and Feet, to Admiration ... They will walk over deep Brooks, and Creeks, on the smallest Poles [logs], and that without any Fear or Concern.

In describing some of the Indian customs he notes that "Their Dances are of different Natures; and for every sort of Dance, the have a Tune, which is allotted for the Dance." Lawson is fascinated by the dancing, music, singing and feasting of the Indians, as well as the games they play. In his depiction of their living quarters he notes:

> These Savages live in *Wigwams*, or Cabins built of Bark, which are made round like an Oven, to prevent any Damage by hard Gales of Wind. They make the Fire in the middle of the House, and have a Hole at the Top of the Roof right above the Fire, to let out the Smoke ... yet I never felt any ill, unsavory Smell in their Cabins, whereas, should we live in our Houses, as they do, we should be poison'd with our own Nastiness; which confirms these *Indians* to be, as they really are, some of the sweetest People in the World.

Lawson is also fascinated that the Indians all work together, have no fences to mark off a corn field or individual plot, and help each other in whatever most benefits the tribe. If a "good" man dies, they have an immense ceremony to honor him and note that "he will have the Enjoyment of handsome young Women, great Store of Deer to hunt, never meet with Hunger, Cold or Fatigue, but everything to answer his Expectation and Desire. This is the Heaven they propose to themselves." He writes of the women as being generally very beautiful, good mothers, and hard workers. He notes that "All the *Indians* give a Name to their Children, which is not the same as the Father or Mother, but what they fancy. This Name they keep, (if Boys) till they arrive to the Age of a Warriour, which is sixteen or seventeen Years; then they take a Name to themselves, sometimes, Eagle, Panther, Allegator, or some such wild Creature." Lawson notes with special interest the governance of the Indian Nation. "The King is the Ruler of the Nation, and has others under him, to assist him, as his War-Captains, and Counsellors, who are pick'd out and chosen from among the ancientest Men of

(Continued)

Case study (continued)

the Nation he is King of. These meet him in all general Councils and Debates, concerning War, Peace, Trade, Hunting . . . where all Affairs are discoursed of and argued *pro* and *con*, very deliberately." He notes further, "The Succession falls not to the King's Son, but to his Sister's Son, which is a sure way to prevent Impostors in the Succession." Lawson seems quite disturbed by what he considers the cruel way they kill an offender of the laws of the tribe or a prisoner of war. The tribal members from near and far come for a "feast like festival" to watch the intense suffering the offender is put through prior to his death. He gives graphic details:

> Their Cruelty to their Prisoners of War is what they are seemingly guilty of Error in, (I mean as to a natural Failing) because they strive to invent the most inhumane Butcheries for them, that the Devils themselves could invent . . . whilst others split the Pitch-Pine into Splinters, and stick them into the Prisoners Body yet alive. Thus they light them, which burn like so many Torches: and in this manner, they make him dance round a great Fire, every one buffeting and deriding him, till he expires . . . The *Indians* are very revengeful, and never forget an Injury done, till they have receiv'd Satisfaction.

Lawson discusses some of the interventions with the white settlers in the area:

> Most of the Savages are munch addicted to Drunkenness, a Vice they never were acquainted with, till the Christians came amongst them . . . Their chief Liquor is Rum, without any Mixture. This the *English* bring amongst them, and buy Skins, Furs, Slaves and other of their Commodities therewith . . . In these drunken Frolicks, (which are always carried on in the Night) they sometimes murder one another, fall into the fire, fall down Precipices, and break their Necks, with several other Misfortunes which this drinking of Rum brings upon them; and tho' they are sensible of it, yet they have no Power to refrain this Enemy.

Lawson goes into great detail to describe hunting, fishing and other pursuits for food by the Indians. Most of the time he has words of admiration for the customs and culture of the Indians. There is no greater account of the life of the Indians of North Carolina prior to the detailed descriptions in Lawson's book. He repeats many of the Native stories of every aspect of their lives and how they dealt with difficulties of weather, natural disasters and diseases. He notes the many roots, herbs, and natural plants that some tribes used to successfully treat the sick. However, the Indians found no remedies to deal with the diseases brought to them by the Europeans. John Lawson ends the chapter of his book about the culture and customs of the Indians with a several-page dictionary of native words from several tribes translated into English. He notes very importantly that "we see that the *Tuskeruro's* are most numerous in *North-Carolina*, therefore their Tongue is understood by some in every Town of all the *Indians* near us." Lawson has an interesting comment suggesting that had the varying Indian Nations communicated in a common language and organized accordingly, the settlers, at least early on, might not have won many battles with the Indians. He also sees the possibility of the use of a common language as a form of peace and tranquility. Many of the settlers of North Carolina settled in the area seeking religious freedom. Yet the irony regarding such freedom of religion is that these settlers, invading the Indian Territory, wanted the Indian tribes to adopt Christianity even though the Indians had their own forms of religion and spirituality. Lawson even suggests that a common Indian language probably would have made it easier for the "Christian" settlers to convince the Indians to adopt Christianity. In addition he adds to the theme of closer Christian/Indian relationships by saying that "Moreover, by the *Indians* Marrying with the Christians, and coming into Plantations with their *English* Husbands, or Wives, they would become Christians . . . Thus we should be let into a better Understanding of the *Indian* Tongue, by our new Converts; and the whole Body of these People would arrive to the Knowledge of our Religion and Customs." He notes at the end of the book that "In my opinion, it's better for the Christians to marry with the Civiliz'd *Indians*, than to suffer the Hardships of four or five years Servitude."[36]

While Lawson understood the Indians and their culture and customs, he failed to recognize that his desire to entice new settlers to North Carolina on the lands that the Indians considered belonged to all mankind and that no man owned, would cause him to lose his life.

John Lawson and the Tuscarora

While John Lawson was in London finishing his book, he was also recruiting new settlers from England and Germany to settle in North Carolina. In addition, in 1709, while still in London, he met with Baron Christoph von Graffenried, a wealthy Swiss nobleman. Graffenried, through a special arrangement with the royalty of England, had been granted 10,000 acres on the Neuse and Cape Fear rivers by the Lords Proprietors of Carolina. On May 13, 1709 Graffenried organized a group of Swiss and German settlers to join him to settle in North Carolina. Since Surveyor General John Lawson knew the area where Graffenried had his land grant, he promised to show Graffenried the area and to suggest the best place to establish a village. Taking his advice, in 1710 Graffenried established a settlement at the confluence of the Trent and Neuse rivers, which the settlers named New Bern (which later would become the first capital of North Carolina) in honor of Graffenried's birthplace, Bern, Switzerland.

By 1710, the Tuscarora Indians, with 15 villages scattered throughout the Pamlico and Neuse Rivers, were becoming concerned about the many new settlers in what they considered to be their land. The settlers were not being fair in trading with the Indians, they raided villages to take slaves, they spread European diseases among the tribes, and most importantly they were encroaching on the land. By the fall of 1711 the Tuscarora Indians retaliated and Carteret, Pamlico, Craven, Lenoir, Jones, Beaufort, and Pitt counties in North Carolina became terrifying places to live. The conflict between the settlers and the Indians would last until 1715.

(Continued)

Once John Lawson was back in North Carolina in 1710, he began taking short trips in and around Bath, and collected new plant specimens and mapped new areas for possible future settlements. For several months beginning in January 2011 he took numerous trips to collect new plant specimens. He also visited new areas in the eastern part of North Carolina as he wanted to survey the water route between the Neuse River and Albemarle Sound. In September 1711, Lawson, Baron Christoph von Graffenried, and two black slaves began a journey up the Neuse River through the territory of the Tuscarora Indians. Up until this point, Lawson had befriended a number of Tuscarora Indians and felt comfortable with taking Baron Christoph von Graffenried on a journey through the tribal lands. But by this time, relations with the Tuscarora Indians had deteriorated.

About the time that John Lawson and Baron Christoph von Graffenried were journeying up the Neuse River, the Tuscaroras and some of the other tribes had united and began to prey on the settlers in eastern North Carolina. In early September 1711 the Tuscaroras took Baron von Graffenried, John Lawson and the two slaves as prisoners.

> The Indians took their prisoners to the village of Catechna, about four miles north of present-day Grifton, in Pitt County [North Carolina]. At Catechna, John Lawson quarreled heatedly with a Coree [Tuscarora tribe ally] chief named Cor Tom. In response, the Indians tortured and killed Lawson. Graffenried was more diplomatic and was given permission to leave and he lived to describe the experience of being captured in words and pictures. He had tried to convince Lawson to back away from the argument which seemed to be a discussion about land rights (Graffenried did not know the Indian language and could not intervene when Lawson talked with the Indians in their language). Known for harboring black fugitives, the Tuscaroras also spared the lives of the slaves.[37]

Just how Lawson was killed remains a mystery. Graffenried was still in the Indian camp but did not see the killing of Lawson. Some historians say that Lawson's throat was cut. Others say he was hanged. Many think he was stuck with pitch-pine needles and set on fire, as Lawson had himself described in his book. Whatever happened, Lawson did not live to see the end of the so-called Tuscarora War, which lasted from 1711 until 1715, when the Tuscarora were defeated.

John Lawson's untimely death at the age of 37 was a major loss. More than anyone else in the "New World" he left a legacy for understanding the flora and fauna of North Carolina, the early history of North Carolina, and knowledge about Native American customs and the culture of North Carolina. Lawson's book has become a classic with respect to American literature, North Carolina history, detailed information on Native Americans, the natural history of the region, and eighteenth-century travel in the Carolinas, Virginia, and Georgia. Certainly, John Lawson has earned the title of Father of Sustainable Travel in America.

Chapter summary

It was noted at the beginning of this chapter that Native Americans had a strong sense of protecting the environment long before it became a major debatable topic in the twentieth and twenty-first centuries. The early civilization that revolutionized the way people would travel in the future was the highly intelligent Sumerian society. Certainly, the Egyptians added a great deal to early travel as well. They made major inroads to cruise travel.

The Phoenicians were the great shipwrights in the early history of travel. Their boats could travel on the great seas, and through using the North Star for navigation purposes they were able to travel great distances. They spread their knowledge and culture throughout the Mediterranean Sea.

The Greeks added a great deal to traveling for sporting events and invented the Olympics. The greatest Greek ancient traveler was Herodotus. He not only traveled under very difficult circumstances, but as he traveled he kept notes on the history, heritage, and culture of the places he visited. He was the first travel writer, and it is through his writings that we know about the culture and history of many different early societies.

Possibly one of the best known early travelers is Marco Polo. He was born in Venice, which during the thirteenth and fourteenth centuries was a major city-state for trade and travel. While Marco Polo traveled to many different countries, he is best known for his travels to and within China. His interactions with the great Chinese leader Kublai Khan are legendary. He wrote an exceedingly popular book depicting in great detail his many travels.

The great naturalist and traveler Charles Darwin is best known for his book *On the Origin of Species*, although the book that made him famous was *The Voyage of the Beagle*. It was on this voyage that he studied the flora and fauna of the many countries he visited. He also took copious notes about every aspect of the culture of the people he came into contact with during his travels.

Charles Lindbergh's solo flight from New York to Paris made him exceedingly famous. He did a great deal for the advancement of air travel. However, just as important are his contributions to the study of environmental science and his special visits to native societies.

The case study in this chapter is all about John Lawson, possibly the father of sustainable tourism in North America (when it was called the New World). While he did not travel great distances, he did take notes on the flora and fauna and the cultures of the Native Americans wherever and whenever he traveled. His book is certainly one of the early accounts of sustainable travel. He generally befriended the Native Americans he met, but an encounter with one of the tribes at the wrong place, at the wrong time, and with the wrong set of circumstances caused his downfall.

Chapter review questions

1 What early society revolutionized the way people were to travel in the future? What did this society develop that would add to the ability of people to travel?
2 How would you describe travel by the Egyptians?
3 With respect to travel, what attributes were the Phoenicians best known for?

4   What major sporting event are the Greeks most famous for in ancient history?
5   Who was Herodotus and what did he have to do with travel?
6   What was the name of the book that Herodotus wrote?
7   Who was Marco Polo? Where was he from? How did he travel?
8   Who did Marco Polo meet in China and why was this person so important?
9   What is the name of the book which Marco Polo wrote?
10 Who was Charles Darwin?
11 What was the name of the first book that Charles Darwin wrote?
12 What did Charles Lindbergh do that made him so famous?
13 What caused Charles Lindbergh to become an environmentalist?

Notes

1   Edgell, Sr., D. L. and Swanson, J. R. (2013) *Tourism Policy and Planning: Yesterday, Today, and Tomorrow* (2nd edition), London: Routledge, pp. 33–34.
2   Ibid., p. 34.
3   Cleary, K., ed. (1996), *Native American Wisdom*, New York: Barnes & Noble, Inc.
4   Edgell and Swanson (2013), p. 34.
5   Pollard, J. (2008) *Wonders of the Ancient World*, New York: Metro Books, p. 18.
6   Ibid., pp. 20–21.
7   Casson, L. (1974) *Travel in the Ancient World*, Baltimore and London: The Johns Hopkins University Press.
8   O'Gorman, K. (2010) *The Origins of Hospitality and Tourism*, Woodeaton, Oxford, England: Goodfellow Publishers Limited, p. 5.
9   Edgell and Swanson (2013), p. 35.
10 Ibid., p. 36.
11 Edgell, Sr., D. L. (n. d.) *The Worldly Travelers* (unpublished book manuscript). Greenville, North Carolina.
12 Herodotus (449 BCE) *The Histories* (Translated by G. C. Macaulay), New York: Barnes & Noble Classics 2004, p. 98.
13 Ibid., p. 109.
14 Edgell (n. d.) *The Worldly Travelers*.
15 Edgell and Swanson (2013), p. 36.
16 Polo, Marco (1300) *The Travels of Marco Polo* (Translated by Ronald Latham), New York: Penguin Books, pp. 84–85.
17 Ibid., p. 126.
18 Ibid., p. 224.
19 Retrieved from http://goodnature.nathab.com/spotlight-on-sustainability-origins-of-ecotourism/, January 10, 2015.
20 Edgell (n. d.) *The Worldly Travelers*, pp. 149–150.
21 Ibid., p. 160.
22 Ibid., p. 161.
23 Ibid., p. 204.
24 Ibid., p. 205.
25 Bak, R. (2000) *Lindbergh: Triumph and Tragedy*, Dallas, Texas: Taylor Publishing Company, p. 219.
26 Berg, S. (1998) *Lindbergh*, New York: G. P. Putnam's Sons, p. 520.
27 Ibid., p. 523.

28 Ibid., p. 536.
29 Whitman, A. (1969) "Lindbergh Traveling Widely as Conservationist." *The New York Times*, June 23, 1969.
30 Powell, W., ed. (2004) *Dictionary of North Carolina Biography*, University of North Carolina Press at Chapel Hill, North Carolina.
31 Retrieved from http://www.ushistory.org/us/5c.asp, June 30, 2015.
32 Retrieved from https://en.wikipedia.org/wiki/John_Lawson_(explorer), June 23, 2015.
33 Retrieved from https://www.nchistoricsites.org/bath/lawson.htm, June 23, 2015.
34 Lawson, J. (1709) *A New Voyage to Carolina; Containing the Exact Description and Natural History of That Country: Together with the Present State Thereof. And a Journal of a Thousand Miles, Travel'd Thro' Several Nations of Indians. Giving a Particular Account of Their Customs, Manners, &c.* London: John Stevens.
35 Retrieved from https://en.wikipedia.org/wiki/Province_of_Carolina, July 1, 2015.
36 Lawson (1709).
37 Retrieved from http://www.waywelivednc.com/before-1770/tuscarora-war.htm, July 3, 2015.

Chapter 3

Sustainable tourism milestones
Twentieth and twenty-first centuries

"Travel and change of place impart new vigor to the mind."
Lucius Annaeus Seneca, *De Tranquillitate Animi*, 60 CE

Chapter 1 introduced elements of the foundation of sustainable tourism through a discussion of ecotourism, geotourism, responsible tourism, and cultural tourism. Chapter 2 presented historical information to set the record straight that certainly the concept of cultural travel has been a part of our global society since ancient times. This chapter contains a fuller explanation of the background and interpretation of sustainable tourism. The focus of the chapter is to present documents that provide the concepts and ideas aimed toward the positive management of sustainable tourism in the twentieth-first century.

As in times past, one of the strongest motivations for travel today is interest in the natural environment and in the heritage, arts, history, language, customs, and cultures of people locally and in other lands. The opportunities to observe how others live, think, and interact socially and within their environment exert a powerful attraction for many visitors. Travelers may seek to experience examples of a locale's arts, sculpture, architecture, celebrations, and festivals, or cultural interests in food, drink, music, or some other special activity during their travels. The attraction may spring from respect for a built environment with significant historic buildings or unique museums, or the natural environment, with a beautiful landscape, pleasant seashore, a magnificent mountain, a lovely forest, the flora and fauna of the area, or simply the social interactions of human beings in their local surroundings. It is this aspect of the environment – natural habitats, built structures, culture, heritage, history, and social interactions – that, with effective policies, strategic planning, and good management, will sustain tourism into the future. It is essential to conserve and maintain sustaining resources for future generations to enjoy.[1]

Certainly, in the twentieth-first century the concept of utilizing sustainable tourism development to stimulate economic growth while maintaining the natural and built environment is receiving greater attention in industry, academia, not-for-profit organizations, and government. In the first edition of *Managing Sustainable Tourism: A Legacy for the Future* (2006) the present author had this to say about sustainable tourism:

> Responsibly managed tourism enhances and enriches natural, heritage, and cultural values and embraces the need to preserve them so that the community and visitor have a quality tourism experience now and in the future ... Sustainable tourism, properly managed, can become a major vehicle for the realization of humankind's highest aspirations in the quest to achieve economic prosperity while maintaining social, cultural, and environmental integrity.[2]

Today, tourism is recognized as one of the fastest growing industries in the world. Within contemporary tourism, growth in sustainable tourism is moving to the forefront of interest in tourism policy, planning, marketing, and management. Such rapid changes in the tourism industry, and its concurrent development practices, have put particular pressure on managing sustainable tourism in all its varied diversities in a dynamic world. The tenet with respect to sustainable tourism is to understand that tourism experiences may be positive, or in some circumstances negative, and to recognize when there is a need for greater guidelines to ensure that the continued growth of tourism will allow for a balanced and positive tourism experience. Comprehensive planning and management decisions and their implementation are requisite to the decision-making process. In effect, sustainable tourism is part of an overall shift that recognizes that orderly economic growth, combined with concerns for the environment and quality-of-life social values, offers the best future for the tourism industry.

The essence of sustainable tourism

Managing sustainable tourism depends on forward-looking policies, good strategic planning, innovative marketing concepts, and sound management philosophies that include building a harmonious relationship among local communities, the private sector, not-for-profit organizations and governments regarding developmental practices that protect the natural and built environments while being compatible with economic growth. As stated earlier, sustainable tourism practices can be a viable means of providing a community or destination with an improved quality of life. There is only a limited environment to work with, and much of that environment is already under siege from the many different industrial, technological, and unplanned tourism developments underway. To preserve environmental resources, to have a positive impact on the social values of the community, and to add to the quality of life of local citizens worldwide and, at the same time, elicit favorable economic benefits for tourism, is indeed a major challenge.

Pleasant climates, scenic wonders, beautiful coastlines and beaches, majestic mountains and valleys, rugged woods interspersed with rolling plains, magnificent natural vistas, and the rhythmic sounds of the sea are all components of the natural environmental attractions that cause large movements of travelers worldwide. Built structures, whether lodgings, museums, art galleries or historic buildings, are a major part of the built tourism environment. Least understood, but an important part of sustainable tourism products, is the enjoyment of different cultures, traditions, and heritages within local communities.

It has been argued that sustainable tourism "incorporates two complementary tracts: the 'natural environment' (ecotourism, geotourism, adventure tourism, agritourism, and rural tourism) and the 'built environment' (history, heritage, culture, arts, and unique structures). There is an expected overlap in this confluence – both within the basic concept of sustainable tourism and a cross-over in the various elements of the definition." The key to balancing the equation of conserving the natural, built, and sociocultural environments on the one hand and adding economic value on the other is a well-planned and well-managed sustainable tourism program.[3]

With orderly economic growth as part of the goal of sustainable tourism, the key is to balance the number of visitors with the *carrying capacity* of the given environment (whether natural or built) in a manner that allows for the greatest interaction and enjoyment with the least destruction. In its most straightforward definition, *carrying capacity* is simply being able to accommodate the largest number of visitors a destination can effectively and efficiently manage within its given environs and management capabilities without an unacceptable alteration in the natural or physical environment or the social fabric of the community or the quality experience of the visitor. When too many people convene at a location and the area cannot handle this influx, the *carrying capacity* of the place is compromised, which, in turn, harms the environment (natural and built) of the destination, has a negative impact on its local citizenry, and the economy of the destination area eventually declines.

Early background in the development of sustainable tourism philosophies and concepts

Most researches in the tourism industry cite the 1987 *Brundtland Report* that emanated from the meeting of the United Nations World Commission on Environment and Development as a starting point for discussing sustainable tourism. As noted in Chapter 2, one could make a case that sustainable tourism had its origins in ancient history. However, in this book, it is the early twentieth century that introduces and molds modern sustainable tourism concepts and philosophies.

This chapter gives the distinction of the first person in the twentieth century to fully understand the sustainability of travel to one of the world's most famous aviators and worldly travelers, Charles Lindbergh. For many years after his historic flight in 1927 he was the best-known celebrity in the United States and in much of the world. In essence, he was the first world superstar. When he visited a country, he would receive treatment usually reserved for royalty or presidents. Having such a world stage allowed him to be a key contributor to the development of world aviation, as well as with respect to other areas of his interest. Some of his positions on national and international issues were very controversial, including his strong support for the conservation of the natural environment.

After Lindbergh's long career in aviation and his promotion of all aspects of air travel, from flying small aircraft to developing an interest in space travel, he turned his attention to environmental concerns. As he studied the impact of aviation on the environment, he thought through possible negative impacts that aviation might have on the environment, causing him to turn his back on the advancement of the aviation industry and to become a staunch environmentalist. He rededicated his life to the protection of flora and fauna throughout the world. Early in the 1960s he fought vigorously against the development of supersonic passenger jets based on his concerns for the environment. He went on to say that "I realized that if I had to choose, I would rather have birds than airplanes." That was an incredible statement for someone who had devoted the greater part of their career to aviation development. In the 1960s and 1970s he became a strong voice for conservation and a supporter of such organizations as the Nature Conservancy, the World Wildlife Fund, the Oceanic Foundation, and the International Union for the Conservation of Nature and Natural Resources. His voice on environmental issues had a major impact on early concepts of sustainable travel.[4]

There were "red flags" in the 1960s regarding the need for the protection of the environment that brought special attention to environmental issues. In 1962 American marine biologist and conservationist Rachel Carson wrote *Silent Spring,* in which she argued that the pesticides and chemicals used in the agricultural industry were impacting on the sustainability of life itself. This book and others of her writings are credited with advancing the global environmental movement and creating intense discussions on all aspects of environmental issues.

The 1970s became the decade of new ideas and concepts with respect to interest in the conservation and protection of the environment. The United States established the Environmental Protection Agency on December 2, 1970 for the purpose of protecting human health and the environment by writing and enforcing regulations based on laws passed by Congress. The agency continues to conduct environmental assessment, research, and education. Then in 1972 the global think tank group the "Club of Rome" (it describes itself as "a group of world citizens, sharing a common concern for the future of humanity") produced a report titled *The Limits to Growth* that analyzed crucial problems facing humanity, including concerns for the environment. The report sold more than 12 million copies and caused high-level politicians, scientists, economists, and others to take notice of interest in the well-being of society, including the environment, in the future. Because of the composition of the Club of Rome (members are current and former heads of state, United Nations personnel, high-level politicians, diplomats, scientists, economists and business leaders from around the globe) its views are taken very seriously.[5] In addition, in 1972 the United Nations General Assembly convened in Stockholm, Sweden a "United Nations Conference on the Human Environment." The idea behind the conference was to cause a global understanding of the need for preservation and enhancement of the human environment. In addition to many principles enunciated at the conference, it noted that "Both aspects of man's environment, the natural and man-made, are essential to his well-being and to the enjoyment of basic human rights and the right to life itself." The stage was set for numerous meetings, conferences, studies, reports, and other activities regarding environmental matters, many of which included travel and tourism, to take place over the next four decades.

An early example of best practices for managing sustainable tourism

While there was much interest in the environment in the 1970s, and there were a number of excellent philosophies and concepts being developed, there was yet, at least in the United States, no significant practical example of an application for the protection of the environment within the travel and tourism industry until 1975. To be sure, there were likely destinations with some form of sustainability of the natural environment in the world but few were well known. In 1975, a futurist, environmentalist, and civil engineer, Stanley Selengut, leased 14 acres above Maho Bay in St. John, U.S. Virgin Islands and developed possibly the best sustainable resort destination anywhere in the world. It was called the Maho Bay Resorts. Over the years, this property has won numerous national and international awards in exemplifying the highest principles of developing and managing a sustainable tourism destination. It has been referred to as "the world's first eco-resort."

In a case study – "Making Paradise Last: Maho Bay Resorts (MBR)" – in the book *Sustainable Tourism: A Global Perspective*, authors Christina Symko and Rob Harris carefully analyzed MBR in terms of its sustainable features. They said this about Stanley Selengut's MBR:

Developing appropriate tourism facilities and accommodations in fragile environments requires inspiration, innovation and technical ingenuity. Ecolodge developers contend both with the challenge of finding ways to build in harmony with nature and the need to engage visitors in nature-based experiences so that they have an enhanced understanding of the environment around them. This case study details how one Ecolodge, Maho Bay Resorts (MBR) in the US Virgin Islands, has sought to address these challenges. In so doing MBR has sought to encompass the philosophy of sustainability in its broadest sense, extending beyond the environmental dimension to embrace economic and social goals linked to surrounding communities ... Market demand for the various MBR products has been strong with occupancy levels approaching 100 per cent in the high season (mid-December to mid-April), while off-season occupancy rates are significantly above the norm for the Caribbean as a whole.[6]

After analyzing Maho Bay Resorts, the article concludes that, in effect, this destination more than meets the standards of development of sustainable resort practices.

A 1996 Yale University Bulletin Series on "The Ecotourism Equation: Measuring the Impacts" included an article by developer Stanley Selengut titled "Maho Bay, Harmony, Estate Concordia, and the Concordia Eco-Tents, St. John, U.S. Virgin Islands." In the article Selengut tells his personal story of the development of the sustainable tourism property Maho Bay. As mentioned earlier in this chapter, most authors discussing sustainable tourism start with the *Brundtland Report* from the 1987 meeting of the United Nations World Commission on Environment and Development. It is interesting to note that Selengut began developing his environmentally sound resort destination in 1975, 12 years earlier. The Yale Series explains the process of developing an ecotourism property in Selengut's words:

I designed a light inexpensive "tent-cottage" which could be built within the existing trees and plants. The walkways [elevated] were built first, on hand-dug footings. Construction materials were wheeled along the walks and carried into place. Pipes and electrical cables were hidden under the walks rather than buried in trenches. The finished walkways flow naturally through the trees and foliage ... We started small with only eighteen units and a modest cash investment. The campground [resort] won the 1978 Environmental Protection Award, was featured in the *New York Times* travel section, and attracted more customers than we could handle. We used the profits to add units a few at a time. Now, with 114 units, Maho Bay is one of the most profitable and highly occupied resorts in the Caribbean . . . The floor decking is made from 100 percent recycled newspaper. The floor is composed of . . . 100 percent recycled newspapers. The siding is made from a composite of cement and recycled cardboard . . . The bathroom tiles and furniture tops are made from 73 percent post-consumer glass bottles.

Asked about the reasons for such a concern for the environment and using recycled building materials, Selengut said that it is ". . . because it is much more profitable! What makes sense from an environmental and conservation point of view also saves money."[7]

The Maho Bay property used recycled materials, wind energy, solar panels and whatever saving-the-environment technologies were available, and the flora and fauna were fully protected. In a postscript to this presentation about the Maho Bay Resort is the sad news that Mr. Selengut's lease on the property expired in 2012 and he was not willing to pay the asking price of $32 million in order to keep the Maho Bay Resort operating. According to Selengut, "An environmentally oriented billionaire who's supposedly going to use it as a family estate" bought the property.

Sustainable tourism development in the 1980s

The 1980s became a decade of recognizing and implementing policies and programs aimed at conserving the environment and natural resources. The world had become concerned with environmental issues and, as a result, the United Nations (UN) decided it was time to seek a consensus of country interests in the problems with respect to protecting the environment. In 1983, the UN Secretary General appointed Gro Harlem Brundtland to chair a World Commission on Environment and Development. The "Brundtland Commission" was established to study and report on the state of the world regarding the environment. In December 1987 the "Brundtland Commission" was officially disbanded after releasing its report in October 1987, titled *Our Common Future*, often referred to as the *Brundtland Report*. This comprehensive report would have a strong impact on the Earth Summit in Rio de Janeiro, Brazil in 1992 and the third UN Conference on the Environment and Development in Johannesburg, South Africa in 2002. The report defined "sustainable development" as the kind of development that meets the needs of the present generation without compromising the ability of future generations to meet their own needs. Even though the *Brundtland Report* does not specifically mention tourism, its concept of sustainability was adopted by many different industries, including many interests in the tourism industry. An excellent discussion of these concepts with respect to sustainable tourism is contained in the research report by the Cooperative Research Centre for Sustainable Tourism titled *Sustainable Tourism: A Critical Analysis* by David Weaver and Laura Lawton.[8]

A special environmental program related to the travel industry which began in France in 1985 received considerable attention. This highly successful endeavor is known as the "Blue Flag" program. In France in 1985 there were concerns raised regarding water quality and sewage disposal at beach destinations. This led to several studies and reports on what kinds of mitigation could be implemented to avoid damaging the environment along the beaches. This effort and interest in France stimulated Europe to initiate a highly successful program referred to as the "Blue Flag Campaign" under the Foundation for Environmental Education in Europe (FEEE). Later FEEE was expanded to include not only European nations but such countries as South Africa, Morocco, Tunisia, New Zealand, Brazil, Canada, and countries in the Caribbean. With this expansion to non-European countries the program was renamed as just the Foundation for Environmental Education (FEE). The FEE, with respect to the "Blue Flag Campaign," has basically four main criteria dealing with: (1) environmental education and information; (2) water quality; (3) environmental management; and (4) safety and services. Each of these criteria has detailed requirements that must be met for a country to qualify to be included in the Blue Flag program. If an appellant destination is from one of the participating countries and meets the criteria, it is eligible to fly, in front of its property, an FEE Blue Flag that, in effect, tells travelers that the destination is certified as environmentally sound.[9]

It was also in the 1980s that destinations began to recognize the economic and social benefits of having an ecotourism type property. As mentioned earlier in this chapter, ecotourism properties like that of Maho Bay had already been developed in the 1970s and had come to maturity in the 1980s. Also, as noted in Chapter 1, the term ecotourism had been coined in 1983 by Héctor Ceballos-Lascuráin. In addition, for example, in the late 1980s Costa Rica (and some other destinations) had already become a popular ecotourism destination.

Sustainable tourism development expands in the 1990s

In the 1990s sustainable tourism became the watchword for the travel industry. No other decade produced so much literature on sustainable tourism. Much of the focus was being driven by local, national, and international studies and a need to manage environmental impacts on destinations and provide sustainable guidelines and practices for the tourism industry. For example, in 1991, the American Society of Travel Agents (ASTA) released *The Ten Commandments of Ecotourism*. These "Ten Commandments" are the most quoted set of ecotourism principles ever released and are a forerunner to sustainable tourism concepts:

1 Respect the frailty of the earth. Realize that unless we are all willing to help in its preservation, unique and beautiful destinations may not be here for future generations to enjoy.
2 Leave only footprints – take only photographs. No graffiti! No litter! Do not take away "souvenirs" from historical sites and natural sites.
3 To make your travels more meaningful, educate yourself about the geography, customs, manners and cultures of the regions you visit. Take time to listen to the people. Encourage local conservation efforts.
4 Respect the privacy and dignity of others. Inquire before photographing people.
5 Do not buy products made from endangered plants or animals, such as ivory, tortoiseshell, animal skin and feathers. Read "Know Before You Go," the U.S. Customs list of products that cannot be imported.
6 Always follow designated trails. Do not disturb animals, plants or their natural habitats.
7 Learn about and support conservation-oriented programs and organizations working to preserve the environment.
8 Whenever possible, walk or utilize environmentally sound methods of transportation. Encourage drivers of public vehicles to stop engines when parked.

9   Patronize hotels, airlines, resorts, cruise lines, tour operators, and suppliers that advance energy and environmental conservation; water and air quality; recycling; safe management of waste and toxic materials; noise abatement; community involvement; and that provide experienced, well-trained staff dedicated to strong principles of conservation.

10 Ask your ASTA travel agent to identify organizations that subscribe to environmental guidelines for air, land and sea travel. ASTA has recommended that these organizations adopt their own environmental codes to cover special sites and ecosystems.[10]

These guidelines helped to further set the stage for future sustainable tourism principles and greater participation by the private sector, which is described later in this section.

In effect, sustainable tourism as a major concept for the travel and tourism industry emanated from the United Nations Conference on Environment and Development, Rio de Janeiro, Brazil, June, 1992. One hundred and seventy-two countries participated, including 108 heads of state. The resulting conference document, called "Agenda 21: The Rio Declaration on Environment and Development, Statement of Forest Principles, United Nations Framework Convention on Climate Change and the United Nations Convention on Biological Diversity," was a very long report with a section of the document that included three basic themes related to sustainable tourism: first, the need for partnerships between the public and private sectors; second, maintaining quality of life without compromising the future well-being of the people or the planet; and, third, an emphasis on preserving environmental sustainability. The report identifies the environment and development issues which threaten to bring about economic and ecological catastrophe and present a strategy for transition to sustainable development practices.[11]

From the outset of the discussions on sustainability, one country that has not only endorsed the precepts and principles of sustainable tourism but has been a leader in sustainable practices and guidelines is Canada. With respect to its national parks, Canada's National Parks Act of 1930 states, "The Parks are dedicated to the people of Canada for their benefit, education, and enjoyment . . . such parks shall be maintained and made use of so as to leave them unimpaired for the enjoyment of future generations." Canada includes in its tourism planning and marketing plans strong statements on sustainable tourism in its vision, mission statement, goal(s), objective(s), strategies and tactics. As early as 1992 Canada has had a "Code of Ethics and Guidelines for Sustainable Tourism":

1   Enjoy our diverse natural and cultural heritage and help us to protect and preserve it.
2   Assist us in our conservation efforts through the efficient use of resources including energy and water.
3   Experience the friendliness of our people and the welcoming spirit of our communities. Help us preserve these attributes by respecting our traditions, customs and local regulations.
4   Avoid activities which threaten wildlife or plant population, or which may be potentially damaging to our natural environment.
5   Select tourism products and services which demonstrate social, cultural and environmental sensitivity.

This "Code" was developed by the Tourism Industry Association of Canada and the National Round Table on the Environment and the Economy.[11] Possibly more than any country in the world, Canada has a strong partnership of the private sector and the government (later in this book, we will describe this relationship as an example of using the term of coopetition).

New directions of sustainable tourism in the 1990s

The 1990s saw a wide range of academic research conducted by universities, international organizations and industry, resulting in numerous reports and articles on sustainable tourism policy, planning, and management. In 1993, with the issuance of the excellent *Journal of Sustainable Tourism*, with articles on a far-ranging number of sustainable tourism issues, a major step to understanding environmental management of sustainable tourism, ecotourism, cultural tourism, and community responsible tourism was reached.

In 1991 the Pacific Asia Travel Association (PATA), at its 40th Annual Conference in Bali, Indonesia, developed a "Code for Environmentally Responsible Tourism" which was approved by the PATA Board of Directors in 1992. PATA has been a key leader in the field of sustainable tourism and produced the following code:

PATA pledges to:

- Promote and recognize best practice in sustainability and corporate social responsibility
- Ensure that PATA events achieve the highest standards of social responsibility and, in turn, create minimal negative environmental impact
- Advance the role of tourism in poverty alleviation, social cohesion, cultural awareness and the preservation and maintenance of human dignity
- Identify and promote the adoption of mechanisms, guidelines and practices to better measure, manage and reduce environmentally harmful impacts and resource depletion
- Establish, undertake and promote education/training programs and knowledge exchange networks aimed at achieving best practice management and operation of travel and tourism activities
- Establish alliances and partnerships with appropriate organizations that strengthen the effectiveness and expand the reach of PATA's environmental and social responsibility programs
- Encourage investment and development of services and infrastructure that minimize adverse environmental impact, support social advancement and community engagement and promote cultural authenticity and preservation[12]

New Zealand is another country, like Canada, Australia, and many countries in Europe, and a few other select countries elsewhere, that has been a leader in the field of sustainable tourism. In 1992 the New Zealand Ministry of Tourism produced an Issues Paper No. 2 on "Tourism Sustainability: A Discussion Paper." It looked at the eco-efficiency of sustainable tourism in the following way:

To practice eco-efficiency, tourism developers need to consider the environment creatively, throughout project design, construction and operation. Failure to do so could be costly and cause adverse public attention. Those who are responsible for delivering products and services to the visitor must examine their operations in light of sustainable resource management. This may involve any of the following actions:

- Protecting the biosphere
- Reducing and disposing of wastes
- Adopting energy efficient practices
- Minimizing environmental risks
- Undertaking "green" marketing
- Mitigating environmental marketing
- Providing complete and credible environmental information for visitors
- Incorporating environmental values in the management of operations
- Conducting regular environmental audits[13]

Also in 1992, the United Kingdom interest group Tourism Concern, in coordination with the World Wide Fund for Nature, published a discussion document titled "Beyond the Green Horizon: Principles for Sustainable Tourism," outlining the following principles, among others:

- *Using resources in a sustainable manner*: The conservation of resources – natural, social, and cultural – is crucial and makes long-term business sense.
- *Reducing overconsumption and waste*: Reduction of overconsumption and waste avoids the costs of putting right long-term environmental damage and contributes to the quality of tourism.
- *Maintaining diversity*: Natural, social and cultural diversity are essential for long-term sustainable tourism and create a resilient base for the industry.
- *Integrating tourism into planning*: Integration into a national and local strategic planning framework and the use of environmental impact assessments increase the long-term viability of tourism.
- *Supporting local economies*: Tourism that supports a wide range of local economic activities and takes environmental costs and values into account both protects those economies and avoids environmental damage.
- *Involving local communities* in the tourism sector not only benefits them and the environment in general but also improves the quality of the tourism experience.
- *Consulting stakeholders and the public*: Consultation between the tourism industry and local communities, organizations, and institutions is essential if they are to work together and resolve conflicts of interest.
- *Training staff*: Staff training that integrates sustainable tourism into work practices, along with recruitment of local personnel at all levels, improves the quality of the tourism product.
- *Marketing tourism responsibly*: Marketing that provides tourists with full and responsible information increases respect for the natural, social, and cultural environments of destination areas and enhances customer satisfaction.
- *Undertaking research*: Ongoing research and monitoring by the industry using effective data collection and analysis tools is essential to solve problems and to bring benefits to destinations, the industry, and consumers.[14]

Key to these broad principles, which underlie the action steps suggested later in this book, is the fact that managed sustainable tourism is often in companies' commercial interests and that responsibility for sustainable tourism is a shared public–private venture. Most private-sector interests in tourism and destinations throughout the world now better understand the necessity and advantages of managing their tourism interests in a sustainable manner.

Other paths to sustainable tourism in the 1990s

Since 1992 the UNWTO has promoted sustainable approaches to tourism development. In 1993 the UNWTO issued a popular sustainable tourism publication titled *Sustainable Tourism Development: Guide for Local Planners*. This report had a strong influence on many countries throughout the world. From that effort going forward, the UNWTO has been a global leader with respect to tourism policy, planning, and the management of sustainable tourism. Later in this book additional information with respect to UNWTO's major contributions to sustainable tourism will be presented.

In 1993 Tony Griffin and Nicolette Boele published an article titled "Alternative Paths to Sustainable Tourism" which outlined five tourism sustainability elements:

1 Preserving the current resource base for future generations
2 Maintaining the productivity of the resource base
3 Maintaining biodiversity and avoiding irreversible environmental changes
4 Ensuring equity within and between generations
5 Maintaining and protecting the heritage (culture/history) of an area, region, or nation[15]

In 1994, the Organisation for Economic Co-operation and Development (OECD) issued a report titled "Tourism Policy and International Tourism in OECD Countries," citing six factors related to sustainable tourism within rural areas:

1 Scenic value including mountains, seashores, lakes, islands, rivers, and special interest scenery such as wetlands or mixed deciduous forest
2 Special wildlife assets
3 Cultural assets including historic buildings, towns, villages, sites and/or ethnic heritage of all types
4 Special facilities for sports including hunting, fishing, skiing, and hiking
5 Ease of access by large populations
6 Effective promotional, commercial, and management skills.[16]

In 1996, the World Travel and Tourism Council, the United Nations World Tourism Organization, and the Earth Council jointly launched an initiative titled *Agenda 21 for the Travel and Tourism Industry: Towards Environmentally Sustainable Development*, that includes:

● Travel & Tourism should assist people in leading healthy and productive lives in harmony with nature
● Travel & Tourism should contribute to the conservation, protection and restoration of the earth's ecosystem
● Travel & Tourism should be based upon sustainable patterns of production and consumption

- Travel & Tourism, peace, development and environmental protection are independent
- Protectionism in trade in Travel & Tourism services should be halted or reversed
- Environmental protection should constitute an integral part of the tourism development process
- Tourism development issues should be handled with the participation of concerned citizens, with planning decisions being adopted at local level
- Nations shall warn one another of natural disasters that could affect tourists or tourist areas
- Travel & Tourism should use its capacity to create employment for women and indigenous peoples to the fullest extent
- Tourism development should recognize and support the identity, culture and interests of indigenous peoples
- International laws protecting the environment should be respected by the Travel & Tourism industry.[17]

The above actions were further reinforced at the 7th Session of the United Nations Commission on Sustainable Development in 1999, which placed increased emphasis on the economic and social aspects of sustainable development, especially in relation to poverty reduction. The Commission urged governments to "maximize the potential for tourism for eradicating poverty by developing appropriate strategies in cooperation with all major groups, indigenous and local communities." The UNWTO and the WTTC became primary organizations to account for the global travel and tourism industry with respect to the Commission's initiative.

A regional approach to sustainable tourism in the 1990s

As noted earlier, regional organizations such as the Organisation for Economic Co-operation and Development, the Organization of American States, the Asia-Pacific Economic Cooperation, and the Caribbean Tourism Organization were all heavily engaged in sustainable tourism activities. At the same time there were bilateral and multilateral agreements between countries that were also involved in sustainable tourism programs. For example, the North American Free Trade Agreement, which included the United States, Canada, and Mexico, under the aegis of the Commission for Environmental Cooperation (CEC – Montreal, Canada) prepared a discussion paper in 1999 titled "The Development of Sustainable Tourism in Natural Areas in North America: Background, Issues and Opportunities." This document suggests that sustainable tourism in natural areas is an opportunity for the three countries to explore cooperation and "perhaps even a common framework, for the promotion of sustainable development through nature-based tourism . . . Underlying the economic benefits of development is a joint commitment to the protection of the ecosystems that attract tourists to natural areas." Under the section of the CEC paper called "Definitions and Context" it was noted that:

- Sustainable tourism is defined, in theoretical terms, as tourism development with minimal negative impacts and maximal positive impacts on the sociocultural and ecological environment through planning and management.
- Ecotourism, or sustainable tourism to natural areas, is a niche market. Numerous definitions of ecotourism are attempting to translate theory into practice.

- Different working definitions of the term "ecotourism" prevail, both within and among Canada, Mexico, and the United States.
- Surveys of ecotourist profiles in Latin America, Canada, and the United States found that the average ecotourist tends to be older, with a graduate degree, a high level of disposable income, and an enjoyment of traveling with family or friends.
- Accurate data on ecotourism are difficult to obtain because of the varying definitions of the term, non-site-specific census methods, and a lack of relevant studies.
- Trends indicate that conventional tourism has grown over the past decade and continues to grow. They suggest a diversification and increase of tourism into alternative and specialized activities such as ecotourism, bird-watching, hiking, canoeing, and visiting natural settings and interesting cultures.
- Key North American natural and cultural tourism assets include ecological regions and landscapes, fauna and flora, protected spaces and species, cultural populations, sites, and artifacts.
- Participation by the local community is key to the long-term viability of tourism.
- History has proven that unplanned, unmanaged tourism that exceeds the carrying capacity of an area is transformed from a non-consumptive renewable resource venture into a short-term "boom and bust" enterprise.
- Promoters of tourism and promoters of nature conservation are bound by three types of relationship conflict, coexistence, or symbiosis. A symbiotic relationship from which both benefit is the ultimate goal.[18]

This paper was very valuable in the sense that it sorted out some of the questions that had been raised earlier in the 1990s. For example, it alluded to the fact that often different countries see ecotourism from many different perspectives. It also focused on the need for planning and management if sustainable tourism is to be successful. Finally, it explained that ultimately a symbiotic relationship is most likely to lead to successful programs in sustainable tourism. It is also interesting to note that it is possible to take three different countries and find in them common ground for a discussion of important sustainable tourism concepts.

As is clear from the above cited reports, in the 1990s there was such an array of activities, meetings, conferences and other events regarding sustainable tourism, too numerous to mention herein and beyond the scope of managing sustainable tourism as addressed in this book. It should be noted, however, that at the same time as the organizations described above were moving forward on sustainable tourism issues in the 1990s, many academic institutions were also conducting significant research on sustainable tourism. In the United States, the University of Colorado established the first U.S. Center for Sustainable Tourism in 1998. The Leeds Metropolitan University in England was establishing a leadership role in responsible tourism. Other universities throughout the world were busily engaged in developing their own versions of what sustainability meant from a travel, tourism, and hospitality perspective.

Several organizations mentioned earlier in this book, like the UNWTO, the Organisation for Economic Co-operation and Development (OECD), the Organization of American States (OAS), the Asia-Pacific Economic Cooperation (APEC), the Caribbean Tourism Organization (CTO) and many others, were holding meetings and conferences and developing research and studies detailing new directions in sustainable tourism. At the same time, such groupings as the Pacific Asia Travel Association and the North American Free Trade Agreement were fostering strong sustainable tourism programs.

In effect, the world's travel and tourism constituencies in the 1990s were all getting on the bandwagon of sustainable tourism.

In 1996 this author prepared the initial report titled *The Organization of American States Sustainable Tourism Development Policy and Planning Guide* for the Department of Regional Development and Environment, Executive Secretariat for Economic and Social Affairs of the Organization of American States (OAS). It was issued as an OAS Inter-American Congress document on January 31, 1997 and discussed at the XVII Inter-American Travel Congress on April 7–11, 1997 in San Jose, Costa Rica. In summary, the document reinforces the concepts of sustainable tourism. The document clearly builds a case that tourism sustainability in essence means seeking growth in a way that does not deplete the natural or built resources, provides a quality product to the visitor, and embraces local involvement. It strongly suggests that responsible tourism management must protect the resources while adding to an area's overall tourism product in such a way that the local area's economic, social, and cultural values are maintained.[19]

Some guidelines for sustainable tourism in the twenty-first century

It is very clear that sustainable tourism today is an integral part of an overall shift that recognizes that orderly economic growth, combined with concerns for the natural and built environment and quality-of-life social values, is the driving force for long-term progress in tourism planning, development, and policies. The concept of utilizing sustainable tourism development to stimulate economic growth and at the same time conserve the natural and built environments is receiving greater attention in industry and government. Consumers of tourism in the new millennium are demanding greater quality in their tourism products. Within the framework of sustainability, they want new and different destinations, greater variety, and more flexibility in their travels. In addition, they want to ensure that their children and future generations can enjoy a wide variety of tourism products. As this book has advocated, positive sustainable tourism development is dependent on forward-looking policies and new management philosophies that seek harmonious relations between local communities, the private sector, not-for-profit organizations, academic institutions, and governments at all levels to develop practices that protect natural, built, and cultural environments in a way that is compatible with economic growth.

Thus far, not much has been said about the marketing of sustainable tourism. While there is a separate chapter in this book on the marketing of sustainable tourism, it is important to note at this point that sensitivity to the environment is rapidly becoming a major component of international tourism marketing strategies. Businesses are recognizing that by forming partnerships with local entities and heeding environmental protection policies, they can create and market quality tourism products.

The new millennium has seen countless new initiatives with respect to the management of sustainable tourism. Mentioning a few such endeavors will illustrate the progress being made with respect to sustainable tourism in the twenty-first century. Following in an approximate chronological order are a few different approaches to the building of sustainable tourism precepts and guidelines for the future.

In 2001 the *National Geographic Society* established *National Geographic's Sustainable Tourism Initiative*. Shortly thereafter, *National Geographic Society*'s popular travel magazine, the *National Geographic Traveler*, and the U.S. Travel Industry

Association of America sponsored a two-part study titled *Geotourism: The New Trend in Travel* to determine how American travelers felt about the conservation of the environment and interest in cultural tourism. A report was issued which mentioned that more than three quarters of American travelers felt it was important that their visits did not damage the environment; 62 percent said it is important to learn about other cultures when they travel, and 38 percent said they would pay more to use a travel company that strives to protect and preserve the environment.[20]

In the meantime, in 2002 *National Geographic's Sustainable Tourism Initiative* partnered with Leeds Metropolitan University (England) to assemble a team of over 300 experts (including this author) in fields related to sustainable tourism and destination quality to survey destinations with respect to their sustainability. The group of "experts" was asked to rate each destination being surveyed based on the following six criteria:

1 Environmental and ecological quality
2 Social and cultural integrity
3 Condition of any historic building and archeological sites
4 Aesthetic appeal
5 Quality of tourism management, and
6 The outlook for the future

The first surveys were conducted in 2003 and the results were published in *National Geographic Traveler* in the March 2004 issue. The cover for the March 2004 issue of the magazine included, in large bold letters, the following: "Exclusive! 115 Places Rated (Our Destination Scorecard Rates Your Favorite Places, Including. . .)." The magazine devoted eight pages of commentary about the sustainability of the destinations under three headings: "The Good," "Not So Bad" and "Getting Ugly." A destination certainly did not want to be in the "Getting Ugly" category. The results were quite revealing, and surprising to many of the destinations, and to many professionals in the travel world. For many destinations the survey was a good measuring stick and an incentive for destinations to take stock and seek improvements, where possible, for the future sustainability of their areas. These surveys took place from 2003 to 2011, with headline covers of the magazine having such statements as "99 Destinations Rated," "133 Destinations Rated," "94 Places Rated," etc. In all, almost 700 different types of destinations were rated, from islands, beaches and coastlines to national parks, grasslands and mountains. These surveys, and the published results, have had a major impact on improving the sustainability of the rated destinations, as well as in causing non-rated areas to be cognizant of the need to be sustainable if they are to offer quality locations and services.[21]

New concepts in sustainable tourism in the twenty-first century

The United Nations designated 2002 "the International Year of Ecotourism." This designation created a great deal of interest in both ecotourism and sustainable tourism. As mentioned earlier in this book, ecotourism is a special subset of sustainable tourism. With such recognition from the United Nations there was greater awareness among public authorities, the private sector, and the general public about tourism issues. This text has already discussed some of the principles of ecotourism from the perspective of

The International Ecotourism Society (TIES). The principles and practices of TIES were more broadly discussed in the 2002 report "Ecotourism: Principles, Practices & Policies for Sustainability" supported by the United Nations Environmental Program and The International Ecotourism Society. The report begins:

> Recognizing the global importance of the issue [ecotourism], the United Nations designated 2002 as the International Year of Ecotourism, and the Commission on Sustainable Development mandated the United Nations Environment Program and the World Tourism Organization to carry out activities for the Year. Its goal is to review the lessons learned in implementing ecotourism, and to identify and promote forms of ecotourism that lead to the protection of critically endangered ecosystems, sharing the benefits of the activity with local communities and respecting local cultures ... Ecotourism is a growing niche market within the larger travel industry, with the potential of being an important sustainable development tool. With billions of dollars in annual sales, ecotourism is a real industry that seeks to take advantage of market trends. At the same time, it frequently operates quite differently than other segments of the tourism industry, because ecotourism is defined by its sustainable development results: conserving natural areas, educating visitors about sustainability, and benefiting local people ... Market research shows that ecotourists are particularly interested in wilderness settings and pristine areas ... ecotourism has a unique role to play in educating travelers about the value of a healthy environment and biological diversity. However, proper planning and management are critical to ecotourism's development.[22]

The United Nations Environmental Program (UNEP), an organization deeply involved in sustaining the environment, continues to support sustainable tourism initiatives. In 2002 UNEP facilitated a multi-stakeholder process that included the World Travel and Tourism Council, the International Federation of Tour Operators, the International Hotel and Restaurant Association, and the International Council of Cruise Lines to produce a very important report titled "Industry as a Partner for Sustainable Development." The report emphasized the importance of management, education, and technology in improving opportunities for local populations, especially in rural areas and elsewhere in better understanding environmental issues. The following quotation summarizes many of the concepts developed in the report from an international travel perspective:

> The challenge is to move from the existing *ad hoc* approach, to one that can integrate the current social, economic, and environmental programs, funds, and initiatives, and evolve new patterns of managing travel and tourism businesses in a more systematic and dynamic way. The inevitable transition to sustainable development strategies gives the travel and tourism industry an opportunity to confirm itself as a solution, rather than a contributor to the economic, social, and environmental challenges facing the future.[23]

This report was exceedingly helpful in that it weighed in on the policy question often raised as to whether the development of sustainable tourism can be economically viable for private companies and local communities. The short answer is yes. This answer was also noted in the earlier discussion in this book with regard to the highly sustainable and profitable Maho Bay Resorts in St. John, U.S. Virgin Islands. That resort and many other tourism entities have shown that a well-developed tourism program that adheres to strong sustainable tourism management principles can be very successful and is likely to have greater success in the future than properties not built according to sustainability practices. Such efforts increase the quality and lifetime value of the tourism products and, hence, increase visitor satisfaction. Satisfied visitors are likely to be repeat visitors and, in the long run, are the key to the overall economic growth of tourism for a local community. If the stakeholders directly involved in a property and local community members partner with each other, and develop sustainable tourism policies, and strategic tourism management plans that include a marketing plan, then the likelihood for success is very high. In general, most of the studies have found that a well-researched, well-planned, and well-managed tourism program that takes into account the natural and built environment has a good chance of improving the local economy and enhancing the quality of life of residents.

Much of the early commentary on sustainable tourism was oriented toward the natural environment. Just as important in sustainable tourism are the history (see Chapter 2), heritage and culture of a destination. Many of the documents researched for this book combine heritage and culture under one banner, cultural tourism. The United Nations Educational, Scientific and Cultural Organization has a special World Heritage program that encourages travel to important cultural and historic destinations. Based on this author's limited research, the best discussion of the similarities and differences of cultural and heritage tourism is contained in the National Trust for Historic Preservation's article "Share Your Heritage: Cultural and Heritage Tourism – The Same or Different?"

> It is not possible to define culture tourism and heritage tourism as two entirely different kinds of tourism. In looking at definitions of both heritage and cultural tourism, there clearly is overlap between the two. Without question, the areas of overlap far exceed the differences ... An informal survey of programs across the country [United States] reveals that "heritage" programs are more often found in rural areas while "cultural" programs are more often found in urban settings. Historic preservation groups are more likely to describe "heritage tourism" programs, while museum and arts groups are more likely to refer to "cultural tourism" programs, though the content is often quite similar ... The primary difference between the two is that heritage tourism is "place" based. Heritage tourism programs create a sense of place rooted in the local landscape, architecture, people, artifacts, traditions and stories that make a particular place unique. Cultural tourism programs celebrate the same kinds of experiences, though with less emphasis on place. Thus, viewing the work of a great master artist in his home and studio is a heritage tourism experience, while viewing those same pieces of art in a traveling exhibition is a cultural tourism experience. The content is the same while the context is different ... This distinction clarifies why preservationists refer to "heritage tourism" while museums and arts organizations are more likely to use the term "cultural tourism." Historic preservation tends to address the built environment and cultural landscape, and preservationists place a high value on maintaining the original context. On the other hand, museums and the arts are more likely to work with collections and performances that can be transported and shared with other communities ... While using the term "cultural heritage tourism" is useful to help bring together all of the partners that need to be working together on this type of an effort (including organizations and individuals representing the arts, museums,

the humanities, historic preservation, heritage areas, ethnic groups and others including tourism partners), it is cumbersome to use in marketing programs to potential visitors. An informal survey reveals that the terms "cultural" and "heritage" have different meaning for the layperson – and for your potential visitors. Thus, based on your audience, it may be more effective to use one term or the other depending upon the image that you are trying to convey.[24]

In Chapter 1 it was noted that the definition of *Geotourism* was "tourism that sustains or enhances the geographical character of a place – the environment, culture, aesthetics, heritage, and the well-being of its residents." *Cultural Tourism* was defined as "traveling to experience the places and activities that authentically represent the stories and people of the past and present." Both such terms are part and parcel of the definition of sustainable tourism, which will be described in more detail later in this chapter.

The impact of the United Nations Educational, Scientific and Cultural Organization on sustainable tourism

A different tactic with respect to cultural and heritage tourism is to review concepts and definitions used by the United Nations Educational, Scientific and Cultural Organization (UNESCO) since most countries of the world seek to have their sites designated as "world heritage sites." At a UNESCO meeting in Paris in 1972 the following was agreed:

- *Noting* that the cultural heritage and the natural heritage are increasingly threatened with destruction not only by the traditional causes of decay, but also by changing social and economic conditions which aggravate the situation with even more formidable phenomena of damage or destruction,
- *Considering* that deterioration or disappearance of any item of the cultural or natural heritage constitutes a harmful impoverishment of the heritage of all the nations of the world,
- *Considering* that protection of this heritage at the national level often remains incomplete because of the scale of the resources which it requires and of the insufficient economic, scientific, and technological resources of the country where the property to be protected is situated,
- *Recalling* that the Constitution of the Organization provides that it will maintain, increase, and diffuse knowledge, by assuring the conservation and protection of the world's heritage, and recommending to the nations concerned the necessary international conventions,
- *Considering* that the existing international conventions, recommendations and resolutions concerning cultural and natural property demonstrate the importance, for all the peoples of the world, of safeguarding this unique and irreplaceable property, to whatever people it may belong,
- *Considering* that parts of the cultural or natural heritage are of outstanding interest and therefore need to be preserved as part of the world heritage of mankind as a whole,
- *Considering* that, in view of the magnitude and gravity of the new dangers threatening them, it is incumbent on the international community as a whole to

participate in the protection of the cultural and natural heritage of outstanding universal value, by the granting of collective assistance which, although not taking place of action by the State [nation] concerned, will serve as an efficient complement thereto,

- *Considering* that it is essential for this purpose to adopt new provisions in the form of a convention establishing an effective system of collective protection of the cultural and natural heritage of outstanding universal value, organized on a permanent basis and in accordance with modern scientific methods . . .

Adopts the Convention with the following definition of "cultural heritage":

Monuments: architectural works, works of monumental sculpture and painting, elements or structures of an archaeological nature, inscriptions, cave dwellings and combinations of features, which are of outstanding universal value from the point of view of history, art or science;

Groups of buildings: groups of separate or connected buildings which, because of their architecture, their homogeneity or their place in the landscape, are of outstanding universal value from the point of view of history, art or science;

Sites: works of man or the combined works of nature and man, and areas including archaeological sites which are of outstanding universal value from the historical, aesthetic, ethnological or anthropological point of view . . .[25]

UNESCO sets out the requirements for nations to maintain and protect the sites that are designated as "World Heritage Sites." UNESCO leaves it to the individual countries to determine how they will define the sites as tourism destinations and promote and market such sites.

Defining sustainable tourism

With the considerable research, documents, and background information contained in this chapter and the four components of sustainable tourism presented in Chapter 1 the question is how to develop a definition of sustainable tourism. Over many years there have been numerous definitions of sustainable tourism. An additional question: "Is it possible to include most of the key precepts of cultural tourism, geotourism, ecotourism and responsible tourism in a single definition?" In the first edition of *Managing Sustainable Tourism: A Legacy for the Future* (Edgell, 2006) sustainable tourism was defined by this author in this way: "To me, the simplest definition of sustainable tourism is achieving quality growth in a manner that does not deplete the natural and built environment and preserves the cultural, history, and heritage of the local community." In this book a slight alteration of this definition works well in the twenty-first century. Thus, "Sustainable tourism is achieving quality growth in a manner that does not deplete the natural and built environment and preserves the culture, history, and heritage of the local community and improves the welfare of the local people." The remaining critical question is: "What is the best way to manage sustainable tourism so that future generations can enjoy quality tourism projects in the future?" Much of the information which will be forthcoming in the next several chapters will help lay the foundation for an answer to this question.

Case study 3: Climate change, sustainability, and impacts on tourism – the Outer Banks of North Carolina

"Adventure is worthwhile in itself."

Amelia Earhart

Background

As mentioned in Chapter 3, in the March 2004 issue of *National Geographic Traveler*, 115 destinations throughout the world were rated in terms of their sustainability. One such rated destination was the Outer Banks of North Carolina. It did not receive a favorable rating. Since the Outer Banks attracts more than five million visitors each year from more than 50 countries and is the principal source of economic development and jobs, there was great concern about the future of tourism to the Outer Banks. As a result, considerable research began. Local meetings were held and numerous surveys were conducted. Several research institutes and universities started to look at all aspects of sustainable tourism on the Outer Banks, including issues related to climate change.

This case study was written by the present author and Carolyn E. McCormick. They began their research in 2004 and continue to research climate change and sustainability with respect to the Outer Banks of North Carolina. After visiting communities along a 115-mile stretch of coastline in the Outer Banks area by vehicle, by walking imperiled areas along the coast, and as passenger-surveyors inspecting the coastline in a small four-seater airplane, it was clear that certain areas of the Outer Banks failed the sustainability criteria developed by the *National Geographic Sustainability Tourism Initiative*. Fortunately, new research and information has become available and researchers are working on a variety of studies that have a bearing on the sustainability of tourism in the Outer Banks. This case study incorporates the research conducted by Edgell and McCormick and adds new information gleaned from other investigations into climate change and sustainability with respect to the Outer Banks.

The Outer Banks is a 200-mile-long string of narrow barrier islands off the coast of the U.S. State of North Carolina that also includes a few miles lying within the U.S. State of Virginia. It begins in the southeastern corner of Virginia Beach, Virginia and stretches along the entire coastline of North Carolina. The Outer Banks is a major tourist destination and is known around the world for its temperate climate and wide expanse of open beachfront. It is also a favorite area for offshore and inshore fishing and provides many additional recreation opportunities. In addition, because there are more than a thousand shipwrecks off the shores of the Outer Banks, it is a popular area for certain types of deep-sea diving.

On June 22, 1587 Sir Walter Raleigh, John White and 116 English colonists were the first English people to sail to Hatteras Island and attempt to settle in the Outer Banks. The colonists were not comfortable with the idea of settling on

(Continued)

Case study (continued)

Hatteras Island and left to settle on Roanoke Island. John White returned to England to gather supplies but due to the Anglo–Spanish War did not return until three years later. By then, the settlement had disappeared, with no trace of the settlers. Today the area is referred to as the "Lost Colony." What happened to the colony continues to baffle researchers who are still looking for clues to the settlement's disappearance.[26]

Without settlers, the Outer Banks became a refuge for pirates who raided Spanish and British ships carrying gold and other valuables on the high seas. It was easy for the pirates to hide in the various inlets along the Outer Banks. The most famous of the pirates was "Blackbeard" (Edward Teach), who made Ocracoke Island his home base.

The Outer Banks is also well known as the place where Orville and Wilbur Wright made the historic first flight in a controlled, powered, heavier-than-air vehicle, which took place on December 17, 1903, at Kill Devil Hills near the seafront town of Kitty Hawk. This historic moment set off a global interest in developing and piloting airplanes. The Wright Brothers National Monument at Kill Devil Hills commemorates the historic flights.

The Outer Banks is also home to maritime forests. According to Dr. Anthony Snider, southern sites manager of the North Carolina Coastal Reserve, and the Bald Head Island Conservancy, "Maritime forests are rare, narrow bands of forest that grow almost exclusively on the stabilized back dunes of barrier islands. They are different from inland forests because of their ability to survive and develop despite their harsh coastal environment." Such woods contain unique kinds of trees and other types of plant life. The woods also provide a habitat for a wide variety of animal wildlife and birds.

The Outer Banks area is the victim of hurricanes and major storms moving up the eastern corridor of the United States. The area is home to the third largest estuary system in the world, the highest sand dunes located on the east coast of the United States, numerous beaches, wildlife preserves, and historical sites. Damage sustained by powerful storms, the frequency of which has increased in recent years, erodes the beaches enjoyed by vacationers, as well as the land on which residences and hotels are built.

Introduction

The changing global climate will pose profound policy challenges and demand strategic decisions from world leaders in coming decades. Climate variability has multiple dimensional impacts depending on the severity of the changes and the vulnerability of the area in question. Few industries are more dependent on the outcome of changes in climate than the tourism industry. For the future growth and sustainability of tourism in the United States, policy responses to climate change are critical. While this study is geared to impacts of climate change on tourism in the Outer Banks of North Carolina, much of the research and analysis contained herein has broad implications for similar coastal tourism destinations throughout the world.

The majority of scientists studying issues related to climate change have stated that global warming is currently taking place and that it is mostly due to human activity. Whether climate change is due to human activity, natural phenomena or both, the fact is that change in the climate will have an enormous impact on the tourism industry. The remarkable growth of tourism throughout the world over the past 25 years has elevated the need for sustainable tourism policy discussions with respect to the repercussions of climate change on the tourism industry. Goeldner and Brent Ritchie (2012) stated that "Compelling evidence indicates that global climate has changed compared to the pre-industrial era – and that it is anticipated to continue to change over the twenty-first century and beyond . . . With its close connections to the environment and climate itself, tourism is considered to be a *highly climate-sensitive economic sector* similar to agriculture, insurance, energy, and transportation."[27] Becken and Hay (2007) pointed out that "Climate change will not only impact on tourism directly by changes in temperature, extreme weather events and other climatic factors, but also indirectly as it will transform the natural environment that attracts tourists in the first place – for example, by accelerating coastal erosion, damaging coral reefs and other sensitive ecosystems and by reducing snowfall and snow cover in mountainous regions. It will also affect the basic services that are so critical for tourism, such as water supplies, especially during periods of peak demand."[28] Former United Nations World Tourism Organization's Secretary General Francesco Frangialli (2007) said, "We [tourism industry] are part of the problem [global warming] and we will be part of the solution."[29]

Until recently, there existed limited research on the potential impact of climate change on specific tourism destinations such as the Outer Banks. A January 17, 2011 Associated Press article titled "Rising Sea Waters Threaten North Carolina's Delicate Coastline" stated, "A North Carolina science panel is predicting the sea level will raise by 1 meter by 2100."[30] This report provided a review of known facts about climate change relevant to the high-density tourist zone of the Outer Banks and promoted a discussion of policy issues at the core of climate change decision-making. Such research is helping to provide a policy agenda for climate change mitigation through sustainable tourism development and management in the United States.

Weather conditions and climatic changes taking place in relation to a tourism destination often dictate why people travel, where they travel, how they travel, and when they travel – and for how long visitors stay at the destination. What tourists want in their tourism products and destinations varies considerably. Generally visitors to beach areas are looking for sunshine and warm waters. Skiers and snowmobilers pray for good snowfalls. Sightseers and outdoor recreationists hope for clear weather and moderate temperatures. The livelihoods of providers of visitor services and products at destinations are often dependent on a certain number of good weather days during the tourism season. Many tourism businesses have failed simply because of weather conditions.

Variances in weather patterns due to climate change may have immediate repercussions for destinations and for the visitors to those destinations. Forest

(Continued)

Case study (continued)

fires destroy the flora and fauna of areas of interest to tourists. Hurricanes and tsunamis change coastlines and often wreak havoc on resort homes, destinations, and tourism services. Floods or droughts can devastate an area once dependent on tourism. These concerns and other factors connected to climate change will often determine the future sustainability of tourism at a destination.

Researcher Bill Birkemeier, a hydraulic engineer at the U.S. Army Corps of Engineers Field Engineer Research and Development Center on the Outer Banks, has said:

> Over the past twenty years there has been a slight rise in both sea temperatures and sea levels due to climate change. Because the Outer Banks are dynamic and ever changing, and since sea-level rise is at present small and gradual, relative to twice-daily tidal variation and surges caused by frequent storms, it is difficult to determine what changes on the coastline are due directly to sea-level rise. A more immediate concern would be whether climate change may increase the number or severity of storms on the coast as storms have a major impact on coastlines.[31]

This Field Engineer Research and Development Center continuously studies the impact of climate change and other sustainability issues on the Outer Banks.

Until global leaders aggressively address issues with respect to climate alterations, the tourism industry is left to its own devices to mitigate or adapt to consequences of such changes. The present author mentioned in the book *Tourism Policy and Planning* (Edgell et al., 2008) that "Tourism administrators must undertake a paradigm shift away from overuse of natural resources toward environmental stewardship . . . Additionally, as global warming comes to the forefront in environmental concerns, tourism managers will need to stay attuned to forecast changes."[32] Individual regions must address the impact of climate change on their specific tourism destinations. Collectively, countries must push for an agenda to address climate change and sustainable tourism development. If nothing is done, the future growth and sustainability of tourism will be at risk. If tourism stakeholders do not define clear-cut policies and plans at this juncture in the growth of tourism, there may never be another opportunity.

Understanding effects of climate change on tourism in the Outer Banks and elsewhere is critical to travel decision-making, environmental stewardship, social evolution, and the economic viability of the travel and tourism industry. Government at all levels and the travel and tourism industry are now more cognizant of the need to address efforts to sustain natural and built resources under changing climate conditions. Given the complexity and breadth of the current science of climate change on the tourism industry, there is an increased need for research to effectively develop action plans in coastal areas. This case study addresses a limited range of climate change issues and sustainability with respect to the Outer Banks tourism industry. However, this research may be useful in providing valuable information applicable to similar tourism destinations throughout the world.

Climate change, tourism, and the Outer Banks

While climate change is increasingly becoming an area of interest in academic research and industry applicability, it still remains a relatively new phenomenon within the mainstream of the tourism industry, as suggested by Becken and Hay.[33] According to the Intergovernmental Panel on Climate Change much of the literature suggests that the majority of scientists are in agreement that the world's climate is warming.[34] What factors are causing the changes in climate is an issue where there is considerable debate. Is it cyclical? Is it caused by the actions of humans? Is it endemic to the universe? Whatever the answer(s), climate change is proceeding at a rate at which there will be unavoidable impacts on the tourism industry. The economic impact alone from climate change on "beach recreation and tourism" is enormous. The question is how the tourism industry will address the issues raised by this movement. Mitigation policies, strategies and management actions will be an important part of any plan to reduce the negative impacts of climate change on the tourism industry.

Tourism is the major economic driver in the Outer Banks. The Outer Banks community must better understand that climate is changing and is having a serious impact on their coastal tourism and recreation economy. Local businesses and management authorities need to recognize the changes and make plans to adapt. The rich complexity of the Outer Banks, a dynamic group of barrier islands and coastline, provides a strong platform for discussion of mitigating impacts of climate change.[35] The Outer Banks tourism industry is particularly sensitive to climate, which can make or break tourism businesses. In effect, the opportunities for visitors to have a quality experience on their visits to the Outer Banks and the resulting infusion of expenditures by visitors is critical to the economic development of the area.[36] A comprehensive research study reporting on the impacts of climate change on fish and wildlife in North Carolina (an important segment of the tourism industry), says, "Coastal wetlands are also highly vulnerable to sea level rise, and loss of this habitat has the potential to adversely affect a number of priority species" in the Outer Banks.[37]

Real-estate development in the Outer Banks is another major economic engine that is in trouble. Many properties developed prior to policies that require buildings not be built beyond the natural sand dunes have already disappeared into the ocean. As additional properties in the barrier islands begin to succumb to the sea, solutions become even more critical.

An article in the Associated Press (reproduced in *The Daily Reflector*, September 24, 2009) titled "Officials Cite Climate Change Threats in South" said that the U.S. Fish and Wildlife Service (Service) "will try to save barrier islands, fight invasive species and work with companies to restore wildlife habitat as they confront the risks posed by climate change." Sam Hamilton, Director of the U.S. Fish and Wildlife Service, said the Service "is on the forefront of climate change threats and that coastal wildlife refuges from North Carolina . . . are endangered. We're seeing sea level rise issues, coastal erosion issues; we're seeing a lot of the sea turtle nesting beaches are stressed and absolutely disappearing."[38] Since unique floral and faunal diversity are reasons why many visitors vacation in the Outer Banks,

(Continued)

Case study (continued)

federal, state, and local agencies are concerned about the critical nature of climate change. Several universities throughout North Carolina, and elsewhere across the country, are investigating the impact of weather and other factors on the mise en scène of the Outer Banks.

In addition to the highly critical research being conducted by the U.S. Corps of Engineers Field Research Facility with respect to climate change and sustainability in the Outer Banks, there is also an important inter-research institute called the University of North Carolina Coastal Studies Institute located on Roanoke Island. It is concerned with the culture and environment of the maritime programs of the Outer Banks. Their research focuses on five main areas:

- Estuarine Ecology and Human Health
- Coastal Engineering and Ocean Energy
- Public Policy and Coastal Sustainability
- Maritime Heritage
- Coastal Processes

These areas are also critical to determining the future sustainability of the Outer Banks, which ultimately will have a major bearing on the sustainability of the tourism industry.

Also studying and conducting important research with respect to the impact of climate and weather on the Outer Banks tourism industry is East Carolina University's Center for Sustainability: Tourism, Natural Resources, and the Built Environment. This innovative center conducts research into the social, economic, environmental and cultural aspects of sustainable tourism. The Center also offers a Master of Science in Sustainable Tourism degree program.

Understanding tourism issues in the Outer Banks using a modified Delphi technique

Studying climate change with respect to the Outer Banks is a connatural composite topic that is both controversial and often misunderstood. This lack of understanding, particularly with respect to local residents, is largely due to the limited information available. This exploratory qualitative case study has utilized a modified Delphi approach (executive judgment based on surveys of experts) as the principal instrument of investigation. The reasoning behind using this research method is that an analysis of the combined experiences of tourism executives, experts from the North Carolina Climate Action Plan Advisory Group, sustainable tourism advocates from the Center, climate scientists, renewable energy experts, and marine conservationists presents ample data and comments to evaluate and better understand the impact of climate change and sustainability issues on the Outer Banks tourism industry.

In the application of the modified Delphi approach, facts and opinions were obtained from a wide variety of persons and groups who have studied and confronted the climate change and sustainability issues or are otherwise interested in climate change impacts on the Outer Banks. Some of the members represent scientific and technical fields and others include business persons in the travel and tourism industry. The research available is quite large and varied. It takes into account scientific work conducted by the Outer Banks Field Research Facility, U.S. Army Corps of Engineers, considered one of the finest national centers for measurements of coastal waters and climate change, as well as other research entities studying the Outer Banks coastal sustainability. Just as important as the quantitative research is the qualitative research based on best practices that have evolved over a number of years. To ensure that sustainable tourism as an economic development strategy in the Outer Banks flourishes in the future, there must be efforts to inspire business and people to accept good practices to conserve the resources that currently exist. A simple poll of visitors, researchers, and students who have visited the Outer Banks in July and August suggests that the physical and natural environment of the coastline during these high-volume tourism months is not capable of handling the needs of the visitors for a quality experience. The automobile traffic is congested, the pollution from the engines is suffocating and the noise is disconcerting. When the visitor and host population are both experiencing exceptionally crowded conditions, the upper limits of the carrying capacity have been surpassed and negative effects of tourism begin to manifest.

A first step in understanding the impact of climate change on tourism in the Outer Banks was to analyze the barrier islands and coastline. These dynamic coastal areas both retreat and accrete, with long-term consequences. They act as buffers to protect the interior of the coast. The authors of this study have a long association with the Outer Banks business and technical community and have had full access to the published research regarding climate change impacts on tourism in the Outer Banks. In addition, as mentioned earlier, they made an aerial reconnaissance to review and better understand the dynamics of the coastal changes. They also walked, or traveled by car, 115 miles of the Outer Banks, including the barrier islands, stopping along the way to gather additional personal comments and data from Outer Banks residents and visitors. Through discussions, interviews, meetings and by other means, the authors accumulated a large amount of published and unpublished facts and intelligence sources, which are used throughout this case study. It also includes data and information available from North Carolina's Climate Action Planning Advisory Group. This research, combined with studies not necessarily directed toward the Outer Banks tourism, along with comments from knowledgeable tourism executives, was included in the case study.

Once the information was gathered, synthesized, and prioritized, further discussions took place with stakeholders, researchers, academics and others to obtain a general consensus on the perceived results of climate change on the Outer Banks. One science panel predicted that the sea level will rise by one meter by 2100. For the Outer Banks that could mean more than 2,000 square miles and adjacent environs would be at considerable risk. Because this area contains some

(Continued)

Case study (continued)

of the most expensive real estate in North Carolina, there could be a $7 billion shock to the residents. East Carolina University's Center for Sustainability, Natural Resources, and the Built Environment and many other research entities are continuing to conduct additional surveys, gathering new information, and seeking to add additional dimensions to the study of climate change impacts and sustainability issues on tourism in the Outer Banks.

Implications for sustainability of tourism in the Outer Banks

The global tourism industry generates trillions of dollars in income, creates millions of jobs, and provides memorable experiences to individuals and families throughout the world. Tourism brings people and families together in both indoor and outdoor venues, including the Outer Banks. Some groups of visitors to this unique set of barrier islands represent several generations of parents, children and grandchildren, and return to the islands over a long time period. The beautiful coastline is a major reason why 5 million visitors from more than 50 countries visit the Outer Banks each year. More than half of leisure travelers to the Outer Banks participate predominately in beach activities. But increasingly natural settings, the history and heritage of the area, and wildlife experiences are becoming important in family vacations to the Outer Banks.

Near the Outer Banks are many attractions, such as the Fort Raleigh National Historic Site, birthplace of English-speaking America in 1587; the Wright Brothers National Memorial, home of man's first powered flight in 1903; Cape Hatteras National Seashore Recreation Area, the nation's first national seashore, established in 1953; Pea Island National Wildlife Refuge; and Alligator River National Wildlife Refuge – all are integral parts of visitor interest in the Outer Banks. Seventy percent of the dynamic barrier islands are owned by the people of the United States and managed by the United States Department of the Interior.

Climate change presents a special challenge to the Atlantic Ocean coastline of the Outer Banks. Weather and climate fluctuations in the region have tremendous impacts on the economic vitality of the area. Tourism is the most important economic activity for the Outer Banks, increasing economic development, creating new jobs, benefiting from a diverse economy, adding new products, generating additional income, spawning new businesses, and contributing to overall economic integration. Economic success in tourism in the Outer Banks is measured by the ability to attract visitors year around, not just during the traditional tourist season. While climate change plays a major role in this industry, just the *perception* of weather conditions as presented by the media impacts heavily on tourism decisions made by visitors.

As mentioned earlier, the Outer Banks are "dynamic." The coastal zone of today is not permanent and will continue to change as it has in the past. It is the fragile fixed human infrastructure that can easily be destroyed by natural processes and climate change. This is a principal reason our coasts are in crisis. In addition, it is important to understand that the Outer Banks area is incredibly varied, with rivers, swamps, estuaries, marshes, barrier islands, inlets, beaches and off-shore shoals and rocks. If the warming climate spawns more frequent and intense hurricanes and other storms, the future will see coastal erosion and associated loss of urban infrastructure, wetlands, and wildlife habitats.[39] Despite the growing knowledge about, and interest in, climate change by a wide variety of interested parties, there appears to be a continuance of a "business as usual" attitude by many coastal destination managers. The question remains as to the best methods for communicating the impact of climate change with the local businesses and communities. Communication through emails, FAQ sheets, blogs, internet, university programs, governmental data, and community meetings are, in addition to research, ways in which scientists, both physical and social, can help the general public better understand the impact of climate change on tourism.

The negative effects of climate change on the Outer Banks have recently been exacerbated by the fact that so many new residents are moving into the area. Such a phenomenon means the area is being inundated with enormous amounts of infrastructure. This wreaks havoc on the natural environment and sets the stage for an even greater crisis as the climate changes. As the climate gets warmer, and more frequent and intense storms take place, it becomes more difficult to evacuate tourists and residents during such crises. Since the barrier islands change and physically move as a result of the storms, what previously seemed possible in terms of alleviating the negative impacts of new residents and businesses may not work in the future.

The question is not whether the Outer Banks climate is changing but rather how to prepare the coastal communities sustainably for the future. How will we be able to protect the native plant and animal species? The very way of life for Outer Banks residents is closely tied to the climate. Beaches are already shrinking. Homes are being lost to the sea. Properties are being flooded. More frequent high waves will damage formerly untouched areas. Coastal wetlands may disappear. If the area environment declines, there will be fewer visitors and the economy will suffer. Coastal erosion and related damage will become commonplace. The natural sand dunes have already been heavily destroyed or altered. Fish and bird life dependent on wetlands will not have their natural habitat. If the heat becomes more intense, public health will be at risk, especially that of children and the elderly. These are all issues for discussion. The implications from such changes are mind boggling. These concerns are a wake-up call for action. Citizens, businesspersons, and political leaders in the community must develop plans of action. Our children and grandchildren are dependent on community action today so they will be able to enjoy the beautiful Outer Banks tomorrow.

It is clear that climate change is a serious threat to humans, fish, and wildlife in the Outer Banks. In response to this threat, efforts to sustain natural resources under changing climate conditions must be forthcoming before it is too late. Otherwise the negative effects of climate change will decrease the quality of life for all concerned. Climate change is a complex set of situations and can be challenging to understand, but good communications, management, planning, and policies can move the community in a positive direction and alleviate some of the pressure on future climate change in the Outer Banks. This case study

(Continued)

Case study (continued)

confirms an urgency to develop policy guidelines and promote long-term planning to offset negative effects of climate change and move forward to conserve and protect resources for the future.

A few initial conclusions

Noted throughout this case study is the fact that few industries are more dependent on an understanding of climate change than tourism. Tourists have many choices with respect to locations and activities and climate plays an important role. Scientific advances have enhanced the accuracy of short-term weather forecasts and seasonal climate predictions. Today, visitors not only visit the internet to view the destination they are interested in, but also Google the weather reports for the area and then make a decision on where they want to spend their holiday.

Considering the impact that seasonal climate variability already has on the tourism industry in the Outer Banks, the projected impacts tied to climate change threaten the longer-term livelihood of many businesses dependent on visitors. Tourism services and products to visitors generate a high per capita consumption of water, energy, and waste management that requires the industry to take responsible steps toward broader sustainability. Covington et al. (2010) mention that

> Local communities dependent on tourism are impacted by climate variability and resource consumption both seasonally and annually, challenging stable business activity and the livelihood of permanent residents throughout the years. The sustainability of tourism is often dependent upon maintaining visitor sense of place, a favorable perception of and attachment to a destination. Central to sense of place is place satisfaction, which is affected by a host of social and local conditions that affect the tourist experience.[40]

Paradoxically, global climate change may not be totally negative to beach tourism; certain coastlines may be able to extend their seasons due to higher water and air temperatures. Regardless, the tourism industry must better understand the interactions of climate change and tourism and respond with responsible plans and policies. In the meantime, mitigation policies and actions to reduce greenhouse gas emissions that contribute to global warming must continue if the long-term impacts of climate change are to be manageable.

The Outer Banks area of North Carolina is disproportionately affected with respect to the climate change impacts on tourism and beachfront real estate. Beach erosion near vacation homes and businesses is already critical, with, for example, more than 109 properties recently lost and 39 currently in peril along one two-mile stretch of beach. Loss of wildlife habitat (due to erosion and the increasingly close links between the land and near shore waters causing decreased water quality) is already at a critical stage. Climate changes affect the quality of the environment, the experience of tourists, wildlife, and the very sustainability of these barrier islands. The potential economic and social consequences could be devastating.

In the long term, successful mitigation policies may stem the tide with respect to global warming and climate change. With respect to the present, we no longer have the luxury of debate. The impact of climate change on the Outer Banks is happening now, and it is necessary to work toward immediate climate change adaptation strategies. Based on the research contained in this case study, and after participating in many meetings and planning sessions with stakeholders along the Outer Banks, the authors concluded that at the very least, a coordinated strategic plan to adapt to climate change should include the following guidelines:

- Assure maintenance of a safe and secure recreational environment
- Examine the need for beach restoration, including beach nourishment
- Study the need for hardened structures along coastline: jetties, groins, seawalls
- Work toward sound policies for wildlife and habitat conservation
- Protect the built environment: history, heritage, and culture of the area
- Develop educational/awareness programs to explain climate change impacts
- Keep abreast of new research on climate trends
- Advocate good waterway and coastal management practices
- Regularly check the health of ecosystems
- Provide developers and agencies with risk assessments to guide development
- Encourage communications and coordination amongst all interested parties
- Review opportunities for resource savings with respect to energy
- Improve data collection and share results with local, state, and national offices
- Be willing to help develop, monitor, and test climate change models
- Expand multidisciplinary education, training and research on marine living resources, particularly in the social and economic sciences

While discussions and controversy about climate change may arise over how best to utilize these guidelines or to make other changes, businesses, developers, tourists, local communities, state and federal agencies, not-for-profit entities, and educational institutions all have a stake in working together toward a healthy, safe, and well-managed coastal environment. If it is not understood now, the stakeholders and community will lose in the future. The Outer Banks waterways and coastline are excellent but fragile laboratories to study climate change and to convince those engaged in coastline activity that now is the critical time for action. It is clear from the research in this case study that climate changes and rising water levels could have a tremendous and devastating impact on tourism in the Outer Banks. Researchers, businesses, and government agencies in the Outer Banks are only recently cooperating more and developing strategies and new ideas to respond to climate change and storm severity. Tourism stakeholders are beginning to understand the need for long-term management of resources and to seek solutions in order to cope with the impact of climate change on tourism in the future.

(Continued)

Case study (continued)

While this case study has focused on the Outer Banks, the research has a bearing on similar coastline strategies to address climate change and sustainability. Goeldner and Brent Ritchie (2012) have expressed many of the global concerns for climate change (which are apropos to the Outer Banks) in these words:

It is essential to emphasize that regardless of the nature and magnitude of climate change impacts, all tourism businesses and destinations will need to adapt to climate change in order to minimize associated risks and capitalize on new opportunities, in an economically, socially and environmentally sustainable manner . . . The unmistakable conclusion of studies in the field have shown that the significance of climate change to tourism is not in some distant and remote future . . . The next generation of tourism professionals will need to contend with virtually all of the broad range of impacts of climate change . . . This is the time for the tourism community to collectively formulate a strategy to address what must be considered the greatest challenge to the sustainability of tourism in the twenty-first century.[41]

In summary, the issue of climate change, and its impact on tourism, is being researched as a potential local security threat to the beautiful Outer Banks area, which welcomes millions of visitors each year. These visitors arrive in carbon-spewing automobiles. They use up energy resources and trample about on natural environments. They don't always understand that their actions have a major bearing on the future sustainability of the area. The question is how to find the right balance such that the visitor has a positive beach experience and, at the same time, the area is not desecrated and the local community is able to maintain a quality lifestyle for its citizens. The ultimate goal is to preserve the Outer Banks, such that future generations of visitors can enjoy their vacation and the local residents will have a better quality of life, and that the natural resources and wildlife will be conserved and protected.

Chapter summary

The first edition of *Managing Sustainable Tourism* set the stage for a better understanding of sustainable tourism with these remarks: "Responsibly managed tourism enhances and enriches natural, heritage, and cultural values and embraces the need to preserve them so that the community and visitor have a quality tourism experience now and in the future."

Carrying capacity is mentioned several times throughout the book – which, in effect, means balancing the number of visitors at a given environment (natural or built). The concept of *carrying capacity* is simply being able to accommodate the largest number of visitors a destination can manage without destroying the environment. With too many visitors in one place the environment is impacted.

While most researchers usually cite the 1987 *Brundtland Report* as a starting point for studying sustainable tourism, there are some other earlier important benchmarks.

In 1962 Rachel Carson wrote *Silent Spring*, which was a wake-up call about the environment. In the 1960s and 1970s Charles Lindbergh was already conducting important work that had an impact on sustainability. In 1979, Stanley Selengut built the "Maho Bay Resorts" – sustainable lodges on St. John in the U.S. Virgin Islands for visitors interested in a "green" vacation. Finally, also of interest was the "Blue Flags" program begun in France in 1985.

One of the early well-recognized documents on sustainability and sustainable travel was the American Society of Travel Agents' *The Ten Commandments of Ecotourism* in 1991. That document, so to speak, opened the floodgates of information on sustainable tourism detailed throughout this chapter. Special mention of Canada with respect to sustainability is included because the Canadian parks programs and Canada's tourism programs always seemed ahead of the rest of the world with respect to sustainable tourism principles and practices.

Another important benchmark was that of the National Geographic Society. The development and use of criteria for rating destinations in terms of their sustainability helped destinations understand sustainability better. In addition, publishing the results of the ratings in *National Geographic Traveler* magazine was a clarion call to action for those destinations with poor ratings.

The case study of the Outer Banks of North Carolina raises different issues of sustainability and introduces some of the concerns about climate change.

Chapter review questions

1 How would you describe the reference to the first edition of *Managing Sustainable Tourism*?
2 Describe what is meant by carrying capacity.
3 Why does carrying capacity have such an effect on a destination?
4 Can you describe the sustainable features of the Maho Bay Resorts?
5 What is the *Brundtland Report* about?
6 Describe the "Blue Flags" program with respect to the environment.
7 What was the name of the document released by the American Society of Travel Agents and what did it have to do with sustainability in travel?
8 Which country's national parks were early proponents of sustainability?
9 Describe each one of the six destination rating criteria from *National Geographic*'s Sustainable Tourism Initiative and explain how they fit with respect to rating sustainable tourism for a destination.
10 Explain what you have learned from reading the case study about the Outer Banks of North Carolina.

Notes

1 Edgell, Sr., D. L. and Swanson, J. R. (2013) *Tourism Policy and Planning: Yesterday, Today, and Tomorrow* (2nd edition), London: Routledge, pp. 147–148.
2 Edgell, Sr., D. L. (2006) *Managing Sustainable Tourism: A Legacy for the Future*, New York: The Haworth Hospitality Press, p. 123.
3 Edgell, Sr., D. L. (2005) "Sustainable Tourism as an Economic Development Strategy along Coastlines." A North Carolina Sea Grant Study, Greenville, North Carolina, September 30, 2005.

4   Berg, A. S. (1998) *Lindbergh*, New York: G. P. Putnam's Sons, pp. 525–532.

5   Edgell and Swanson (2013), pp. 150–151.

6   Symko, C. and Harris, R. (2002) "Making Paradise Last: Maho Bay Resorts." In R. Harris, T. Griffin, and P. Williams (eds.) *Sustainable Tourism: A Global Perspective*, New York: Butterworth-Heinemann, p. 273.

7   Miller, J. A., ed. (1996) "The Ecotourism Equation: Measuring the Impacts." New Haven, Connecticut: Yale University Bulletin Series Number 99.

8   Weaver, D. and Lawton, L. (1999) *Sustainable Tourism: A Critical Analysis*, Australia: National Library of Australia Cataloging in Publication Data, 1999.

9   Edgell and Swanson (2013), p. 156.

10 Ibid., p. 151.

11 Ibid., p. 155.

12 Pacific Asia Travel Association (1991) "Code for Environmentally Responsible Tourism." San Francisco, California: PATA.

13 New Zealand Ministry of Tourism (1992) "Tourism Sustainability: A Discussion Paper." Issues Paper No. 2. Wellington, New Zealand.

14 Eber, S. (1992) *Beyond the Green Horizon: Principles for Sustainable Tourism*, Surrey: United Kingdom and the World Wide Fund for Nature.

15 Griffin, T. and Boele, N. (1994), "Alternative Paths to Sustainable Tourism," *The Annual Review of Travel*. New York: American Express Travel Related Services.

16 Edgell (2006), p. 95.

17 World Travel and Tourism Council, World Tourism Organization, and Earth Council (1996) "Agenda 21 for the Travel and Tourism Industry: Towards Environmentally Sustainable Development."

18 Commission for Environmental Cooperation (1999) "The Development of Sustainable Tourism in Natural Areas in North America: Background, Issues and Opportunities," Montreal, Canada.

19 Organization of American States (1997) "Sustaining Tourism by Managing its Natural and Heritage Resources." XVII Inter-American Travel Congress, Turismo – doc. 11/97. January 31, 1997.

20 *National Geographic Traveler* and Travel Industry Association of America (2003) "The Geotourism Study: Phase I. Executive Summary." Washington, D.C.: Travel Industry of America.

21 Edgell (2006), pp. 18–19.

22 Wood, M. E. (2002) "Ecotourism: Principles, Practices & Policies for Sustainability." New York: United Nations Publication.

23 World Travel and Tourism Council (2002) "Industry as a Partner for Sustainable Development," United Kingdom.

24 National Trust for Historic Preservation (2001) "Share Your Heritage: Cultural and Heritage Tourism – The Same or Different?" Washington, D.C.

25 United Nations Educational, Scientific and Cultural Organization (1972) "Convention Concerning the Protection of the World and Natural Heritage," Paris, France.

26 For more information, see http://www.outerbeaches.com/OuterBanks/AllAboutOBX/History/ (accessed March 11, 2015).

27 Goeldner, C. and Brent Ritchie, J. (2012) *Tourism: Principles, Practices, Philosophies*, (12th edition), Hoboken, New Jersey: John Wiley & Sons, Inc., p. 382.

28 Becken, S. and Hay, J. (2007) *Tourism and Climate Change: Risks and Opportunities*, Clevedon, England: Channel View Publications, p. xvii.

29 Frangialli, F. (2007) Keynote Address: "Tourism Can Help in Global Action on Climate Change and Poverty," Bali, Indonesia, December 12, 2007.

30 The Associated Press (2011) "Rising Sea Waters Threaten North Carolina's Delicate Coastline," January 17, 2011.

31 Birkemeier, B. (2008) "Personal Interview of Bill Birkemeier by David L. Edgell, Sr., November 5, 2008," U.S. Army Corps of Engineers, Engineer Research and Development Center, Duck, North Carolina.

32 Edgell, Sr., D., Swanson, J., DelMastro, M., and Smith, G. (2008) *Tourism Policy and Planning: Yesterday, Today, and Tomorrow*, Oxford, England: Elsevier, p. 351.

33 Becken and Hay (2007).

34 Intergovernmental Panel on Climate Change (2007) "Climate Change 2007: The Physical Science Basis." Contribution of Working Group I to the Fourth Assessment Report. Cambridge, UK: Cambridge University Press.

35 Riggs, S., Culver, D., Ames, D., Mallison, D. and Walsh, J. (2008) "North Carolina's Coasts in Crisis: A Vision for the Future," Center for Sustainable Tourism, East Carolina University, Greenville, North Carolina.

36 Curtis, S., Arrigo, J., Long, P. and Covington (2009) "Climate, Weather and Tourism: Bridging Science and Practice," Center for Sustainable Tourism, East Carolina University, Greenville, North Carolina.

37 DeWan, A., Dubois, N., Theoharides, K. and Boshoven, J. (2010) "Understanding the Impacts of Climate Change on Fish and Wildlife in North Carolina," Washington, D.C.: Defenders of Wildlife.

38 *The Daily Reflector*, September 24, 2009 article "Officials Cite Climate Threats in South" (repeated from an article from the Associated Press).

39 Riggs, S., Ames, D., Culver, S. and Mallinson, D. (2011) *The Battle of North Carolina's Coast*, Chapel Hill, North Carolina: The University of North Carolina Press.

40 Covington, R., Arrigo, J., Curtis, S., Long, P. and Alderman, D. (2010) "Tourists' Climate Perceptions: A survey of preferences and sensitivities in North Carolina's Outer Banks," *The North Carolina Geographer*, 17, 38–53.

41 Goeldner and Brent Ritchie (2012), pp. 383–385.

Chapter 4

Sustainable tourism and the United Nations Millennium Development Goals

"Tourism in the twenty-first century will be a major vehicle for fulfilling people's aspirations for a higher quality of life . . . tourism also has the potential to be one of the most important stimulants for global improvement in the social, cultural, economic, political and ecological dimensions of future lifestyles."

David L. Edgell, Sr., *International Tourism Policy*, 1990

Turbulence, strife, poverty, conflicts, and unrest aptly describe much of today's world. Nearly 80 percent of the world's population is in poverty, 70 percent is illiterate and more than 50 percent suffer from hunger and malnutrition. Issues relating to world hostility and conflict, economic crises, misdistribution of wealth, belligerency, global warming, disaster relief, impoverishment, sickness, and ineffectiveness of governments to find solutions to problem areas are demanding creative leadership and policy attention by governments and international organizations.[1]

Poverty exists throughout the world – in some countries more than others – representing differing degrees of being poor. Many areas lack basic food, shelter, clothing, healthcare, education, and the physical means of improving one's life. The concern is not a new one but what has changed is the transformation of leadership interests by the United Nations in the problem of poverty alleviation, and the role that tourism policy plays in these efforts.

Politicians, humanitarians and religionists – for example, the late Mahatma Gandhi, Mother Teresa, Norman Borlaug and others – have pleaded the case for poverty alleviation. Mahatma Gandhi as a political figure, humanitarian, and strong advocate for the poor was successful in obtaining the Mahatma Gandhi National Rural Employment Guarantee Act. Norman Borlaug, biologist and humanitarian and the "father of the Green Revolution" (agriculture), and Mother Teresa, simply by her interactions with the poor and her gifted ability to explain the needs of the poor, were able to garner support for programs and actions aimed at reducing poverty.

What appears to be a fairly recent movement is the increased transformation by some of the world's business leaders in utilizing their immense wealth to enrich the global well-being of the poor throughout the world. For example, Microsoft mega-billionaire Bill Gates, in partnership with billionaire Warren Buffett, initiated a multi-billion-dollar challenge to other billionaires of the world to use their wealth to fund global social change. Operating through the Bill and Melinda Gates Foundation, many of the world's billionaires are contributing money, ideas, and strategies toward innovative programs to reduce poverty and disease and increase the world's food supply and drinkable water.

In addition, there are many local groups working toward increasing the literacy level in their communities to provide them with the education and training needed for obtaining employment to improve their quality of life. There are social and religious groups, charity organizations, and specialized agencies conducting special country missions to provide medical assistance and other support to help the world's neediest populations. While considerable progress is being made, much of the world's population lives each day under extreme poverty conditions.

The United Nations Millennium Development Goals

There are several questions for this chapter to address, including: What is being accomplished by world organizations with respect to reducing poverty? Where does global tourism policy fit with respect to poverty alleviation? and How is the leadership in the tourism industry responding to the policy challenge of reducing world poverty?

The United Nations (UN) has accepted the world's leadership role in advocating equality, equity, human rights, peace, sustainability, and programs for the general well-being of the world. At the UN Millennium Summit in 2000 (at the time of this meeting, it was the largest gathering of world leaders in history), the 189 member states (there are now 193) supported the UN in setting eight international development goals that are referred to as the *United Nations Millennium Development Goals* (MDGs) to be reached by 2015 and which are listed below:

1   To eradicate extreme poverty and hunger
2   To achieve universal primary education
3   To promote gender equality and empower women
4   To reduce child mortality
5   To improve maternal health
6   To combat HIV/AIDS, malaria, and other diseases
7   To ensure environmental sustainability
8   To develop a global partnership for development[2]

The UN identified world poverty alleviation as one of the most important and challenging issues.

This chapter will summarily address the MDG goals 1, 3, 7, and 8 from an international tourism perspective.

In 2011, the UN issued *The Millennium Development Goals Report*, which informed the world about the progress that had been made toward the 2015 goal of reducing extreme poverty. The report was mostly positive, stating that millions of people had been lifted from severe poverty conditions. Despite real progress, however, the document noted that the most vulnerable cases of poverty were still in dire need of help. Some of the severely disadvantaged live in remote rural areas, where about three quarters of the two billion people under extreme poverty conditions are located, and are simply hard to reach. This reality has left disparities in progress made toward poverty reduction between urban and rural areas. In addition, those poor who were living in zones where conflicts were taking place had an increased likelihood of becoming even more distressed (the current situations in Yemen and Syria are good examples of this difficulty).[3]

On September 25, 2013, the UN issued a status report titled "A Life of Dignity for All." The member states adopted the report and renewed their commitment to meet the MDG targets and agreed to meet in September 2015 to adopt a new set of goals, building on the achievements of the MDGs to date.[4] Earlier the UN had called upon all of its organizational units to help with programs aimed to reduce poverty, including the UN's specialized agency, the United Nations World Tourism Organization (UNWTO).

The United Nations World Tourism Organization and poverty alleviation

One key agency of the UN in addressing world poverty is the UNWTO, which is the policy agency responsible for the promotion of responsible, sustainable, and universally accessible tourism. As the leading international organization in the field of tourism, UNWTO promotes tourism as a driver of economic growth, inclusive development and environmental sustainability, and offers leadership and support to the sector in advancing knowledge and tourism policies worldwide. UNWTO is committed to promoting tourism as an instrument in achieving the UN Millennium Development Goals, geared towards reducing poverty and fostering sustainable development. UNWTO's membership includes 155 countries, 7 territories and more than 400 affiliate members representing governments, the private sector, education institutions, tourism associations, and local tourism authorities. This organization, as the global body for tourism policy, has a major focus on economic development, international understanding, peace, prosperity, sustainability, and universal respect for human rights and fundamental freedoms through world tourism policies.[5]

The UNWTO responded to the UN goal with recommendations for action in its "Tourism and Poverty Alleviation" report. The initiative cited in the report suggests that one approach toward poverty alleviation takes place through the provision of assistance in sustainable tourism development projects. The UNWTO has in its definition of sustainable tourism in Part 3 "Ensure viable, long-term economic operations, providing socioeconomic benefits to all stakeholders that are fairly distributed, including stable employment and income-earning opportunities and social services to host communities, and contributing to *poverty alleviation*."[6]

The UNWTO recognized the transformative powers and fundamental roles that tourism can play in addressing global poverty issues. Over the years, UNWTO has made a mark in utilizing tourism development as an opportunity to increase the welfare of peoples throughout the world. Because tourism is forecast to grow substantially in developing countries, where much of the poverty exists, there is interest in utilizing tourism as a tool for poverty reduction.[7]

While most of the economic advantages of tourism in the world take place in developed nations, the growth of tourism in the least developed countries (LDCs) is increasingly being recognized for its economic potential to contribute to the reduction of poverty. Many LDCs have a comparative advantage over developed countries in tourism as they often have not yet desecrated their scenic beauty, natural landscapes, wildlife, cultural heritage, and other sustainable-tourism-related attributes to the same extent as has happened in developed nations. Because tourism is so diverse and creates jobs and income more quickly than most other industries, it can provide LDCs with much-needed foreign exchange. Tourism is generally labor intensive, offering employment opportunities for both skilled and unskilled persons, especially with respect to women and young people in LDCs. Tourism is an industry largely composed of small businesses and the start-up costs and barriers to entry are usually less than is true in the manufacturing sector. Tourism development, if properly planned for and supported, can provide an economic opportunity for LDCs and help alleviate unemployment and the resulting poverty.[8] In addition, the tourism industry provides more jobs for women and youth than most other industries.

The United Nations Environmental Program and tourism sustainability

The United Nations Environmental Program (UNEP) has a major role to play in sustainable tourism development and toward the reduction of poverty. UNEP has introduced what it calls the "green economy" – defined as an economy that results in *improved human well-being and social equity, while significantly reducing environmental risks and ecological scarcities*. UNEP produced a report titled "Tourism: Investing in Energy and Resource Efficiency" in 2008 that also addressed the issue of tourism and poverty, as well as environmental programs related to tourism. UNEP, in partnership with UNWTO, elaborated in the report the important economic impact that sustainable tourism can have on small and medium-sized businesses. The report also stated:

> In greening the tourism sector, therefore, increasing the involvement of local communities, especially the poor, in the tourism value chain can contribute to the development of local economy and poverty reduction ... There is increasing evidence that more sustainable tourism in rural areas can lead to more positive poverty-reducing effects ... Governments and international organizations can facilitate the financial flow ... with an emphasis on contributions to the local economy and poverty reduction.

UNEP basically has three principles to be followed in the definition of sustainable tourism:

Thus, sustainable tourism should

1   Make optimal use of environmental resources that constitute a key element in tourism development, maintaining essential ecological processes and helping to conserve natural heritage and biodiversity.

2 Respect the socio-cultural authenticity of host communities, conserve their built and living cultural heritage and traditional values, and contribute to inter-cultural understanding and tolerance.

3 Ensure viable, long-term economic operations, providing socioeconomic bene-fits to all stakeholders that are fairly distributed, including stable employment and income-earning opportunities and social services to host communities and contributing to poverty alleviation.

UNEP also fosters guidelines to support ecotourism programs, keeping in mind the importance of including the social-cultural aspects of tourism development. In addi-tion, the organization calls for strong political leadership aimed toward bringing together diverse stakeholders so that sustainable tourism development will be endorsed by the entire community. The ultimate goal is to maintain a high level of visitor satisfaction through a superior sustainable tourism product that will increase the number of repeat visitors as well as promote sustainability to a larger world mar-ket. This can best be accomplished by strong strategic alliances with local community involvement, support by governments at all levels, developing private-sector partner-ships and utilizing help from organizations such as the UNWTO.[9] If all the entities buy into the concept of sustainability and work together, some definite headway can be made in reducing poverty. This approach fits some of the concepts of "pro-poor tourism" described in the next section.

Pro-poor tourism and the Millennium Development Goals

This chapter would not be complete without mentioning the concept of *pro-poor tourism* (PPT) in connection with the MDGs. The simplest definition of pro-poor tour-ism which fits this section is that given by the Center for Responsible Travel: Pro-poor tourism is "Tourism that results in increased net benefit for the poor people in a destination."[10] An excellent review of the background and main concepts and princi-ples of PPT is included in Chapter 3, "Tourism and the Explicit Concern with Poverty Reduction: A Review" (by Ferry van de Mosselaer and René van der Duim) in the book *Sustainable Tourism & the Millennium Development Goals* (Bricker, Black, and Cottrell, 2013).

As mentioned earlier, the UN, at its Millennium Summit in 2000, identified poverty as one of the most important world challenges, and issued the MDGs. The UNWTO adopted the PPT concept and launched the *Sustainable Tourism – Eliminating Poverty Initiative* in 2002 at the World Summit on Sustainable Development in Johannesburg, South Africa. UNWTO included poverty reduction as a part of the overall approach to sustainable tourism development. "During that occasion, the UNWTO invited UN agencies, governments, donor agencies, nongovernmental organizations and other stakeholders to unite in a concerted effort to use the benefits that derive from tourism to actively combat poverty throughout the world."[11] A number of approaches aimed at providing resources and directions that would ultimately benefit smaller enterprises in LDCs were introduced. (Note Case Study 1 in this book regarding the ecotourism project aimed to benefit the Kalingo Indians in the Commonwealth of Dominica.)

There are many different ways to review the PPT concept but the three pathways mentioned below (Mitchell and Ashley, 2010) are good starting points:

1 *Direct effects from tourism to the poor*: Labor income from tourism jobs or small enterprise, other forms of tourism income, and nonfinancial livelihood changes (negative as well as positive).
2 *Secondary effects from tourism to the poor*: Indirect earnings from non-tourism sectors that supply tourism (e.g. food). Added to these are induced effects from tourism workers re-spending their earnings in the local economy.
3 *Dynamic effects on the economy*: Impacts on entrepreneurialism, market factors, other export sectors, or the natural environment are all included here.[12]

For a more complete explanation of these pathways and PPT, see the article mentioned earlier by Ferry van de Mosselaer and René van der Duim (2013).

While the concept of PPT continues to be debated, defined and redefined, it is a rallying point for attention to the role that tourism can play in poverty alleviation. The energy for addressing PPT must come from many sources, including regional and world organizations, governments, not-for-profit organizations, academia, volunteer agencies, and most importantly a strong endorsement from the private sector. Since much of the hard-to-reach poverty is in rural areas, and because many rural areas have beautiful landscapes, often large amounts of unique flora and fauna, interesting history, heritage and culture, such areas offer tourism development opportunities. A key to reducing poverty through tourism is providing more jobs and income.

Community-based tourism, sustainability, and poverty

Even though many of the small communities in outlying locations in the LDCs tend to have the most severe poverty, tourism's impact in rural areas is often overlooked. As a result, from an economic and tourism development perspective, little attention is being paid to community-based tourism in many poverty-stricken areas of the world. Yet, as Edgell (1990) noted, "Rural environments [often] have vast expanses of land and water and wide diverse topographies (mountains, plains, forests, grasslands, and deserts) that provide outstanding settings for tourism."[13] Later in *Tourism Policy: The Next Millennium*, Edgell (1999) mentions that "Almost every local community in the world has some resource, attraction, activity, event or special interest or adventure opportunity that can motivate a traveler."[14] This was followed by Edgell (2002) saying that "Rural travel destinations still offer the most diversity in beauty, experience, culture, heritage."[15] It tends to be more difficult to find leaders in small remote communities that have the interest or ability to recognize the great potential of tourism as an economic development tool. Even defining community-based tourism can be difficult. A definition from the Jamaica Social Investment Fund describes community-based tourism as follows:

> Community-based tourism (CBT) has at its core, the aim of achieving sustainable development for communities often removed from traditional market economies including tourism. CBT involves increasing local peoples' contribution to the tourism value chain by providing cultural interaction experiences for domestic and foreign

tourism, hospitality services including tours and accommodations or products that complement the industry such as agriculture and handicrafts. As a sustainable development tool, its criteria for success should be based on triple bottom line [social, environmental and financial] thinking with a focus on environmental and social goals, and economic viability, without which the CBT initiative cannot achieve its purpose, which is to be sustainable in providing development benefits.[16]

An excellent discussion of CBT and poverty issues is described in a case study by Edwards, Galaski, and Dodds (2013) titled "Connecting Communities to the Tourism Supply Chain." The case study notes that "Community-based tourism has emerged out of efforts to apply tourism as a development tool in rural areas in many developing countries."[17] The case study noted that not many CBT projects are likely to be successful unless considerable pre-planning takes place and that sustainable financial plans are identified and are taken into account at the outset of the project and that there is a good understanding of the market for the specific community-based destination under consideration. The case study notes that CBT is most likely to be successful "in partnership with a tour operator."[18]

For many communities, the early best approach may be to consider following carefully the precepts mentioned earlier in this book regarding ecotourism. Case Study 1 highlights ecotourism and its potential impact on the community of the Kalinago Indian Territory in the Commonwealth of Dominica. While this project has taken into consideration financial planning, destination marketing and other ecotourism parameters it remains to be seen if in the long run it will be sustained and profitable. Utilizing ecotourism as a transforming tool to alleviate conditions of poverty and to provide jobs within the Kalinago Indian Territory is certainly a good experimental initiative.

The Millennium Development Goals and employment in the tourism industry

Employment in the tourism industry has a major impact on two of the United Nations Millennium Development Goals (MDGs): "To eradicate extreme poverty and hunger" and "To promote gender equality and empower women." Certainly a person, young or old, male or female, who has a job is less likely to be suffering from "extreme poverty." One of the socioeconomic advantages of tourism over many other industries is that it is labor intensive and growing much faster than most other sectors of the world's economy. Tourism employment is concentrated mainly in the services sector rather than in the goods-producing sector; the tourism industry accounts for more than a third of the total global services trade. Generally speaking, the service sector of the world's economy creates jobs much faster and requires less capital than is true in most manufacturing sectors. In addition, the tourism industry is among the world's top creators of jobs that require varying degrees of skill and allow for quick entry into the workforce by youth, women and migrant workers.[19]

The travel and tourism industry is one of the leading job creators in the world, accounting for nearly one in every eleven jobs worldwide. According to reports from the World Travel and Tourism Council, job growth in the travel and tourism industry is "forecast to average 1.9 percent per year over the next decade, compared with 1.2 percent annual growth forecast for total jobs in the global economy . . . travel & tourism is a particularly attractive option for stimulating development in rural and low-income countries and regions that have previously relied heavily on subsistence agriculture, natural resource extraction, or informal self-employment."[20] Such progress in job production by the tourism industry fits well with accomplishing the MDG goal of poverty alleviation, even though, like many other industries, the tourism industry tends to follow economic cycles, increasing in good times and decreasing when the economy is in a downturn.

Possibly the most important UN MDG in which the tourism industry makes the most contribution is with respect to "promot[ing] gender equality and empower[ing] women." According to the joint UNWTO/UN Women report titled "Global Report on Women in Tourism 2010" women have a higher percentage of jobs in the tourism industry than in any other economic sector, averaging close to 50 percent of global employment in the tourism industry. Key findings of the report state:

> Although much information is still missing, the results of the initial survey suggest that tourism is worth investing in; it has the potential to be a vehicle for the empowerment of women in developing regions. Tourism provides better opportunities for women's participation in the workforce, women's entrepreneurship, and women's leadership than other sectors of the economy. Women in tourism are still underpaid, under-utilized, under-educated, and under-represented, but tourism offers pathways to success.[21]

While the tourism industry serves as a good harbinger for creating jobs and supporting the MDGs, it will only work if there is good coordination and cooperation at the local and national levels that includes leadership in communities, commitments by governments, and most importantly private-sector involvement. While many of the lesser developed countries offer potential for developing and maintaining sustainable tourism sites, there must be a commitment by the private sector to invest in such locations. More success stories available to build from will encourage greater support by all interested stakeholders in tourism development projects.

Safety and security and the Millennium Development Goals

On any given day, the world is fraught with wars, turbulence, strife, conflicts and unrest. There is nothing more threatening to the travel industry than tourists who are afraid to travel to certain destinations because they are concerned for their personal safety and security when traveling. In the opinion of this author, the issue of safety and security is possibly the most important concern in meeting the Millennium Development Goal of "reducing poverty." In the book *Tourism Policy and Planning: Yesterday, Today, and Tomorrow* (Edgell and Swanson, 2013) the authors point out that

> Concern for the safety and security of world travelers remains an extremely important issue for the travel and tourism industry. Providing safety and security in the travel industry will continue to be a major challenge for tourism policy and planning. In brief, safety and security are vital elements in the provision of quality tourism. A tourism destination that is not considered to be safe and secure is not going to survive very long.[22]

Many of the countries that are suffering from the deepest poverty are those where conflicts of one kind or another are taking place.

Many countries provide their citizens with travel advisories suggesting places they do not consider safe for their citizens to travel. Unfortunately, many LDCs are on travel advisory lists, which impacts negatively on their opportunities to increase tourism and decrease poverty. Like many other countries throughout the world, the United States provides a daily list of "Alerts and Warnings" to its citizens, suggesting they may want to use considerable caution in traveling to countries that are on the list. Examples of "travel warnings" include countries with an unstable government, civil war, ongoing intense crime or violence, or frequent terrorist attacks. "Travel Warnings" remain in place until the situation changes; some have been in effect for years. "Travel Alerts," on the other hand, include short-term events that a citizen should be aware of as they plan their trip. Reasons for a "Travel Alert" might include an election season that is bound to have many strikes, demonstrations, or disturbance; a health alert like the outbreak of Ebola; or evidence of an elevated risk of terrorist attacks. When such short-term events are over, the "Travel Alert" is canceled. In 2015 the average daily "Travel Warnings" was about 35 countries and "Travel Alerts" averaged about 5 countries. Most of the countries on the lists were LDCs. The result is that these countries are driven further into poverty and their citizens suffer further.

The book *Safety and Security in Tourism* (Hall, Timothy, and Duval, 2003) says that

> security concerns not only affect individual tourism decision-making but also have a broader influence on economic and political confidence, which in turn affects the wider environment within which the tourism industry operates . . . Although crime, terrorism and national security concerns will continue to be important . . . health, social and environmental issues are also becoming a part of the lexicon of tourism security and are also becoming related to ideas of sustainable development.[23]

This concern in reinforced in the book *Tourism, Security and Safety* (Mansfeld and Pizam, 2006), in which they note that "Tourism and security incidents are inevitably interwoven phenomena. When security incidents such as wars, terrorism, crime, and civil unrest take place at or close to areas where tourism forms an important land use, the tourism industry, tourists, and the local community are always affected."[24] The lack of safety and security in the world, and especially in the LDCs, may very well be a principal reason for poverty in many areas. The more peaceful the world is, the greater the opportunity for poverty reduction.

Partnerships in sustainable tourism development and the Millennium Development Goals

One of the MDGs is "To develop a global partnership for development." This section will briefly mention a few global partnerships within the tourism industry aimed toward sustainable tourism development. Much of this effort is being led by the UNWTO, but there are many additional partners as well. Already mentioned in this chapter is the special work being accomplished by the UNEP in sustainable tourism development.

An excellent review of many global partnerships for sustainable tourism development is contained in Rosemary Black's chapter "Partnership in Practice: Ecotourism and Sustainable Accreditation and Certification Programs" in the book edited by Bricker et al. (2013) titled *Sustainable Tourism & the Millennium Development Goals*. It mentions that in addition to UNWTO, UNEP, the World Bank and the European Union there are some unique examples of global partnerships in sustainable tourism development. The section of the chapter titled "The Partnership Model in Practice: Examples of Sustainable Tourism and Ecotourism Certification and Accreditation Programs" contains an excellent critique of the principles of the *Protected Area Network of Parks* program developed by the World Wide Fund for Nature; it includes an interesting discussion of the *Sustainable Tourism Certification Network of the Americas* regional program that includes North America, the Caribbean, and South America; it introduces and provides details of the initiative referred to as the *Global Sustainable Tourism Council*; and ends with a discussion of the relatively new *Global Partnership for Sustainable Tourism*. All of these programs add importantly to partnerships in sustainable tourism development and ultimately impact on the MDGs.[25]

There are many other regional and international partnership programs in sustainable tourism development. Mentioned earlier in this book is *The International Ecotourism Society*, which is a well-known and well-developed program working on sustainable and ecotourism projects throughout the world. Two well-known conservation organizations that have an important bearing on sustainable tourism development include the *Nature Conservancy* and the *World Conservation Union*. There is also the *International Institute for Peace through Tourism*, which has a major sustainable tourism component and which is described in considerable detail later in this book. The National Geographic Society, independently and through its Center for Sustainable Destinations, has contributed immensely to identifying and critiquing global tourism destinations and adding to a better understanding of sustainability. The relatively new Center for Responsible Travel has added a very special dimension to strengthening knowledge about sustainable tourism. Regional organizations described earlier in this book like the Organisation for Economic Co-operation and Development, the Organization of American States, the Asia-Pacific Economic Cooperation and the Caribbean Tourism Organization have been working for some time on sustainable tourism issues and concepts. The U.S. Agency for International Development has provided easy global access to its online tool kit and resource series on "Sustainable Tourism: International Cooperation and Development." From a more private-sector approach we have partners for sustainable development through such organizations as the World Travel and Tourism Council, the International Federation of Tour Operators, the International Hotel and Restaurant Association, and the International Council of Cruise Lines. While this list is not complete, it does emphasize that there are numerous partnerships in sustainable tourism development which also assist to some degree in the MDGs.

It is absolutely clear in the management of sustainable tourism that now and in the future there will be a greater use of public-private partnerships. In 2003, at the Global Travel and Tourism Summit, the World Travel and Tourism Council introduced a *Blueprint for New Tourism* report, which noted the importance of partnerships in sustainable tourism development. Such partnerships must take place at all levels – at the local level, the state/province level, the regional level, the national level and the global level – and are illustrated in Figure 4.1.

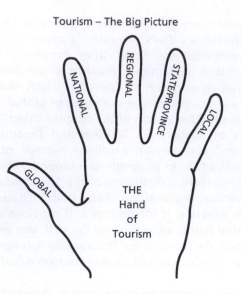

Figure 4.1 Prepare for globalization in sustainable tourism through partnerships at all levels

Adapted from the book *Coopetition: Global Tourism beyond the Millennium* (Edgell and Haenisch, 1995).

Case study 4: Cuban tourism at the crossroads of the modern era of sustainability

"Tourism is a simple continuation of politics by other means."

Jean-Maurice Thurot, *Economia*, May 1975

Introduction

With regard to the United States and Cuba re-establishing diplomatic relations, a new era of tourism development is on the horizon. According to a Pew Research Center report in January 2015, "Two-thirds of Americans favor an end to the decades-long U.S. trade embargo on Cuba."[26] Before the Cuban Revolution of 1959, Americans traveled to Cuba in droves and Cuba's earnings from tourism outpaced the rest of the Caribbean.

In October 1959 Fidel Castro spoke to the American Society of Travel Agents (ASTA) convention . . . in Havana. "We have sea," said Castro. "We have bays, we have beautiful beaches, we have medicinal waters in our hotels, we have mountains, we have game and we have fish in the sea and the rivers, and we have sun. Our people are noble, hospitable, and most important, they hate no one. They love visitors, so much in fact that our visitors feel completely at home."

The U.S. Ambassador, Philip Bonsai, speaking at the same conference, had this to say: "Cuba is one of the most admirable countries in the world from the point of view of North American tourism and from many other points of view."[27] Then, of course, shortly after 1959 Cuban-American relations soured and in 1961 the U.S. imposed a punishing embargo on Cuba, banned U.S. citizens from visiting Cuba, except under very special conditions, and diplomatic relations were severed.

In 1961 Cuba turned to a socialistic type of government and began receiving large amounts of economic aid from the Union of Soviet Socialist Republics (USSR). Fidel Castro reversed his earlier tourism policy (as expressed at the ASTA convention), considering tourism to be a bourgeois activity not appropriate for Cuban political and economic policy. The tourism policy for Cuba was to no longer market tourism as an integral part of its economy. Cuba went from being the number one Caribbean tourist market in 1958 to a little-known tourism destination with only 12,000 visitors in 1974.[28] In 1989 the USSR began to fall apart, thus cutting off Cuba's generous economic package, and the Cuban economy declined drastically. To earn foreign currency and to bolster a failing economy, Cuba re-introduced tourism as part of its economic policy in the 1990s. Cuban tourism began to gradually rebound, even without its major U.S. market. By 2014 Cuba was receiving approximately 3 million visitors and approaching earnings of $3 billion from international tourism, Canada being the largest market, followed by European visitors.

In 2015 the results of the new détente between the U.S. and Cuba is already beginning to have an impact on the tourism industry. While there are still considerable restrictions regarding Americans traveling to Cuba and U.S. travel companies operating in Cuba, the current political climate is opening up new opportunities. For example, on July 7, 2015 it was announced that the Carnival cruise-ship company intends to begin traveling to Cuba in May 2016.

Canadian and European tourists have been the mainstay for revving Cuba's tourism program since the 1990s. Both of these markets are most interested in the "sun, sand, and sea" in Cuba. However, Cuba is more than just sun and beaches. It has a rich heritage, with cultural attractions, and has opportunities for expanding its nature tourism or ecotourism sites. Cuban music and dancing as part of its tourism product is exceedingly popular, locally and internationally. Cuba has had a fairly strong conservation and environmental protection policy. However, Cuba has lacked funding for restoration, and some of the beautiful historic buildings in Old Havana are in desperate straits and in need of immediate attention. Cuba is quite aware of its responsibilities to protect its environment and has participated in global meetings on sustainability and climate change. Cuba is a party to numerous international agreements with respect to the environment such as the Antarctic Treaty, Biodiversity Agreement, Climate Change – Kyoto Protocol, Decertification, Endangered Species, Environmental Modification, Hazardous Wastes, and Law of the Sea, Maritime Dumping, Ozone Layer Protection, Ship Pollution and Wetlands Protection.

Background

"It is said that when Christopher Columbus arrived at the northeast coast of Cuba on October 27, 1492, startled by the island's beauty, he exclaimed: 'It is the most

(Continued)

Case study (continued)

beautiful land human eyes have ever seen!'"[29] The island of Cuba was inhabited, several thousand years before Christopher Columbus arrived, by numerous Mesoamerican tribes such as the Gauanajatabeys, Ciboneys, and others. By the time Columbus arrived he met a fairly advanced tribe called the *Tainos*. "They are the best people in the world," Columbus recorded of the Indians [Columbus thought he was in India so misnamed the inhabitants of Cuba *Indians*], "without knowledge of what is evil; nor do they murder or steal . . . All the people show the most singular loving behavior . . . and are gentle and always laughing."[30]

That scenario did not last long.

> The enslavement, torture, murder, and extermination of the native people of the West Indies followed quickly on the heels of Columbus and his men. It was obvious from Columbus's journal that the Tainos were not as used to battle and warfare as the Spaniards. Columbus notes that "with 50 men you could subject everyone and make them do what you wished . . . and that the natives were such cowards and so fearful . . ." that they were, therefore, easy to rule.[31]

Columbus and his compatriots had only one thing on their minds – to find gold or silver in Cuba. Their fruitless quest for gold in Cuba made them angry, thinking that the natives were not cooperating in the search for gold. During this early period a priest named Batolomé de las Casas summed up the cruelty of these early Spaniards in these words:

> The Indians came to meet us, and to receive us with victuals, and delicate cheere . . . the Devill put himself into the Spaniards, to put them all to the edge of the sword in my presence, without any cause whatsoever, more than three thousand souls, which were set before us, men, women and children. I saw there so great cruelties, that never any man living either have or shall see the like.[32]

Cuba was claimed by Columbus to be a possession of Spain, and it became a Spanish colony ruled by a Spanish governor in Havana. Most of the local Cubans were unhappy under Spanish rule but were not strong enough to oust the Spanish. When the U.S. colonies successfully rebelled from the British, and with the victory of the French Revolution of 1789, many Cubans sought, unsuccessfully, to rebel against the Spanish.

In 1762, Havana was briefly occupied by Great Britain, before being returned to Spain in exchange for Florida. This brief respite from Spanish control only increased the unrest in Cuba. Many Cubans supported the idea of an American-style economy and government and were interested in being annexed by the U.S. This fit U.S. interests as well. With the United States winning its War of Independence from England and obtaining the Louisiana Purchase, it began to look south toward Cuba with interest. As early as 1805 President Thomas Jefferson secretly negotiated with the Spanish governor in Havana to annex Cuba. "Thus in 1809 Thomas Jefferson wrote, 'I candidly confess that I have ever looked upon Cuba as the most interesting addition that can be made to our system of States, the possession of which would give us control over the Gulf of Mexico and the countries and isthmus bordering upon it.' . . . Jefferson had attempted to purchase Cuba from Spain in 1808 (he was the first of four Presidents to do so)."[33] He was not successful and while three other U.S. presidents also tried to obtain Cuba, they also were unsuccessful.

A series of rebellions by the local Cubans during the nineteenth century failed to end Spanish rule. However, increased tensions between Spain and the United States led to the Spanish–American War in 1898, won by the U.S., which, after a couple of years, gave Cuba its independence; however, the U.S. remained as a domineering presence in Cuba, almost as if Cuba were a U.S. colony. This arrangement left a sour taste in the mouths of the Cuban people and there were many demonstrations and other forms of unrest. Nothing really notable happened until the 1950s, when General Fulgencio Batista was elected as president of Cuba. Early on, conditions for Cuba seemed to be improving but Batista, seeing that he was losing the presidential campaign in 1952, dissolved the legislative body and took over the country as a dictator. That set the Cuban people against him and a young lawyer named Fidel Castro offered himself as a popular alternative. He organized a strong resistance to overthrow Batista and for several years (1953–1959) led the revolution that ousted Batista in 1959. Fidel Castro became the president of Cuba and governed the island through the Communist Party. The current president of Cuba is Raúl Castro, Fidel Castro's brother.

A new policy shift in U.S.–Cuba relations

The United States severed diplomatic relations with Cuba on January 3, 1961, and instituted a trade embargo on February 3, 1962. President John F. Kennedy's administration extended the ban on February 8, 1963, forbidding U.S. citizens to travel to Cuba. While the trade embargo is still in effect, relations between the two countries began to thaw when in April 2009 U.S. President Barack Obama expressed his intention to relax the existing travel restrictions by making it legal for Americans to travel to Cuba if they met certain conditions.

On December 17, 2014 President Obama announced that he was seeking a new policy between the U.S. and Cuba. During the historic meeting between Obama and Raúl Castro in Panama on April 11, 2015 a new détente resulted, and new policies began to be developed between the two countries. This reconciliation between the two countries has already begun, with an agreement to reopen embassies in Washington and Havana on July 1, 2015. This shift in U.S. and Cuban policies is already making it easier for U.S. citizens to travel to Cuba.

The U.S. executive branch of government has taken the first steps in making it easier for Americans to travel to Cuba. However, for Americans to travel to Cuba completely free of U.S. restrictions will require the U.S. Congress to repeal the Helms–Burton Act of 1996. Currently, Americans can visit Cuba for numerous approved reasons without having to have special permission from the U.S. Government. Since the U.S.–Cuba travel market is currently in transition, both countries have time to plan for the future. Cuba is not yet fully ready to handle a

(Continued)

Case study (continued)

huge increase of travel from the U.S. Even moving slowly in the transition process, by 2016 U.S. travel to Cuba will likely surpass Canada as the number-one market, and will grow rapidly once more if the restrictions are lifted. There is pent-up demand from U.S. travelers wanting to travel to Cuba. In addition, of importance to many travelers, Cuba is considered a very safe destination.

Economics of tourism in Cuba

According to the June 19, 2015 Caribbean Tourism Organization's latest tourist arrival statistics for the year of 2014, the Dominican Republic, at 5.1 million visitors, leads all Caribbean nations. The largest market for visitors to the Dominican Republic is U.S. tourists. In second place is Cuba, with 3 million tourists and their largest market are visitors from Canada. Every indication is that, with the likelihood of increased numbers of U.S. visitors to Cuba in 2015, Cuba will become the number-one market in the Caribbean within a few short years. For example, tourism arrivals to Cuba for January through April of 2015 are up over 14 percent for the same time period in 2014. Arrivals are up over 6 percent for the Dominican Republic for the same time period. Expenditures by visitors in Cuba approached $3 billion and accounted for about 125,000 jobs. These numbers for Cuba will continue to increase as travel restrictions for U.S. travelers are relaxed.

The Cuban infrastructure is not yet in good enough condition to handle large numbers of visitors. In addition, Cuba must also guard against some of the negative impacts of large-scale mass tourism that may lead to environmental degradation, economic inequality, and cultural erosion. "The government is playing an active role in encouraging visitors to engage in tourism activities away from the resorts, which will be essential for small tourism entrepreneurs in the future as one way to battle the potential dangers of mass tourism."[34] However, thus far, the big draw for visitors has been Havana and the Varadero Beach area.

Cuba has all of the ingredients for a successful sustainable tourism program

While Cuba desperately needs to earn hard currency from its tourism industry, it has an excellent opportunity to pursue the best sustainable tourism program in the Caribbean. As a large island, Cuba has numerous natural areas, of interest to a broad spectrum of visitors, in addition to its beautiful beaches. Cuba has a very interesting culture and heritage, of great interest to visitors. So far Cuba has had a positive program of protecting the environment and its wonderful natural assets, including the island's fauna and flora. In contrast to most of the rest of the Caribbean, Cuba's beaches, mangroves, coral reefs and seagrass beds remain relatively well conserved. One question is: Can Cuba continue to maintain its successful sustainability in concert with large increases of visitors? One advantage that Cuba has that might in the long run help the Cubans to understand the need for a successful sustainable tourism program is that Cuba has the second highest literacy rate in the world, 99.8 percent (the Vatican City, at 100 percent, is the highest). Having a well-educated population will likely lead to more interest in the environment and natural resources.

Cuban culture is incomparable and quite different from most of the rest of the Caribbean. For example, Cuban music, dance, and art is unique to the country. Much of the art depicts the fascinating Cuban history, its special culture and heritage. The music includes both Latin American and African influences. Cuban dance, in rhythm with the fast-paced Salsa music, is beautiful to watch. Also, something which exists nowhere else in the world, and which adds a special nostalgia for American visitors, is Cuba's large collection of American automobiles from the 1950s. Harsh economic realities and Cuban ingenuity in repairing old automobiles has resulted in Cuba keeping antique American cars in working order, operated and displayed on the streets of Havana.

United Nations Educational, Scientific and Cultural Organization: Cuba's sustainability

Cuba also has an advantage in protecting its environment through the required maintenance of its United Nations Educational, Scientific and Cultural Organization (UNESCO) sites. The Caribbean region has 17 UNESCO locations, and 9 reside within Cuba. In fact, Cuba has more UNESCO sites than Egypt. Being a UNESCO site is an advantage for promoting sustainable tourism in that UNESCO certification emphasizes special cultural, natural and/or historical significance for a destination. The following Cuban locations, taken from a UNESCO website,[35] are listed under two UNESCO categories: *Cultural* and *Natural*:

Cultural

1 "Archaeological Landscape of the First Coffee Plantations in the South-East of Cuba: The remains of the 19th-century coffee plantations in the foothills of the Sierra Maestra [mountains] are unique evidence of a pioneer form of agriculture in a difficult terrain. They throw considerable light on the economic, social, and technological history of the Caribbean and Latin American region."

2 "Historic Centre of Camagüey: One of the first seven villages founded by the Spaniards in Cuba, Camagüey played a prominent role as the urban centre of an inland territory dedicated to cattle breeding and the sugar industry. Settled in its current location in 1528, the town developed on the basis of an irregular urban pattern that contains a system of large and minor squares, serpentine streets, alleys and irregular urban blocks, highly exceptional for Latin American colonial towns located in plain territories. The Spanish colonizers followed medieval European influences in terms of urban layout and traditional construction techniques brought to the Americas by their masons and construction masters."

(Continued)

3 "Old Havana and its Fortification System: Havana was founded in 1519 by the Spanish. By the 17th century, it had become one of the Caribbean's main centres for ship-building. Although it is today a sprawling metropolis of 2 million inhabitants, its old centre retains an interesting mix of Baroque and neoclassical monuments, and a homogeneous ensemble of private houses with arcades, balconies, wrought-iron gates and internal courtyards."

4 "San Pedro de la Roca Castle, Santiago de Cuba: Commercial and political rivalries in the Caribbean region in the 17th century resulted in the construction of this massive series of fortifications on a rocky promontory, built to protect the important port of Santiago. This intricate complex of forts, magazines, bastions and batteries is the most complete, best-preserved example of Spanish-American military architecture, based on Italian and Renaissance design principles."

5 "Trinidad and the Valley de los Ingenios: Founded in the early 16th century in honour of the Holy Trinity, the city was a bridgehead for the conquest of the American continent. Its 18th- and 19th-century buildings, such as the Palacio Brunet and the Palacio Cantero, were built in its days of prosperity from the sugar trade."

6 "Urban Historic Centre of Cienfuegos: The colonial town of Cienfuegos was founded in 1819 in the Spanish territory but was initially settled by immigrants of French origin. It became a trading place for sugar cane, tobacco and coffee. Situated on the Caribbean coast of southern-central Cuba at the heart of the country's sugar cane, mango, tobacco and coffee production area, the town first developed in the neoclassical style. It later became more eclectic but retained a harmonious overall townscape."

7 "Viñales Valley: The Viñales valley is encircled by mountains and its landscape is interspersed with dramatic rocky outcrops. Traditional techniques are still in use for agricultural production, particularly of tobacco. The quality of this cultural landscape is enhanced by the vernacular architecture of its farms and villages, where a rich multi-ethnic society survives, illustrating the cultural development of the islands of the Caribbean, and of Cuba."

Natural

1 "Alejandro de Humboldt National Park: Complex geology and varied topography have given rise to a diversity of ecosystems and species unmatched in the insular Caribbean and created one of the most biologically diverse tropical island sites on earth. Many of the underlying rocks are toxic to plants so species have had to adapt to survive in these hostile conditions. This unique process of evolution has resulted in the development of many new species and the park is one of the most important sites in the Western Hemisphere for the conservation of endemic flora."

2 "Desembarco Del Granma National Park: Desembarco del Granma National Park, with its uplifted marine terraces and associated ongoing development of karst topography and features, represents a globally significant example

(Continued)

Case study (continued)

of geomorphologic and physiographic features and ongoing geological processes. The area, which is situated in and around Cabo Cruz in south-east Cuba, includes spectacular terraces and cliffs, as well as some of the most pristine and impressive coastal cliffs bordering the western Atlantic."

Strategizing for the future of Cuba's sustainable tourism program

For Cuba to have a successful sustainable tourism program in the future, it would be beneficial if they implemented policies and strategies that emphasize the four sustainable tourism components mentioned in Chapter 1, which are:

- Ecotourism: responsible travel to natural areas that conserves the environment and improves the welfare of the local people;
- Geotourism: tourism that sustains or enhances the geographical character of a place – its environment, culture, aesthetics, heritage, and the well-being of its residents;
- Cultural Tourism: traveling to experience the places and activities that authentically represent the stories and people of the past and present;
- Responsible Tourism: tourism that maintains the benefits to local communities, minimizes negative social or environmental impacts, and helps local people conserve fragile cultures and habitats or species.

If Cuba's tourism program used these four pillars of sustainable tourism to guide its development, it would have the best such program in the Caribbean, and possibly in the world. Now is the time for Cuba to develop such a sustainable tourism policy before it is too late.

Chapter summary

We know that poverty exists throughout the world, but often it is not realized how much really exists and whether the tourism industry is capable of making a dent in the level of poverty. This chapter has addressed this concern. It is a complicated issue and one that has been with the global community for a long time.

There appears to be an opportunity to address a few of the UNMDGs through sustainable tourism practices, although it is much too early to determine just how the vast tourism resources can best impact such goals. The agency assigned to work toward the UNMDGs is the UNWTO. The UNWTO has responded with recommendations for action in its "Tourism and Poverty Alleviation" report.

One key to making some impact on the poverty issue is to review opportunities for tourism development in less developed countries (LDCs). Many LDCs have areas in them that offer opportunities for sustainable tourism development, but they may not have the technical skills to address such development. This situation can be alleviated to some degree by technical help from the UNWTO or other international organizations.

Often overlooked in international sustainable tourism development is the United Nations Environmental Program (UNEP). Yet this organization has the technical expertise to address questions regarding tourism and the environment. Fortunately UNWTO and UNEP are working together regarding sustainable tourism and the UNMDGs.

Working toward the alleviation of poverty through tourism is a very complicated endeavor. There are a few success stories but the difficulties are many. Most success has come from forming partnerships with interested parties at all levels. Developing sustainable tourism projects, especially in LDCs, won't work well unless the tourism projects have strong local support followed by resources and cooperation at the governmental level and in partnership with the private sector.

The case study for this chapter relates to a "new" relationship between Cuba and the United States. It is not yet clear what impact this relationship will have on the tourism industry between these two countries and the rest of the world. Certainly Cuba has many potential opportunities with respect to sustainable tourism development and promotion.

Chapter review questions

1 Discuss your thoughts with respect to the amount of poverty you may be aware of and some methods you think may be helpful in alleviating poverty.
2 What is your opinion on the United Nations Millennium Development Goals?
3 Do you think the tourism industry can help reduce poverty, and if so, how?
4 Describe how you think the UNWTO might be able to help alleviate poverty through sustainable tourism development.
5 What does UNEP stand for and what is the involvement of this organization with respect to sustainable tourism development?
6 Describe what the term LDC stands for. What is your opinion of LDCs?
7 Why are partnerships so important with respect to sustainable tourism?
8 Are you aware of the new political relationship between Cuba and the United States and how it might impact on the tourism industry?
9 Can you describe some of the potential tourism destinations in Cuba?
10 Did you know about the United Nations Educational, Scientific and Cultural Organization sites in Cuba?

Notes

1 Edgell, Sr., D. L. and Swanson, J. R. (2013) *Tourism Policy and Planning: Yesterday, Today, and Tomorrow* (2nd edition), London: Routledge, p. 265.
2 United Nations (2000) *Millennial Declaration*, New York, September 6–9, 2000.
3 United Nations (2010) *The Millennium Development Goals Report*, New York, September 20–22, 2010.
4 United Nations (2013) *A Life of Dignity for All*, New York, September 23–25, 2013.
5 United Nations World Tourism Organization, retrieved April 1, 2015 from http://www2.unwto.org/content/who-we-are-0.
6 Yunis, E. (2004) "Tourism and Poverty Alleviation," Madrid, Spain: United Nations World Tourism Organization.
7 Edgell and Swanson (2013), p. 267.

8 United Nations World Tourism Organization (2011) "Report to the United Nations . . . Global Review of the Program of Action for Least Developed Countries for the Decade 2001–2010."

9 Edgell and Swanson (2013), p. 268.

10 Bricker, K., Black, R., and Cottrell, S., eds. (2013) *Sustainable Tourism & the Millennium Development Goals,* Burlington, Massachusetts: Jones & Bartlett Learning, pp. 42–43.

11 United Nations World Tourism Organization (2002) "Sustainable Tourism–Eliminating Poverty" at the World Summit on Sustainable Development in Johannesburg, South Africa.

12 Mitchell, J. and Ashley, C. (2010) *Tourism and Poverty Reduction: Pathways to Prosperity,* London: Earthscan.

13 Edgell, Sr., D. L. (1990) *International Tourism Policy*, New York: Van Nostrand Reinhold.

14 Edgell, Sr., D. L. (1999) *Tourism Policy: The Next Millennium*, Urbana, Illinois: Sagamore Press.

15 Edgell, Sr., D. L. (2002) *Best Practices Guidebook for International Tourism Development for Rural Communities*, Provo, Utah: Brigham Young University.

16 Jamaica Social Investment Fund (2011) *Community Based Tourism Policy*, Kingston, Jamaica: World Bank.

17 Edwards, R., Galaski, K., and Dodds, R. (2013) "Connecting Communities to the Tourism Supply Chain," in K. Bricker, R. Black, and S. Cottrell (eds.) *Sustainable Tourism & the Millennium Development Goals*, Burlington, Massachusetts: Jones & Barlett Learning, pp. 265–276.

18 Ibid., p. 276.

19 United Nations Women and United Nations World Tourism Organization (2011) "Global Report on Women in Tourism 2010," Madrid, Spain: United Nations World Tourism Organization.

20 Turner, R. and Sears, Z. (2013) "The Travel & Tourism Competitiveness Report 2013," World Economic Forum Annual Meeting 2013, Davos-Klosters, Switzerland, January 23–27, 2013.

21 United Nations Women and United Nations World Tourism Organization (2011) "Global Report on Women in Tourism 2010," Madrid, Spain: United Nations World Tourism Organization.

22 Edgell and Swanson (2013), p. 285.

23 Hall, C., Timothy, D., and Duval, D., eds. (2003) *Safety and Security in Tourism*, Binghamton, New York: The Haworth Hospitality Press, p. 13.

24 Mansfeld, Y. and Pizam, A., eds. (2006) *Tourism, Security and Safety*, Oxford, England: Elsevier Butterworth-Heinemann, p. xiii.

25 Bricker et al. (2013), p. 285.

26 Retrieved from http://pewresearch.org/fact-tank/2015/05/28/what-we-know-about-cubas-economy/.

27 Baker, C. (2000) *Cuba*, Emeryville, California: Moon Handbooks, p. xxiv.

28 Sanders, E. and Long, P. (2002) *Economic Benefits to the United States from Lifting the Embargo*, Boulder, Colorado: University of Colorado.

29 Retrieved from http://cubanfishingcenters.com/cuba.php, July 5, 2015.

30 Baker (2000), p. 22.

31 Retrieved from http://www.glencoe.com/sec/socialstudies/btt/Columbus/native_peoples.shtml, July 6, 2015.

32 Baker (2000), p. 23.

33 Ibid., p. 28.

34 Hingtgen, N., Kline, C., Fernades, L., and McGehee, N. (2015) "Cuba in Transition: Tourism Industry Perceptions of Entrepreneurial Change," *Tourism Management*, 50, 184–193.

35 Retrieved from http://whc.unesco.org/en/statesparties/CU/, July 6, 2015.

Chapter 5

Rural tourism and sustainability

"Two roads diverged in a wood, and I – I took the one less traveled by"

Robert Frost

In the complex world of global tourism, the primary emphasis is on metropolitan areas, where mass tourism generates large economic benefits, both for the community and for the businesses involved. Often rural communities get ignored with respect to tourism development. Rural locales are often seen as areas too difficult or too expensive to develop or market. There are certainly many exceptions to this view, such as exotic lodges, beautiful resorts, and unique bed and breakfast properties in rural locations. For the most part rural areas in much of the world are somewhat neglected with respect to tourism development in general, and specifically in terms of sustainability. This chapter will discuss many of the problems of tourism development and sustainability in rural environments and then present principles and practices to help mitigate some of the difficulties in these areas. While the chapter relies heavily on information about rural tourism in the United States, much of the research in this regard is apropos of other parts of the world as well.

Rural tourism is not easily defined. It usually means tourism that takes place in the countryside. However, Lane (1994) says,

> Rural tourism is a complex multi-faceted activity: it is not just farm-based tourism. It includes farm-based holidays but also comprises special-interest nature holidays and ecotourism, walking, climbing and riding holidays, adventure, sport and health tourism, hunting and angling, educational travel, arts and heritage tourism, and, in some areas, ethnic tourism.[1]

Almost every rural community in the world has some resource, attraction, activity, event, or special interest or adventure opportunity that can motivate a traveler. It may be a special fishing site, a hunting trip, a unique place for taking photographs or painting, a backpacking or horseback trail experience, a good location for ballooning, a white-water river-rafting adventure, an unusual or distinct festival, or simply a place for rest and relaxation. Rural environments have vast expanses of land and water and wide diverse topographies (mountains, plains, forests, grasslands, rivers, lakes, and deserts) that provide outstanding settings for tourism and recreation development. The point is that there is hardly a place in a rural area in the world that is not conducive to a form of tourism development.[2]

The problems of tourism development in rural areas are well documented. Many rural populations have aged and have experienced a population loss and a decline in local businesses. This is especially true with respect to the better-educated young and skilled workers who leave for greater economic opportunities in the cities. Residents of rural communities often lag behind in education, especially in the less-developed countries of the world. The economic competitiveness of rural locations is generally declining, in part because rural communities depend upon too few sources of income and lack certain necessary facilities. In addition, many rural areas can no longer prosper from mining or harvesting trees as they did in the past.

However, not all rural areas are suffering. Many are using imagination, ingenuity, and innovation in the hopes of capturing some of the tourism dollars that are most often connected with urban sites. Furthermore, global interest in sustainable tourism has changed the image of many rural areas to that of a very special destination for visitors seeking ecotourism and geotourism experiences. Bernard Lane (1994) saw this movement early on and noted that "While there are many problems in developing and managing rural tourism it does offer one positive way of introducing new investment, employment and enterprise into the countryside. A sustainable approach to tourism seeks to avoid an unbalanced approach to economic growth by using tourism as a tool for broader economic progress, actively seeking alternatives to tourism. It also tries to involve local business and communities in ownership, decision-making and benefits."[3]

International rural tourism development principles and practices

Rural tourism takes place throughout the world, with a multitude of different approaches depending on the location and the development and management of the site. The practices of rural tourism are as varied as there are countries in the world. In 1990, Elizabeth Boo of the World Wildlife Fund wrote *Ecotourism: The Potentials and Pitfalls*, offering practical guidelines of use to rural tourism planners. While the following guidelines were written for park management, they are highly useful for rural tourism areas or for setting the stage for sustainable tourism practices.

- The success of nature tourism depends on the conservation of nature. Many parks are threatened, and it is critical for everyone involved with nature tourism to realize that intact natural resources are the foundation of the product.
- Nature tourism sites need revenue for protection and maintenance, much of which can be generated directly from entry fees and sales of products. Many protected areas charge nominal or no entrance fees and provide few if any auxiliary services.

- Tourists are a valuable audience for environmental education ... Whether "hard-core" nature tourists or "new" visitors with little background in natural history, all tourists can enhance their appreciation of the area through information brochures, exhibits and guides.
- Nature tourism will contribute to rural development when local residents are brought into the planning process. For nature tourism to be a tool for conservation and rural development, a concerted effort must be made to incorporate local populations into development of the tourism industry.
- Opportunities are emerging for new relationships between conservationists and tour operators ... as more tourists come to parks and reserves, tour operators have the opportunity to become more actively involved with conservation of these areas through education for their clientele and donations to park management.[4]

One of the best examples of a global tour operator utilizing the right practices for eco-travel to remote rural areas and nature sites is Lindblad Expeditions, which has developed a highly successful model approach for its positive overarching sustainable tourism policies:

- Preserve a destination's natural assets to ensure its ongoing value to the travel industry and the local community
- Maintain positive relations with local government officials who determine business regulations
- Attract and retain employees who possess key skills
- Build and expand a loyal customer base[5]

One of the many international organizations reporting on rural tourism principles is the Organisation for Economic Co-Operation and Development (OECD – located in Paris, France – see Chapter 1 for more details on this organization). In its 1991–1992 report on tourism, the OECD (which released the report in 1994) stated that six factors determine the suitability of rural areas for tourism development:

1 Scenic value, including mountains, seashores, lakes, islands, rivers, *and* special interest scenery such as wetlands or mixed deciduous forest
2 Special wildlife assets
3 Cultural assets, including historic buildings, towns, villages, sites and/or ethnic heritage of all types
4 Special facilities for sports, including hunting, fishing, skiing, and hiking
5 Ease of access by large populations
6 Effective promotional, commercial, and management skills

While these six factors were not designed for sustainable tourism development in rural areas, for the most part they represent good sustainable tourism practices in today's world.[6]

Agritourism as a part of the rural tourism product

A special subset of rural tourism that has become relatively popular in the new millennium is "agritourism." Agritourism is most often connected with working farms and ranches, although it can also include wineries, outdoor camps, target-shooting facilities, fee-based pond fishing, leased hunting, rural weddings, and other recreation venues where visitors can enjoy the outdoors. Visitors may buy local farm products, enjoy outdoor entertainment, and stay overnight. Rural entrepreneurs may become involved in agritourism as a way of supplementing their income, while others want to share outdoor experiences with visitors. Agritourism exists in almost every country of the world. In the U.S., for example, activities related to agritourism account for more than 25,000 sites and generated services and products valued over a billion dollars. Agritourism is big in Hawaii, where people enjoy a standard Hawaii beach or adventure vacation and include some agritourism activity during their vacation. Wine tours in the Napa Valley of California, and in many countries throughout the world, have become very popular. The Tuscany region in Italy was one of the first regions in the world to become exceedingly popular as an agritourism destination. Many of the old farmhouses have been converted into inns and gained a reputation for offering an authentic and quaint Italian countryside experience. Tuscany's famous wineries and excellent local foods make it one of Europe's best agritourism destinations. In other areas related to agritourism it may be the scenery or opportunities to see wild animals or fishing or hunting or photography or bird watching that is the attraction. In addition, there are couples that like the idea of a rural outdoor or farm-based wedding with a beautiful setting as their dream.

Rural tourism policy in the United States

As increasing numbers of people were leaving rural areas in the United States in the 1970s and 1980s there was a national concern for the loss of the unique heritage and culture of the countryside values of America. There were numerous reasons for the migration of rural populations leaving the countryside for more urban areas. The most significant phenomenon was a decrease in employment opportunities in rural areas. Employment in traditional industries such as mining, logging, and agriculture were changing. Once the minerals and trees began disappearing the jobs in mining and logging were gone as well. The family farm with a few hundred acres was being altered due to new technology in agriculture equipment requiring less labor and a general move toward corporate farming, whereby thousands of acres were managed by corporations located in large cities. A need arose to investigate new opportunities for the survival of rural America, and the field of rural tourism emerged.

In one sense, rural tourism was not new. The United States, in the eighteenth century, had been founded on values of small rural communities. Much of the history and heritage of America is immersed in rural economic development. What is new is that over the past 25 years there began a resurgence of interest in tourism as an alternative product base in rural communities. The current interest in sustainable tourism has increased interest in tourism policies that support rural tourism development. In this respect it has been noted that rural areas often have a comparative advantage because of their natural resources, as well as, in many cases, authentic history, and heritage and cultural attributes of interest to potential visitors.[7]

Research by many economists in rural development in the United States suggests that non-metropolitan, pastoral locales that are dependent on tourism, retirement income, and governmental expenditures that improve facilities at parks and recreational sites, exhibit greater stability than those that rely on rural manufacturing, mining, and logging. Agriculture is still the most important industry in rural America, but due to its high use of mechanization, it employs relatively few people full time. As a result, rural communities continue to seek alternatives to economic development other than the once-dominant industries of farming, ranching, timber production and mining. Many areas are looking toward more sustainable resources as developmental tools. Sustainable tourism is a highly viable option because its implementation often relies on an area's history, heritage, culture, geographic resources, and natural uniqueness.[8]

After the U.S. *National Tourism Policy Act* of 1981 was passed, a strong interest emerged on the part of the U.S. Government, through the newly established United States Travel and Tourism Administration, in fostering programs to increase tourism throughout the U.S., and specifically to increase international tourism to the U.S. As visitors sought more variety in their tourism products they began to note the special qualities in rural areas that offered opportunities for ecotourism, adventure experiences, cultural attractions, and the peace and tranquility of the countryside. Investigations (e.g. Long and Edgell, 1997) of rural areas noted that many rural communities were hampered in their efforts to develop tourism due to a lack of the human, financial and technical resources necessary to establish a sustainable tourism industry acceptable to residents and businesspeople, as well as their travelling guests.[9]

At the beginning of 1989, the U.S. Congress, seeking answers for making rural areas more economically viable, "directed the United States Travel and Tourism Administration (USTTA) to undertake a two-part national study to determine:

- The ways in which small businesses in rural areas can be promoted through travel and tourism, and,
- Whether there is a need for federal policy concerning the development and promotion of small businesses in rural communities through travel and tourism, and whether or not there should be a federal program to support such a policy."[10]

The USTTA contracted with the consulting firm of Economic Research Associates to prepare the *National Policy Study on Rural Tourism and Small Business Development*, which was conducted during the six-month period between April and September, 1989. The study noted in its "Executive Summary" that "there is no coherent national policy on rural tourism development and little systematic coordination between federal agencies whose programs and actions affect tourism enterprises in rural areas . . . there are at least four important reasons that lend support in favor of a federal policy on rural tourism.

- The federal government already has a major presence in rural tourism [National Park Service etc.];
- Tourism should play an important contributing role in the national agenda for rural economic development;
- There are no explicit federal policies or programs that focus on rural tourism; and
- There is an apparent broad-based interest in creating a federal rural tourism policy."[11]

The comprehensive study discussed, in some detail, the broad issues in rural America, rural tourism development (travel/recreation industry integration), lack of rural infrastructure, leadership in rural communities, and many other areas relevant to the development of rural tourism. The major conclusions emanating from the study were that:

- "Yes, there is a need for federal policy on rural tourism; travel and tourism could be an important tool for rural economic revitalization, and it should be an essential component of the broader rural economic development strategies; and
- Yes, strategic responses on the part of the federal government are needed if the new policy is to be implemented effectively on behalf of the nation's rural areas."[12]

The *Study* concludes with "policy recommendations" for the U.S. Congress, as follows:

- "Specifically recognize tourism as a legitimate and important element of rural economic development by referencing 'growth and development of travel and tourism' in all policies and programs relating to rural development.
- Specifically recognize rural travel and tourism as a legitimate and important element of domestic travel and tourism policies by revising the language, where appropriate, of the *National Tourism Policy Act of 1981*, to include 'growth, development, and promotion of travel and tourism in rural areas.'
- Specifically instruct appropriate federal agencies to accord due importance in their programs that target small business/economic development and foster the travel and tourism industry."[13]

While the study itself did not specifically refer to sustainable tourism in its final report, much of the research conducted within the study discussed aspects of rural areas and tourism that fit well within the parameters of sustainable tourism. For example, the study mentions that many senior Americans were interested in national parks, historical sites, scenic beauty and special events and festivals depicting the culture of rural communities. In other words, cultural tourism, ecotourism, and geotourism, three of the pillars of sustainable tourism, were of popular interest in rural areas in the 1980s. The study cited many success stories of small rural towns that utilized "sustainable" tourism as a means of economic revitalization through the interest of visitors in the natural environment and the history, heritage, and culture of the area. Amongst many examples in the study of the relationship of rural tourism to sustainability is the following:

> Near Park Rapids, Minnesota in 1984, it took 12 women at a baby shower with an idea (and determination) to create the Village of Smokey Hills, which became a big attraction in a very short time. They created a pioneer village near a mountain site "out in the woods," where no roads existed; no power had been extended to the site. But within six weeks the Village of the Smoky Hills became a reality, a kind of crafts shopping area in which artists and craftsmen demonstrated their skills and sold their crafts. They also provided a hands-on experience, encouraging visitors to participate and learn the craft as well to buy hand-made items. Forecasting 20,000 visitors in the first year, 100,000 showed up. It grew from there into a thriving rural community.

The study also mentioned a fledgling program that began in the late 1980s and was codified through Congressional legislation in 1991 as the National Scenic Byway program. The program was designed to preserve and protect the nation's scenic but less-traveled roads and promote tourism and economic development. The most scenic of the rural road byways are designated as **All-American Roads** if the road meets at least two of six qualities: **scenic quality; natural quality; historic quality; cultural quality; archeological quality;** and **recreational quality**. The concept behind the National Scenic Byway is to get people off the highways and on to the rustic rural roads for more enjoyable travel. The National Scenic Byway program has become an integral part of sustainable tourism in the United States.

The U.S. Congress response to the study was partially imbedded in the establishment of the National Rural Tourism Foundation (NRTF) as part of the *Tourism Policy and Export Promotion Act* of 1992. Amongst other provisions, the Act noted:

- "Many local communities with significant tourism potential are unable to realize the economic and employment opportunities that tourism provides because they lack the necessary local resources and expertise needed to induce tourism trade;
- Increased efforts directed at promotion of rural tourism will contribute to the economic development of rural America and further the conservation and promotion of natural, scenic, historic, scientific, educational, inspirational, and recreational resources for future generations of Americans and foreign visitors; and,
- Exporting those goods and services which United States industry can produce at a comparative cost advantage, such as travel and tourism services, will be in the Nation's long-term strategic interest."

The Act directed the NRTF to provide "planning, development, and implementation of projects and programs which have the potential to increase travel and tourism export revenues by attracting foreign visitors to rural America." This provision included:

- "Participation in the development and distribution of educational and promotional materials pertinent to both private and public attractions located in rural areas of the United States, including Federal parks and recreational lands, which can be used by foreign visitors;
- Development of educational resources to assist in private and public rural tourism development; and
- Participation in Federal Agency outreach efforts to make such resources available to private enterprises, state and local governments, and other persons and entities interested in rural tourism development."[14]

The past chairman and past president of the NRTF, Dr. Patrick Long, in congressional testimony had this to say: "Although the Foundation was never publicly funded and consequently has been unable to reach its full potential, it stands ready to meet its goals should Congress see fit to revisit the Foundation's role and consider providing appropriate resources." Dr. Long went on to say that "strengthening the Foundation will create opportunities to increase export earnings from tourism and transportation services traded internationally and will encourage the development of the tourism industry in rural communities which have been severely affected by the decline of agriculture, family farming, the extraction of manufacturing industries, or by the closing of military bases."[15] The NRTF concept was a good idea. However, because the initial legislation authorized NRTF to be a charitable and non-profit corporation without receiving any federal funds, this has hampered the NRTF from carrying out its mission. The U.S. Congress should rectify this shortcoming.

Greensburg, Kansas: A unique sustainable rural community success story

On May 4, 2007, a powerful EF5 tornado (winds in excess of 200 miles per hour) struck the rural community of Greensburg, Kansas, destroying 95 percent of the town and killing 13 people out of a population of less than 1,600. "We lost half the population [to relocation] right away," recalls Greensburg Mayor Bob Dixson. "They had no place to live. A lot of older residents moved to neighboring communities. But we were very blessed – 2.8 million of our friends and neighbors came to help us," he says, referring to the population of Kansas.[16]

In the weeks and months following the tornado devastation, the remaining residents met and discussed plans for the future. They turned a horrifying disaster into an opportunity – not just for Greensburg but for other rural communities throughout the world. The community developed a *Sustainable Comprehensive Master Plan*, stating that "A truly sustainable community is one that balances the economic, ecological, and social impacts of development." The City Council of Greensburg passed a resolution requiring all new city buildings larger than 4,000 square feet to meet U.S. Green Building Council LEED Platinum certification and reduce energy consumption by 42 percent as compared to standard buildings. LEED stands for "Leadership in Energy and Environmental Design" and includes four levels: Certified, Silver, Gold, and Platinum (the highest level). Today, Greensburg, Kansas, with a Platinum certification, has the most LEED-certified buildings per capita in the world. More than any other rural community, this small rural village captures the true values of sustainability in its goals in the Master Plan:

- Be progressive while remaining unassuming
- Open doors to newcomers while maintaining traditional cultural heritage
- Provide opportunities for young people – education, jobs, a future back home
- Value the natural environment, balanced with growth and economic development
- Build a variety of durable, healthy, energy-efficient houses and buildings
- Look to renewable sources of energy, such as Greensburg's plentiful wind
- Treat each drop of water as a precious resource
- Remain affordable.

These eight goals fit perfectly with respect to the principles and practices of sustainable tourism. Today, visitors from around the world visit Greensburg, Kansas to see how a truly sustainable community operates. Greensburg Mayor Bob Dixson says: "The biggest success story in Greensburg to me, has been the resiliency and determination of our citizens to make a difference in their world. We're new pioneers in the sustainability movement."[17] A side note to this story is that actor/environmentalist Leonardo DiCaprio (who drives a hybrid and powers his L.A. home with solar panels) produced *Greensburg*, a 13-part series on the new Planet Green network, about the rebuilding of Greensburg, Kansas.

Coopetition and clustering as tools for sustainable rural tourism development

For a developed country like the United States of America, rural tourism development remains possibly the single largest lacuna in rural development efforts throughout the country. Furthermore, only limited credible research has been accomplished so far to suggest new innovative and creative approaches to rural tourism development. "The neglect of tourism as a rural business activity has also been compounded by the absence of any theoretical research published in mainstream tourism journals."[18]

The present author, representing the United States Travel and Tourism Administration, was engaged in a number of rural tourism projects throughout the United States in the 1980s and 1990s. He wrote a series of rural tourism articles based on his personal experiences. One common theme he noted in many of the rural communities he visited was a lack of cooperation among such communities when marketing their destinations in a competitive environment. It became clear that if rural communities within a region were to be more successful in reaching a larger marketplace for their tourism products, and in being more competitive, they would have to cooperate more fully. This led to the use of the term *coopetition*, sometimes spelled as co-opetition, which is a portmanteau term that combines the words cooperation and competition. Coopetition occurs when companies, destinations, or other groups interact with partial congruence of interests to benefit both groups. The present author was the first person to introduce *coopetition* as an important means to facilitate economic and competitive growth in tourism. The definition of the word coopetition in the tourism vernacular is the need for *coop*eration among tourism destinations in order to better market their tourism product effectively and meet the com*petition* (hence *coopetition*) at the regional or global level. In other words, tourism entities cooperate with each other to reach a higher value of competitive advantage in the marketplace. By working together, such entities can share knowledge and research and outsmart competitors in a market they could not reach as a single entity. The author was able to convince a number of rural tourism destinations that were competing against each other to form partnerships or strategic alliances to better market their tourism products and to increase the number of visitors from greater distances. Other examples were included in the book *Coopetition: Global Tourism beyond the Millennium* (Edgell and Haenisch, 1995).[19]

A 1996 book titled *Co-opetition*, co-authored by Adam M. Brandenburger (Harvard University) and Barry J. Nalebuff (Yale University), advanced the concept of coopetition by noting that "When a business strategy is so new in design, a new word must be coined to capture its value. Such is the case with *co-opetition*, a method that goes beyond the old rules of competition and cooperation to combine the advantages of both. Co-opetition is a pioneering, high-profit means of leveraging business relationships."[20]

Charles R. Goeldner and J. R. Brent Ritchie, in their book *Tourism: Principles, Practices, Philosophies* (12th edition, 2012), included a special focus on *partnerships*, saying that "This [view of partnerships] highlights the high degree of interdependency among all destination stakeholders, as well as the need for alliances and working relationships that build cooperation – sometimes with competitors as well as colleagues. Edgell's concept of coopetition . . . captures the value of partnership in a unique way."[21]

Another form of partnership not too dissimilar from that of "coopetition" is the use of tourism *clusters* or *cluster mapping* in rural areas. This concept is relatively new with respect to its applications to rural tourism. One of the early pioneers in the application of "clustering" in rural tourism was Michael Porter, of the Institute for Strategy and Competitiveness at the Harvard University Business School. He noted, in a research study (2004) titled *Competitiveness in Rural U.S. Regions: Learning and Research Agenda*, that "Many experts highlight the common misperception that agriculture is the dominant source of employment and income in rural economies [in the U.S.]. In fact, agriculture is important in only a small number of rural counties, and its overall impact on rural regions in the U.S. is negligible." His study included a "Cluster Mapping Project" – clusters that consist of related industries within a sector that are prone to co-locate. He noted that traded clusters with the highest absolute level of employment in regions included hospitality and tourism. The study indicated that "rural tourism" in its broadest sense not only includes scenic beauty but offers the potential for "special clusters" like the "California Wine Cluster" in the Napa Valley, which also encompasses a "scenic rural tourism tour cluster" in the beautiful countryside where the grapes are grown. Combining the "scenic beauty" of the Napa Valley with its heavy production of wine throughout the region makes for an impressive area for marketing rural tourism.[22] Clustering of tourist attractions and activities in certain areas can attract more tourists to each area and induce them to stay longer and spend more money than would have been possible without clustering.

The best sustainable tourism tour in a rural environment

One of the rapidly expanding types of tourism in rural areas is special interest and adventure tourism. Special interest rural tourism, or adventure tourism, usually refers to tourists in small groups who are visiting a specific area to learn about and experience something special in the area. A specific type of special interest theme may include nature or environmental themes that relate to flora, fauna, geology, scenic beauty, or biological attributes of the area. An example of this kind of rural tourism is described below.

While there is still a great deal of progress to be made in stimulating pro-environmental and ecological behaviors in tourism, recreation, and leisure, this author recently (May 16, 2015) participated in possibly the best example of a rural sustainable tourism tour anywhere in the world: the "Black Bear Tour" in eastern North Carolina. This guided black bear tour took place in the Pocosin Lakes National Wildlife Refuge located in northeastern North Carolina, a very rural area of the state and home to the largest black bear population in the world. The "Wildlife Refuge" is administered by the U.S. Fish and Wildlife Service, U.S. Department of the Interior, whose mission is "working with others to conserve, protect and enhance fish, wildlife and plants and their habitats for the continuing benefit of the American people. By accomplishing this goal, the Service helps protect a healthy environment for people to enjoy."[23] The message is clear: "Wildlife First."

The Pocosin Lakes National Wildlife Refuge in and of itself has an interesting history: The term "Pocosin" is an Algonquian Indian word meaning "swamp on a hill." It contains more than 100,000 acres, with a variety of forests, wetlands, lakes, ponds, and swamps. The density of wildlife is incredible, containing a wide variety of amphibians, reptiles, mammals, and birds. The list of such wildlife is long but a few of the more recognizable species include alligators, many varieties of turtles and snakes, opossums, black bears, red wolfs, raccoons, weasels, mink, red and gray foxes, coyotes, bobcats, otters,

Figure 5.1 A mother and baby black bear in Pocosin Lakes National
Wildlife Refuge
(Photo: Elaine Barr)

squirrels, beavers, rabbits, deer, and more than 200 species of birds. The guidelines for visiting the refuge are simple and practical: Don't disturb nesting birds; respect the wildlife and habitats; don't litter the area. Watching and photographing wildlife is particularly popular at the refuge.

The black bear tour the author had the privilege of participating in began at about 6 p.m. in the afternoon and finished by 8 p.m. The tour is limited to a dozen participants and takes place three times a year from mid-May to late June, a time of considerable activity and movement by the bear population. Our tour was guided by a biologist assigned to the refuge and to nearby areas. She was well versed and knowledgeable about the area and knew the habits and locations of the black bears. She also provided excellent background information on the environment and about the flora and fauna of the area. As a result, during the tour, our group saw more than a dozen black bears, as well as other wildlife species, and noted different kinds of vegetation including a wide variety of trees, plants, and bushes. The entire visit to the refuge was representative of what an excellent pro-environmental sustainable tourism tour in a rural environment should promote.

Planning for sustainable tourism in a rural environment

Today, the concept of sustainability as a resource development and management philosophy is permeating all levels of policy and practice relating to tourism, from local to global. Sustainable management of the natural and physical environment, more than ever before, must coexist with economic, sociocultural, and health and safety objectives of localities and nations.[24] For planning a sustainable tourism project or destination in a rural area, the most important single component is in having a large segment of the community involved in the very beginning of the planning process.[25] This fact is stressed in almost every practical guideline on sustainable tourism in a rural area.

Edgell (1978), writing about sustainability of tourism and tourism that includes rural areas, said that

> if this country [the U.S.] is . . . to maintain our nation's natural beauty and other vital resources, planning is essential . . . With proper planning, reserves can be set aside in the form of national parks, seashores, and forests, both to protect finite scenic resources from overuse or exploitation and to increase travel opportunities for tourists . . . [planning] can aid in maintaining our historical and cultural heritage, preserving and restoring traditions, while at the same time adding to the quality of life of those who wish to enjoy the benefits of such important social aspects of this great country.[26]

To be successful in a rural community, the tourism plan must be an integral part of a community's total economy and it must be sustainable, even if only on a seasonal basis. To be sustainable, it must be properly planned and managed, to ensure a continuing high-quality experience for the visitor.[27] The plan needs to highlight the importance of authenticity in the attractions. The publication *A Training Guide for Rural Tourism Development* defines authenticity as "the lifestyle of a community that emerges in response to its physical and social nature, its significant historical and economic events and the special qualities of the people who live in and develop the community."[28] Planning is essential. Inskeep (1994) notes that

> It is now recognized that tourism must be developed and managed in a controlled, integrated and sustainable manner, based on sound planning . . . The experience of many tourism areas [including rural areas] in the world has demonstrated that, on a long-term basis, the planned approach to developing tourism can bring benefits without significant problems, and maintain satisfied tourist markets. Places that have allowed tourism to develop without the benefit of planning are often suffering from environmental and social problems.[29]

In order to plan properly, the rural tourism destination community should conduct an economic, environmental and social impact study as part of the planning process. The key here is to maintain the sustainability of the tourism destination and to ensure that it adds to the quality of life of the local residents. Edgell (2006) suggests that "By managing the development, marketing, and promotion of sustainable tourism through a strategic sustainable tourism plan, the community is able to project itself as a very special place that tourists will want to visit, return to, and possibly even to retire to."[30]

Possibly one of the greatest stories with respect to sustainability in the United States takes place in an unlikely area in the state of Kansas. It has to do with the disappearing grasslands that once covered about 40 percent of North America. The two best efforts to educate visitors about the history, heritage, and sustainability of the prairie grass are through the Tallgrass Prairie Preserve, discussed in the case study at the end of this chapter, and the Flint Hills Discovery Center.

Discovering the Flint Hills of Kansas

One of the most fascinating areas for sustainable tourism in the United States with respect to the four pillars of sustainability advocated in Chapter 1 of this book – geotourism, cultural tourism, responsible tourism, and ecotourism – exists in the Flint Hills of Kansas. The case study in this chapter, titled *Experiential Tourism*, will discuss the Flints Hills in considerable detail. However, the best way to understand the Flint Hills is to make a visit to the Flint Hills Discovery Center in Manhattan, Kansas. This unique interactive museum is dedicated to the exploration of the magnificent Flint Hills, highlighting the science, history, and culture of the ecoregion, from prehistory to the present day.

The "vision" of the Discovery Center says that "We aim to serve as a principal place for learning and understanding about the Tallgrass prairie and the Flint Hills ecoregion in particular; to assure its long-term preservation." The "mission" of the Discovery Center reads, *"The Flint Hills Discovery Center* inspires people to celebrate, explore, and care for the Flint Hills." This "vision" and "mission" fit perfectly with respect to the concepts of sustainable tourism as explained in this book.[31]

This book has stressed in numerous chapters the importance of "authenticity" as a cornerstone within the concept of sustainability. The Discovery Center's displays, exhibits and educational programs present an exciting and authentic story about the origin of the grasslands, including the Native Americans who lived and hunted buffalo several hundred years ago. The Native American history itself is a fascinating account of the development of the state of Kansas. The original inhabitants of Kansas include eight Indian tribes: Arapaho, Comanche, Kansa, Kiowa, Missouri, Osage, Otoe, and Pawnee. The toponym "Kansas" was derived from the Kansa Indian tribe that roamed the area where the Discovery Center is located. The first European to visit Kansas was the Spanish explorer Vázquez de Coronado in 1542, who was hoping to reach the mythical Seven Cities of Gold. He was amazed to view the thousands of buffalo grazing on the grasslands of Central Kansas. One of the mixed-blood Native Americans of Kansas, Charles Curtis, became Vice President of the United States under President Herbert Hoover.

Even the design of the Discovery Center is an example of "sustainability." The internal structure of the building was designed with ecosystems in mind, using criteria from the Leadership in Energy and Environmental Design (LEED) certification program of the U.S. Green Building Council. The *Discovery Center* received the LEED Gold certification in January 2013, making it the first city building to achieve LEED status.

Case study 5: Experiential tourism – the Flint Hills and the Kansas Tallgrass Prairie National Preserve

"I shall certainly withdraw from Heaven – for the soul prefers freedom in the prairie."[32]

Walt Whitman

(Continued)

Case study (continued)

Introduction

The native grasslands that were once prevalent throughout the world have almost disappeared. In North America, native grasslands once covered 40 percent of the land but have been decreasing greatly over the past few decades. Mismanagement of water and other resources have had a numbing impact on the grasslands of India, Tibet, Mongolia, China, Africa, Russia, South America and elsewhere across much of the world. The European Commission reports that 12.8 percent of its grasslands have disappeared. There are currently international efforts to protect the remaining grasslands. One of the leaders in this respect is Dr. John Head, who wrote the book *Global Legal Regimes to Protect the World's Grasslands* (2012). He notes that "the [special] kinds of grasslands [that] can make [a difference] to the overall health of the planet are really quite substantial."

In North America, the grasslands are generally known as "prairie" grass, from the French word for "meadow." In the U.S. the grasslands are sometimes referred to as "tallgrass prairie" (a partial misnomer as most of the grass is not really very tall). At one time nearly 400,000 square miles of tallgrass prairie stretched from the U.S. state of Ohio to the Rocky Mountains in the western part of the U.S., and from the country of Canada to the U.S. state of Texas. Less than 4 percent of that prairie remains today, much of it in the rolling Flint Hills located in the U.S. states of Kansas and Oklahoma. The Flint Hills are named for the abundant residual flint eroded from the bedrock that lies near the surface. According to Ken Salazar, former U.S. Secretary of the Interior, "[The Flint Hills Legacy Conservation Area] will protect land, water, and wildlife while creating new opportunities for economic prosperity in the Region [ecoregion]." Fortunately, the Nature Conservancy became involved as a major partner in the Flint Hills project. The Nature Conservancy's definition, which fits experiential tourism, is "environmentally responsible travel to natural areas, in order to enjoy and appreciate nature and accompanying culture features [both past and present] that promote conservation, have a low visitor impact and provide for beneficially active socioeconomic involvement of local peoples." In addition, there is a Flint Hills Discovery Center in Manhattan, Kansas, a science and history museum which focuses on all aspects of the Flint Hills and explains in detail all about the prairie flora and fauna and the history and heritage of the area. The Discovery Center's vision states: "We aim to serve as a principal place for learning and understanding about the tallgrass prairie and the Flint Hills ecoregion in particular; to assure its long-term preservation."

Within the Flint Hills ecoregion is the first U.S. national park dedicated to the tallgrass prairie and the people who lived on it – the Kansas Tallgrass Prairie National Preserve. On November 12, 1996, Public Law 104-333, the Tallgrass Prairie National Preserve Act of 1996, was enacted and the newest national park was established. The Tallgrass Prairie National Preserve protects a nationally significant remnant of the once vast tallgrass prairie and its cultural resources. It has numerous hiking trails, cultural sites, views of flora and fauna, and education about the native populations that lived in the region. This case study principally concentrates on "experiential tourism" connected with the preserve, which is explained in a separate section in the case study.

Experiential tourism defined

In Chapter 1 of this book there was an explanation of the relationship of eco-tourism, geotourism, responsible tourism and cultural tourism to sustainable tourism. This same explanation basically applies to experiential tourism. A more extensive and comprehensive definition of experiential tourism is provided by the organization "Nature and Outdoor Tourism Ontario" [Canada]:

> Experiential tourism has become the current term that encompasses a variety of tourism and traveler categories, including the following: cultural tourism, ecotourism, educational travel, experimental tourism, heritage tourism and nature tourism, where activities are environmentally sensitive, displaying respect for the culture of the host area and looking to experience and learn rather than merely stand back and gaze. Experiential tourism involves active participation, involvement, even immersion.[33]

In other words, experiential travelers are usually seeking experiences that allow them to learn first hand about nature, culture, history, geography, and heritage in rural areas.

FERMATA, an international nature tourism consulting group, prepared a study titled *Experiential Tourism Strategy for the Kansas Flint Hills* (September, 2005), which defined experiential tourism in these words:

> At once recreational and educational, experiential tourism revolves around venues and activities that allow tourists to be active participants in (rather than only passive beneficiaries of) their travel experiences. Experiential tourism relies on *in situ* natural, cultural and historical resources, and helps people learn not only about the world around them but about themselves as well. It includes activities that draw people outdoors such as birding, and other wildlife viewing, hiking, camping, learning about the history of a region, and nature photography, in addition to other cultural, historical, or nature-based activities.[34]

Most studies on experiential travel have noted that it is prodigiously expanding. It also has helped to reinvigorate the economic vitality of rural areas. A few of the objectives of experiential tourism include:

1 People create meaning through direct experience.
2 The experience includes the people met, the places visited, the activities participated in and the memories created.
3 Experiential tourism draws people into local nature, culture and history.

(Continued)

Case study (continued)

4 Experiential tourism is low-impact, low-volume, and high-yield.
5 Experiential tourism is very personal, unique and individual for each visitor.
6 Experiential tourism opportunities allow for personal growth and reflect the values and interests of the individual visitor.
7 The desired outcome of experiential tourism is to achieve a complete participatory experience that provides new knowledge and authentic experiences.[35]

Experiential tourism and the Kansas Tallgrass Prairie National Preserve

James E. Sherow, Professor of History at Kansas State University, captures the essence of the need for preserving the Flint Hills in these words:

> It is one of the most endangered ecosystems on the face of the planet . . . If we learn how to sustain a human-grass relationship that gave rise to the tallgrass prairies, then we've learned how to sustain a living ecosystem. If we learn how to do that, perhaps we can also extend that lesson to the earth itself.

Within the Flint Hills, the Kansas Tallgrass Prairie National Preserve is one attempt to help people learn about the tallgrass prairies and the human connection to the ecosystem. The Preserve's brochure follows this line of reasoning: "Whether you are visiting from the next county, a distant state, or another country, you now have a prairie destination, rich in the unique history, culture, and ecology of the Great Plains." It is visits to and education about the Preserve's rich history, culture, and ecology which in effect define experiential tourism in this case study.

The (U.S.) National Park Trust, a non-profit organization dedicated to supporting national parks in the U.S., and the U.S. National Park Service dedicated the Tallgrass Prairie National Preserve in the scenic Flint Hills of central Kansas on May 31, 1997. Capturing the history and heritage of the tallgrass prairie into a national park system demonstrated a very special need for protecting an important resource and educating visitors about the role that grasslands play in supporting the "health of the planet." For more than forty years, dedicated individuals who understood the importance of the prairie grass had been interested in preserving the rich natural and cultural past by setting aside land for prairie tallgrass. The Flint Hills of Kansas was a natural site for such an effort and for studying the rich history of Native American cultures and the pioneer spirit of America.[36]

The Preserve is 10,894 acres of rolling grassland located in northern Chase County, Kansas, in the heart of the Flint Hills region. The area was once the hunting grounds for the Kansa and Osage Indians, and contains hills and prairie streams that are home to a wide variety of life. This incredible ecosystem hosts 400 species of plants, 150 kinds of birds, 29 types of reptiles and amphibians, and 30 species of mammals. The prairie flora and fauna, along with the historic buildings, the Native American cultural history, and the rich legacy of ranching, are all preserved for present and future generations to enjoy.[37]

Experiential visitors and others that visit the preserve have noted not just the culture and history of the area but the "vistas and views" of seeing the relationship of earth and sky, the vastness, and openness of the landscape and feeling of nature. To view a herd of bison (buffalo) on the preserve and think about the millions of bison who use to roam the prairie is a unique experience, as is an image of the Native Americans living in the area several thousand years ago, or imagining what Francisco Vázquez de Coronado must have said of the prairies when he crossed Kansas in 1541. *National Geographic* magazine, in their April 2007 issue, had a large section titled "Splendor of the Grass: The Prairie's Grip is Unbroken in the Flint Hills of Kansas" in which is described the "vast ecosystem" of the prairie. The article suggests to the experiential traveler that you "see the tallgrass prairie for itself, and you begin to suspect that grasses are what hold this world together . . . Where the tallgrass survives, so does night dark enough to reveal the glittering banner of the Milky Way flung against the sky. Stars wheel above us seen or not, but if we don't see – and treasure – the last of the prairie, it may vanish from underfoot."[38]

Marketing experiential tourism and the Kansas Tallgrass Prairie National Preserve

Nature, culture, and heritage destinations have long been appealing to travelers interested in an authentic and adventurous experience. There has been a rise in the volume of tourists who seek adventure, culture, history, geology, archeology, and interaction with local people. Cultural, nature, and heritage tourism are generally understood as a type of special interest tourism – for example, museums, ancient buildings, viewing sites and artifacts, as well as hiking, bird watching and other types of outdoor activities. This interest – which is, in effect, experiential tourism – bodes well for destinations like the Kansas Tallgrass Prairie National Preserve. The research information currently available supports the concept of experiential tourism and its growth.

In the United States there are also distinctive social groups that are most likely to be experiential travelers – for example the "Baby Boomers" (the 78 million Americans born between 1946 and 1964). Baby Boomers are an active and vigorous generation, which started the fitness craze in earlier years. Now that most have retired, they want a vacation that fits into their active, health-conscious lifestyle. Nature travel, hiking, and visiting cultural areas is high on their agenda. Then there are the Millennials (also called Generation Y or the echo boomers), born between 1977 and 2000, the children of the Baby Boomers, who number 83 million. They have grown up with active parents and an appreciation of the environment. They are looking for adventure and green destinations. They are the experiential travelers of tomorrow.

In 2003 the Travel Industry Association of America prepared a study titled *Geotourism: The New Trend in Travel*, which was sponsored by *National*

(Continued)

Case study (continued)

Geographic Traveler magazine and which provided a wide range of information related to experiential travel. The study noted that "More than half of the traveling American public consider it important to experience or learn about cultures other than their own when they travel ... Authenticity is a primary theme when examining travelers' wants and needs ... Travelers' positive attitudes about culture and history extend to the activities they choose to do at home and while traveling."[39]

An April 2015 report, "The Case for Responsible Travel: Trends & Statistics 2015" by the Center for Responsible Travel, noted these facts:

- "A significant number of international travelers seek out nature- and culture-based experiences, such as visiting historic sites (40% of overseas travelers), cultural sites (23%) and national parks (20%)," according to the U.S. Government's 2012 National Travel & Tourism Strategy.
- The 2012 National Travel & Tourism Strategy found similar trends among Americans traveling abroad: "Nature-based, culture-based, heritage and outdoor adventure travel represent a significant segment of the outbound tourism market as well."
- In 2014, domestic and international travelers made over 292 million recreation visits to the 370 recreation areas administered by the U.S. National Park Service.

This is pretty clear evidence that travel related to experiential tourism is growing throughout the world. It is a trend that is likely to continue in the future.

Experiential tourism is a strong component of sustainable tourism

As noted earlier, experiential tourism takes into account aspects of the four pillars of sustainable tourism – that is, ecotourism, geotourism, cultural tourism, and responsible tourism. One of the people who has contributed a great deal to an understanding of these components of sustainable tourism and how they can be incorporated into experiential tourism is Jonathan Tourtellot, Geotourism Editor of *National Geographic Traveler*. He not only developed the term "geotourism" but, in numerous studies of sustainable tourism, applied the term liberally to what has been described in this case study as "experiential tourism." As an expert in the field, he has had this to say:

> In a growing number of destinations, the business leaders, citizens, and government authorities are realizing that safeguarding their distinctive sense of place – cultural assets, natural habitats, historic features, scenic appeal – is essential for reaping the benefits of responsible tourism. A trend to encourage.

Possibly no country in the world is more advanced in understanding sustainable tourism and, in effect, experiential tourism than Canada. While much of the rest of the world was just learning about "sustainable tourism," Canada had already (1992) produced a "Code of Ethics and Guidelines for Sustainable Tourism." This "Code" was produced and adopted by the Tourism Industry Association of Canada. The section on a "Code of Ethics for Tourists" generated the following guidelines:

1 Enjoy our diverse natural and cultural heritage and help us to protect and preserve it.
2 Assist us in our conservation efforts through the efficient use of resources including energy and water.
3 Experience the friendliness of our people and the welcoming spirit of our communities. Help us to preserve these attributes by respecting our traditions, customs, and local regulations.
4 Avoid activities which threaten wildlife or plant populations, or which may be potentially damaging to our natural environment.
5 Select tourism products and services which demonstrate social, cultural and environmental sensitivity.

These guidelines, which certainly fit well with explaining experiential tourism, were well ahead of such an understanding in most of the rest of the world.

Canada's national parks are very advanced in connecting Canadians to their natural and cultural heritage. Parks Canada's vision statement (2010) is: "Canada's treasured natural and historic places will be a living legacy, connecting hearts and minds to a stronger, deeper understanding of the very essence of Canada." In addition, the Canadian national tourism vision is: "Canada will be the premier four-season destination to connect with nature and to experience diverse cultures and communities." This statement could easily be interpreted as a general explanation of an experiential tourism component for sustainable tourism.

Chapter summary

Rural tourism is sometimes overlooked with respect to economic development and as regards sustainable tourism. Businesses usually look to the higher density areas for tourism development, with the thought of generating more visitors and profits. There are certainly many exceptions to this line of reasoning as there are wonderful ecotourism lodges, bed and breakfast properties and other accommodations that show off the beauty and charm of rural locations.

One of the early advocates and knowledgeable persons about nature and rural tourism was Elizabeth Boo of the World Wildlife Fund. She developed several helpful principles and practices related to rural tourism development. She noted some of the needs in park management as many parks are located in rural areas.

Also mentioned in the chapter was Lindblad Expeditions because this company utilizes the right sustainable tourism practices in rural and nature environments. Two special points in this regard noted by Lindblad Expeditions are to preserve the natural resources and to maintain good relations with the local community. This chapter also mentioned a rural tourism report by the Organisation for Economic Co-operation and Development which included six factors with respect to rural tourism development.

It was 1989 before the United States had a coherent rural tourism policy. As mentioned earlier, rural tourism has not really received the attention it deserves. Once the U.S. launched a study of rural tourism policy and the U.S. Congress passed legislation to support rural tourism development, new progress on rural tourism development increased. However, some of the attention has been short lived and rural tourism needs to be re-stimulated in the U.S.

As far as sustainability is concerned, Greensburg, Kansas is one of the best places in the U.S. This little community was not at all on the "tourism" map before it was devastated by a tornado that nearly destroyed the entire community. Today, visitors are curious about just what has happened to this community to cause all the excitement about sustainability. One person outside the community who helped tell the Greensburg story was actor/environmentalist Leonardo DiCaprio.

Two concepts that have been applied to rural tourism areas and that have worked rather well are "coopetition" and "clustering." Clustering is a fairly well-known concept and has been in vogue for many years. Coopetition has been taking place for some time but wasn't well defined with respect to the tourism industry until the mid-1990s.

From a very narrow perspective, the black bear tour described in this chapter is an excellent example of sustainable tourism in a rural area, but it does not generate very much revenue to the area. On the other hand, the experiential tourism project in the Flint Hills of Kansas described in the case study is also a good example of sustainable tourism and does generate revenue. The Kansas Tallgrass Prairie National Preserve administered by the U.S. National Park Service and the Flint Hills Discovery Center tell a wonderful story about the tallgrass prairie that was almost extinct but is now being preserved.

Chapter review questions

1 If you have visited a rural tourism location, what is your general opinion of rural tourism?
2 What are some of the practical guidelines for rural tourism cited in the chapter?
3 What do you think about the tourism practices of the World Wildlife Fund and Lindblad Expeditions?
4 Are you familiar with the term agritourism? If so, give some examples.
5 Were you aware of the U.S. rural tourism policy initiative?
6 What are your opinions with respect to rural tourism?
7 Were you aware that actor Leonardo DiCaprio is a strong environmentalist and has been involved in a sustainable tourism development project?
8 Have you ever heard of Greensburg, Kansas?
9 Were you aware of the terms clustering and coopetition before reading this chapter?
10 After reading this chapter, do you think you would like to visit Greensburg, Kansas, or Pocosin Lakes National Wildlife Refuge, or the Kansas Tallgrass Prairie National Preserve, or the Flint Hills Discovery Center?

Notes

1 Lane, B. (1994) "What is Rural Tourism?" *Journal of Sustainable Tourism*, 2(1–2), 7–21.
2 Edgell, Sr., D. L. (1990) *International Tourism Policy*, New York, New York: Van Nostrand Reinhold, p. 30.
3 Lane, B. (1994).
4 Boo, E. (1990) *Ecotourism: The Potentials and Pitfalls*, 2 vols. Washington, D.C.: World Wildlife Fund.
5 Edgell, Sr., D. L. (2006) *Managing Sustainable Tourism: A Legacy for the Future*, New York: The Haworth Hospitality Press, p. 46.
6 Organisation for Economic Co-Operation and Development (1994) "Tourism Policy and International Tourism in OECD Countries 1991–1992," Paris: OECD.
7 Edgell, Sr., D. L. (2011) "Investigating Best Practices for Rural Tourism Development," in the *Journal of Hospitality and Tourism*, 9(2), 2.
8 Ibid., p. 3.
9 Long, P. and Edgell, Sr., D. L. (1997) "Rural Tourism in the United States: the Peak to Peak Scenic Byway and KOA," published in S. Page and D. Getz (eds.) *The Business of Rural Tourism: International Perspectives*, London: International Thomson Business Press.
10 Economic Research Associates (1989) *National Policy Study on Rural Tourism and Small Business Development*, Washington, D.C.
11 Ibid., p. I-8.
12 Ibid., p. I-4.
13 Ibid., p. I-9.
14 Tourism Policy and Export Promotion Act of 1992, Public Law 102–372, September 30, 1992, Washington, D.C.
15 Long, P. (2008) "Testimony Before the Subcommittee on Commerce, Trade and Consumer Protection of the Committee on Energy and Commerce, U.S. House of Representatives," September 11, 2008.
16 Retrieved from www.usatoday.com/story/news/greenhouse/2013/04/13/greensburg-kansas.
17 National Renewable Energy Laboratory (2009) *Greensburg, Kansas: A Better, Greener Place to Live*, U.S. Department of Energy, Office of Energy Efficiency and Renewable Energy, October, 2009.
18 Page, S. and Getz, D. (1997) *The Business of Rural Tourism: International Perspectives*, Boston, Massachusetts: International Tomson Business Press, p. 3.
19 Edgell, Sr., D. L. and Haenisch, R. (1995) *Coopetition: Global Tourism beyond the Millennium*, Kansas City, Missouri: International Policy Publishing.
20 Brandenburger, A. and Nalebuff, B. (1996), *Co-opetition*, New York: Doubleday.
21 Goeldner, C. and Brent Ritchie, J. (2012), *Tourism: Principles, Practices, Philosophies* (12th edition), Hoboken, New Jersey: Wiley, p. 295.
22 Porter, M. et al. (2004) *Competitiveness in Rural U.S. Regions: Learning and Research Agenda*, Cambridge, Massachusetts: Institute for Strategy and Competitiveness, Harvard University Business School.
23 U.S. Fish and Wildlife Service (2002) "Pocosin Lakes National Wildlife Refuge," September 2002.
24 Weaver, G. (1993) *Tourism Development: A Guideline for Rural Communities*, Columbia, Missouri: University of Missouri, p. 44.

25 Weaver, G. (1991) *Tourism USA: Guidelines for Tourism Development*, Columbia, Missouri: University of Missouri, p. 1.

26 Edgell, Sr., D. L. (1978) "International Tourism and Travel," in H. F. van Zandt (ed.) *International Business Prospects 1977–1979*, Indianapolis, Indiana: Bobbs-Merrill Educational Publishing, pp. 164–165.

27 U.S. Department of Commerce (1994) *Rural Tourism Handbook: Selected Case Studies and Development Guide*, Washington, D.C., p. 1.

28 Koth, B., Kreag, G., and Sem, J. (1991) *A Training Guide for Rural Tourism Development*, Saint Paul, Minnesota: Tourism Center, University of Minnesota, p. 4.

29 Inskeep, E. (1994) *National and Regional Tourism Planning: Methodologies and Case Studies*, World Tourism Organization publication, London: Routledge, p. 3.

30 Edgell (2006), p. 105.

31 Retrieved from www.flinthillsdiscovery.org.

32 Grier, E., ed., (1984) *Notebooks and Unpublished Prose Manuscripts*, New York: New York University Press.

33 Retrieved from http://noto.ca/info_for_your_business/experiential_tourism, July 9, 2015.

34 FERMATA (2005) *Experiential Tourism Strategy for the Kansas Flint Hills*, Austin, Texas.

35 Retrieved from http://noto.ca/info_for_your_business/experiential_tourism, July 9, 2015.

36 Edgell (2006), p. 100.

37 Ibid., p. 102.

38 Klinkenborg, V. (2007) "Splendor of the Grass," *National Geographic*, 211(4).

39 Travel Industry Association of America (2003) *Geotourism: The New Trend in Travel*, Washington, D.C.: Travel Industry Association of America.

Chapter 6

Sustainable tourism and the prospects for peace

"The world is a book and those who do not travel read only one page."

Saint Augustine (4th century CE)

Seventeen centuries have passed since the above quotation, attributed to Saint Augustine, was noted, and yet the message of travel in the twenty-first century is the same – travel to turn the page and learn something new about the world. At the International Institute for Peace through Tourism's World Symposium, held in Ekurhuleni (adjacent to Johannesburg International Airport), South Africa, on February 16–19, 2015 the two keynote addresses by Dr. Taleb Rifai and Mr. David Scowsill, in effect, reinforce the quotation from St. Augustine. Dr. Rifai, Secretary General of the UN World Tourism Organization, had this to say: "Travel is the language of peace." He went on to say that the fundamental experience of tourism – visiting new places and meeting new people – is a transformative force that breaks down cultural barriers and builds bridges between people, communities, and nations. Mr. Scowsill, President and CEO of the World Travel and Tourism Council, noted in his address: "Beyond economics, it is the unparalleled power of travel and tourism to bring people together, to open minds and share experiences which makes it a driver of peace connecting people and facilitating direct interaction between cultures."[1] The world leader in *peace through tourism* Louis D'Amore, who organized the Peace through Tourism World Symposium, is President and Founder of the International Institute for Peace through Tourism and a strong proponent of travel and tourism initiatives that contribute to international understanding, cooperation among nations, and improved quality of the environment, and other attributes aimed at sustainable tourism and the prospects for peace.

The comments by the world's travel and tourism leaders not only reflect the message in Saint Augustine's quotation above, but also reinforce a statement from one of the worldly travelers of yesteryear, Samuel Clemens (aka Mark Twain), who noted in his bestselling book *The Innocents Abroad*:

> Travel is fatal to prejudice, bigotry, and narrow-mindedness, and many of our people need it sorely on these accounts. Broad, wholesome, charitable views of men and things cannot be acquired by vegetating in one little corner of earth all one's lifetime.[2]

Following this same theme is the quotation from Pope John Paul II in 1985 (mentioned earlier in this book):

> The world is becoming a global village in which people from different continents are made to feel like next-door neighbors. In facilitating more authentic social relationships between individuals, tourism can help overcome many real prejudices, and foster new bonds of fraternity. In this sense tourism has become a real force for world peace.[3]

New directions in the literature on peace and tourism

The old adage "When peace prevails, tourism flourishes" (author unknown) has a strong and truthful ring to it. In other words, the more peaceful the world, the greater the opportunity for tourism to grow. The opportunities for peace and international tourism growth depend on many different factors, including the development of effective policies, plans, and management of the tourism industry. If greater world cooperation takes place, there is the potential for tourism to be one of the most important stimulants for global improvement in the social, cultural, economic, political, and ecological dimensions of future lifestyles, adding to the possibilities of a more peaceful world.

Peace and tourism have interesting conceptual ties. Traveling to foreign lands increases understanding and cooperation between visitors and hosts. Tourism, also, can be hindered by the lack of peace in a destination. Thus, tourism can be seen as a generator and beneficiary of peace. Peace is an important part of the foreign policy processes across nations.[4]

The tourism industry has gradually noted the importance of the concept of tourism and peace, and new literature on the topic is evolving, in the academic community and elsewhere. A significant new imprint of peace through travel and tourism in the new millennium includes the *Journal of Tourism and Peace Research*, launched in 2010. Researchers interested in the subject of peace as it relates to travel, tourism, and hospitality have a new avenue to express their views on the broad ramifications of "tourism and peace research."

In addition, in 2010 an important book titled *Tourism, Progress and Peace* (edited by Omar Moufakkir and Ian Kelly and published by CABI) became available to researchers and others interested in a wide range of topics on tourism and peace. This book set the stage for a better understanding of the ingredients necessary in the quest for a more peaceful world through the medium of travel and tourism. The book provides new information and concepts to help researchers establish a solid foundation in peace education as it relates to travel and tourism.

This philosophy of peace and prosperity through travel is further identified in the book *Tourism Policy and Planning: Yesterday, Today, and Tomorrow* (2nd edition, co-authored by Edgell and Swanson, 2013). The co-authors noted that "Tourism cannot flourish without political stability and safety, which are restricted when peace is absent.

Without peace, tourism is diminished; therefore, tourism is a beneficiary of peace. Through creating cultural awareness, tourism can be a stimulus for peace."[5]

In January 2014 a book titled *International Handbook on Tourism and Peace* became available. This book was a collaboration of efforts by the UNWTO and the Government of Austria. It contains contributions from experts around the world and provides an overview of important areas of tourism as a potential tool in peace-building efforts. There is a particularly interesting article titled "Peace through Tourism: An Historical and Future Perspective" by Louis D'Amore. The book was published by the Centre for Peace Research and Peace Education of the Klagenfurt University (Austria) in cooperation with the UNWTO.

International organizations advocating peace through tourism

It is absolutely clear in today's travel and tourism market that tourism cannot flourish without political stability and safety, which are restricted when peace is absent. Edgell (1990) noted in *International Tourism Policy* that "International tourism in the twenty-first century will be a major vehicle for fulfilling people's aspirations for a higher quality-of-life . . . laying the groundwork for a peaceful society . . . tourism will be a principal factor for creating greater international understanding and goodwill and a primary ingredient for peace on earth . . . and provide a foundation for peace and prosperity."[6]

A quotation from the Secretary-General of the UNWTO was mentioned at the beginning of this chapter. The UNWTO is vested by the United Nations with a central and decisive role in promoting the development of responsible, sustainable, and universally accessible tourism, with the aim of contributing to economic development, international understanding, peace, prosperity, and universal respect for and the observance of human rights and fundamental freedoms. The United Nations has further engaged the UNWTO in promulgating opportunities for considering the advantages that tourism has in reducing poverty in many of the less developed countries. In addition, the UNWTO has sponsored many different meetings and conferences that include important references to tourism and peace. Forums that advocate peace through tourism will be mentioned later in this chapter.

Also noted earlier in this chapter was the World Travel and Tourism Council (WTTC), which includes the CEOs and presidents of the most important travel and tourism companies throughout the world. WTTC leadership not only emphasizes the important economic attributes of travel and tourism, but also advocates balancing this with people, culture, environment, and the impact that tourism can have on peace. The WTTC clearly recognizes that the absence of peace disrupts global trade in tourism, which has a negative impact on economic growth through tourism. Therefore, tourism benefits from peace and the global economy benefits from tourism development. Travelers rank safety and security as key factors in planning a vacation or going to a convention, such that destinations and countries not considered very "safe" or not at "peace" suffer the economic consequences of a decline in their tourism industries.

Today, there is an organization exclusively devoted to peace through tourism, the International Institute for Peace through Tourism. The IIPT is a not-for-profit organization dedicated to fostering travel and tourism initiatives that contribute to international understanding, cooperation among nations, an improved quality of environment, cultural enhancement and the preservation of heritage, poverty reduction, reconciliation and healing wounds of conflicts – and through these initiatives, helping to bring about a peaceful and sustainable world. It is founded on a vision of the world's largest industry, travel and tourism becoming the world's first global peace industry; and the belief that every traveler is potentially an "Ambassador for Peace." It was this organization that organized the International Institute for Peace through Tourism's World Symposium, cited at the beginning of this chapter.

International conferences toward peace through tourism

Over the years there have been many international conferences related to peace and tourism. Most have been forgotten through the annals of time but it is important to note some of the early vestiges of the peace through tourism concepts which took place. This section will start with the *Helsinki Accords* and go on to highlight a few other international conferences that have a bearing on peace and tourism. Much of the information in this section originated from research conducted by Edgell and Swanson (2013) and published in the book *Tourism Policy and Planning: Yesterday, Today, and Tomorrow.*

1975 *Helsinki Accords*[7]

The *Helsinki Accords* were the final act of the Conference on Security and Cooperation in Europe held in Helsinki, Finland, during July and August 1975. Thirty-five nations, including the United States, Canada, and all European states except Albania and Andorra, signed the pact in an attempt to improve relations between the communist bloc and the West (this was during the Cold War between the United States and Western-bloc countries and the Soviet Union and Eastern-bloc countries, which were on opposite sides of the ideological political spectrum). While the *Helsinki Accords* were not a legally binding concord, as they did not have treaty status, they neverthe-less carried an aura implying a moral pledge to abide by the decisions taken at the conference. The *Accords* dealt with tourism provisions in the human-rights section of the document.

The lengthy details of the *Helsinki Accords* covered a broad range of issues. However, peace, security, and human rights were mentioned many times in the document. The tourism section of the *Accords* acknowledged that freer tourism is essential to the development of cooperation amongst nations. Specific to tourism, the signatories to the *Accords*, among other points, included:

(a) Their intentions to "encourage increased tourism on both an individual and group basis";
(b) The desirability of carrying out "detailed studies on tourism";
(c) An agreement to "endeavor, where possible, to ensure that the development of tourism does not injure the artistic, historic and cultural heritage in their respective countries";
(d) Their intention "to facilitate wider travel by their citizens for personal or professional reasons";
(e) An agreement to "endeavor gradually to lower, where necessary, the fees for visas and official travel documents";

(f) An agreement to "increase, on the basis of appropriate agreements or arrangements, cooperation in the development of tourism, in particular, by considering bilaterally, possible ways to increase information relating to travel and other related questions of mutual interest"; and,

(g) Their intention "to promote visits to their respective countries."

At the time, this agreement was considered a revolutionary move to support tourism exchanges among the signatory countries. The *Helsinki Accords* helped to begin a process of greater interest in the world with respect to peace and sustainable tourism. It is likely that the discussions that took place in Helsinki in 1975 reverberated throughout the world and were helpful in instituting the UNWTO in 1976.

1980 *Manila Declaration*[8]

As noted earlier, the UNWTO became an official world tourism organization in 1976. It held its first major world conference on tourism in Manila, Philippines, September 27–October 10, 1980. It included the participation of 107 delegations of states and 91 delegations of observers, in order to clarify the nature of tourism in all aspects and the role tourism would be playing in a very dynamic world. The popular and often-cited document that emanated from this conference became known as the *Manila Declaration on World Tourism*.

The *Manila Declaration* set the stage for developing future research on issues related to peace and sustainable tourism. The next couple of paragraphs quote extensively from the *Manila Declaration*, adding to the theme of peace through tourism and promulgating ingredients basic to developing sustainable tourism.

> **Considering** that world tourism can develop [best] in a climate of peace and security which can be achieved through the joint effort of all States in promoting the reduction of international tension and in developing international cooperation in a spirit of friendship, respect for human rights, . . . **Convinced** that world tourism can be a vital force for world peace and can provide the moral and intellectual basis for international understanding and interdependence, . . . **Convinced** further that world tourism can contribute to the establishment of a new international economic order that will help to eliminate the widening economic gap between developed and developing countries and ensure the steady acceleration of economic and social development and progress, in particular of the developing countries, . . . **Aware** that world tourism can only flourish if based on equity, sovereign equality, non-interference in internal affairs and cooperation among all States, irrespective of their economic and social systems, and if its ultimate aim is the improvement of the quality-of-life and the creation of better living conditions for all peoples, worthy of human dignity.

If the document had closed with this last statement, it would still have been one of the great tourism policy documents. However, the document continued in a similar vein, advocating best practices for implementing such policies that included peace precepts and a foundation for discussing sustainable tourism.

For example, Step 1 of the *Manila Declaration* declares:

> Tourism is considered an activity essential to the life of nations because of its direct effects on the social, cultural, educational and economic sectors of national societies

and their international relations. Its development is linked to the social and economic development of nations and can only be possible if man has access to creative rest and holidays and enjoys the freedom to travel within the framework of free time and leisure whose profoundly human character it underlies. Its very existence and development depend entirely on the existence of a state of lasting peace, to which tourism itself is required to contribute.

The *Manila Declaration* is also important because it set the stage for later documents to build on the peace through tourism principle. One such document, for example, is the *Columbia Charter* (1988), which discusses "world peace through tourism" (discussed later in this chapter). Item 13 of the *Manila Declaration* has this to say: "With respect to international relations and the search for peace, based on justice and respect of individual and national aspirations, tourism stands out as a positive and ever-present factor in promoting mutual knowledge and understanding and as a basis for reaching a greater level of respect and confidence among all the peoples of the world."

Item 18 of the *Manila Declaration* helped to form a foundation for a discussion of sustainable tourism several years before the *Brundtland Report* (1987) was issued. This comment is made here because it is the *Brundtland Report* (which did not mention tourism) that many researchers refer to as the starting point with respect to the beginnings of sustainable tourism discussions. The *Manila Declaration* was also a major policy document in the tourism industry with respect to sustainable tourism before the United Nations Conference on Environment and Development (Agenda 21) took place (see Chapter 3) in 1992. This element of the *Manila Declaration* document states that:

> Tourism resources available in the various countries consist at the same time of space, facilities and values. These are resources whose use cannot be left uncontrolled without running the risk of their deterioration, or even their destruction. The satisfaction of tourism requirements must not be prejudicial to the social and economic interests of the population in tourist areas, to the environment or, above all, to natural resources, which are the fundamental attraction of tourism, and historical and cultural sites. All tourism resources are part of the heritage of mankind. National communities and the entire international community must take the necessary steps to ensure their preservation. The conservation of historical, cultural and religious sites represents at all times, and notably in time of conflict, one of the fundamental responsibilities of States.

The *Manila Declaration* is fundamental to understanding the foundation for the international peace through tourism initiatives and as a basis for the study of sustainable tourism.

The UNWTO, as the leader in global tourism principles, practices, and policies, is grounded in the *Manila Declaration*, as noted in Items 19 and 25: "International cooperation in the field of tourism is an endeavor in which the characteristics of peoples and basic interests of individual States must be respected. In this field, the central and decisive role of the World Tourism Organization [UNWTO] as a conceptualizing and harmonizing body is obvious," and in the last point of the document, "The Conference urges the World Tourism Organization [UNWTO] to take all necessary measures, through its own internal, intergovernmental and non-governmental bodies, so as to permit the global implementation of the principles, concepts and guidelines contained in this final document."

1985 *Tourism Bill of Rights and Tourist Code*[9]

The *Tourism Bill of Rights and Tourist Code*, developed at the World Tourism Organization's Sixth General Assembly held in Sofia, Bulgaria, in September 1985 also has references to peace through tourism and support information on sustainable tourism. A discussion of the development of a tourism bill of rights and a tourist code began shortly after the conference in Manila in 1980. The document developed in Sofia was broken down into two parts: the *Tourism Bill of Rights* and the *Tourist Code*.

Most of the member nations of the World Tourism Organization wanted to foster tourism growth and development, but in a balanced way of "sustainability" to avoid potential negative impacts from tourism. This interest was partially addressed in Article III of the Bill by "a) encourage the orderly and harmonious [sustainable] growth of both domestic and international tourism; b) integrate their [national] tourism policies with their overall development policies at all levels – local, regional, national and international – and broaden tourism cooperation within both a bilateral and multilateral framework, including that of the World Tourism Organization [UNWTO]."

While the present benchmark for concerns with respect to terrorism is most often cited as September 11, 2001, terrorism was a major problem in the 1980s, with airplane hijackings, hostage takings, and ship interferences taking place. The Bill, in Article IV c), addressed this concern, saying that nations must "ensure the safety of visitors and the security of their belongings through preventive and protective measures." These concerns added to the discussion of peace and tourism. The issue of safety and security is discussed in more detail later in this book.

Even though the *Manila Declaration* addressed sociocultural and environmental issues, many nations felt it should be reinforced with a *code* for tourist behavior. Article VI of the Bill stated that tourists had responsibilities to the host community in these words: "They [host communities] are also entitled to expect from tourists understanding and respect for their customs, religions and other elements of their cultures which are part of the human heritage." At the same time, tourists had the right to expect (included in Article VII) that "The population constituting the host communities in place of transit and sojourn are invited to receive tourists with the greatest possible hospitality, courtesy and respect necessary for the development of harmonious human and social relations."

There was also a concern that visitors often did not respect the destination they were visiting. The Code, through Article X, noted that: "Tourists should, by their behavior, foster understanding and friendly relations among peoples, at both the national and international levels, and thus contribute to lasting peace." Discussions on the concept of peace and sustainability were an integral part of the Bill and Code.

1989 *The Hague Declaration on Tourism*[10]

In April 1989, possibly inspired by the global progress made in tourism policy, sustainable tourism, and peace through tourism noted in the *Manila Declaration* and the *Tourism Bill of Rights* and *Tourist Code*, the Inter-Parliamentary Union (IPU) – a worldwide organization of 112 national parliaments founded in 1889 – and the UNWTO organized a global conference on tourism which took place in The Hague, Netherlands. The results of this convocation set the most comprehensive global tourism principles that existed at the time. *The Hague Declaration on Tourism* is much too long to summarize but it is worth noting some selected sections of the "principles" that evolved from the conference in the next few paragraphs demonstrate just how important this document was in communicating the importance of peace and sustainability concepts in the tourism industry. *The Hague Declaration on Tourism* is of such importance as a policy document that it is presented in its entirety, with a discussion of key concepts, in the book *Tourism Policy and Planning: Yesterday, Today, and Tomorrow* (Edgell and Swanson, 2013).

In Principle I of *The Hague Declaration on Tourism* it is useful to observe, "All Governments should work for national, regional, and international peace and security which are essential to the development of domestic and international tourism." The word "peace" shows up often in world meetings on tourism.

Principle II of *The Hague Declaration on Tourism* is an effort to encourage countries to develop a strategic plan for tourism to balance the socioeconomic growth of tourism with concerns for the environment. Principle III is extremely important in that it sets the stage for many of the current views on sustainable tourism. The principle of sustainable tourism is summarized in this section as: "An unspoilt natural, cultural and human environment is a fundamental condition for the development of tourism. Moreover, rational management of tourism may contribute significantly to the protection and development of the physical environment and the cultural heritage, as well as to improving the quality-of-life." This principle is in essence the foundation for sustainable tourism as discussed throughout this book.

There have been many more meetings, conferences and forums in which the UNWTO has been involved where the issues of "peace" and "sustainability" have been presented and discussed. However, the examples above demonstrate that the UNWTO has been intimately involved in many different policy issues, including issues of the environment and safety. In the next section a few notes related to the *Columbia Charter* are discussed. This effort was an initiative by the International Institute for Peace through Tourism (IIPT). A more detailed discussion of IIPT is contained as part of Case Study 6, at the end of this chapter. While IIPT has no official status connected to the UNWTO, there is considerable collaboration by both organizations on tourism peace issues.

1988 The *Columbia Charter*[11]

The *Columbia Charter* is devoted to the issues of peace through tourism and sustainable tourism, and emanated from a conference titled "The First Global Conference: Tourism – A Vital Force for Peace" and convened in Vancouver, British Columbia, Canada, October 23–27, 1988. It was the first major event of the International Institute for Peace through Tourism (IIPT, founded in 1986), taking place during the "United Nations International Year of Peace" (1988). The convocation was partly aimed at the concern of the tourism industry with respect to major terrorism events that took place in 1985 and 1986. The year 1986 was the peak year for terrorism, and from that point forward traveler safety and security were major issues and dealt with in many different forums and with many types of international agreements. IIPT held two additional global conferences, in Montreal, Canada (1994) and Glasgow, Scotland (1999). These three conferences and other meetings and activities provided the information and impetus for the "First Global Summit on Peace through Tourism" held in Amman, Jordan (2000). IIPT has also worked toward mobilizing the travel and tourism industry as a leading force for poverty reduction.

The *Columbia Charter* built on the philosophies and principles expressed in the 1980 *Manila Declaration* and other documents related to peace and tourism and sustainable tourism. It expressed "the urgent reality that peace is an essential precondition for tourism . . . promotes tourism which is in harmony with the world's natural and cultural resources . . . advocates the development of educational systems both in institutions and in the community, in which everyone from industry leaders and government, to individual tourists, can learn the possibilities and the value of tourism as a force for peace." While the charter is generally thought of as a "peace through tourism" document, it also addressed other important tourism concerns:

- Promotes mutual understanding, trust and goodwill;
- Reduces economic inequities;
- Develops in an integrated manner with the full participation of local host communities;
- Improves the quality-of-life;
- Protects and preserves the environment, both built and natural, and other local resources;
- Contributes to the world conservation strategy of sustainable development.

2000 *Amman Declaration on Peace through Tourism*[12]

The first world tourism peace summit was held in Amman, Jordan, on November 8–11, 2000 and the resulting document is known as the *Amman Declaration on Peace through Tourism*. This conference was the first of a series of world peace summits sponsored by the International Institute for Peace through Tourism. It was the most important such event ever held and is referenced as follows:

Amman Declaration on Peace through Tourism:

We the representatives and participants at the Global Summit on Peace through Tourism, assembled in Amman, Jordan, from 8–11 November 2000 . . . **recognize** that travel and tourism is a worldwide social and cultural phenomenon, engaging people of all nations as hosts and guests, and as such is one of humanity's truly global activities.

. . . and that travel and tourism is one of the world's largest and fastest growing industries, creating one in eleven jobs, contributing to intentional and regional economic growth, bridging disparities between developed and developing countries, and bringing prosperity which fosters peace.

. . . and that peace is an essential precondition for travel and tourism and all aspects of human growth and development.

. . . and the development of tourism as a global vehicle for promoting understanding, trust and goodwill among peoples of the world requires an appropriate political and economic framework.

. . . Do hereby **declare** our commitment to building a Culture of Peace through Tourism, and support the following principles:

1 That tourism is a fundamental human activity engaging social, cultural, religious, economic, educational, environmental, and political values and responsibilities.
2 That the right of people to travel is a fundamental human right which should be exercised without undue restriction including the facilitation of travel for those with disabilities and special needs.

3 That community livelihood should be enhanced and local cohesion encouraged and that all peoples and communities be recognized as being manifestations of a heritage.

4 That human differences be respected and cultural diversity celebrated as a precious human asset and that peaceful relationships among all people be promoted and nurtured through sustainable tourism.

5 That historical monuments and landmarks be protected and where necessary restored and rehabilitated and made accessible to everyone as valuable assets for humanity and legacies for future generations.

6 That the preservation and wise use of the environment and ecological balance, are essential to the future of tourism, and that ancient wisdoms of Indigenous Peoples and care for the Earth be acknowledged and respected.

7 That the global reach of the tourist industry be utilized in promoting "dialogues on peace" and in bridging the have and have-not societies of the various regions of the world.

. . . and **acknowledge** the legacy of His Majesty The Late King Hussein of Jordan in laying the foundations of peace in the region and for his effort to make the Hashemite Kingdom of Jordan "a land of peace" and a place of welcome for the peaceful traveler; the commitment of His Majesty King Abdullah II to strengthen and expand King Hussein's Legacy of peace; and to the Government and people of Jordan, for their hospitality and support and their generous contributions to the success of the conference.

. . . and **commend** the IIPT for giving scope to the vision of peace through tourism and for its untiring effort toward that end, and to the title sponsor and other sponsors and contributors, for advancing the cause of Peace through Tourism.

. . . and **welcome** the declaration by the United Nations of the International Year for the Culture of Peace (2000) and the International Decade for a Culture of Peace and Non-Violence for the Children of the World (2001–2010).

. . . and **commit** ourselves to the realization of the goals and objectives as enshrined in the United Nations Declaration of Program of Action on a Culture of Peace through our activities and initiatives.

Adopted at Amman November 11, 2000

Bilateral tourism agreements

The *Helsinki Accords* mentions the opportunity for countries of the world to enter into bilateral tourism arrangements or agreements to assist in moving visitors across borders more conveniently and with fewer barriers, and in fostering positive political and socioeconomic issues in tourism. While often the concept behind a tourism agreement is to promote greater trade in tourism between the two nations, bilateral tourism agreements also serve additional national policy objectives, such as encouraging international understanding, friendly relations, and goodwill. There also have been efforts made by several countries to recognize that tourism activities of a national tourism office constitute a legitimate diplomatic and consular function within the meaning of

Article 3 of the Vienna Convention on Diplomatic Relations. Such recognition would put tourism on a more equal footing with other industry sectors covered by the convention.[13]

Usually bilateral tourism agreements begin with a preamble or policy statement indicating the reason for negotiation of a tourism arrangement between the two nations. This statement would then be followed by specific articles of the agreement. There follow a few selected principles taken directly from a number of different bilateral tourism agreements to illustrate some of the items that might be included in an agreement:

- Aim to increase two-way tourism
- Support efforts by the national tourism organization's travel promotion office
- Improve tourism facilitation
- Encourage investments in each other's tourism industry
- Promote the sharing of research, statistics, and information
- Recognize the importance of the safety and security of tourists
- Suggest mutual cooperation on policy issues in international tourism
- Provide for regular consultations on tourism matters
- Acknowledge benefits from education and training in tourism
- Enhance mutual understanding and goodwill

Many bilateral tourism agreements are very brief, simply expressing a need for a better understanding of tourism exchanges between the two countries. In some cases, specific provisions are written into the agreement to allow, for example, tourism personnel of one country, with their international tourism office located in the other country, to be provided with diplomatic privileges. Other interests might include support for permitting greater air and sea access. Also, the agreement might have a provision to make it easier for cultural groups from one country to enter another country without having to obtain a visa. It was noted in one agreement that two countries agreed to cooperate in joint marketing of tourism. There is no lack of creativeness in what a bilateral tourism agreement might contain. Sometimes a key provision, mentioned above, regarding the sharing of research and information will help promote sustainability in the two countries. Once such an agreement is properly negotiated and signed, it is usually valid for five years, with an opportunity to renew or extend the arrangement, or to amend it in one form or another.

Peace through tourism and sustainable tourism

The record for peace through tourism has not been a very good one. Currently there are more than 40 conflicts or other situations that are not conducive to peaceful tourism that are a major distraction from the concept of peace through tourism, and yet tourism is increasing at a substantial rate. Of course, without such conflicts taking place, tourism would grow even faster and the concern for safety and security would diminish. The author of this book is a strong believer in the concept of peace through tourism. The case study to this chapter introduces a little history and a few world leaders who have believed in a strong connection between peace and tourism.

The issue of sustainable tourism is receiving major attention in the twenty-first century. Many in the tourism industry, including global organizations and academicians, are focused on sustainable tourism issues. Discussions about climate change and global warming have pushed the "sustainability" issue to the forefront and the leaders in the tourism industry have responded. A key question for the tourism leaders is how best to mitigate the negative features of tourism development so that sustainable tourism progress can move forward.

There appear to be a number of individual countries that have made considerable progress toward sustainable tourism over the past several years. Certainly Canada has been one such country, Australia another, also New Zealand, and note that Costa Rica and Dominica are leaders in ecotourism and nature tourism. There are many other countries that could be added to this list but the countries mentioned above make for good models to follow toward the principles of sustainability.

Case study 6: Travel, the language of peace and sustainability

"I have watched the cultures of all lands blow around my house and other winds have blown the seeds of peace, for travel is the language of peace."

Mahatma Gandhi

Introduction

Global travel and tourism has grown enormously over the past forty years, and is likely to continue to grow in the future. The travel and tourism industry is one of the largest contributors to the world economy. A question that arises is: Can such an enormous travel and tourism community utilize its economic capacity to impact in a positive manner, helping to create a global environment that is conducive to increasing sustainable tourism and at the same time planting *the seeds of peace*? This case study is partially based on a journal article by the present author (Edgell, 2014) titled "Travel and Tourism, the Language of Peace."[14]

Over the years a few of the great leaders of the world have noted opportunities for travel and tourism to have a positive impact in creating a more peaceful world. Mahatma Gandhi, certainly from a philosophical perspective, was one of them. Others, like the late Pope John Paul II (now Saint John Paul II), a holistic global thinker, noted in his address to the World Travel Congress of the American Society of Travel Agents held in Rome, Italy, November 14, 1985 that: "The world is becoming a global village in which people from different continents are made to feel like next-door neighbors. In facilitating more authentic social relationships between individuals, tourism can help overcome many real prejudices, and foster new bonds of fraternity. In this sense tourism has become a real force for world peace" (see note 3).

In April 2013, at the 13th World Travel and Tourism Council's (WTTC) Global Summit, former U.S. President Bill Clinton had this to say: "I actually believe that simply expanding tourism and doing it in a way that is good economics . . . can have a profoundly positive impact . . . on every economy. I have seen that peace works better than conflict and one of the best manifestations of this is in travel and tourism." Later, in September 2013 at the WTTC Asia Regional Summit, former Prime Minister of the United Kingdom Tony Blair stated: "Travel & Tourism is an industry which can genuinely help to bring about not only more commerce and prosperity, but more peace, security and understanding." These statements certainly support the premise that the growth in global travel and tourism can be a contributor to the concept that *travel is the language of peace*.

The travel and tourism industry is poised to be a driving influence toward greater international people-to-people cultural exchanges that will lead to opportunities for friendlier global relations and world understanding, ultimately providing an environment for peace in the world. Within the past few years we have seen, throughout our modern society, global conflicts spreading and noted that many traditional societal structures and securities are fraying, thus creating uncertainty, and in some cases anxieties. Travel and cultural interchanges as part of sustainable tourism have the potential to be the antidote to these circumstances. The concern is whether the current travel and tourism industry leadership has the capacity and interest to effect positive change and advance the social, economic, environmental and cultural well-being of local and global communities, and utilize increased travel to transform our society into a more peaceful world.

This case study will briefly investigate certain travel and tourism policy movements throughout history that portend that global travel in the twenty-first century may be a major factor to lead to a more peaceful world. The theme of the case study suggests that travel has the potential power to impact in a positive way toward a more peaceful world. The book *International Tourism Policy* (Edgell, 1990) noted in the beginning of the first chapter:

> International tourism in the twenty-first century will be a major vehicle for fulfilling people's aspirations for a higher quality of life, a part of which will be through "facilitating more authentic social relationships between individuals" and, it is hoped, laying the groundwork for a peaceful society through global touristic contacts. International tourism also has the potential to be one of the most important stimulants for global improvement in the social, cultural, economic, political, and ecological dimensions of future lifestyles. Finally, tourism will be a principal factor for creating greater international understanding and goodwill and a primary ingredient for peace on earth.

This augurs well in keeping with the old adage (author unknown) that says, "When peace prevails, tourism flourishes."

Peace through travel in ancient times

Peace through travel is not a new idea. While there appears to be no single moment in the history of travel and tourism that pinpoints a sole foundation for the idea of peace through travel, there are references to the concept in ancient times. The research for this article begins with information from the book *The Histories*, written in 440 BCE (Before the Common Era) by the Greek historian Herodotus (484–425 BCE), a worldly traveler and travel writer. Herodotus noted that the

(Continued)

Case study (continued)

many city-states of Greece (politically and economically independent communities) were almost continuously at war with each other, except during the Olympic Games.

The Olympic Games (Games) began in 776 BCE in Olympia to celebrate and honor Zeus (the king of the Greek gods) and were by far the largest international gathering of spectators from differing backgrounds and interests in ancient times. The Games, now known mostly for their athletic contests, in earlier times also included a celebration of the arts, dance, storytelling, and other cultural activities. The athletes (males only in the early Games) were from Greece but the spectators and non-athletic participants represented individuals from many different nations and communities. People traveled long distances, mostly by walking or by donkey, to participate in the most popular festivities of the era, those associated with the Games of ancient Greece.

The problem, as noted previously, was that the city-states of Greece were in perpetual conflict with each other. As a result, the roads to Olympia (and throughout most of Greece) were not safe from bandits and marauders. The kings of the major Greek city-states (often at war with each other), noting the importance of the Games, and in an effort to protect the athletes and travelers to the "Games," instituted what has become known as the *Olympic Truce*, which early on proclaimed: "May the world be delivered from crime and killing and be free from the clash of arms." Under the conditions of the truce, warring factions would cease all warfare and hostilities seven days prior to the opening of the Games, during the Games, and seven days after so that athletes, artists, and visitors could travel in total safety to participate in or attend the Games. Unfortunately, this truce expired after the Games and often old conflicts resumed and new ones developed.

Travel in ancient times was rarely peaceful for the journeyer. There is ample evidence, as shared by Herodotus, of the difficulty of travel in age-old Greece. The traveler had to have stamina, patience, and an insatiable desire to travel in order to overcome the many obstacles in his path. He prayed for good weather and hoped the treacherous pirates on the high seas or brigands on land would not attack. Travel was so perilous that many travelers, including Herodotus, hoping for peaceful travel, made sacrifices and said prayers to their favorite gods before embarking on a journey.

A few global leaders that advocated peace through travel

From ancient times to the present, the world has been in perpetual turmoil. On any given day in the modern world many conflicts are taking place somewhere on the planet. Pirates still exist on the high seas, attacking commercial and private vessels. Bandits and terrorists prey on unknowing travelers in many parts of the world. Wars and hostilities are a common occurrence. A question to be asked is what role have world leaders played toward ensuring a more peaceful world through travel? Three global leaders are mentioned below who were notably impacted by the horrors of World War II and who strongly advocated that travel has the potential to be *the language of peace*.

During World War II, General Dwight David Eisenhower, as the Supreme Allied Commander in Europe, witnessed the horrific impact of war on people and cultures and the destruction of much of Europe. Memories of the devastation and suffering that took place during the war haunted him for the rest of his life. He said that this situation must never happen again. He stated: "People want peace so badly that someday governments are going to have to get out of the way and let them have it." After being elected U.S. President, he established the non-profit corporation People to People International (PTPI) on September 11, 1956, with the aim of enhancing international understanding and friendship through educational, cultural, and humanitarian travel activities involving the exchange of ideas and experiences of people of different countries and diverse cultures. President Eisenhower felt very strongly that everyday citizens of the world wanted peace and could attain it much more effectively without government interference. The mission of PTPI "is to enhance international understanding and friendship through educational, cultural and humanitarian activities involving the exchange of ideas and experiences directly among peoples of different countries and diverse cultures." In June 2006, PTPI's Student Ambassador Programs became the first organization to receive the Cavaliere per la Pace (Knight of Peace Award). Until very recently, People to People International was led by President and Chief Executive Officer Mary Jean Eisenhower, granddaughter of President Eisenhower. The outcome of such a program as PTPI is to utilize travel to help create a more peaceful world (Edgell, 2013).[14]

President Eisenhower's administration was followed by that of President John F. Kennedy, who also had personally witnessed the atrocities of World War II and saw travel as a direct path toward peace. He endorsed President Eisenhower's PTPI program, saying, "The nature of People to People activities is as varied as the individuals involved. The housewife whose recipe contains the yeast of kindness, the soldier whose arms embrace homeless waifs, the doctor who heals with humility, all assert a single theme – the power of people, acting as individuals, to respond imaginatively to the world's need for peace." In addition, in 1963, President Kennedy said, "Travel has become one of the greatest forces for peace and understanding in our time. As people move throughout the world and learn to know each other, to understand each other's customs and to appreciate the qualities of individuals of each nation, we are building a level of international understanding which can sharply improve the atmosphere for world peace."

Another great leader and worldly traveler who also barely survived the barbarous conditions of World War II eventually became Pope John Paul II, known and referred to as the "traveling pope." As pope he completed 104 foreign trips, traveling more than 725,000 miles, more than all the previous popes combined. He believed that if the peoples of the world could interact more frequently and learn about each other's culture they would form a strong human fraternity. His comments on peace through tourism were noted earlier in the introduction to this case study.

(Continued)

Case study (continued)

Twentieth-century landmark policies on peace through tourism

Peace and tourism was discussed at many different conferences during the twentieth century. After World War II a new kind of long-term war came into being, commonly known as the "Cold War," which included the communist bloc, led by the Union of Soviet Socialist Republics (USSR), and the democratic Western bloc led by the United States (US). In July, 1955, in Geneva, Switzerland a meeting was held between US President Dwight D. Eisenhower and USSR Premier Nikita Khrushchev in which it appeared that the Cold War was beginning to thaw a little. In his report to the nation after the meeting, President Eisenhower said: "The subject that took most of my attention was the possibility of increased visits overseas by the citizens of one country into the territory of the other nation. In this subject there was the fullest possible agreement between the West and the Soviet Union." Twenty years later, in July/August 1975, many countries on both sides of the Cold War, including the US and the USSR, gathered in Helsinki, Finland for a Conference on Security and Cooperation in Europe and signed the document known as the *Helsinki Accords*. Peace, security, tourism and human rights were mentioned many times in the *Helsinki Accords*, which acknowledged that freer travel is essential to the development of cooperation and peace.

The world organization that has impacted the most in global tourism policy is the World Tourism Organization (UNWTO). Founded in 1976, UNWTO has a major focus on economic development, international understanding, peace, prosperity, sustainability, and universal respect for human rights and fundamental freedoms through world tourism policies. With a membership that includes 156 countries, 6 associate members and more than 400 affiliate members, representing governments, the private sector, educational institutions, tourism associations, and local tourism authorities, the UNWTO promotes the concept of peace through tourism at its general assembly meetings, as well as through conferences and additional mediums of communication.

The International Institute for Peace through Tourism

Possibly the most important and influential international organization dedicated to the concept of "peace through tourism" is the International Institute for Peace through Tourism (IIPT), founded by Louis D'Amore in 1986 during the "United Nations International Year of Peace." Its mission statement includes: "The IIPT is a not for profit organization dedicated to fostering and facilitating tourism initiatives which contribute to international understanding and cooperation, an improved quality of environment, the preservation of heritage, and through these initiatives, helping to bring about a peaceful and sustainable world."

Initially, IIPT held three major international peace through tourism conferences, starting with Vancouver, Canada in 1988, Montreal, Canada in 1994, Glasgow, Scotland in 1999, and many smaller meetings, all of which brought together global travel and tourism leaders to discuss and formulate ideas and programs that would lead to a more peaceful world through the medium of travel. The discussions at these various venues laid the groundwork for the "First Global Summit on Peace through Tourism" held in Amman, Jordan, November 8–11, 2000.

The *Amman Declaration on Peace through Tourism* is possibly the most important recent statement linking peace and tourism, and, as mentioned earlier in this chapter, it includes "that peace is an essential precondition for travel and tourism and all aspects of human growth and development" and "Do hereby declare our commitment to building a Culture of Peace through Tourism." The "Culture of Peace through Tourism" includes numerous principles supporting a broad dialogue on peace related to the tourism industry. Since the Amman summit, there have been other global conferences continuing to build on the initial foundation of peace through tourism. There have also been many new developments – such as, for example, the Global Peace Parks Program.

In addition, the IIPT introduced the *Credo of the Peaceful Traveler,* which embraces this article's theme, *Travel and Tourism, the Language of Peace.* The script of the *Credo* reads: "Grateful for the opportunity to travel and experience the world and because peace begins with the individual, I affirm my personal responsibility and commitment to:

- Journey with an open mind and gentle heart
- Accept with grace and gratitude the diversity I encounter
- Revere and protect the natural environment which sustains all life
- Appreciate all cultures I discover
- Respect and thank my hosts for their welcome
- Offer my hand in friendship to everyone I meet
- Support travel services that share these views and act upon them and,
- By my spirit, words and actions, encourage others to travel the world in peace"

The United Nations Millennium Development Goals and tourism

The United Nations (UN) is the global body that has accepted the world's leadership role in advocating policies and programs aimed toward equality, equity, human rights, peace, and sustainability, all essential factors for the peace and general well-being of the world. The UN promotes numerous activities that support the foundation for a more peaceful world. At the Millennium Summit in 2000 the UN identified world poverty alleviation as one of the most important and challenging issues. The 189 member states supported the UN in setting as one of its goals "to free humanity from extreme poverty, hunger, illiteracy and disease by 2015." Such goals are indispensable to establishing world peace and hence, growth in tourism.

The UN called upon all of its organizational units to help with programs aimed to reduce poverty, including the UN's specialized agency, the UNWTO. As noted earlier, the UNWTO is the principal global tourism policy body that promotes responsible, sustainable, and universally accessible tourism as well as international understanding and peace. The UNWTO fully endorsed the idea of using tourism

(Continued)

Case study (continued)

as a mechanism for poverty reduction, principally through economic development in small and medium-size enterprises in poverty-stricken countries.

The UNWTO responded to the UN goal with recommendations for action in its "Tourism and Poverty Alleviation" report. The initiative cited in the report suggests that one approach toward poverty alleviation should take place through the provision of assistance in sustainable tourism development projects. The UNWTO has in Part 3 of its conceptual definition of sustainable tourism to "Ensure viable, long-term economic operations, providing socioeconomic benefits to all stakeholders that are fairly distributed, including stable employment and income-earning opportunities and social services to host communities, and contributing to poverty alleviation." This effort depends on and supports the contribution that tourism can make toward a more peaceful world.

A peaceful world also makes it easier to utilize tourism as an economic development tool in the poorer nations of the world. Thus, the more peaceful the world, the greater are the opportunities for helping to reduce poverty. Areas of the world where conflicts are taking place tend to exacerbate the problems of the poor. If the UN can realize its goals, with the support of the UNWTO and other organizations, the basic elements for a more peaceful world will have been achieved. Changing society to better respond to global social responsibilities is complicated, but the UN is on the right path. To create a global environment where the majority of people can grow, thrive, and live in peace and prosperity has been a challenge for a long time. Travel, as the *language of peace*, has a major role to play in helping the UN to reach its goals.

Conclusion

This case study suggests that peace and travel have interesting and essential conceptual ties. Traveling to foreign lands and learning about other cultures can lead to greater understanding and cooperation between guests and hosts which may eventually lead to a more peaceful world. The tourism industry depends on a more peaceful world in order to have quality growth in travel and tourism. What is critically needed at this juncture is a greater emphasis by world leaders and others on tourism policies and strategic plans that promote and cultivate the ingredients necessary for a more peaceful world.

The author of this case study first became acquainted and interested in tourism policy and its relationship to peace after reading a letter addressed to U.S. President Dwight D. Eisenhower by U.S. Presidential Assistant Clarence B. Randall in his 1958 report *International Travel*. Randall stated, "I hold the strong conviction that tourism has deep significance for the peoples of the modern world, and that the benefits of travel can contribute to the cause of peace through improvement not only in terms of economic advancement but with respect to our political, cultural, and social relationships as well." This message is as valid today as it was when written 57 years ago.

International travel is vital to global trade. The absence of peace disrupts world trade and when global trade is disrupted, travel declines, which then leads to a decline of global Gross Domestic Product, which in turn results in greater world poverty. Therefore, tourism benefits from peace and the global economy profits from tourism development. International tourism, through effective sustainability policies, strategic planning, and positive management, has the potential to be one of the most important stimulants for global improvement in the social, cultural, economic, political, and ecological dimensions of future lifestyles. In other words, *travel is certainly a contributor to the language of peace*.

Interests in the contribution of travel and tourism to a more peaceful society have been expressed in many different ways in the different sections of this case study. The opportunity that tourism offers for positive economic, environmental, and social benefits toward a more peaceful world for tomorrow will depend on the decisions being made today. We can plan well for the development of peace through travel or let it happen haphazardly and hope for the best. As noted earlier in this document, "Ultimately, the highest purpose of tourism policy and planning is to integrate the economic, political, cultural, intellectual, and sustainability benefits of tourism cohesively with people, destinations, and countries in order to improve the local and global quality-of-life and provide a foundation for peace and prosperity."

Chapter summary

A common theme that permeates this book is that the more "peaceful" the world, the greater the opportunities for developing sustainable tourism. It is very difficult to even think of developing sustainable tourism while a country is at war or attending to a situation of civil strife or another kind of conflict. This concern has been addressed by the world leadership in the tourism industry.

The old adage "When peace prevails, tourism flourishes" has such a truthful ring to it. It is so obvious yet not always addressed in key documents or books about tourism. We can have the best principles, policies, plans, management, and marketing of tourism but without a peaceful world, tourism will not grow for very long. Peace is basic to progress.

There have been many meetings, conferences, and special events within the realm of discussions or documents related to peace and tourism. This chapter highlighted a few of the key ones over a period of years. However, the organization that has been most upfront about peace and sustainable tourism is the International Institute for Peace through Tourism.

The case study in this chapter included references to peace and tourism that go as far back as the Olympic Games in Greece in 776 BCE. While the *Olympic Truce* was short lived, it does demonstrate the interest in ancient times of peace as it relates to tourism. This chapter cited two former world leaders, President Dwight D. Eisenhower and President John F. Kennedy, and their interest in peace and travel.

Chapter review questions

1 Thinking in very broad terms, what is your view on peace and sustainable tourism?
2 Were you aware of the old adage "When peace prevails, tourism flourishes" before you read this chapter?

3 Before you read this chapter, were you aware of the International Institute for Peace through Tourism?
4 Were you aware of the many meetings and conferences that have taken place over the years which included aspects of peace and tourism?
5 What are your thoughts on the *Olympic Truce*?
6 Did you ever participate in any of the People to People International programs?
7 Why is the *Manila Declaration on World Tourism* so important?

Notes

1 International Institute for Peace through Tourism's World Symposium (2015), Ekurhuleni, South Africa, February 16–19, 2015.
2 Twain, M. (1869) *The Innocents Abroad*, Hartford, Connecticut: American Publishing.
3 American Society of Travel Agents (1985) "Address of Pope John Paul II to the Participants in the World Travel Congress of the American Society of Travel Agents," Rome, Italy, November 14, 1985.
4 Edgell, Sr., D. L. (2014) "Travel and Tourism, the Language of Peace," *Journal of Hospitality and Tourism*, 12(2), 30–41.
5 Edgell, Sr., D. L. and Swanson, J. (2013) *Tourism Policy and Planning: Yesterday, Today, and Tomorrow*, London, England: Routledge, p. 129.
6 Edgell, Sr., D. L. (1990) *International Tourism Policy*, New York: Van Nostrand Reinhold.
7 *Helsinki Accords.* Conference on Security and Cooperation in Europe, Helsinki, Finland, July–August, 1975.
8 *Manila Declaration on World Tourism*, World Tourism Organization, September 27–October 10, 1980.
9 *Tourism Bill of Rights and Tourist Code*, World Tourism Organization, Sofia, Bulgaria, September 17–26, 1985.
10 *The Hague Declaration on Tourism*, Inter-Parliamentary Union and the World Tourism Organization, The Hague, Netherlands, April 10–14, 1989.
11 The *Columbia Charter*, International Institute for Peace through Tourism, Vancouver, British Columbia, Canada, October 23–27, 1988.
12 *Amman Declaration on Peace through Tourism*, Amman, Jordan, November 8–11, 2000.
13 *Vienna Convention on Diplomatic Relations*, Vienna, Austria, April 18, 1961.
14 Edgell, Sr., D. L. and Swanson, J. R. (2013) *Tourism Policy and Planning: Yesterday, Today, and Tomorrow* (2nd edition), London, England: Routledge, p. 43.

Chapter 7

Strategic planning for sustainable tourism

"Before he sets out, the traveler must possess fixed interests and facilities to be served by travel."

George Santayana (1863–1952)

Just as a traveler must strategically plan his trip through information and education about the chosen destination in order to obtain the optimum value from his travel, so must a nation, community, or destination plan well for the future success of their sustainable tourism programs. From a sustainable tourism perspective it is known that one of the strongest motivations for the traveler is interest in the natural environment, historic structures, heritage, arts, history, language, customs, and cultures of people. The most efficient way to respond to building a sustainable tourism program for any destination is through a strategic planning process. Utilizing strategic planning for sustainable tourism development evolved from some of the new planning tools of the 1990s. Edward Inskeep (1994), in *National and Regional Tourism Planning*, had this to say about strategic planning:

> A planning approach which has received considerable attention in recent years, and is applicable to some tourism areas, is strategic planning. While the outcomes of strategic and long-range comprehensive planning may be very similar, [strategic planning] focuses more on identification and resolution of immediate issues. Strategic planning typically is more oriented to rapidly changing future situations and how to cope with changes organizationally. It is more action oriented and concerned with handling unexpected events . . . if used within the framework of integrated long-range policy and planning, the strategic planning approach can be very appropriate . . . Emphasis is given to formulating and adopting tourism development policies and plans for an area in order to guide decision-making on development

actions. The planning of tourism, however, should also be recognized as a continuous and flexible process.[1]

Today, the strategic planning process has become a major mainstream planning tool and includes the economic, environmental, and sociocultural factors within a sustainable tourism framework designed to provide direction for a tourism organization or destination. This chapter presents some of the practical steps in the strategic planning process for sustainable tourism.

In managing sustainable tourism, it is recognized that careful strategic planning is necessary. Edgell (2006) explains the importance of planning and management in developing sustainable tourism goals and objectives, noting that "In general, most studies have found that a well-researched, well-planned, and well-managed tourism program that takes into account the natural and cultural environment has a good chance of improving the local economy and enhancing the quality of life of residents."[2] In brief, tourism planning is essential to building a successful sustainable tourism program in the future and it must seek to foster the conservation of the resources that tourism is dependent on and improve the quality of life for the local residents. Strategic planning also lays the foundation for effective management of tourism, which is essential for the long-term success of sustainable tourism. Since planning looks to the future of the destination's growth it helps to define the markets that would yield the greatest profits and provide the most benefits to the local community. Strategic planning must always keep in mind that a key goal is to both provide a special experience for the visitor and at the same time protect the natural environment. In short, strategic planning is critical to the sustainability of the destination as it monitors the visitor impact on the environment so that it can be better managed.

For the travel and tourism industry to move in the direction of greater attention toward the growth and management of sustainable tourism, it will require progressive planning guidelines and goal-setting. There will need to be good leadership and effective strategies if the future for sustainable tourism is to grow; otherwise the progress toward sustainability may well be limited to a haphazard approach that lacks a set of strategic goals aimed to benefit local communities. For many local communities, tourism is vital to economic growth; those benefits include generating income, creating jobs, spawning new businesses, spurring economic development, promoting economic diversification, developing new products, and contributing to economic integration. In addition, if local and national governments are committed to broad-based tourism policies that provide citizens with a higher quality of life while generating sustained economic, environmental, and social benefits, then strategic planning must proceed in a logical order to move sustainable tourism to the forefront of their policy agendas.

This chapter will approach strategic planning for sustainable tourism, with some divergences, utilizing the classic strategic tourism planning model that includes a vision and mission statement. The vision statement should be just a few words that describe where local or national tourism strategy wants to be, while the mission statement explains how to get there. The vision and mission statements are followed by a set of goals, objectives, strategies and tactics.

A look at strategic planning for sustainable tourism within a nation mandates that policymakers, planners and managers must understand the need for developing wide-ranging strategies and long-term plans, adjusted as conditions fluctuate or mature. Carefully planned sustainable tourism programs should fulfill economic, environmental, and social goals while maintaining cultural integrity and an ecological balance.

However, it also involves making hard political choices based on complex social, economic, and environmental tradeoffs. It requires a broader, longer-term vision than that traditionally used in community planning and decision-making.

Tourism planning takes place at all levels of organizations. In the book *National and Regional Tourism Planning* (1994), Edward Inskeep says:

> The importance of effective tourism planning in ensuring economic benefit and sustainability is now widely recognized ... The discussion takes into account economic, environmental and socio-cultural factors in achieving sustainable development ... tourism must be developed and managed in a controlled, integrated and sustainable manner, based on sound planning. With this approach, tourism can generate substantial economic benefits to an area, without creating any serious environmental or social problems. Tourism's resources will be conserved for continuous use in the future.[3]

Planning accomplished in a rational manner helps maintain a high quality of the natural and built environment that is essential for successful tourism programs at the community level. Inskeep (1994) also explained that

> The effective development, operation and management of tourism requires certain institutional elements. These elements include:

> - Organizational structures, especially government tourism offices and private sector tourism associations such as hotel associations.
> - Tourism-related legislation and regulations, such as standards and licensing requirements for hotels and tour and travel agencies.
> - Education and training programs, and training institutions to prepare persons to work effectively in tourism.
> - Availability of financial capital to develop tourist attractions, facilities, services and infrastructure, and mechanisms to attract capital investment.
> - Marketing strategies and promotional programs to inform tourists about the country or region, and induce them to visit it, and tourist information facilities and services in the destination areas.
> - Travel facilitation of immigration (including visa arrangements), customs and other facilities and services at the entry and exit points of tourists.

> The institutional elements also include consideration of how to enhance and distribute the economic benefits of tourism, environmental protection measures, reducing adverse social impacts, and conservation of the cultural heritage of people living in the tourism areas.[4]

Strategic tourism planning, an introduction

Strategic tourism planning in its simplest definition is envisioning a desired future for a destination, tourism organization, or other entity and then organizing and implementing the steps to get there. Alternatively, think of strategic planning as a "roadmap" to lead tourism related organizations or destinations from their present level of tourism development to where they would like to be in the next five years, or at some other future date. Strategic tourism planning is not a mysterious difficult theory left only to experts to develop, prepare, and implement. It is simply a process or tool intended to optimize the benefits of tourism so that the result is a balance of the appropriate quality and quantity of supply with the proper level of demand.[5] In effect, strategic tourism planning is a framework designed to provide direction for a tourism organization or destination at any level – local, regional, or national.

There are many different approaches to strategic sustainable tourism planning, depending on the desired end goals the organization seeks to accomplish. In the past, what is generally referred to as a *strategic plan* today was often called a *master plan*. Master plans sometimes conjure up an image of being static, whereas strategic planning for sustainable tourism is dynamic and future-oriented. However, many master plans do include a section or chapter on, for instance, a "strategic vision" or key strategic challenges and constraints, or other sections that meet the same pragmatic aims as a strategic plan. Businesspeople sometimes prepare a strategic plan, then develop a brand, produce a business plan, generate a marketing scenario, and determine a budget for the organization. The strategic plan presents a broad picture of what the organization desires to accomplish and provides the identifiable paths to follow to achieve that end. As opposed to a business plan with lots of numbers, the strategic plan usually consists of words explaining the key decisions that an organization will need to make in future years. It looks at where the organization has been, where it wants to go, how it will get there, what resources will be needed and when the process will begin.[5]

Before setting out to develop a strategic plan for sustainable tourism it is necessary for the organization or destination to have an overall tourism policy. Goeldner and Brent Ritchie (2012) noted that

> In effect, tourism policy seeks to provide a framework within which the destination can provide high-quality visitor experiences that are profitable to destination stakeholders while ensuring that the destination is not compromised in terms of its environmental, social, and cultural integrity ... Planning follows the policy process ... Good policy and sound planning must be conducted to ensure that a destination will be both competitive and sustainable.[6]

Strategic tourism planning for sustainable tourism is a collaborative management tool that can be used to help determine a destination's vision, mission, goals, objectives, strategies, and tactics. It also lays the groundwork for a destination to develop a brand identity as it moves forward in preparing a marketing plan. It drives the organization to produce fundamental decisions and actions for the future.

Depending on the circumstances and the needs of the destination, strategic tourism planning may be either a simple straightforward decision-making process or in some cases a complex set of multiple decision directions, each of which has a bearing on the ultimate plan. It helps to encourage the destination management organization to be responsive to the needs of the community and the stakeholders, and contributes to organizational stability and growth. Strategic planning seeks to obtain an overall consensus of the members of the community as a foundation for long-term planning and goal-setting.

The strategic sustainable tourism planning process

The process of strategic sustainable tourism planning takes into account that a destination must be able to adjust to new trends, changing markets, sustainable tourism products, and a competitive market environment. Destinations that have planned well for sustainable tourism usually have a competitive edge in the marketplace. A plan focused on the sustainability of the tourism destination will ensure consistent quality of the tourism product(s) and yield the most benefits. In addition, good planning will override short-term goals aimed solely at profit motivations and emphasize many of the important future attributes that are more positive for the entire community. Strategic planning to better manage sustainable tourism is receiving increased attention. In brief, tourism planning is essential to the sustainability of the destination in the future, and must foster the conservation of the resources that tourism is dependent on, as well as improve the quality of life of local residents.

In the past, tourism planning did not receive the same kind of interest by the destination management organization in managing the destination as it does today. The history of the travel, tourism, and hospitality industries is replete with examples of tourism areas and destinations that deteriorated or failed as a result of a lack of planning or because of poor planning. Much of this decadence can be traced to haphazard planning and development, which has motivated modern tourism managers to insist on more careful planning. Good tourism planning gives a destination many advantages, six of which are mentioned below:

1 There is a close relationship between policy and planning; strategic tourism planning strengthens an area's or organization's tourism policies.
2 Strategic tourism planning is a highly organized effort of rational thinking and, like tourism policy, is future-oriented.
3 Strategic tourism planning contains many steps, which begin with inventorying an area's tourism product and end with a blueprint for future development.
4 Strategic tourism planning balances economic goals with the need for conserving the environment, built and natural, and improving the quality of life of local residents.
5 Strategic tourism planning fosters the conservation of the resources that tourism is dependent on for future growth.
6 Strategic tourism planning emphasizes quality, efficiency and effectiveness throughout the process to improve the organization's operations and marketing success.[7]

Those who work in the field are accustomed to seeing myriad variations of the strategic tourism planning process. The author of this book, with considerable experience in tourism planning, has often used different approaches to strategic tourism planning, depending on the circumstances, the destination, and the community. One strategic plan may focus on organizational capacity, while another aids in building the appropriate supply components. A strategic tourism plan may concentrate on visitor research, or may work toward developing stakeholder involvement, or may recommend ways to spend the marketing budget. A comprehensive strategic tourism plan will incorporate all of these elements and address others as well.

Strategic planning in the tourism industry is usually a policy/planning/management tool to assist the tourism entity (national tourism office, destination, local community) in organizing its resources to accomplish its goals. In effect, it is a blueprint to help shape and guide the entity in reaching its future goals. A good example of a well-organized and effective strategic tourism planning document is the Canadian Tourism Commission's *2015–2019 Corporate Plan Summary: Marketing Canada in an Ever-Changing World*. Canada has successfully been producing effective tourism plans that include the sustainability of its tourism products for many years.

As a practical matter, a strategic plan for sustainable tourism should, at a minimum, include a vision, mission statement, goal(s), objective(s), strategies, and tactics in one form or another. Some plans may use different descriptive words from those above, such as, for example, priorities, aims or targets, but the ultimate usage is the same, to improve the destination's position in the tourism marketplace. A destination's brand usually reflects its vision and should be included in a discussion of strategic tourism planning.[8]

The process of strategic tourism planning includes several steps. If the destination (whether it is at the local, regional or national level) is comfortable with its brand image then it simply needs to identify the brand at the beginning of the planning cycle and move forward to the next step. Usually the brand is an effort to portray the uniqueness of the destination. The entity's brand's tagline is usually very short (so that most people can remember it), just a few words – for example, *Canada, Keep Exploring*; *Virginia is for Lovers*; *Dominica, The Nature Island*; *The British Virgin Islands, Nature's Little Secrets*; *There's Nothing Like Australia*; *100% Pure New Zealand*; *Essential Costa Rica*. A brand identification phrase that is easy to remember is very important for long-range planning. A good branding campaign will bring attention to the destination, and an effective marketing plan will help promote the brand. The brand itself is not necessarily a specific part of the strategic planning for sustainable tourism, but as noted in relation to the brands mentioned above, many have direct or implied sustainable tourism messages. In the next several paragraphs each of the strategic tourism planning components will be examined: a vision, mission statement, goal(s), objective(s), strategies, and tactics.

Developing the vision statement

As noted above, in this chapter there is a set order of procedures, starting with a "vision" (or vision statement) and ending with "tactics." In some planning publications the "mission statement" is the starting point and the plan may have only a set of objectives rather than "goal(s), objective(s), strategies and tactics." This section will first include the development of the "vision statement."

Determining the vision is the first step of the strategic tourism planning process whereby a community, country, destination, or other entity develops a vision statement. Usually composed of just a few words, the vision statement will depict an image of what the destination or other entity should be like in the future. It is the image of what the destination wants to be, no matter how idealistic it may seem. It may be inspirational, letting the world know how the destination wants to be known. It should provide a common ideal or dream that all the stakeholders can endorse. Goeldner and Brent Ritchie (2012) note the development of a strategic vision as "a stimulating, intellectual process that often attracts and should involve the relevant stakeholders of a destination . . . After the visioning process is complete, the organization will take that information and come up with a more specific mission statement to also help guide the organization."[9]

According to the Sustainable Tourism Cooperative Research Centre,

> The process of developing a **Vision Statement** can be a valuable process in developing a shared view of where tourism is heading for a community or region [destination or country]. To be effective, it must be more than simply words. It needs to be assimilated into council's [stakeholders'] culture and *it should inform the direction*

key decisions take in relation to tourism planning and development ... Often, a vision statement is mistaken for a mission statement. The 'Vision' describes a future identity and the 'Mission' describes why it will be achieved ... Developing a vision statement for tourism in your community or region should be an engaging process that evolves over a number of weeks and months.[10]

When penning a vision, the vision author needs to have a thorough understanding and knowledge of the destination or area and the desired plans for future development and promotion of the tourism products. There are a number of different techniques that can be used in preparing a vision. It might evolve from a simple brainstorming session, where the stakeholders gather to discuss their ultimate interests in the destination. In some circumstances, it makes sense to use focus groups to share a wide range of different opinions in building the vision. This may also be a good time to utilize the services of an experienced strategic planning/marketing consultant who can help with developing the vision, mission statement, and branding of the destination.[11]

Examples and comments about vision statements are easily found online using most search engines and may shed some light on the modus operandi for developing a vision. For example, the vision statement for Costa Rica reads like this: "To become the leading ground operator in the region and our client's best partner, always providing the best possible product, with the highest quality of services, and demonstrating faithfully our commitment towards social and environmental responsibility." Now, Costa Rica's mission statement is "To provide memorable holidays in Costa Rica, social and environmentally responsible, satisfying the needs of our clients and always exceeding their expectations." Noting the comment in the previous paragraph that "often, a vision statement is mistaken for a mission statement," this is the case with respect to Costa Rica's vision and mission statements. On the other hand, New Zealand's Tourism Strategy 2015 has a vision statement: "In 2015, tourism is valued as the leading contributor to a sustainable New Zealand economy." While it is a good, concise vision statement, it implies a short-term vision (2015) when the strategic plan should be looking years into the future. New Zealand's mission statement – "to motivate our target market to come now, do more, and come back" – suggests a longer-term plan. The basic point is that the vision should send a highly positive message, which all the stakeholders are in agreement with, but short enough to be inspirational and hopefully address the issue of long-term sustainability.

The mission statement

Usually the next step in the strategic tourism planning approach is to develop a mission statement. Some comments have already been made about the mission statement but more clarification is needed at this point. A mission statement is an agreed-upon statement by the organization that supports the vision and that helps to explain the pathway(s) to accomplishment. It helps chart a course of action to support the vision for the destination and it provides grounding for setting goals and objectives. Compared to the vision statement, the mission statement is generally (but not necessarily) longer, in that it outlines how to get there – much like a road map. The mission statement is usually goal-oriented and designed to inspire people to make decisions and take actions.[12]

As with the vision statement, there needs to be a wide range of people involved in preparing the mission statement – certainly the stakeholders, and possibly outside experts to help guide the process. A few examples should suffice to get the message across about developing the mission statement. The British Virgin Islands has a short but powerful mission statement: "To foster, develop and promote a sustainable tourism industry for the British Virgin Islands." Such key words as "foster, develop and promote" are certainly "goal oriented" and the message on sustainability is a good one. The mission statement for Saint Vincent and the Grenadines is much longer but very clear, and a good example of where the mission statement wants to lead the tourism sector in that country: "To provide an enabling environment for the economic growth and sustainable development of the tourism and other productive sectors in St. Vincent and the Grenadines, through the formulation and administration of policies and plans to regulate the tourism and industry sectors, by working with stakeholders to promote greater economic diversification and sectoral linkages, international competiveness, improved productivity and investment." It brings to bear more than just what the tourism industry wants, but also touches on the tourism industry's interconnectedness with other "industry sectors" – letting the reader know that the tourism industry is a part of the entire country's industry. It also addresses two very important aspects of tourism: "economic growth" and "sustainable tourism." The Republic of Malta has an excellent short mission statement, as follows: "Our mission is to establish and execute a tourism policy which is based on the principles of sustainable tourism development to contribute to economic growth whilst respecting the heritage and environment of the Maltese islands." A mission statement for a specific country doesn't get much better than this. It includes a very important word – "policy." As noted earlier in this chapter, policy and planning must go hand in hand in order for there to be overall positive management of the country's tourism sector.

Planning goals

Tourism planners do not always agree on the next steps in strategic tourism planning. Experience by many experts in strategic tourism planning suggests the following scenario: goals, objectives, strategies, and tactics as an outline approach in the strategic tourism planning process. There are some planners that combine goals and objectives, and others that combine strategies and tactics. This section and the next three will break it down into four groups: goals, objectives, strategies, and tactics. Figure 7.1 depicts this approach.

Of the four parts mentioned above, the most important one is goal setting. The goal(s) are the driving force of what the strategic plan intends to achieve – and, therefore, need careful crafting to be effective. If goal setting is accomplished in the right vein, it will help establish a target level for tourism development, marketing, promotion, and

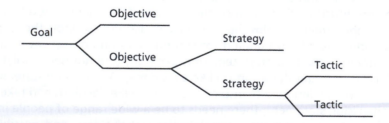

Figure 7.1 Tree diagram: goal-oriented tourism planning

sustainability for the destination. For most tourism destinations, there may be several goals, which represent the aim or purpose intended by stakeholders when the decision to develop the destination is initially visualized, or an already developed destination may want to change the direction of its programs. The goal-oriented method utilized may be short-term (one to two years) or long-term (usually not more than five years before being reviewed and possibly revised). The goals should be measureable – for example, "it is expected that growth in visitation to the destination will be a certain percent each year or in a future year the organization will reach a certain number of visitors."

As mentioned earlier, Canada does as good a job in strategic sustainable tourism planning as any entity. The Canadian Tourism Commission has been working on tourism planning for a long, long time; reference the *2015–2019 Corporate Plan Summary: Marketing Canada in an Ever-Changing World*, an excellent document to read with respect to tourism planning and specifically in terms of goal setting. In the "Plan Summary" it is noted that the Canadian Tourism Commission's ultimate goal is "To grow tourism export revenue in markets offering the highest return and where the Canada brand lands." It clearly spells out the economic goal without ignoring the brand of *Canada, Keep Exploring*. In the corporate plan, the goal is followed by three specific "objectives" cited in the next section. The complete corporate report explains in detail just how Canada plans to reach its goal.[13] On the other hand, the British Virgin Islands, mentioned earlier in this chapter, have numerous goals, three of which are mentioned below:

1　Increase the economic contribution of tourism to the British Virgin Islands
2　Provide a superior destination experience for visitors by developing and expanding the number and quality of product offerings
3　Adapt and promote a more sustainable approach to tourism development[14]

Planning objectives

Objectives support the goal(s); they are the stepping stones to reach the goal and are concrete, real, practical steps or intentions that define expected achievements in the strategic tourism plan. Objectives are specific-oriented targets of the destination that can be implemented and made operational in meeting the goal(s) of the plan. Generally the objectives are in priority order, such that the available resources earmarked to achieve the highest-priority objectives are dealt with first. The idea is to think about the overall goal(s) and seek out innovative approaches and creative guidelines (objectives) to reach or go beyond what is expected.

Again, using the Canadian Tourism Commission Corporate Plan Summary 2015 as an example, it lists three "Immediate Outcome Objectives" as follows:

1　Generate demand for Canada's visitor economy
2　Support Canadian Tourism Businesses to sell Canada
3　Advance corporate excellence and efficiency

The objectives are short, clear-cut, and followed with "activities" (strategies) and "targets" (tactics) for reaching these objectives. Again, to understand just how all this works, it is advisable to review the complete Canadian planning documents.

Even though Saint Vincent and the Grenadines is a much smaller market than, for example, Canada, it is important that the country carefully spells out its tourism planning objectives. The objectives for the Saint Vincent and the Grenadines Ministry of Tourism are as follows:

- To ensure that there is a high quality visitor experience for all consumers of Saint Vincent and the Grenadines tourism product.
- To advance the knowledge of Saint Vincent and the Grenadines in major source markets as a desirable tourism destination.
- To ensure that data collection and analysis (qualitative and quantitative) are of a high enough standard to afford effective planning and development of the tourism sector.
- To expand the opportunities of visitors' expenditure in order to maximize the return from expenditure in tourism development and marketing.[15]

These objectives are clear-cut and fit the marketplace for Saint Vincent and the Grenadines.

Planning strategies

Strategies relate to actions and operations that are necessary to meet the objectives included in the strategic tourism plan. In some circumstances, the strategy may include the development of new products or special programs for implementing the objectives. The strategy should also identify key target audiences that are a part of the overall planning process. One strategy might be to provide the leadership necessary to accomplish the objectives or set the criteria for measuring the quality of the tourism product. Strategies also involve identification of funding needs and sources, as well as a review of existing resources related to the objectives of the plan. Furthermore, a strategy might include forming a partnership or collaborating with other interested entities or introducing new technology. The key is that the strategies are aimed towards reaching the identified goals and objectives.

Planning tactics

The last item in the strategic tourism planning system is tactics. The tactics are the short-term actions (usually less than six months) for immediate achievements related to the plan. They are, in effect, the activities for securing the objectives designated by the strategy. Tactics are the day-to-day activities and details, whether setting the agenda for the stakeholders' meeting or making arrangements to support the planning process to be used to achieve the strategic planning goal.

Implementing the strategic tourism plan

The beauty of achievement, on finalizing a strategic tourism plan, lies in the knowledge that tough decisions have been made concerning the most important issues and that the destination can now move forward proactively. From this point on, the strategic planning process and tools of implementation for a strategic plan for *sustainable tourism* are similar to any other strategic tourism plan. The sustainability aspects of the plan would have already been accounted for in the vision, mission statement, goals and objectives.

Moving ahead with the strategic plan, there is considerable analysis that must take place. Many tourism planners use many different tools within the planning process. The well-known SWOT (strengths, weaknesses, opportunities, and threats) analysis is often utilized in strategic planning. Another tool, SMART (specific, measurable, achievable, relevant, and time-bound), may be used to help set and monitor the goals. Most strategic tourism planners will build into the process a situational analysis (or needs assessment), a competitive analysis, a monitoring device, an evaluation, built-in performance measures, and research to improve the process. Branding the destination can also be included in the strategic tourism planning process.

The strategic tourism planning approach is dependent on the conditions existing in the destination/organization and the marketplace. Commonly, the planner or leader will hold numerous brainstorming sessions to enable all stakeholders to reach a consensus on which tools are best suited for the specific strategic plan in question. This supports the notion of continuously monitoring and evaluating the strategic plan, as dynamic processes or changes in the market may be taking place while the plan is being developed and implemented.[16]

Governments (at all levels), destinations, advisers, planners, and consultants have many different tools for organizing a strategic tourism plan, depending on the needs, circumstances, and size of the project. For example, the author of this book organized an action plan document for a project he was working on by first developing a schematic diagram similar to Figure 7.1, which allowed him to think through the various steps to take in developing a strategic tourism plan for a specific destination. A diagram helps explain to the stakeholders the marketing framework for analyzing the destination's desire to increase sales in their target customer segments of the marketplace. Later, this marketing planning approach evolved into an article, "Strategic Marketing Planning for the Tourism Industry."[17] While some of the steps utilized in this particular example are similar to a classic strategic tourism plan, the framework approach taken has many differences as well. It was not designed as an overall strategic tourism plan but was, instead, at the time, a strategic marketing plan effort for a specific destination and for purposes of illustration. This strategic marketing planning approach, including a special diagram, will appear in Chapter 8.

Internal analysis in the strategic planning process[18]

Internal analysis in the strategic planning process reviews the factors that characterize the destination. Characteristics may include highway demand, heritage, sports facilities, outdoor recreation activities, the natural environment, or proximity to major metropolitan areas, among many other factors that serve to drive tourism demand to the destination. Not only is it important to understand a destination's tourism product, or supply, it is equally important to identify the community's organization structures that will influence tourism development. A few steps that can be incorporated into the internal analysis of tourism strategic planning are the following.

Strategic planning for sustainable tourism

(a) Analyze the destination's natural environment:
  1 Assess the area's geography to identify opportunities and threats to tourism development.
  2 Evaluate previous and predicted climate issues that could affect visitation to the area.
  3 Gauge residents' attitudes towards tourism and tourism development by enabling community members to voice their views and concerns through either a local community meeting or a web-based survey.
  4 Measure the general condition of service provided by the tourism industry workforce, addressing relevant training needs.
  5 Identify meaningful elements of the area's culture that could be incorporated into the overall tourism experience.
  6 Review the history of the area to maintain or revive critical characteristics important to heritage tourism.

(b) Examine the assembled elements:
  1 Identify current mission, goals, objectives, strategies, and tactics of key community organizations; areas of concordance, overlap, and conflict; and common and shared human financial resources related to tourism development.
  2 Review budgets and funding of comparable destination management organizations as a benchmark to identify enhanced and sustainable funding opportunities for a destination-related organization.
  3 Identify specific tourism-related infrastructure needs or opportunities that may not meet visitor expectations and may detract from the destination's appeal.
  4 Analyze the signage and transportation routes to and through the destination to ensure ease of access for visitors to attractions and other supply components.
  5 Assess the use of technology by destination promoters in the areas of customer relationships, packaging, booking and travel planning, demographic information, promotion, communications and revenue management, among other areas.
  6 Review quality, availability, and distribution of visitor information about the destination.
  7 Evaluate the community's existing crisis contingency plan to ensure it is proactive and can handle a wide array of incidents that could arise at any time.

(c) Conduct extensive visitor research:
  1 Plan visitor research studies by working with destination managers to establish and understand the survey objectives.
  2 Design and test what type of visitor survey instrument is used to collect data from visitors.
  3 Complete interviews with the general population as well as additional interviews with those who have visited the destination.
  4 Prepare a summary report to include descriptive statistics of the data along with tests of the hypotheses stated in the original study design phase.
  5 Identify existing and new market segments and decision patterns that will increase visitation to the region.

(d) Investigate industry-operating sectors:
  1 Inventory businesses in all tourism operating sectors (accommodations, meeting spaces, transportation, activities and entertainment, food services, outdoor recreation, visitor services and shopping) in order to determine quality and quantity.

2　Identify opportunities for improvement in all operating sectors.

3　Meet with selected tourism industry members, including supply operators, tourism managers and developers.

4　Conduct a web-based survey of local industry members to identify tourism development issues and concerns important to the stakeholders.

5　Gather information on new attractions and expansions that may be planned.

6　Examine the potential to repackage existing tourism products and develop new special events and niche tourism supply (convention center, heritage, military, sports, nature trails, and agritourism and industrial activities, among others) that may bolster tourism in the shoulder and off-season months.

7　Evaluate the impacts of existing outdated facilities and inadequate supply, including the aesthetic appeal of architectural design standards, such as streetscape, gateway, signage and façade improvements.

The above are just a few additional steps that may need to be included in the strategic tourism planning mechanism, depending on the destination, organization, and accessible information.

External environmental scan in strategic planning[19]

It is crucial for a destination to understand how it fits in the larger tourism industry and how various factors at all levels may have an impact on visitation at the local level. This is done by studying industry trends at the local, regional, national and international levels. Competitive analysis is also a vital activity when pursuing a sound tourism development strategy.

(a) Explore details of large tourism systems:
1　Identify the "outside" (non-destination) stakeholders and design an effective and efficient means of outreach to them. Outside organizations may include neighboring destination-management organizations, local and national tourism entities, economic development, environmental and transportation agencies, among other groups.

2　Review current and anticipated industry trends in terms of visitation, origin of demand, revenues, supply development, consumer preferences, safety and security and other indicators at the local/national and international levels.

3　Research trends in particular activities and industries important to the destination.

(b) Perform competitive analysis:
1　Examine competitive destinations in the region.
2　Determine the competitive position of the destination against similar areas in terms that may include current and historical visitation, tourism revenue, market segmentation, markets-of-origin, marketing expenditures and/or other pertinent data.

Strategic tourism planning recommendations should lead towards optimized tourism in the destination. Research should focus on determining the future of tourism in the region and how it can achieve its highest and best goal within the context of infrastructure and environmental constraints in the destination, and in accordance with the wants and needs of area visitors and community stakeholders. This disciplined process of scanning the internal and external environments and formulating tourism strategies calls for a certain order and pattern to keep it focused and productive. It should raise a sequence of questions to help planners examine the tourist's experience, test viable interpretations of certain data, incorporate information about the present, and anticipate the destination's future impact on the tourism marketplace. In effect, as mentioned earlier, the strategic tourism plan is no more, and no less, than a set of decisions about what the desires of the organization are, what to accomplish, and how it will get there.

Strategic tourism planning is, in summary, a practical, intensive, ideas-packed approach to improving a destination's opportunities for sustainability of its tourism programs over a long period. It is a thought-out system that aims to stretch the available resources through careful planning, monitoring, and evaluation. It is an action-oriented plan to benchmark and counter competitors' strategies with built-in performance measures. Strategic tourism planning proposes to develop a coherent strategy to build upon destinations' strengths and to learn from the past while correcting for the future in order to increase tourism's positive impacts upon the organization and community. The overall goal is to match tourism supply and demand – to provide adequate and appropriate facilities, amenities, services and events (supply) after identifying what visitors want and need (demand) in consideration of what is wanted and needed within the community. Successful implementation of good tourism development strategies will result in the creation of new jobs, additional visitor expenditures and increased incomes. Tourism development, if planned carefully, can improve an area's quality of life, which will be appealing to new residents, companies, and entrepreneurs.

Case study 7: Peru: the Condor Lodge Ecotourism Project

"The journey not the arrival matters."

T. S. Eliot

Background

The focus of this case study is on the Condor Lodge Ecotourism Project in Apurimac Canyon, Peru (Andean Mountain range – a refuge for the Andean condor). However, to understand certain aspects of the location of the Condor Lodge, information about tourism in Peru is helpful. Transportation to the lodge starts from Cuzco, which is a fascinating community and an example of sustainable tourism from a history/heritage perspective. This case study partially relies on updated and new information from a journal article prepared in 2011 by David Urias and the present author (Urias and Edgell, 2011).[20]

Tourism to Peru

Peru is a very beautiful South American country with a diversity of land, weather, and people. The country has 11 ecoregions that include magnificent mountains, lush jungles, and long ocean coastlines. The weather varies from tropical in the east to dry desert in the west, and cold in the Andes Mountains. Peru was home to many pre-Columbian indigenous Amerindians, including the well-known Incas. Later the Spaniards conquered Peru and settled throughout the country. Also, other immigrants arrived from many parts of the world. The integration of these many different cultures in Peru makes for a very fascinating heritage of interest to tourists.

Tourist arrivals to Peru approach 4 million visitors. Tourism in Peru is the third largest industry, behind fishing and mining. The culture and heritage of Peru includes the Incas, Chancas, Chachapoyas, Mochicas and Warl, and the art, dances and customs handed down from generation to generation. Three of the main areas visited by tourists include the capital city of Lima, the Inca ruins of Machu Picchu (which receives about half of the visitors to Peru), and the ancient city of Cuzco. Machu Picchu now ranks as one of the "New Seven Wonders of the World" (of the original Seven Wonders of the World, only the pyramid at Giza in Egypt remains). Machu Picchu is well known to travelers but less is known about the interesting city of Cuzco. Cuzco is 11,000 feet above sea level in the heart of the Andes Mountains. It is considered the archeological capital of the Americas due to its Inca heritage. Cuzco was at the center of the Inca Empire. It is a United Nations Educational, Scientific and Cultural Organization (UNESCO) World Heritage Site. A World Heritage Site is a place that is listed by UNESCO as being of special cultural or physical significance. Since the Condor Ecotourism Lodge is near to Machu Picchu and Cuzco, it has the potential to draw adventure tourists from those two locations who might have a special interest in seeing the nesting area of the Andean Condor. The Andean Condor, found mostly in the Andes Mountains, is a fascinating bird, one of the world's largest flying birds, with a wingspan up to 10 feet. The species is listed by the World Conservation Union as "vulnerable" to extinction as it has been gradually losing much of its habitat.

Peru and sustainability

More recently, with a general interest in sustainability, Peru, like many other countries, has become more cognizant of the advantages of sustainable tourism that also includes ecotourism. The country has many opportunities for developing its natural areas for ecotourism activities such as hiking, bird watching, adventure, nature observation, local cultural festivals, heritage, and other forms of nature-based and cultural tourism and recreation. Peru, the third largest country in South America and bordered by Brazil, Bolivia, Chile, Columbia, and Ecuador, is rich in history, heritage, and natural beauty. With respect to flora and fauna, Peru's variety of climates and ecosystems ranks the country amongst the world's top eight nations in terms of biodiversity, where one can find 84 of the 104 life zones existing throughout the globe. The country is home to more than 400 species of mammals, 300 reptiles, 1,700 birds and more that 50,000 plants registered to date (Tomos and Elgegren, 2006).[21] The emphasis on Peru's natural beauty and

(Continued)

Case study (continued)

historic sites has led to increases in international tourism to Peru. Not many people realize that the world's largest river, the Amazon, has its beginnings in Peru, starting from the Mantaro River. The lodge fits this move toward interest in the natural environment by international visitors. Almost all of the lodge's visitors are from outside Peru.

The Condor Lodge Ecotourism Project

The Condor Lodge Ecotourism Project follows the recent emphasis on sustainability of tourism destinations. While the lodge has been operational since 2006, it is in some respects still in a developmental stage. The lodge has not generated the numbers of visitors that had been hoped for over the last several years. The highest year of visitation to the lodge was 80 visitors in 2006, with the lowest year being 2008, with just 37 ecotourists, and the next lowest year 2014, with 54 tourists. These numbers have caused the owner to review why the low numbers, what changes need to be made, and how to better market the lodge. This case study will not attempt to answer these concerns, but rather to use the lodge as a discussion piece for ecotourism.

This case study will review aspects of sustaining ecotourism in the context of the lodge. Responsibly managed ecotourism enhances, enriches, and embraces the need to preserve nature, heritage, and cultural values. In so doing, ecotourism adds value to the community, such that the local citizens and visitors have a quality tourism experience (Edgell, 2006).[22] In addition, a well-designed ecotourism project strongly promotes conservation, education, and awareness of the natural environment, as well as the history, heritage, and culture at the targeted location (Wright, 1993).[23] Ecotourism projects, properly designed and managed, can add economic value – creating local jobs, producing additional income, and adding to the economic development of the area. When well planned and executed, ecotourism development provides an incentive to preserve the best features a community or destination has to offer, including its wildlife habitats, historic areas, scenery, local culture and heritage, and the flora and fauna of the area.

Defining ecotourism in relationship to the Condor Lodge

The principle of ecotourism development, with the overall framework of sustainable tourism, has achieved considerable prominence and greater acceptance in recent years. The term ecotourism has existed for a long time and over the years it has been looked at in many different circumstances. Goeldner and Brent Ritchie (2012) have noted that

> Ecotourism, geotourism, nature tourism, green tourism, low-impact tourism, adventure travel, alternative tourism, environmental preservation, symbiotic development, responsible tourism, soft tourism, appropriate tourism, quality tourism, new tourism, sustainable development, and sustainable tourism all

are monikers for similar types of tourist activities and developments. Of all the terms, *ecotourism* and *sustainability* are most frequently used. The principle of both is to sustain or even enhance the quality and attractiveness of the natural environment.[24]

Ecotourism is connected to the natural environment and implies that visitors should have an opportunity to have a pleasant nature experience but in such a way that it is sustained for future generations to also enjoy and that it contributes to the economy of the local community. McCool and Moisey (2008) note that "Furthermore, ecotourism, nature-based tourism, responsible tourism and green tourism are all terms applied to what is being referred to as a gentler, more socially and environmentally sensitive type of tourism."[25] Ecotourism as it relates to the lodge basically utilizes the definition of ecotourism as presented by The International Ecotourism Society (TIES): "responsible travel to natural areas that conserves the environment and sustains the well-being of local people."[26] This ecotourism concept, as used in the context of the lodge in this case study, explains that such development must respect traditions and cultures in the area, protect and preserve the environment, and educate visitors about their surroundings. A major object of ecotourism at the lodge is to provide an ecotourism-type environmental education experience for visitors and to manage this activity in a sustainable fashion. An education component serves to provide information about the natural history and culture of a site, while also promoting a conservation ethic that may infuse tourists with stronger pro-environmental attitudes.[27] The lodge did not meet all of the TIES principles cited earlier in this book but it did attempt to apply the following principles:

1   Minimize impact [on the site where the lodge is located].
2   Build environmental and cultural awareness and respect.
3   Provide positive experiences for both visitors and hosts.

Sustainable tourism, authentic and educational

The relationship between sustainable tourism, including ecotourism, and destinations is one which is concerned with ensuring that destinations deliver authentic interpretations of environmental, cultural, and heritage values (Honey and Gilpin, 2009; Urias and Russo, 2009).[28] This concept has been inherent in sustainable tourism for a long time. The World Tourism Organization noted in 1993 a strong message with respect to authenticity: "Respect the sociocultural authenticity of host communities, conserve their built and living cultural heritage and traditional values, and contribute to intercultural understanding and tolerance." Such "respect" and "understanding" largely results through the education of the visitor about the destination. Education in this context is more than just a one-way transfer of information. It is about explanation, revelation, and understanding in a manner that personally involves the ecotourist in an interesting and enjoyable fashion with respect to the location of the visit.

(Continued)

Case study (continued)

The Condor Lodge

The lodge is in the Andes mountain range that is heir to ancient civilizations and rich colonial traditions. Peru, as mentioned earlier, has a rich biodiversity and is a melting pot of different cultures. Peru consists of four distinct geographical features: coastal, jungle, desert, and sierra. Sierra is the name given to the Andean highland region, where the Andes mountain range runs through the country north to south, dividing the coastal area from the jungle. The Sierra makes up over 30 percent of the nation's territory. The Sierra region offers a wide diversity of landscapes, which vary according to the altitude. The average altitude is 14,000 feet above sea level. The lodge is just outside Cuzco (about a two-hour drive and then a hike or horseback ride up the mountain to the lodge), high up in the Sierra region of the Apurimac River Canyon. The lodge is located in the Apurimac region near to the very small rural village called Antilla. This little community is about 12,000 feet above sea level, with a panoramic view of the Andes Mountains. The terrain in the area is extremely steep, formed by narrow, deep valleys with impressive abysses, cold plateaus, and high mountain peaks. There are snow-capped mountains, mountain forests, beautiful lakes, and many different species of flora and fauna like the Intimpa pine tree, the Andean fox, and the Andean deer. In brief, the area is an idyllic location for a nature-based, culture-heritage ecotourism project. It is an area where there are many Andean condors, hence the name of the Condor Lodge.

Antilla has about 2,000 inhabitants, most of whom are Peruvian Indians with an Inca heritage and who speak the Quechua language, although some also speak Spanish. Most of the families live in small adobe homes, usually with dirt floors, no running water, and no indoor plumbing. The community is mostly engaged in activities related to agriculture: raising horses, mules, cows, pigs, and chickens. Thus far, there has not been much of an opportunity to engage this local population in any major way with respect to the lodge.

The lodge was established in 2006 and has been a leader in ecotourism in the region. The lodge offers an opportunity for a visit to the ancient city of Cuzco and then transportation to the Condor Lodge in the mountains (see www.thecondorlodge. com). Efforts have been made to contact the general tourism community and to welcome both Peruvians and international visitors interested in a nature-based experience in the mountains. The lodge offers an exciting opportunity to observe the Condors fly over the Apurimac River Canyon and to see their mountain nesting areas. The programs at the lodge offer photography, hunting, horseback riding, nature walks, fishing, rural tourism, and magnificent scenery. They also present an opportunity to examine the history, ecological diversity, conservation efforts, biogeography, and the Peruvian culture.

To date, most of the visitors have been from Europe and generally already had a predisposition to enjoy nature and the outdoors. The three biggest interests at the lodge thus far have been observing the Condors as they soar through the mountains (and seeing the beautiful scenery at the same time), hiking, and horseback riding. In addition, most such visitors to the lodge have also visited Cuzco to get a flavor of this wonderful ancient Inca city. The visitor surveys note guest satisfaction with the lodge and the visits in Cuzco. For special visitors who want to study or research a natural area with a wide diversity of geography, it is an ideal location. Following most of the precepts of ecotourism, efforts are being made to develop programs to financially help the local school and to educate the local population about conservation measures. The lodge offers a rural experience, transport service by van and horseback, excellent traditional food provided by locals, use of knowledgeable, local guides, and modern lodging. The visitor has the opportunity of understanding and appreciating the cultural reality of indigenous life in the rural Andes. It is an opportunity to practice and research the principles of ecotourism in a wonderful environment.

Evaluating the lodge as an ecotourism destination

Possibly a new approach to the study of an ecotourism destination is through an innovative concept called destinology: The multidisciplinary "art and science" of planning, designing and constructing not just buildings and rides, but entire destination experiences. In other words, "a way of thinking of ways to engage people during a visit, and to make sure they take something away after they leave."[29] Therefore, put the lodge under a microscope and develop a plan of action to improve and possibly expand the activities at the lodge. Data to evaluate the lodge has been generated through both activities participated in and general observations by the visitors. A few open-ended surveys were developed, as well as discussions and informal interviews with the visitors. One suggestion that received considerable attention was to develop an education center adjunct to the lodge, where visitors could study and learn more about the environment and come up with ideas to expand the promotion and conservation of the area more effectively. With respect to the lodge's environmental impact and sustainability, the "good news" is that the lodge (a) checks water consumption and uses regulating equipment on facets/showers; (b) utilizes locally produced food when available; (c) encourages visitors to stay on pathways; (d) has a recycling program in place; (e) purchases in bulk when possible; (f) serves beverages in recyclable containers; (g) removes waste from natural areas; and (h) gives preference to equipment which has a long life and can be repaired. Most of these environmentally protective devices fit well with the principles of ecotourism.

The lodge is an excellent laboratory for studying all aspects of ecotourism, including understanding the Peruvian culture, learning about flora and fauna unfamiliar to most visitors, and observing unique natural areas not in existence elsewhere. It is the only place in South America where one can observe the nesting places of the Andean condor. The lodge has spectacular recreational activities to participate in. One major weakness of the lodge is that it has not had an effective marketing campaign. Visitation has not improved over several years. The lodge needs to develop a strong target-marketing approach, improve its website, and interact with the various suppliers of adventure vacations, green travel, and nature visitors. One of the best market opportunities is to attract not

(Continued)

Case study (continued)

just those visitors who enjoy the mountains, but also market visitors of Cuzco and Machu Picchu.

The growth in nature-based tourism and ecotourism is likely to continue, with increased global environmental awareness, more emphasis on outdoor recreation, and a better educated population with respect to conservation of natural and built resources. This case study has examined some of the main concepts of ecotourism in a real experience through the Condor Lodge in Peru. It took into consideration that ecotourism is responsible travel to natural areas that conserves the environment and seeks an understanding of the local community. A visit to the Condor Lodge is a unique experience in an undisturbed natural environment, with the visitors viewing flora, fauna, birds, animals, landforms, scenery, and natural beauty. This aspect of the Condor Lodge ecotourism reinforces the fact that sustainable tourism development is development that has been carefully planned and managed. Because the world's resources are limited, the future of tourism growth depends on a good understanding of sustainable tourism. As Goeldner and Brent Ritchie have noted (2012), "The environment is the resource base for tourism, and without protection, the natural attraction that brought the tourist in the first place will be lost."[30]

Chapter summary

There are many different kinds of planning, from regular planning to comprehensive planning, or long-range planning, or strategic planning. This chapter concentrates on strategic planning. Strategic planning focuses more on planning in dynamic situations where changes are taking place.

Edward Inskeep, writing in *National and Regional Tourism Planning*, says: "The importance of effective tourism planning in ensuring economic benefit and sustainability is now widely recognized." Strategic planning fits well with concerns for sustainable tourism. In effect, strategic tourism planning is a framework that can be used to provide direction for a tourism organization or destination at any level: local, regional, and national.

In developing a sustainable tourism project, good policy and strategic planning are important. Tourism policy looks at the big picture and long-range aspects of the project, while planning follows the policy process and focuses on the details of the project. Strategic planning helps in understanding the overall management of a destination. As a practical matter, a strategic plan for sustainable tourism should include a vision, mission statement, goals, objectives, strategies, and tactics.

A "vision" and a "mission statement" are closely entwined. The vision is a "dream" of what one might like to obtain from a sustainable tourism project. The mission statement helps us to understand what is needed to reach that dream. A vision is sometimes incorporated into a brand tagline or a "slogan" that portrays an image that is described in just a few words so that it can be remembered.

The "mission statement" supports the vision and helps explain how to reach the vision. After the vision and mission statement are agreed by the stakeholders, the more formal planning takes place, with goals, objectives, strategies and tactics. Tactics are what needs to be done in the very short term (maybe within the next six months).

Most strategic plans include the popularly known SWOT (strengths, weaknesses, opportunities, threats) analysis. Some plans also include SMART (specific, measureable, achievable, relevant, and time-bound) analysis, which can be used to help monitor the strategic plan. There are numerous other tools available in the planning process, including "Internal Analysis" and the "External Environmental Scan."

The case study on the Condor Lodge Ecotourism Project in Peru illustrates some of the aspects of a sustainable tourism project. There was a general attempt in the project to follow some of the guidelines and principles available from The International Ecotourism Society. The project is still in the process of being improved.

Chapter review questions

1   How would you differentiate strategic planning from other types of planning?
2   Why is there a particular need for planning with respect to sustainable tourism development?
3   What is the difference between policy and planning?
4   How would you define a "vision"?
5   What would your definition of "mission statement" be?
6   What is the difference between a goal and an objective?
7   Describe what you think a "strategy" might be in a sustainable tourism project.
8   Is a "tactic" long-term or short-term in the planning process?
9   What does SWOT stand for?
10 What does SMART stand for?
11 How would you describe the country of Peru?
12 Are you familiar with The International Ecotourism Society?
13 How would you describe the Condor Lodge Ecotourism Project?

Notes

1   Inskeep, E. (1994) *National and Regional Tourism Planning*, World Tourism Organization Publication, London and New York: Routledge, pp. 8–9.
2   Edgell, Sr., D. L. (2006) *Managing Sustainable Tourism: A Legacy for the Future*, New York: The Haworth Hospitality Press, p. 32.
3   Inskeep (1994), pp. i, 6.
4   Ibid.
5   Edgell, Sr., D. L. and Swanson, J. (2013) *Tourism Policy and Planning: Yesterday, Today, and Tomorrow* (2nd edition), London: Routledge.
6   Goeldner, C. and Brent Ritchie, J. R. (2012) *Tourism: Principles, Practices, Philosophies* (12th edition), Hoboken, New Jersey: John Wiley & Sons, Inc.
7   Edgell and Swanson (2013), p. 248.
8   Edgell and Swanson (2013), p. 249.
9   Goeldner and Brent Ritchie (2012), pp. 337–338.
10 Sustainable Tourism Cooperative Research Centre (2015) "Step 3 Resource: Creating a Vision Statement Factsheet."
11 Edgell and Swanson (2013), p. 249.
12 Edgell and Swanson (2013), p. 250.

13 Canadian Tourist Commission (2015) *2015–2019 Corporate Plan Summary: Marketing Canada in an Ever-Changing World,* Vancouver, British Columbia: CTC.
14 Retrieved from http://www.bvitourism.co.uk/vision-mission.
15 Saint Vincent and the Grenadines, Ministry of Tourism, Sports and Culture, *Discover St. Vincent and the Grenadines.*
16 Edgell and Swanson (2013), p. 252.
17 Edgell, Sr., D. L., Ruf, K. M., and Agarwal, A. (1999) "Strategic Marketing Planning for the Tourism Industry," *Journal of Travel & Tourism Marketing*, 8(3), pp. 111–120.
18 Edgell and Swanson (2013), pp. 254–255.
19 Ibid., pp. 255–256.
20 Urias, D. and Edgell, Sr., D. L. (2011) "The Managerial and Educational Aspects of Sustaining Ecotourism in the Context of the Condor Lodge Conservation Project in Peru," *Asian Journal of Tourism and Hospitality Research*, 5(2).
21 Tolmos, R. and Elgegren, J. (2006) "Peru's System of Natural Protected Areas: An Overview." Paper presented at the OECD workshop on Distribution Issues in Biodiversity Policy, 26–27 April, Oaxaca, Mexico.
22 Edgell, D. (2006).
23 Wright, P. (1993) "Ecotourism: Ethics or Eco-sell?" *Journal of Travel Research*, 31(3), 3–9.
24 Goeldner and Brent Ritchie (2012), p. 386.
25 McCool, S. and Moisey, R., eds. (2008) *Tourism, Recreation and Sustainability* (2nd edition), Oxfordshire, United Kingdom: CABI Publishing, p. 283.
26 The International Ecotourism Society (2008), www.ecotourism.org.
27 Urias and Edgell (2011).
28 Honey, M. (2008) *Ecotourism and Sustainable Development: Who Owns Paradise?* (2nd edition), Washington, D.C.: Island Press; Honey, M. and Gilpin, R. (2009) *Tourism in the Developing World: Promoting Peace and Reducing Poverty*, Washington, D.C.: United States Institute of Peace; Urias, D. and Russo, A. (2009) "Ecotourism as an Educational Experience." Paper presented at the Association of International Education Administrators Annual Meeting, Atlanta, Georgia.
29 Hill, S. (2015) "Thrill Seekers," *Kansas Alumni*, Issue 4, 2.
30 Goeldner and Brent Ritchie (2012), p. 391.

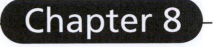

Chapter 8

Marketing the sustainable tourism product

"Every morning in Africa, a gazelle wakes up. It knows it must run faster than the fastest lion or it will be killed. Every morning in Africa, a lion wakes up. It knows it must run faster than the slowest gazelle or starve to death. It doesn't matter if you are a lion or a gazelle, when the sun comes up, you had better be running."

Maurice Greene, American athlete (1974–)

The above quotation is apropos of the marketing of sustainable tourism in today's marketplace. Tourism in general, and sustainable tourism in particular, is a very competitive business. New marketing tools are becoming available faster than most destinations can keep up. Sustainable tourism destinations have a strong incentive to move quickly to preserve the best things the destination has to offer – from its scenic coastlines to its wildlife habitats, its historic districts, its local culture, folklore and heritage – in order to compete with other destinations. As noted earlier in this book, if a sustainable tourism destination is properly integrated as part of an overall local economic strategy, tourism can provide a local community with economic development, environmental sustainability and social benefits. A destination that maintains its sustainable tourism products will have a clear marketing advantage over its competitors.

Sustainable tourism policy to support marketing goals

The marketing of sustainable tourism products takes into account the need for a good policy, a powerful strategic plan and a well-managed destination. From a marketing standpoint, sustainable tourism might mean giving up current revenues from tourism, by limiting capacity, to ensure there will be demand and supply of the tourism product in the future. This idea of giving up profits in the short term to ensure that sustainability of the destination remains intact for the future often presents difficulties of acceptance by stakeholders. It means that the sustainable tourism destination must have a strong tourism policy that all the stakeholders agreed to at the beginning. One of the best examples of such a policy is that contained in the City of Cape Town Responsible Tourism Policy, which includes the following principles for a positive sustainable tourism destination:

- Makes positive contributions to the conservation of natural and cultural heritage embracing diversity.
- Minimizes negative economic, environmental and social impacts.
- Provides more enjoyable experiences for tourists through more meaningful connections with local people, and a greater understanding of local, cultural, social and environmental issues.
- Is culturally sensitive, encourages respect between tourists and hosts, and builds local pride and confidence.
- Generates greater economic benefits for local people and enhances the well-being of host communities.
- Provides accurate information about accessibility of facilities and infrastructure for people with disabilities (visual, communication, mobility) to customers.
- Involves local people in decisions that affect their lives and life chances.
- Improves working conditions and access to the industry.[1]

Sustainable tourism planning and marketing

Chapter 7 detailed the requirements for long-term strategic planning, which included the need for a vision, mission statement, goals, objectives, strategies, and tactics. Long-term planning is necessary in preparing marketing concepts for sustainable tourism properties before they develop a marketing plan. One of the keys to sustainable tourism is to prevent problems that occur when carrying capacity (the amount of tourism a destination can handle) is exceeded. In *Marketing for Hospitality and Tourism* (2014), Kotler, Bowen, and Makens note that

> From a marketing standpoint, sustainable tourism can mean giving up current revenues from tourism by limiting capacity to ensure there will be demand for tourism in the future . . . Sustainable tourism is a concept of tourism management that anticipates and prevents problems that occur when carrying capacity is exceeded. Carrying capacity can be determined by an environmental impact assessment (EIA). The EIA analysis fits well to complete during the planning process. The authors suggest that an EIA typically follows these steps:

1 Inventories the social, political, physical, and economic environment.
2 Projects trends.
3 Sets goals and objectives.
4 Examines alternatives to reach goals.
5 Selects preferred alternatives.
6 Develops implementation strategy.
7 Implements strategy.
8 Evaluates outcome.[2]

These eight steps are basic to the sustainable tourism planning process before a marketing strategy is developed. Morrison (2013) notes in his book *Marketing and Managing Tourism Destinations* that

> The Ministry of Jobs, Tourism and Innovation in British Columbia, Canada suggests that a destination's long-term plan for tourism should also include:
>
> - Vision, mission, objectives (goals) and strategies
> - Organizational structure
> - Budget and sources of funding
> - Target markets
> - Brand positioning
> - Priority product and destination development categories and strategies
> - Priority promotional strategies
> - Research and evaluation
> - Tactics and implementation plan.[3]

Once the policy is set and the planning is complete, positive destination management practices need to be identified before a marketing plan is prepared. Goeldner and Brent Ritchie (2012) note that management should review its competitiveness and sustainability:

> The Competitiveness of a destination refers to its ability to compete effectively and profitably in the tourism marketplace. Sustainability pertains to the ability of a destination to maintain the quality of its physical, social, cultural, and environmental resources while it competes in the marketplace. A major concern in this regard is to avoid the false appearance of economic profitability, a profitability that is derived from the subtle, often invisible (in the short run) depletion of the destination's *natural capital*. Conversely, sustainability may be viewed as encouraging "natural capital investment" – that is, refraining from current consumption in order to protect the environment, and the restoration of natural stocks (those that are renewable), thus ensuring the availability of such resources for future consumption.[4]

The ten "P's" of sustainable tourism marketing

The sustainable tourism agenda in the new millennium advances some profound challenges for the marketing of sustainable tourism. Customers of tourism products and services are demanding higher quality in their tourism experiences. They want greater variety and more flexibility in their travels. New approaches to the marketing of sustainable tourism must be examined and added to our repertoire of marketing tools.

The most common practices in the field of marketing are the time-honored four "P's" of marketing: *product, price, place,* and *promotion*. In *Tourism is Your Business: Marketing Management*, published by the Canadian Hotel and Restaurant Association, five more "P's" were included: *partnership, packaging, programming, positioning,* and *people*. Edgell (1999) added *planning* as one more "P" to complete "the ten 'P's' of sustainable tourism marketing" presented below (based on an earlier article).[5]

1 **Product**: The sustainable tourism product is quite different from most other products because it depends on attributes not usually associated with other kinds of travel and tourism products; such intangibles as the natural beauty, history, heritage and culture or other special features that can be difficult to define as an integral part of the product. In addition, the destination must position its tourism offerings in ways to compete with similar types of destinations.

2 **Price**: Pricing sustainable tourism products is a highly complex topic. There are so many special factors to consider, ranging from positioning of the product (defining such characteristics as nature, history, heritage and culture) to seasonal variations, and ascertaining the competition. A multitude of pricing options exist, including adjusting the price to fit the season, timing of the product offering, and responding to changes in climate.

3 **Place**: Since the tourism products, in general, and especially sustainable tourism products in particular, cannot be physically displayed for the customer to see or touch, the destination must market an "image" of the "place" where the product is located and find unique ways to market and sell the product.

4 **Promotion**: Promotion is one of the most important of the ten "P's" for sustainable tourism marketing. Like many other products, advertising, trade shows, public relations, and technology (websites, viral marketing, and so on) are important tools to entice interest by the potential customer. Possibly just as important is the branding of the product. The destination must find ways to present its sustainable tourism product through good branding or other techniques such that the customer can remember the product.

5 **Partnership**: Forming partnerships or strategic alliances with other entities can boost the marketing opportunities for sustainable tourism products. Another word for partnership is "coopetition" – a word developed by Edgell and Haenisch (1995) to explain how small rural communities could cooperate with their neighbors so that they could compete in the larger marketplace and obtain visitors from greater distances. Edgell and Haenisch (1995) combined the words *cooperation* and *competition* to form the word coopetition, and wrote the book *Coopetition: Global Tourism beyond the Millennium*.[6]

6 **Packaging**: Although tourism services related to a sustainable tourism destination are not physically packaged, the packaging of various services and activities at the site or in connection with the transportation to the destination is extremely important. It is difficult to package some aspects of sustainable tourism – for instance, scenery, history, heritage, and culture.

7 **Programming**: Programming special activities like hiking, fishing, bird watching and the like at a sustainable tourism destination will enhance and enrich the opportunities for the visitor. If the destination has targeted certain types of customers, then the programming should be geared to providing unique experiences for these visitors.

8 **Positioning**: Finding a special niche for the sustainable tourism product will increase the market share for the destination. The marketing team must plan where to position their tourism products for the greatest advantage in selected target markets.

9 **People**: The people who ultimately sell the sustainable tourism product are extremely important in the overall scheme of marketing. Word-of-mouth promotions by the staff on the property or site can be powerful. Staff members who understand distribution channels like online marketing and social media marketing tools like viral marketing and buzz marketing are essential in increasing market

share. The staff also play a critical role in delivering quality tourism services and products and creating an image of such quality in the minds of the potential customers.

10 **Planning**: Developing a strategic marketing plan is key to understanding how to best meet the needs of the sustainable tourism visitor. Once all is said and done, it is the annual strategic marketing plan that is the roadmap for increasing the number of visitors to a sustainable tourism site. Such planning depends heavily on good research, analysis, and pertinent information about the destination.

These ten "P's" of sustainable tourism marketing go a long way towards providing for the marketing of sustainable tourism products. They are not all-encompassing, but they do introduce different approaches for use in the marketing plan. It is the annual marketing plan that gives the direction for marketing sustainable tourism products. These "Ten P's for Sustainable Tourism Marketing" are essential for the marketing director to consider in the overall marketing program and as potential elements for the strategic marketing plan. They also demonstrate how complex the marketing director's job is if he/she is to be successful in increasing market share and in meeting the competition.

Strategic market planning for the sustainable tourism product

Strategic market planning for sustainable tourism products is a comprehensive systematic process with numerous steps to follow to achieve success (see Figure 8.1). Because of the uniqueness of the sustainable tourism market, the strategic plan needs to communicate and target the message of the product more carefully to the potential visitors. With the new technology and social media being developed, including smartphones, viral marketing, Facebook, Twitter, and other new equipment, the field of marketing sustainable tourism is changing rapidly. These changes in communication technology will challenge the way we market sustainable tourism in the future. To find out just which direction a destination needs to take regarding its sustainable tourism products requires extensive research and analysis. According to Edgell, Ruf, and Agarwal (1999), "Tourism marketing is research-based, analytic, goal-oriented, strategic, and directed."[7] Customer research is a critical piece of the analysis and involves learning the needs, likes and dislikes, perceptions, and satisfaction levels of tourists through qualitative and quantitative research methods. This step involves both primary and secondary research, as well as data mining, customer segmentation, and target market(s) identification.

With the crowded international tourism marketing landscape, maintaining and increasing competitiveness is crucial for successful sustainable tourism destinations. Maintaining competitiveness means keeping a positive market position relative to other destinations in terms of price and quality, profitability, sustainability, and meeting visitors' needs. Remaining competitive in the marketplace involves creating new supply and refreshing existing supply while still maintaining sustainability. The sustainable tourism destination should develop an action plan showing some of the steps that might be helpful for a marketing plan. In a marketing project that the author was involved in the schematic diagram shown as Figure 8.1 was first developed by all the stakeholders involved. Such a diagram helps to better explain to all involved in the planning process what the marketing framework is about for analyzing the destination's

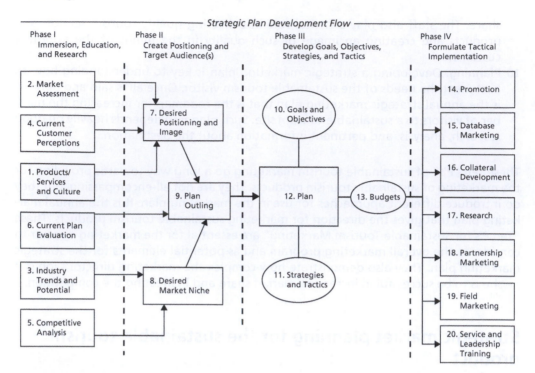

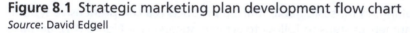

Figure 8.1 Strategic marketing plan development flow chart
Source: David Edgell

desire to target specific segments in the marketplace. While some of the steps utilized in this particular example are similar to a classic strategic tourism plan, the framework approach taken here has many differences as well. The flowchart in Figure 8.1 was not designed as an overall strategic tourism plan but was, instead, at the time, a strategic tourism marketing plan effort for a specific destination and for purposes of illustration. However, while it is not a model, it is a practical example of one destination's strategic marketing plan.

Target marketing (market segmentation) for sustainable tourism destinations

This section will introduce, in a limited way, target marketing with respect to sustainable tourism destinations. Target marketing is sometimes also referred to as "niche" marketing or "market segmentation." With respect to sustainable tourism destinations, it is recognized that not all such destinations can appeal to all travelers in the marketplace. Many destinations today are moving away from mass marketing and toward target marketing – identifying market segments, selecting one or more of them, and approaching each individually. As Kotler et al. note in *Marketing for Hospitality and Tourism* (2014), "Instead of scattering their marketing efforts (the 'shotgun' approach), firms are focusing on the buyers who have great interest in the values they create well (the 'rifle' approach)."[8] For example, if geotourists are a target market, advertising in geographic-oriented magazines would give comprehensive coverage of this market. This "rifle approach" is aimed at only the market of interest. Morrison (2013), in *Marketing and Managing Tourism Destinations*, notes that "Greater marketing success follows from pursuing specific groups of tourists (target markets) rather than trying to appeal to the mass market."[9] Goeldner and Brent Ritchie (2012) mention in *Tourism: Principles, Practices, Philosophies* "that few vacation destination areas are universally acceptable and desired . . . The target market is that segment of a total potential market to which the tourism attraction would be most salable."[10]

In a strategic marketing plan development approach, the marketing goals and objectives are represented by the sustainable tourism market targets to determine the numbers of tourists to be attracted to the destination. The target markets are set in the marketing plan and if the plan is implemented properly, the opportunities for reaching the goals and objectives are greatly improved. While the target markets may look into the future for the next five years, they should be updated each year. The target markets should be specifically aimed at visitors with the characteristics that match what is being offered at the destination. In some cases this may be very narrowly defined, such as, for example, attracting "bird watchers" to a very specific location. Goeldner and Brent Ritchie (2012) discuss some of the bases for market segmentation: geographic, demographic, socioeconomic, psychographic, behavior patterns, consumption patterns and consumer predispositions.[11] Morrison (2013) lists seven sets of segmentation criteria, as follows:

- *Trip purpose*: Defining the market segment by the visitor's main purpose for the trip, with four main divisions – business, meetings, conventions, and so on; pleasure, vacation or leisure; visiting friends or relatives; and personal.
- *Geography*: Describing markets by place of residence.
- *Socio-demographics*: Profiling tourists according to census-style characteristics such as age, education, occupation, income, household composition, and so on.
- *Psychographics*: Dividing up visitors by their psychological orientations, lifestyles or activities/interests/opinions.
- *Behavior*: Differentiating among groups of visitors based upon past purchasing and travel behaviors or future travel purchase intentions.
- *Product-related*: Using some aspect of the product to define the market segment, such as ski slopes.
- *Channel of distribution*: Applying different criteria, specific travel trade intermediaries are divided into sub-groups.[12]

Although Kotler et al. (2014) introduce some of the same kinds of market segmentations as described above, they approach target marketing a little differently. They include broad variables of segmentation such as geographic, demographic, psychographic and behavioral, with numerous sub-categories that address a wide range of characteristics. These authors also have a classification of visitor segments. Without going into the specific definitions of each (most are obvious), the categories are: "Organized mass tourists; Individual mass tourists; Explorers; Drifters; Visiting friends and relatives; Business travelers; Pleasure travel; Business and pleasure travelers; Tag-along visitors; Grief travel; Education and religious travel; and, Pass-through tourists."[13] While this discussion focused on target marketing or segmented markets, the point is that many of the categories described fit, in some form or another, with sustainable tourism destinations. A successful sustainable tourism destination must have a brand that speaks to the target markets and inspires travelers to choose a very special sustainable tourism destination.

Branding the tourism product

Branding the tourism product doesn't always get as much attention as it should in strategic marketing planning of the sustainable tourism product. Strategic planning, as was discussed in Chapter 7, is essential to managing and growing any brand, business or organization effectively. The brand must relate to the target market and communicate a specific message that can be clearly understood by the visitor. A good branding slogan with a simple and short memorable phrase can go a long way in attracting potential visitors. It's all about creating a difference of one destination from another. The process of branding must be carefully planned, developed and managed. Sometimes, in developing a brand campaign, a slogan that travelers can remember is helpful, such as, for example, "Fly the Friendly Skies" – a brand promotional tool used by United Airlines. Actually, United Airlines had dropped the slogan 20 years earlier and found they needed a slogan that focused on the customer, and decided that "Fly the Friendly Skies" was well known and had the right feel for their new efforts of being more friendly to customers. With the crowded international tourism marketing landscape, maintaining and increasing competitiveness is crucial for successful destinations, and having a good brand can make a big difference.

Certain countries, and some specific destinations, have established a special identity that sets them apart from their competitors. Canada, for example, with a brand of "Canada – keep exploring," markets and promotes its natural beauty, history, and heritage and is well known for having many sustainable tourism destinations. Canada promotes many outdoor tourism products, their Native American culture, their English/French heritage, and many other special characteristics related to sustainable tourism. Also many of Canada's national parks earn high marks for stewardship, such as, for example, Gwaii Haanas National Park Reserve and Haida Heritage Site, which helps authenticate the branding message.

Many destinations in Australia and New Zealand also get high marks for marketing sustainability. Costa Rica has created a strong brand as a world leader in ecotourism. Certainly Dominica, with its brand "Dominica – the nature island," promotes a clear sustainable tourism message. There are many other countries with unique sustainable tourism products that have developed special brands. Building a brand takes a long time in obtaining a constituency for the product and means that year in and year out the destination must produce a high-quality sustainable tourism product if the brand is to be believed. The destination must develop a brand that has emotional appeal to the potential visitor and then must deliver on a promised experience.

Marketing a sustainable tourism destination: Big Cedar Lodge

Big Cedar Lodge, a wilderness resort near Branson, Missouri that offers rustic outdoor activities, has developed an excellent marketing strategy. The lodge rests in the heart of the Ozark Mountain country, a region distinctively characterized by rugged remoteness, natural beauty, diverse features, and rich history. The resort respects the sanctity of nature and fosters most of the concepts expected of a sustainable tourism destination. Big Cedar Lodge overlooks a body of water, Table Rock Lake, with 43,000 acres of clear blue-green expanses along nearby heavily wooded areas. The lodge is a tribute to man's ability to blend built structures with a strong presence of their own into a natural setting.

The guiding philosophy behind the continued development and marketing of Big Cedar Lodge is the idea that the principal asset of the resort is its wilderness setting. It is important that the natural habitat, which is an integral part of Big Cedar Lodge, is not a victim of development, but rather a beneficiary. In this regard, the preservation of plants and wildlife is of primary concern. Every effort is made to accommodate animals relocated from cleared areas, utilities are located underground, the integrity of natural waterways is maintained, new plant life is introduced appropriately, and the buildings are designed to respect the environment and cultural heritage of the existing community.

Big Cedar Lodge, and the surrounding cabins, are a part of Bass Pro Shops, which was founded by John L. Morris, a businessman and a recognized international conservation leader. After he bought the property, Big Cedar Lodge, he purchased an additional 2,230 acres to expand the natural environmental area. Shortly thereafter he increased this effort to expand the natural environment by purchasing 10,000 acres to develop a private wilderness refuge, the Dogwood Canyon Nature Park. This park, 20 minutes' drive from Big Cedar Lodge, represents a special commitment to the preservation of nature. Archeologists unearthed Indian burials, artifacts, and ancient cliff-dwelling remains on the property. Mr. Morris reintroduced the buffalo and elk that once roamed the area. He also added a herd of Texas longhorn cattle. Furthermore, in 1997, Big Cedar Lodge added a "naturalist" Top of the Rock golf course. The golf course, like Big Cedar Lodge and Dogwood Canyon Nature Park, was built in wilderness splendor, preserving the pristine beauty of the area. The course's commitment to the environment has been recognized as an Audubon Signature Course by Audubon International.

Today, Big Cedar Lodge is a model of how a sustainable tourism destination can be profitably marketed by following the principles of sustainable tourism development. People want to visit the lodge and cabins in their pleasant natural surroundings, enjoy their many outdoor activities and learn about the rich heritage and history of the area. It is sustainable tourism at its finest. Big Cedar Lodge takes special advantage of marketing itself through the numerous Bass Pro Shops throughout the country, as well as producing an excellent website and utilizing the latest e-commerce tools.

The strategic sustainable tourism marketing plan

The strategic sustainable tourism marketing plan is what brings all the details of market planning together in one place. Whether the aim is a sustainable tourism destination or another type of destination, the process is very similar. Ideally the marketing plan should flow from a policy framework, include the vision, mission statement, goal(s), objective(s), strategies, and tactics used in strategic planning, and set the agenda for managing and implementing the marketing goals. It should be future-oriented, but updated each year and include the source of funding for the plan.

Kotler et al. (2014) note that

> Success in the marketplace is not guaranteed by understanding marketing concepts and strategies. Successful marketing requires planning and careful execution . . . A marketing plan serves several purposes within any hospitality [tourism] company:
>
> - Provides a road map for all marketing activities of the firm for the next year.
> - Ensures that marketing activities are in agreement with the corporate strategic plan.
> - Forces marketing managers to review and think through objectively all steps in the marketing process.
> - Assists in the budgeting process to match resources with marketing objectives.
> - Creates a process to monitor actual against expected result.[14]

In actuality the marketing plan usually relates to a five-year "strategic tourism plan" but is updated each year as the markets, products, and competition change.

A good example of a tourism strategic plan that relates to a marketing plan is that of the U.S. state of Tennessee. The *Tennessee Tourism Strategic Plan* has a good sustainable tourism ring to it, stating in the opening paragraph that

> Tennessee delivers an authentic American experience to every generation through its rich culture and heritage, iconic world-class attractions and incredible scenic beauty, all embodied by original music – spanning time and genre – born in Tennessee. Our state is treasured by its people and cherished by its guests. In Tennessee, lifetime memories are made.[15]

Case study 8: Sustainable tourism and Ambergris Caye, Belize

Introduction

The book *National and Regional Tourism Planning: Methodologies and Case Studies* (1994), developed for the World Tourism Organization (WTO) with the assistance of WTO consultant Edward Inskeep and published by Routledge, contains several case studies. One of them is titled "Master Plan for Ambergris Caye, Belize" and was developed in 1989.[16] It is an example of integrated planning for a sustainable tourism-based island community. Planning is directed toward preserving the community's distinctive informal character, while still allowing for the controlled growth of tourism.

Edgell (2004–2015) has researched and followed tourism activities on Ambergris Caye for the past twelve years. In this case study, the author follows the content in the master plan with comments on the master plan based on updated information, research and visits to the island. Ambergris Caye has some absolutely beautiful scenery.

Background

Belize was the site of several Maya city-states until their decline at the end of the first millennium CE. The British and Spanish disputed the region in the seventeenth and eighteenth centuries. It formerly became the colony of British Honduras in 1854. Territorial disputes between the United Kingdom and Guatemala delayed the independence of Belize until 1981. Guatemala refused to recognize the new nation until 1992 and the two nations are involved in an ongoing border dispute.

Belize is located in Central America, fronting onto the Caribbean Sea. It shares a boundary with Guatemala on the west and the Yucatan Peninsula of Mexico on the north. The population of about 347,389 (July 2015 estimate) is primarily English-speaking, with Spanish also widely used. The capital of Belize is Belmopan, and the largest community is Belize City, situated on the coast. Offshore, and part of Belize, is the Belize Barrier Reef, the second largest coral reef system in the world after the Great Barrier Reef in Australia. On this reef are several islands or cayes, of which the largest is Ambergris Caye in the north.

Belize has struggled to maintain its environment and has had to contend with considerable deforestation and water pollution from sewage. However, Belize is quite aware of its needs with respect to the environment and has signed numerous international environmental agreements, including the Biodiversity, Climate Change, Climate Change–Kyoto Protocol, Decertification, Endangered Species, Hazardous Wastes, Law of the Sea, Ozone Layer Protection, Ship Pollution Wetlands, and Whaling. These agreements have been signed but most have not yet been ratified.

Tourism has become the mainstay of the economy of Belize. International arrivals were 222,000 in 1990 and by 2014 had reached 321,217, according to the Caribbean Tourism Organization. Of this total, 199,321 of the tourists were from the U.S., 26,397 from Canada, 38,904 from Europe and the remaining 56,595 from the rest of the world. Tourism to Belize is still largely focused on beach and marine activities, although there has been a gradual increase in nature tourism, with ecotourists visiting the jungle areas that include visits to the ruins of Maya temples. Belize has more Maya ruins than any of the other countries with a Maya heritage: Mexico, Guatemala, Honduras, and El Salvador. These five countries have entered into a joint promotion of *La Ruta Maya* (The Maya Route), which links by road several of the Maya sites in Belize with Maya locations in the other four countries.

Ambergris Caye and San Pedro Town

Ambergris Caye is the largest island of Belize, located in the northeast of the country in the Caribbean Sea. Its name comes from "ambergris' – a wax-like substance that originates as a secretion in the intestine of the Sperm Whale and is found floating in tropical seas. Its main use is in the manufacture of perfumes, producing a fragrance much like musk. It is considered a natural aphrodisiac by some cultures.

(Continued)

Case study (continued)

Ambergris Caye, a beautiful tropical island that is part of the Belize Barrier Reef, is about 25 miles long and a mile wide. Actually, Ambergris Caye is not really an island but rather the end of the Yucatan Peninsula extending from Mexico. The narrow channel that separates Mexico and Belize was dug by the Maya to provide a trade route from the bay of Chetumal to the Caribbean. It is the principal tourism destination within Belize and is a popular location for tourists interested in scuba diving, snorkeling, fishing and other water- and beach-related activities. Of interest to some tourists is visiting an excavated site where a Maya community once lived in pre-Columbian times and whose residents made distinctive polished red ceramics.

When Madonna sang her song "La Isla Bonita" in 1987, about her dreams of San Pedro, she was referring to Ambergris Caye, which has since been nicknamed La Isla Bonita. San Pedro Town is the largest settlement, with a population of 10,000, and is the only town on Ambergris Caye. San Pedro has a small but modern airport serviced by Tropic Air and Maya Island Air and can be reached by plane from Belize City (in 20 minutes) as well as by numerous sea ferries. Tourism is by far the number-one industry in what was once a fishing village. It is not the over-crowded noisy tourism of Cancun or the skyscraping hotels of Waikiki since no building is higher than a tall coco palm, or three stories. Although there are a few vehicles in town, golf carts, bicycles and walking are the principal modes of trans-portation. Almost everyone is barefoot or in sandals and any type of clothing is acceptable, although shorts and tee-shirts are the predominant form of dress. Away from the center of town there is an abundance of flora and fauna and the waters are full of aquatic wildlife. The local population mingles well with the tourists and a familiar sign in town is "Welcome to San Pedro, where you won't be a stranger for long." In some respects San Pedro Town is a replica of the relaxed Caribbean lifestyle of 30 or 40 years ago, before international travel to the Caribbean became a fast, crowded, and noisy form of tourism.

The Ambergris Caye Master Plan for Development

After research and field surveys were completed in 1989 by the United Nations Development Program and the World Tourism Organization, in conjunction with the Belizean government, a report was issued: *Ambergris Caye Master Development and Zoning Plan – Belize*, which was a comprehensive study of Ambergris Caye. Tourism on Ambergris Caye was reviewed with respect to several factors – the national context; general characteristics; specific tourism statistics; tourist attrac-tions; and accommodations and other tourist facilities. Extensive field surveys were carried out and meetings held with government agencies, the private sector and community leaders. The key development objectives included:

- "Provide opportunities for the future natural expansion of tourism in keeping with the general character, environment and the unspoilt nature of the island.
- Generate jobs for the future natural increase of the resident population, as a minimum level of jobs needed.

- Maintain as far as possible the existing character of urban and rural environments.
- Protect sensitive ecologies from excessive human activity.
- Avoid levels of immigration that put an undue social strain on the community or its facilities.
- Plan for the ordered expansion of San Pedro town to meet existing and future population needs.
- Establish a context for the systematic planning and development of tourist accommodations and associated facilities.
- Inhibit speculation in and the high cost of land."[17]

The basic concepts of the plan have considerable value but are so general as to be difficult to measure. What was desired was planned growth that balanced social and economic costs with benefits for the community and for the country of Belize. Belize wants to take advantage of the economic opportunities, jobs, income, foreign currency and economic integration available through tourism to Ambergris Caye, but not destroy the environment and social infrastructure in the process. Ideally, from a visitor's viewpoint, Ambergris Caye is most often noted as a relaxed, small-scale tourism program which residents and visitors both appear to enjoy. Like many sustainable destinations, it has many positive points and some negatives. In a very unscientific manner there are some attributes of Ambergris Caye than can be measured from a sustainable tourism perspective. The present author, based on considerable expertise in sustainable tourism and numerous visits to Ambergris Caye, has made his own judgments about measuring sustainable tourism on Ambergris Caye.

Measuring sustainable tourism on Ambergris Caye

There is not a specific set of principles or practices to measure the sustainability of tourism on Ambergris Caye. In Chapter 1 of this book four components of sustainable tourism were introduced and explained: ecotourism, geotourism, cultural tourism, and responsible tourism. Certainly Ambergris Caye, as an island destination, meets some of the criteria for each one of these components. This recognition of sustainability is not a form of measurement but it does indicate that Ambergris Caye has the potential to be a noteworthy sustainable tourism destination. One set of criteria that could be used to measure sustainable tourism on Ambergris Caye is that used by National Geographic's Center for Sustainable Destinations.

It was mentioned in Chapter 3 of this book that in 2002 National Geographic's Center for Sustainable Destinations developed a set of measurement criteria for evaluating destinations throughout the world. The Center partnered with Leeds Metropolitan University in the United Kingdom to assemble a panel of 340 well-traveled experts (including this author) in a variety of fields related to sustainable tourism – ecology, sustainable tourism, geography, planning, travel writing and photography, historic preservation, cultural anthropology, archeology, and related disciplines – to survey destinations throughout the world with respect

(Continued)

Case study (continued)

to their sustainability. The ratings of the destinations (out of 100) were then published once a year in *National Geographic Traveler* magazine from 2004 to 2010. The group of "experts" were asked to rate each destination being surveyed based on the following six criteria:

1 Environmental and ecological quality.
2 Social and cultural integrity.
3 Condition of any historic building and archeological sites.
4 Aesthetic appeal.
5 Quality of tourism management.
6 The outlook for the future.

The March 2004 issue of *National Geographic Traveler*'s section on "115 Places Rated" noted that none of the 115 destinations rated 90 or above and none fell under 20. Under the title of "Reef and Islands of Belize" (not specifically mentioning Ambergris Caye, although it was definitely the "main" island included) the rating received was a middling score of 58. For each destination, symbols showed which factors most influenced the experts' judgments. The "symbols" for the rating of "Reef and Islands of Belize" suggested that more efforts needed to be made in the tourism management of the islands. That rating was 10 years ago. The question is what has happened in the last 10 years with respect to Ambergris Caye. As one of the "experts" on the *National Geographic* panel for six years, the present author is familiar with the criteria, and in 2015, based on his observations and personal visits to Ambergris Caye, attempted his own rating of the island based on the six *National Geographic* criteria:

1 *Environmental and ecological quality*. With some exceptions, Ambergris Caye would receive a rating of "good" when you compare it with other islands in the Caribbean region. Ambergris Caye, as home to the Belize Barrier Reef, would not attain a score as high as that for the Great Barrier Reef in Australia, but then Australia has one of the strongest sustainable tourism policies in the world. Belize could learn a great deal from studying the management techniques utilized for the Great Barrier Reef in Australia.
2 *Social and cultural integrity*. Ambergris Caye deserves a good score on this criterion. The citizens of Belize on Ambergris Caye are friendly and gracious hosts to the visitors. Ambergris Caye would almost be in the same category as Dominica and the Grenadines in the Caribbean, which received excellent ratings based on this criterion.
3 *Condition of any historic building and archeological sites*. While Ambergris Caye doesn't have many truly historic buildings, the island does a credible job with respect to the Maya archeological locations and findings on the island.
4 *Aesthetic appeal*. The beach areas on Ambergris Caye need attention with respect to cleanliness. There is too much debris along much of the occupied coastal areas. The rating in this category would be weak if it weren't for the fact that recently a number of local volunteers have stepped up and are attempting

to address this situation (this is a form of "voluntourism" where individuals volunteer on projects which give back to the community). The local community has stepped up and organized trash pickups and other activities to beautify the area.

5 *Quality of tourism management.* Ambergris Caye fails in this category, as was true in 2004. Trying to locate information with respect to sustainable tourism management plans or other information about sustainable tourism for Belize or Ambergris Caye is extremely difficult.

6 *The outlook for the future.* In 2004 the islands and reef of Belize received a weak rating in this regard. However, with respect to only Ambergris Caye and the Belize Barrier Reef, progress has taken place in the last few years. If Belize has a good sustainable tourism management plan for Ambergris Caye, the outlook for the future could be favorable. The government of Belize and the private sector are quite aware of the economic importance of Ambergris Caye and know they cannot afford to overlook the future sustainability of the island.

Ambergris Caye has the opportunity and potential to be a good sustainable tourism destination in the future. If it continues to meet the needs and interests of visitors today and fosters an image of a place to relax and enjoy the beauty of the island, then a positive future is in store. The most difficult aspect of many island destinations is to not risk destroying the very places that visitors love the most. Islands are worlds unto themselves – with their own traditions, ecosystems, cultures, landscapes and environments. It is up to the visitors, governments, private-sector and not-for-profit organizations to work together to maintain the economic, social, cultural, and environmental integrity of Ambergris Caye for future generations to enjoy.

Chapter summary

Marketing sustainable tourism may be the most difficult aspect for almost any destination. It may take special marketing tools to get the message across about a sustainable tourism destination. Many such destinations are small and have only limited marketing resources. However, there are also many bright spots, such as Costa Rica, where word-of-mouth marketing has been so effective in getting across the ecotourism message.

In terms of good sustainable tourism policy concepts to support a marketing program, the example of the *City of Cape Town Responsible Tourism Policy* is one of the best. In addition to setting the stage for the marketing of sustainable tourism it is useful to utilize the "environmental impact assessment" (EIA) approach noted in the book *Marketing for Hospitality and Tourism*. This approach helps define the carrying capacity for a destination.

It was the opinion of this author that in marketing sustainable tourism it may be necessary to consider more than the basic business school four "P's" of marketing: Product, Price, Place, and Promotion. The four "P's" are certainly very important, but adding Partnership, Packaging, Programming, Positioning, People, and Planning for sustainable tourism marketing seemed to make sense. There are other items that might be added, but the 10 listed in the chapter are a good starting point.

A diagram of an actual strategic marketing plan flow chart is included. Each project needs its own blueprint; however, the one shown in this chapter just happened to fit well for the project it was designed for. It was utilized by a specific destination for organizing a marketing campaign.

Alastair Morrison, in his book *Marketing and Managing Tourism Destinations*, lists seven sets of segmentation criteria. Most or all of these criteria should be considered in segmenting a market for sustainable tourism purposes. If the market segments are well understood, targeting the right markets will be much easier.

Branding a tourism product is exceedingly important. If the brand name is short, with a tag line or slogan that people can easily identify with or remember – like, for instance "Just Do It" – then marketing the product becomes a whole lot easier. United Airlines had a good, memorable tagline: "Fly the Friendly Skies." Then they dropped the tagline about 20 years ago. However, the airline finally figured out how valuable that tagline was and brought it back into use again.

One destination that has struggled with its sustainability is Ambergris Caye in Belize. This very beautiful island has so much to offer as a sustainable tourism destination. Currently it needs a strong sustainable tourism policy, a good strategic plan, and good management. It is one of those destinations to watch in terms of its future sustainability.

Chapter review questions

1   What is your opinion with regard to the "environmental impact assessment" steps for sustainable tourism destinations?
2   Had you heard of "The Ten 'P's' of Sustainable Tourism Marketing" before reading this chapter?
3   What is your opinion about strategic planning diagrams?
4   What do you know about market segmentation, or target marketing, or niche marketing?
5   In general, do you believe the tourism industry does a good job in branding their tourism products?
6   Are you familiar with the United Airlines "Fly the Friendly Skies" tagline?
7   Prior to reading this chapter did you know anything about "Big Cedar Lodge" and "Dogwood Canyon" as sustainable tourism destinations?
8   Were you aware that the second largest barrier reef in the world is in Belize?
9   Did you know that of the five countries with Maya ruins Belize has the most?
10   Had you ever heard of Ambergris Caye?

Notes

1   Cape Town, South Africa (2009) "Responsible Tourism Policy for the City of Cape Town," November 2009.
2   Kotler, P., Bowen, J., and Makens, J. (2014) *Marketing for Hospitality and Tourism* (6th edition), Upper Saddle River, New Jersey: Pearson Education, Inc, p. 511.
3   Morrison, A. (2013) *Marketing and Managing Tourism Destinations*, New York: Routledge, p. 45.

4 Goeldner, C. and Brent Ritchie, J. R. (2012) *Tourism: Principles, Practices, Philosophies* (12th edition), Hoboken, New Jersey: John Wiley & Sons, Inc., p. 329.
5 Edgell, Sr., D. L. (1999) "The 10 'P's' of Hospitality & Tourism Marketing," *Ingram's magazine*, Kansas City, Missouri, February 1999.
6 Edgell, Sr., D. L. and Haenisch, T. (1995) *Coopetition: Global Tourism beyond the millennium*, Kansas City, Missouri: International Publishing.
7 Edgell, Sr., D., Ruf, K., and Agarwal, A. (1999) "Strategic Marketing Planning for the Tourism Industry," *Journal of Travel & Tourism Marketing*, 8(3), 111–120.
8 Kotler et al. (2014), p. 209.
9 Morrison (2013), p. 71.
10 Goeldner and Brent Ritchie (2012), p. 434.
11 Ibid., p. 435.
12 Morrison (2013), p. 88.
13 Kotler et al. (2014), p. 527.
14 Kotler et al. (2014), p. 543.
15 The Tennessee Tourism Committee (2013) *Tennessee Tourism Strategic Plan*, August 2013.
16 Inskeep, E. (1994) "Master Plan for Ambergris Caye, Belize," in *National and Regional Planning: Methodologies and Case Studies*, World Tourism Organization Publication, London and New York: Routledge.
17 Ibid., pp. 217–218.

Chapter 9

Managing sustainable tourism in the new millennium

"Travel teaches us to tolerate the ideas and customs of societies we are unaccustomed to in our daily lives."

David L. Edgell, Sr., *The Worldly Travelers*

The key to sustainable tourism growth is to manage the destination effectively within a given natural, built, or cultural environment in order to provide benefits to the local population, to enrich the visit of the tourist, and to preserve the tourism products for future generations to enjoy. Natural areas must be preserved and flora and fauna protected. Customs and traditions must not be discarded and privacy and dignity must be maintained.[1]

As in times past, one of the strongest motivations for travel today is interest in the natural environment and in the heritage, arts, history, language, customs, and cultures of people locally and in other lands. The opportunity to observe how others live, think, and interact, socially and within their environment, exerts a powerful attraction for many visitors. Travelers may seek to experience a locale's arts, sculpture, architecture, celebrations and festivals, or cultural interests in food, drink, music, or other special activities of travel, tourism, and hospitality. The attraction may be a built environment with significant historic buildings or unique museums, or the natural environment, with a beautiful landscape, pleasant seashore, a magnificent mountain, a lovely forest, the flora and fauna of the area, or simply the social interactions of human beings in their local surroundings. It is this aspect of the environment – natural habitats, built structures, culture, heritage, history, and social interactions – that, with effective policies, sound planning, and good management, will sustain tourism into the future.[2] Edgell (2006) noted:

> Responsibly managed tourism enhances and enriches natural, heritage and culture values and embraces the need to preserve them so that the community and visitor

have a quality tourism experience now and in the future . . . Sustainable tourism, properly managed, can become a major vehicle for the realization of humankind's highest aspirations in the quest to achieve economic prosperity while maintaining social, cultural, and environmental integrity.[3]

Today, tourism is recognized as one of the fastest growing industries in the world. Within contemporary tourism, growth in sustainable tourism is moving to the forefront of interest in tourism policy, planning, and management. Such rapid changes, and concurrent development practices, have put particular pressure on sustainable tourism planning, policy and management. The key tenet with respect to sustainable tourism is to understand that tourism experiences may be positive, or in some circumstances negative, and to recognize when there is a need for strategic planning, policy guidance, and management practices to ensure that the continued growth of tourism will allow for balanced and positive tourism experiences. In effect, sustainable tourism is a part of an overall shift that recognizes that orderly economic growth, combined with concerns for the environment and quality-of-life social values, offers the best future for the tourism industry.[4] The management of all resources in such a way that economic and sociocultural concerns are fulfilled is an important aspect of the managing of sustainable tourism in the new millennium.

Sustainable tourism principles and practices

Managing sustainable tourism depends on forward-looking polices and sound management philosophies that include building a harmonious relationship among local communities, the private sector, and governments regarding developmental practices that protect the natural and built environments while being compatible with economic growth. As stated earlier in this book, sustainable tourism practices can be a viable means of providing a community or destination with an improved quality of life. There is only a limited environment to work with, and much of that environment is already under siege from the many different industrial, technological, and unplanned tourism developments underway. To preserve environmental resources, to have a positive impact on the social values of the community, and to add to the quality of life of local citizens worldwide, and, at the same time, to elicit favorable economic benefits for tourism, is indeed a major management challenge.

Pleasant climates, scenic wonders, beautiful coastlines and beaches, majestic mountains and valleys, rugged woods interspersed with rolling plains, magnificent natural vistas, and the rhythmic sounds of the sea are all components of the natural environmental attractions that cause large movements of travelers worldwide. Built structures, whether lodging, museums, art galleries or historic buildings, are a major part of the built tourism environment that attracts many tourists. Least understood, but an important part of sustainable tourism, is the enjoyment by certain visitors of the different cultures, traditions, and heritages within local communities.

It has been argued that sustainable tourism "incorporates two complementary tacks: the 'natural environment' (ecotourism, geotourism, adventure tourism, agritourism, and rural tourism) and the 'built environment' (history, heritage, culture, arts, and unique structures). There is an expected overlap in this confluence – both within the basic concept of sustainable tourism and a cross-over in the various elements of the definition."[5] Recent research "stresses that positive sustainable tourism development is dependent on futuristic policies and new management philosophies which seek to include a harmonious relationship among local communities, the private sector, not-for-profit organizations, academic institutions, and governments at all levels in developmental practices that protect natural, built, and cultural environments compatible with economic growth."[6]

A common misconception about sustainable tourism is that it is "consumed" by the visitor but then is instantaneously renewed. The key to renewable sustainable tourism is to balance the equation of conserving the natural, built, and social environments on the one hand, and adding economic value on the other, with a well-planned and well-managed sustainable tourism program. Simply put, sustainable tourism means achieving quality growth in a manner that does not deplete the natural and built environments and preserves the culture, history and heritage of the local community in order to improve the quality of life of the local citizens. Sustainable tourism references the natural surroundings plus the built environment, which consists of a montage of influences from history, heritage and culture to new and modern structures. In this same vein, Bricker, Black, and Cottrell, in *Sustainable Tourism & the Millennium Development Goals* (2013), note that "Sustainable tourism requires an intricate balance of social, environmental, and economic efforts to support positive change from a very local to a very global perspective."[7]

Defining sustainable tourism from a management perspective

There are many different definitions of sustainable tourism, depending on how the organization or author wants to define it. A few examples will suffice to get the general message of the variations defining sustainable tourism. The International Council on Monuments and Sites notes that "Sustainable tourism refers to a level of tourism activity that can be maintained over the long term because it results in a net benefit for the social, economic, natural and cultural environments of the area in which it takes place."[8] That definition certainly captures the essence of "sustainability" as far as tourism is concerned. The United Nations Environmental Program uses this definition of sustainable tourism: "Sustainability principles refer to the environmental, economic, and socio-cultural aspects of tourism development and a suitable balance must be established between these three dimensions to guarantee its long-term sustainability."[9] That also is a good definition. East Carolina University's Center for Tourism has this working definition of sustainable tourism: "Sustainable tourism contributes to a balanced and healthy economy by generating tourism-related jobs, revenues, and taxes while protecting and enhancing the destination's social, cultural, historical, natural, and built resources for the enjoyment and well-being of both residents and visitors."[10] This definition fulfills almost all the conceptual concerns with respect to sustainable tourism; however, the sustainable tourism definition produced by the World Tourism Organization (UNWTO) in conjunction with the United Nations Environmental Program (UNEP) is the one most widely accepted and quoted.

The UNWTO/UNEP publication *Making Tourism More Sustainable – A Guide for Policy Makers* (2005) notes at the beginning: "Most governments, international development agencies, trade associations, academic institutions and non-governmental organizations acknowledge that, without sustainability, there cannot be development that generates benefits to all stakeholders, solves serious and urgent problems such as extreme poverty, and preserves the precious natural and man-made resources on which prosperity is based." The UNWTO/UNEP "conceptual definition" of sustainable tourism is: "Sustainable tourism development guidelines and management practices are applicable to all forms of tourism in all types of destinations, including mass tourism and the various niche tourism segments. Sustainability principles refer to the environmental, economic, and socio-cultural aspects of tourism development, and a suitable balance must be established between these three dimensions to guarantee its long-term sustainability." The "niche tourism segments" include the four components of sustainable tourism mentioned in Chapter 1 of this book: ecotourism, geotourism, cultural tourism, and responsible tourism.

Thus, sustainable tourism should:

1   Make optimal use of environmental resources that constitute a key element in tourism development, maintaining essential ecological processes and helping to conserve natural heritage and biodiversity.
2   Respect the socio-cultural authenticity of host communities, conserve their built and living cultural heritage and traditional values, and contribute to inter-cultural understanding and tolerance.
3   Ensure viable, long-term economic operations, providing socioeconomic benefits to all stakeholders that are fairly distributed, including stable employment and income-earning opportunities and social services to host communities, and contributing to poverty alleviation.[11]

Special concepts in managing sustainable tourism

With orderly economic growth as part of the goal of sustainable tourism, the key is to balance the number of visitors with the *carrying capacity* of the given environment (whether natural or built) in a manner that allows for the greatest interaction and enjoyment with the least destruction. This must be accomplished in the milieu of interdependency of the tourism industry with many other industries locally and globally. There are many opinions on how this can be attained; however, there is general agreement that establishing a workable sustainable tourism policy, plan, and management strategy is a starting point. In its most straightforward definition, *carrying capacity* is simply being able to accommodate the largest number of people a destination can effectively and efficiently manage within its given environs and management capabilities. When too many people convene at a location and the area cannot handle this influx, the *carrying capacity* of the place is compromised, which, in turn, harms the environment of the destination, has a negative impact on its local citizenry, and the economy eventually declines. To meet this concern, effective planning steps must be taken in conjunction with overall management guidelines.[12]

The concept of sustainability as a resource development and management philosophy is permeating all levels of policy and practice relating to tourism, from local to global. More than ever, sustainable tourism management of the natural and physical environments must coexist with economic, sociocultural, health, safety and security objectives of localities and nations. Finding a balance between economic growth and protecting the natural and built resources is challenging governments and businesses alike to cooperate in sustainable tourism development. The additional broad challenge of cooperation among the members of the tourism community to support sustaining tourism is also coming to the fore. The concept of utilizing sustainable tourism development as an economic stimulator to achieve growth while maintaining the natural and built environment is receiving greater attention and emerging simultaneously from industry, government and academia.

Trends in sustainable tourism

Environmental responsibility and land planning are two very important factors in adopting and managing sustainable tourism practices, and it is through such accomplishments that a "sense and respect of place" can be achieved. One development that has proceeded in this vein is found at Bald Head Island (BHI), North Carolina in the United States. BHI is actually a village, located off the coast of Brunswick County, North Carolina, with a land mass of 4.3 square miles and a water mass of 1.5 square miles. The only access to BHI is by a catamaran ferry boat. There are 14 miles of pristine beaches. Transportation on BHI is limited to a tram system, electric carts, bikes, or walking. Only emergency construction and supply vehicles are allowed on the island's extensive network of mini-roadways, which wind through the protected maritime forests and dune fields. Bald Head Woods Coastal Reserve, a maritime forest located in the center of the island, Bald Head Island Natural Area, the estuarine waters next to Middle Island, and a significant parcel of land on the island's southeast point have been designated by the State of North Carolina as protected lands. Also overseeing the sustainability of the natural habitat of the barrier island are the Smith Island Land Trust and the Bald Head Island Conservancy, both originating locally. Four other areas are designated as Significant Natural Heritage Areas, as defined by the North Carolina Division of Parks and Recreation.

In a letter (February 20, 2015) to the Bureau of Ocean Energy Management regarding an energy issue with respect to BHI, the following management concepts on BHI were noted:

> Like many coastal communities, BHI is a combined residential community and popular tourist destination. Unlike most, however, BHI property owners not only make a financial investment in their homes, they also make an unspoken commitment to "live in harmony with nature." This community considers environmental stewardship to be the hallmark of its existence and places an extremely high value on the scenic and aesthetic value of their homes, of their beaches and of the island as a whole. The presence of pristine beaches, lush forests and a healthy, vibrant marsh are supported by strict regulations in these areas. They include minimal impact during development and the monitoring of lighting across the island. Because these principles are important to property owners, the Village of Bald Head Island is in the midst of applying for designation in the Audubon International's Sustainable Communities Program. This program helps communities take steps to ensure that they are healthy and vibrant places in which to live, work, and play – both today and tomorrow. That vision is founded in the three pillars of sustainability – a healthy local environment, quality of life for citizens and economic vitality.[13]

On the cultural side of sustainable tourism, the country of New Zealand is proactively highlighting its Maori culture while preserving and promoting Maori traditions and the environment. The Maori people live throughout New Zealand, and many are actively involved with keeping their culture and language alive. Maori culture is rich and varied, and includes traditional and contemporary arts such as weaving and carving. New Zealand's unique Maori culture is one of the main reasons why many visitors go to New Zealand. The Maori culture is second only to the beautiful landscapes of New Zealand as a key part of the management and marketing of tourism.

In addition to cultural, historic, heritage and arts sites, ecosystems – reefs, forests, arctic tundra, rivers, coasts, islands, plains, lakes and mountains (with all their varied flora and fauna) – are powerful attractions to holidaying travelers. Almost no other industry is as dependent on the quality of the environment as tourism. In taking all necessary steps to ensure the protection and enhancement of the natural and built environments through sustainable tourism management, we increase the carrying capacity of such valuable sites.

Choosing a sustainable tourism management approach or combination of approaches is a complex process, requiring the evaluation of economic, environmental, cultural, heritage and social factors. Whether working in the public or private arena, the objective must be to design the least intrusive form of intervention that results in efficient, effective and equitable decisions on tourism development and use of natural and built resources. Success depends on fostering practical, acceptable and profitable tourism destinations while preventing damage to the local environment. These choices become critical in determining long-term tourism sustainability. New innovative approaches to the precepts of sustainable tourism management are needed throughout the tourism industry.

Other issues impacting on the ability to manage sustainable tourism

A major management issue is preparing for the impact of climate change on sustainable tourism.

> Compelling evidence indicates that global climate has changed compared to the pre-industrial era – and that it is anticipated to continue to change over the twenty-first century and beyond . . . With its close connections to the environment and climate itself, tourism is considered to be a *highly climate-sensitive economic sector* similar to agriculture, insurance, energy, and transportation. The manifestations of climate change will be highly relevant for tourism destinations and tourists alike, requiring adaptation by all major tourism stakeholders.[14]

Especially vulnerable to the impact of climate change with respect to tourism are the world's coastal areas and islands. For example, already highly concerned with respect to impacts of climate change are such islands as the Republic of Kiribati, the Republic of the Maldives, the Republic of Fiji, the Federated States of Micronesia, the Republic of Palau, the Republic of Cape Verde, and the Republic of Seychelles. Tourism is a key industry for most of these islands. Some of the information in the following paragraph appeared earlier in this book, but in the opinion of the author climate change is such a critical issue with respect to sustainable tourism that the thoughts are worth repeating.

The tourism industry has identified climate change as a key issue that must be addressed in policy circles, strategic plans, and management practices. Weather conditions and the climate of a tourism place often dictate why people travel, where they travel, how they travel, and when they travel, and for how long visitors stay at the destination.

Generally visitors to beach areas are looking for sunshine and warm waters. Skiers and snowmobilers pray for good snowfalls. Sightseers and outdoor recreationists hope for clear weather and moderate temperatures. Many tourism businesses have failed simply because of weather conditions. "Until we adequately address the issue of climate change, tourism managers will have to develop a comprehensive destination policy, strategy, and management framework that adapts to and accommodates the reality of long-term . . . climate change."[15]

Coopetition and partnerships in the management of sustainable tourism

Coopetition, sometimes spelled *co-opetition*, is a portmanteau word that combines cooperation and competition. Ray Noorda, founder of the networking software company Novell, is credited as the first person to use the term in the business world. Coopetition occurs when companies, destinations, or other groups interact with partial congruence of interests to benefit all parties. Edgell and Haenisch were the first (1995) to introduce *coopetition* as an important means to explain "partnerships" or "strategic alliances" in the tourism industry in their book *Coopetition: Global Tourism beyond the Millennium*.[16] It has numerous applications in sustainable tourism as businesses compete to increase their profitability but at the same time cooperate with governments (at all levels) and non-profit entities to protect and preserve the environment. It is a proactive approach that fits the creative strategies needed in the area of sustainable tourism management. This "coopetition" relationship in the managing of sustainable tourism is illustrated as an example in Figure 9.1.

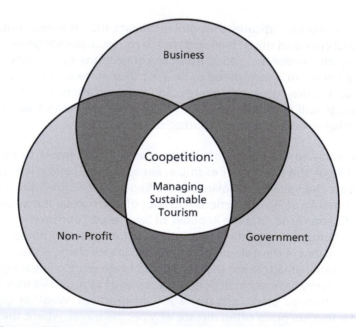

Figure 9.1 Coopetition strategy for managing sustainable tourism

Goeldner and Brent Ritchie (2012) include a major focus on *partnerships* in their book *Tourism: Principles, Practices, Philosophies* and noted that "This [partnership] highlights the high degree of interdependency among all destination stakeholders, as well as the need for alliances and working relationships that build cooperation – sometimes with competitors as well as colleagues. Edgell's concept of coopetition . . . captures the value of partnership in a unique way."[17]

The UNWTO also advocated the need for partnerships in the management of sustainable tourism: "Tourism being an extremely competitive industry requires a coordinated management approach based on collective vision and strong partnerships." In this respect, the UNWTO identified five benefits of following a professional destination management approach:

- Establishing a competitive edge
- Ensuring tourism sustainability
- Spreading the benefits of tourism
- Improving tourism yield
- Building a strong and vibrant brand identity[18]

These "five benefits" are essential management concepts for a sustainable tourism destination to be successful in today's competitive environment.

Tourist destinations that encompass sustainability in their tourism products add a special dimension to economic growth and quality-of-life benefits for the community. Unspoiled natural ecosystems, well-maintained historic sites, and cultural heritage events lead to satisfied visitors. The concern in some quarters of interest in sustainable tourism is whether governments, private-sector entities, local communities, not-for-profit organizations, and others are ready to accept, plan for, participate in, lobby for, and manage tourism programs that support sustainable tourism principles and practices. To ensure that sustainable tourism as an economic development strategy flourishes in the future, there must be efforts to inspire businesses and people to accept good practices, whether they choose to enhance the natural scenic beauty as it intermingles with flora and fauna or enrich the built environment. In that respect, a major challenge is to provide best practices to help guide the management process and provide future generations with the opportunity to enjoy and benefit from sustainable tourism.

Sustainable tourism strategies and guidelines

It is important to consider sustainable tourism strategies and guidelines as an area contemplates tourism development. It is important in the planning and development process to consider every aspect of sustainable tourism that might be considered by all the different stakeholders. Edgell (2006) developed a few basic guidelines to keep in mind:

1 The first requisites are to inventory, assess and seek to develop as many visitor attractions as possible with roots in the local community or which complement local activities. If properly developed and maintained, local cultural and heritage initiatives can improve the overall ambiance of the area and add to the quality of community life. At the same time, local pride and cleanliness of the area may evolve with good leadership as tourism moves throughout the community.

2 Development within each local community should strive to keep the uniqueness of the environment preserved. If there are period historical buildings, special natural resources or sensitive cultural traits available, a community should capitalize on such resources. This approach keeps the authenticity of the area intact, which enriches its value to the visitors and local people alike.

3 Any realistic guidelines for sustainable tourism development must include community involvement. Not only is it good public relations to canvass the local population in the tourism development process but it also will result in the ultimate success of the endeavor. The community then becomes an effective force in assisting in the implementation of the program.

4 A local community should seek to measure tourism development in the light of environmental and social costs and benefits to the area. Sustainable tourism should be viewed in terms of short-term and long-term values to the community. Intangible values such as "quality of life" should be added or included in the overall quantification of sustainable tourism development.

5 Marketing of sustainable tourism must utilize e-commerce tools as well as take advantage of "coopetition" (partnerships, strategic alliances). Most sustainable tourism destinations will rely heavily on "niche" (target) marketing or other forms of database marketing. An effective, regularly updated website will be important in the marketing mix for the local tourism products. Other marketing tools such as viral marketing, buzz marketing and others will need to be utilized.[19]

The key to sustainable tourism is to manage the destination within the given natural and/or built environment effectively to provide benefits to the local population, to enrich the visit of the tourist and to preserve the tourism products for future generations to enjoy. Natural areas must be preserved and flora and fauna protected. Customs and traditions must not be discarded, and privacy and dignity must be maintained. Ultimately, properly managed sustainable tourism will add far more value than its cost, in effort and planning, to the quality of life of local citizens, visitors, and tourism employees alike. That is the reason for today's urgent call to develop management strategies and guidelines to ensure that this phenomenon happens.

Recognizing sustainability warning signs

Sometimes a destination which is receiving large numbers of visitors and is heavily dependent on tourism does not see the signs of overdevelopment, or the potential negative impact on the sustainability of the area. Thus, tourism areas with large visitor numbers need to constantly monitor the impact of intense demand on the natural and built environment, and on their social and cultural values. The following are a few warning signs to watch for:

- Erosion of the natural environment as a result of overdevelopment or intensive use
- Pollution of ocean, lake, and river environments through boating, littering, or other tourism-related activities
- Visual, noise, and air pollution from overdevelopment (hotels blocking scenic views), tourism traffic (congestion), or unregulated air quality (smokestacks, emissions)

- Utility shortages caused by overuse or capacity limitation during peak visitation or according to time-of-day usage (particularly electricity, sewage, and water usage)
- Traffic congestion at airports, roadways, and tourist sites during high tourism season (or because of a lack of adequate facilities)
- Lack of public facilities (restrooms, trash disposal, parking)
- Inadequate attention to the safety and security needs of visitors
- Friction and resentment between the host community and tourists
- Social problems, including general crime, drug abuse, and prostitution
- Overcrowding and damage to national shrines, monuments, and historical structures[20]

It is important to look at how we prevent such problems, which already exist in many parts of the world, and provide for sustainable tourism development that avoids such issues.

Sustainable tourism practices as part of the management of sustainable tourism

In 2007 East Carolina University developed a Center for Sustainable Tourism, and in 2010 a Master of Science Degree in Sustainable Tourism. The center was created as an interdisciplinary and collaborative approach where complex sustainable tourism issues could be addressed. It became a place where concepts and ideas for sustainable tourism management principles and practices could be introduced, discussed and implemented. In 2012, the Center for Sustainable Tourism at East Carolina University, in conjunction with Miles Media, issued the document *Pledge to Travel Green*. It included "10 Ways to Care":

1 **Learn About Your Destination** – Enjoy a rewarding experience by learning more about the natural environment, culture and history that makes every destination unique.
2 **Don't Leave Your Good Habits at Home** – While traveling, continue to recycle, use water wisely, and turn off lights as you would at home.
3 **Be a Fuel-efficient Traveler** – Book direct flights, rent smaller cars and keep your own vehicle operating at maximum efficiency. Once in your destination, walk or bike where possible.
4 **Make Informed Decisions** – Seek out destinations or companies that engage in energy efficiency or recycling programs and that take actions to preserve their communities and the natural environment.
5 **Be a Good Guest** – Remember that you are a guest in your destination. Engage with locals but respect their privacy, traditions and local community.
6 **Support Locals** – As a visitor, the money you spend on your trip can help support the local artisans, farmers and business owners whose livelihood depends on tourism.
7 **Dispose of Your Waste Property** – Leave a beautiful place for others to enjoy – recycle where possible and always dispose of your waste with care.
8 **Protect Your Natural Surroundings** – Be mindful of the plants, animals and ecosystems that you impact. Avoid feeding wildlife, stay on designated trails and strictly follow all fire restrictions.

9 **Make Your Travel Zero Emissions** – As an additional step, consider the option of purchasing carbon credits to fully offset your travel's impact on climate change.

10 **Bring Your Experiences Home** – Continue practicing your sustainable habits at home and encourage friends and family to travel with the same care.

If these 10 suggestions are utilized in the management of sustainable tourism throughout the world, progress will have been made. Other organizations have produced similar principles and practices, all of which add to the protection of the natural and built environments. The need for good management of sustainable tourism is imperative if the future for positive tourism experiences is to take place.

Case study 9: The managerial and educational aspects in the context of sustainable tourism – Contentnea Creek

"He who does not travel does not know the value of men."

Moorish proverb

Introduction

This case study discusses the managerial and educational aspects of Contentnea Creek in North Carolina in the context of sustainable tourism. It is based on a journal article prepared in 2014 by the present author (Edgell, 2014).[21] The case study includes information discussed earlier in this book, but which needs to be revisited for the purposes of discussing the managerial and educational aspects in the context of sustainable tourism in the Contentnea Creek area. It is noted that, when strategically well planned and executed, tourism provides an economic stream both into and within a community or area, and an incentive to preserve the best features a community, or destination, has to offer, from its wildlife habitats to its historic districts, and from its scenery to its local culture and heritage. Responsibly managed ecotourism enhances, enriches, and embraces the need to preserve nature, heritage, and cultural values. In so doing, ecotourism adds value to the community such that the local citizens and visitors have a quality tourism experience (Edgell, 2006).[22] In addition, a well-designed ecotourism project strongly promotes conservation education and awareness of the natural environment, as well as the history, heritage, and culture at the targeted location. Properly integrated as part of an overall local economic strategy, tourism can provide economic development, environmental sustainability, social benefits, and an improved quality of life for the local citizens. A Contentnea Creek ecotourism project may have the potential to offer a unique opportunity to showcase the areas in and around the creek as potential ecotourism destinations.

This case study discusses the grass-roots development of Contentnea Creek as an ecotourism site in North Carolina (N.C.); it notes the N.C. counties (areas) through which the creek flows; it reviews the application of The International Ecotourism Society (TIES) principles; it analyzes benefits to the area; and it suggests policies to increase its future sustainability. The case study also addresses the need for greater education, appreciation, and awareness in developing, maintaining, and managing sustainable ecotourism type projects. The Contentnea Creek area offers itself as an excellent case study site. However, the author of this piece, a member of TIES and an active ecotourism practitioner, believes this case study offers important information for other possible ecotourism projects throughout the world.

Early history of the area: Heritage tourism

The Contentnea Creek area contains beautiful scenery and a magnificent natural environment, richness in flora and fauna, and a built environment steeped in history, heritage and culture. One of the early non-Indian explorers of the region was the naturalist, writer and surveyor John Lawson from England. On December 28, 1700 Lawson was commissioned by colonial authorities in the New World to explore the interior of the Carolina "country" (now North and South Carolina). Starting in Charleston (South Carolina) and traveling by canoe and on foot through the Carolina wilderness, he covered nearly 600 miles in 57 days, ending at the mouth of the Pamlico River (North Carolina). His travels took him near to parts of the Contentnea Creek area.

Lawson made detailed notes about all aspects of his travels, and in 1709 he returned to London to write a book about his explorations. The book (written in archaic English) was titled *A New Voyage to Carolina; Containing the Exact Description and Natural History of That Country: Together with the Present State Thereof. And a Journal of a Thousand Miles, Travel'd Thro' Several Nations of Indians. Giving a Particular Account of Their Customs, Manners, &c.* and was published in London in 1709. In essence, the book is a benchmark for what many members in the tourism industry today refer to as sustainable tourism: travel related to the natural and built environments. It is a primer for discussing sustainable travel. As he traveled, Lawson took careful note of the vegetation, wildlife and, in particular, the many Indian tribes he encountered. He also befriended a powerful Indian nation known as the Tuscarora. The book was an instant bestseller, and was translated into German and French.

John Lawson spent many years in what is now North Carolina and South Carolina, studying the flora and fauna, the native cultures, and the environment – and, through written accounts, passed this information along to his peers in England. By 1710 many new settlers from England, Germany, and Switzerland settled near Contentnea Creek, in an area dominated by the Tuscarora Indians. Initially relations between the Tuscarora Indians and the settlers were friendly, until the settlers began to take over land that was considered to belong to the Tuscarora Indians.

During the summer of 1711, Lawson and Christoph von Graffenried, a wealthy Swiss-German explorer and writer, took a trip up the Neuse River toward Contentnea Creek. Perhaps due to the proximity of the river and creek to the lands inhabited by the Tuscarora, Lawson and von Graffenried were seized by the natives and taken to Catechna Village, the Tuscarora town of Chief Hancock, on

(Continued)

Case study (continued)

Contentnea Creek. After questioning the prisoners, the Indians decided to set them free. But before they were to leave the following day, the captives were questioned again. The chief reproached Lawson and von Graffenried for wrongful acts committed against the Tuscarora. Lawson responded angrily to the Chief's charges. A general quarrel followed in which von Graffenried did not take part, but which resulted in both he and Lawson again being confined. At another council meeting, the Indians decided to execute Lawson and to free von Graffenried, who had promised presents in exchange for his freedom. The natives were very secretive about the manner of Lawson's death, and von Graffenried did not see it. Some said he was hanged and others said his throat was slit with a razor he carried with him. However, it was generally believed that the Indians "stuck him full of fine small pitch pine splinters and so set him gradually on fire" (Hudson, 1992).[23]

Ecotourism

Generally, ecotourism is considered as a subset of the larger term "sustainable tourism" – as are, for example, geotourism, pro-poor tourism, responsible tourism, and ethical tourism. The United Nations World Tourism Organization's concept of sustainable tourism is tourism that leads to the management of all resources in such a way that economic, social, and aesthetic needs can be fulfilled while maintaining cultural integrity, essential ecological processes, and biological diversity, and contributing to poverty alleviation. One of the first known successful practices of sustainable tourism (ecotourism) development took place in the Maho Bay Campground project on St. John, U.S. Virgin Islands, which won the 1978 Environmental Protection Award (Yale University, 1996).[24]

Over the past 30 years there have been many definitions of ecotourism. Possibly the first accepted definition of ecotourism was made in 1983 by the Mexican architect Héctor Ceballos-Lascuráin, who defined it as follows:

> That form of environmentally responsible tourism that involves travel and visitation to relatively undisturbed natural areas with the object of enjoying, admiring, and studying the nature (the scenery, wild plants and animals), as well as any cultural aspect (both past and present) found in these areas, through a process which promotes conservation, has a low impact on the environment and on culture and favors the active and socioeconomically beneficial involvement of local communities
>
> (Ceballos-Lascuráin, 1998)[25]

Most subsequent interpretations and definitions of ecotourism include most of the ingredients described in the above definition.

Most researchers today use the definition of ecotourism presented by The International Ecotourism Society (TIES). Ecotourism is defined by TIES (1990) as "responsible travel to natural areas that conserves the environment and improves the well-being of local people."[26] In addition, for this paper, the TIES "Principles of Ecotourism" are used as follows:

Ecotourism is about *uniting conservation, communities, and sustainable travel*. This means that those who implement and participate in ecotourism activities should utilize the following ecotourism principles:

- Minimize impact.
- Build environmental and cultural awareness and respect.
- Provide positive experiences for both visitors and hosts.
- Provide direct financial benefits for conservation.
- Provide financial benefits and empowerment for local people.
- Raise sensitivity to host countries' political, environmental, and social climate.

Another definition of ecotourism, used by the Nature Conservancy, is the definition articulated by the World Conservation Union (IUCN): "Environmentally responsible travel to natural areas, in order to enjoy and appreciate nature (and accompanying cultural features, both past and present) that promote conservation, have a low visitor impact and provide for beneficially active socioeconomic involvement of local peoples" (ICUN, 1993).[27]

Ecotourism focuses on socially responsible travel, appreciation of natural habitats, environmental sustainability, cultural appreciation, and the creation of economic opportunities for local communities. Ecotourists seek to enjoy and learn from the natural and built environments they visit in a responsible manner.

Possibly the most popular and most often quoted guidelines for ecotourism travel are those provided by the American Society of Travel Agents (ASTA), which are titled: "The Ten Commandments of Ecotourism":

1 Respect the frailty of the earth. Realize that unless all are willing to help in its preservation, unique and beautiful destinations may not be here for future generations to enjoy.
2 Leave only footprints. Take only photographs. No graffiti! No litter! Do not take away souvenirs from historical sites and natural areas.
3 To make your travels more meaningful, educate yourself about the geography, customs, manners and cultures of the regions you visit. Take time to listen to the people. Encourage local conservation efforts.
4 Respect the privacy and dignity of others. Inquire before photographing people.
5 Do not buy products made from endangered plants or animals, such as ivory, tortoiseshell, animal skins, and feathers.
6 Always follow designated trails. Do not disturb animals, plants or their natural habitats.
7 Learn about and support conservation-oriented programs and organizations working to preserve the environment.
8 Whenever possible, walk or use environmentally-sound methods of transportation. Encourage drivers of public vehicles to stop engines when parked.
9 Patronize those (hotels, airlines, resorts, cruise lines, tour operators and suppliers) who advance energy and environmental conservation; water and air quality; recycling; safe management of waste and toxic materials; noise

(Continued)

Case study (continued)

abatement, community involvement; and which provide experienced, well-trained staff dedicated to strong principles of conservation.

10   Encourage organizations to subscribe to environmental guidelines. ASTA urges organizations to adopt their own environmental codes to cover special sites and ecosystems.

Essentially, travel is a natural right of all people and is a crucial ingredient of world peace and understanding. With the right to travel comes responsibilities. ASTA, as noted above, encourages the growth of peaceful tourism and environmentally responsible travel (ASTA, 1991). It is this sense of ecotourism which will drive tourism development along the banks of Contentnea Creek. The ideal of keeping the creek basin pristine and the natural areas relatively undisturbed could make Contentnea Creek developments unique and sustainable. In addition, if developed and managed responsibly, ecotourism can provide much-needed revenues to the municipalities and counties along the creek.

Describing Contentnea Creek

Contentnea Creek is 100 miles in length; flows across five North Carolina counties – Wilson, Greene, Pitt, Lenoir, and Craven; includes six municipalities – Wilson, Stantonsburg, Snow Hill, Hookerton, Grifton, and Kinston; and may have the potential to be developed and promoted as an aquatic recreation and ecotourism initiative. The tourism development focus would likely need to highlight nature-based tourism, agritourism, and cultural heritage and history tourism (Edgell, 2008).[28]

Through East Carolina University's Center for Geographic Information Science, a complete digital data collection and mapping of Contentnea Creek was conducted in 2008. This mapping and analysis of Contentnea Creek demonstrated that with water quality improvements and conservation of the environment surrounding the creek the area would lend itself to being developed as a recreation site based on best practices of ecotourism principles (Mulcahy, 2008).[29]

An experiment along Contentnea Creek

An ecotourism development project that includes a few of the principles of ecotourism described in this article began to take place along Contentnea Creek in 2009, when the small rural community of Grifton (population of 2,659 in 2011), North Carolina, situated along the creek, received a Small Towns Economic Prosperity grant from the North Carolina Rural Economic Development Center. The town decided to utilize some of the grant money to focus on tourism as a development tool to improve their economic growth and cultural well-being. This approach was captured in an earlier article titled "Investigating Best Practices for Rural Tourism Development" (Edgell, 2011)[30] which indicated that many rural areas have a comparative advantage in tourism development because of their natural environment, authentic history and heritage, and cultural attributes of interest to potential visitors. Tourism is a highly viable economic development option because its implementation relies on an area's cultural, historic, ethnic, geographic, and natural uniqueness. Grifton is just one small example of the possibilities that being near Contentnea Creek offers for potential development. It personifies many such areas that exist throughout the world.

It just so happens that the Contentnea Creek area contains rich historic and cultural resources that if developed, and promoted, would bring many additional visitors to the area. The opportunity to study the Contentnea Creek area's history, culture, and ecology provides a special educational component for such an ecotourism project. In effect, Contentnea Creek provides a unique context for implementing educational programs in a living laboratory or "real life" setting. It is clear in today's world that most travelers are now looking for "greener" destinations and places where there is an emphasis on the history, heritage and culture of the local people.

The overriding goal for a potential Contentnea Creek Project would be to utilize tourism as a generator of economic development and to promote the area as an aquatic recreation and ecotourism initiative. To accomplish this goal will take considerable research, some technical assistance, involvement of interested community members, finding potential entrepreneurs, locating initial financial resources, developing a good strategic plan, and later building brand identification and presenting a marketing strategy for the area in question. The overall mission of the project is that it must seek to improve the quality of life for the local citizens, add economic development to the community, and provide a special experience for visitors interested in ecotourism type experiences.

By utilizing the example of Contentnea Creek as a potential ecotourism location, this case study noted research and best practices guidelines for the growth of ecotourism. It is an attempt to explain what ecotourism means and why it is such an important part of sustainable tourism. It also demonstrates that people want to experience nature; they want to know about responsible travel and to learn to appreciate cultures different from their own. The case study notes that ecotourism is distinguished by its emphasis on conservation, education, and benefits for the local community. It denotes the fact that increased tourism to sensitive natural areas without appropriate planning and management can threaten the integrity of ecosystems and local cultures. Finally, ecotourism can provide a viable economic development alternative for local communities. Ecotourism also presents educational benefits in that it reminds us that tourism involving visiting fragile, pristine, and relatively undisturbed areas that must be protected and conserved for future generations to enjoy.

Chapter summary

The following quotation, taken from the first edition of this book (Edgell, 2006), is a good summary for managing sustainable tourism in the new millennium:

> Responsibly managed tourism enhances and enriches natural, heritage and culture values and embraces the need to preserve them so that the community and visitor

have a quality tourism experience now and in the future . . . Sustainable tourism, properly managed can become a major vehicle for the realization of humankind's highest aspirations in the quest to achieve economic prosperity while maintaining social, cultural, and environmental integrity.

Managing sustainable tourism must always be looking toward the future. The tourism industry is constantly changing and the management of sustainable tourism must be able to adjust to new directions.

Bricker et al. note that "Sustainable tourism requires an intricate balance of social, environmental, and economic efforts to support positive change from a very local to a very global perspective." The key is to manage that "balance" and ensure that the local community has an improved quality of life as a result of tourism development. If the community is not gaining or sharing in the benefits of tourism development in their area, then tourism development should not happen.

The concern for *carrying capacity* is raised again in this chapter. It is just so important to make sure a tourism development project in an area can handle the influx of visitors without damaging the environment. The world is full of examples where the number of visitors has exceeded the *carrying capacity* and caused a decline of the natural and built environments. On the other hand, there are also some excellent examples of sustainable tourism destinations like Bald Head Island in North Carolina where most of the precepts for good sustainable tourism development are adhered to. The efforts by New Zealand to preserve the culture of its native population and include it as part of a sustainable tourism approach is another positive example.

Climate change and global warming are contemporary issues that will likely be with us for some time, and will have a major impact on the tourism industry. Island nations and coastlines from a tourism perspective will be the first to feel the brunt of global warming. Already many island destinations are preparing for the problems that will come with global warming.

Coopetition was mentioned earlier in the book. It is a good illustration of the need for "partnerships" representing businesses, governments, and non-profit organizations in order to manage sustainable tourism. Sustainable tourism management is dependent on all the stakeholders at all levels working together to avoid damaging the environments.

Many organizations have developed guidelines aimed at protecting the natural and built environment. In 2012 East Carolina University's Center for Sustainable Tourism developed the document *Pledge to Travel Green* with "10 Ways to Care." It has some good practices that most travelers can relate to.

The short case study regarding the possibilities for a sustainable tourism project along Contentnea Creek in North Carolina is just in the beginning thought process at this stage. It may be too difficult to develop at the present time but it may present an opportunity in the future. It does, however, provide an opportunity to think about what might be included in such a project.

Chapter review questions

1 In a few words, describe what you would say are the key factors for managing sustainable tourism.
2 What would you include in the "built environment" with respect to a tourism destination?

3 What would you include in "quality of life" for a local community that is developing a tourism destination?
4 What do you think of the description of Bald Head Island, North Carolina?
5 Where do you think the biggest problems with respect to climate change and global warming are likely to take place?
6 Do you understand the term "coopetition"?
7 What is your opinion of East Carolina University's *Pledge to Travel Green*?
8 What would you add to a proposed sustainable tourism project like Contentnea Creek?

Notes

1 Edgell, Sr., D. L. (2006) *Managing Sustainable Tourism: A Legacy for the Future*, New York: The Haworth Hospitality Press.
2 Edgell, Sr., D. L., Allen, M., Smith, G., and Swanson, J. (2008) *Tourism Policy and Planning: Yesterday, Today, and Tomorrow*, Oxford, United Kingdom: Butterworth-Heinemann, pp. 181–182.
3 Edgell (2006), p. 123.
4 Edgell, Sr., D. L. and Swanson, J. (2013) *Tourism Policy and Planning: Yesterday, Today, and Tomorrow* (2nd edition), New York: Routledge, pp. 147–148.
5 Edgell, Sr., D. L. (2005) "Sustainable Tourism as an Economic Development Strategy along Coastlines." A North Carolina Sea Grant Study, Greenville, North Carolina, September 30, 2005.
6 Edgell (2006), p. 4.
7 Bricker, K., Black, R., and Cottrell, S., eds. (2013) *Sustainable Tourism & the Millennium Development Goals: Effecting Positive Change*, Burlington, Massachusetts: Jones & Bartlett Learning, p. 3.
8 Retrieved from http://www.iztzg.hr/en/odrzivi_razvoj/sustainable_tourism/
9 United Nations Environmental Program document on sustainable tourism.
10 Retrieved from www.sustainabletourism.net.
11 World Tourism Organization and United Nations Environmental Program (2005) *Making Tourism More Sustainable – A Guide for Policy Makers*, Paris, France: UNEP/WTO, pp. 11–12.
12 Edgell and Swanson (2013), p. 150.
13 Bald Head Island, North Carolina Association letter (dated February 20, 2015) to the Bureau of Ocean Energy Management in Herndon, Virginia.
14 Goeldner, C. and Brent Ritchie, J. (2012) *Tourism: Principles, Practices, Philosophies* (12th edition), Hoboken, New Jersey: John Wiley & Sons, Inc., p. 382.
15 Ibid., p. 383.
16 Edgell, Sr., D. L. and Haenisch, R. (1995) *Coopetition: Global Tourism beyond the Millennium*, Kansas City, Missouri: International Policy Publishing.
17 Goeldner and Brent Ritchie (2012), p. 419.
18 World Tourism Organization (2012) "Destination Management & Quality Programme," Madrid, Spain.
19 Edgell (2006), pp. 93–94.
20 Ibid., pp. 104–105.
21 Edgell, Sr., D. L. (2014) "The Managerial and Educational Aspects of Developing and Sustaining Ecotourism in the Context of the Contentnea Creek Project in North Carolina," *Journal of Hospitality and Tourism*, 12(1), 33–42.

22 Edgell (2006).
23 Hudson, M. (1992) "Among the Tuscarora: The Strange and Mysterious Death of John Lawson, Gentleman, Explorer, and Writer," *North Carolina Literary Review*, 1, 62–82.
24 Malek-Zadeh, E., ed. (1996) *The Ecotourism Equation: Measuring the Impacts*, New Haven, Connecticut: Yale University.
25 Ceballos-Lascuráin, H. (1998) *Ecoturismo, Naturaleza Y Desarrollo Sostenible*, Mexico: Editorial Diana.
26 The International Ecotourism Society (1990) "What is Ecotourism?" Retrieved from http://www.ecotourism.org/what-is-ecotourism.
27 World Conservation Union (1993) "Ecotourism Defined."
28 Edgell, Sr., D. L. (2008) "Contentnea Creek: Its Richness, Its New Beginning: Strategic Overview of Tourism Opportunities," prepared for the North Carolina Clean Water Management Trust Fund.
29 Mulcahy, K. (2008) "Contentnea Creek: Digital Data Collection and Analysis of Neuse Sub Bain 2007 for Water Quality Improvements and Linear Park System," Center for Geographic Information Science, East Carolina University.
30 Edgell, Sr., D. L. (2011) "Investigating Best Practices for Rural Tourism Development," *Journal of Hospitality and Tourism*, 9(2), 1–15.

Chapter 10

Future world issues that will impact on managing sustainable tourism

"Coming events cast their shadows before."

Thomas Campbell

Worldwide tourism has grown enormously over the past 10 years and will likely continue to do so in the future. Research conducted by Oxford Economics (an arm of the Oxford University Business School) for the World Travel and Tourism Council, explained that travel and tourism is among the world's largest industries, at US$7.6 trillion in 2014, accounting for 9.8 percent of Global Development Product and generating more than 277 million jobs in 2014 (1 in 11 of the world's total jobs). By 2025, the number of global jobs in tourism is forecast to reach 356 million.[1]

The World Tourism Organization (UNWTO) reported that international tourist arrivals in 2014 grew by 4.7 percent over 2013, reaching 1.138 billion. International tourism receipts reached a new record of US$1.245 trillion. Data provided by the UNWTO over a period of years shows enormous growth trends for tourist arrivals and tourist expenditures. International tourist arrivals are forecast to reach 1.8 billion by 2030.[2] Of equal importance is the fact that tourism, as an export, is of critical importance to both industrialized and developing nations. As an economic factor, tourism is growing faster than the rest of the world economy in terms of export, output, value added, capital investment, and employment.

The opportunity that tourism offers for positive economic and social benefits for tomorrow will depend on the decisions being made today. One of the key issues today is understanding how to develop tourism in a sustainable manner without compromising the interests of future generations in the opportunity to enjoy the benefits of tourism. To accomplish the management of sustainable tourism for the future will require transforming some of our current thinking, practices and behavior in such a way as to not have negative interventions on the natural and built environment.

215

There are concerns with major issues like climate change that will impact on the tourism industry in ways that we don't yet understand. If global warming is indeed a likelihood in our future, certain destinations, especially island locations, will be unusually vulnerable. The U.S. National Oceanic and Atmospheric Administration's July 2015 international report confirms that 2014 was earth's warmest year on record and that "climate markers" continue to show a global warming trend. Noticeable increases in litter, rubbish, and fuel spillages in the oceans have been observed. The transportation sector's greenhouse gas emissions are a cause for concern. How are the issues to be dealt with now and in the future? What are some of the key leaders in the travel and tourism industry saying about sustainable tourism?

Leadership in the cause of sustainable tourism

In reviewing international tourism meetings and conferences over the recent past, some of the main topics discussed are questions and concerns about sustainable tourism. The leadership in the tourism industry is certainly aware of the issues with respect to sustainable tourism. A few of the global leaders in the travel and tourism industry were asked about their opinions with respect to sustainable tourism in July 2015. Here is what they had to say.

Dr. Taleb Rifai, Secretary-General, World Tourism Organization (UNWTO), noted:

> More than 1 billion tourists traveled to an international destination in 2014; by 2030, UNWTO expects this number to reach 1.8 billion. Tourism growth and sustainability are non-zero sum game; when properly and responsibly managed, tourism can contribute to the prosperity of communities around the world by fostering development and creating much needed jobs while championing the conservation of our natural and cultural heritage. As world leaders gather to adopt a new universal sustainable agenda, the tourism sector is committed to be part of the solution of a more equitable and sustainable future.[3]

David Scowsill, President and CEO, World Travel and Tourism Council (WTTC), said:

> For 25 years WTTC has worked to raise the status of our sector and to benchmark its contribution against others. We now know that our sector contributes almost 10 percent of world GDP and 1 in 11 of all jobs on the planet, but such economic importance must be accompanied by responsibility in the way we run our businesses and how we tell that story. As our sector continues to expand, we need to ensure that this growth is sustainable and inclusive. What are the challenges for the long-term sustainability of our industry? It is about looking after the environment, it is about engaging with the communities that host us, and yes it is about holistic business models which combine "people, planet and profit". According to our own data, our sector will create 26 million more jobs over the next 10 years. Without the right people to fill these jobs we will not be sustainable, not as businesses, not as destinations and not as guardians of our planet. Travel and Tourism is a dynamic industry, we are resilient, adaptable and growing. We need to harness this huge capacity to innovate to ensure that we are sustainable as we grow. Over the years WTTC has worked closely with Travel and Tourism industry leaders, represented by members, to ensure long-term considerations are prioritized over the short-term

gains. Tourism for Tomorrow served as a platform for collaboration with private sector, policymakers, NGOs and communities and proved vital in making all industry players understand the need for a more coordinated approach. Whilst doing so, WTTC has emphasized that sustainable growth in the Travel and Tourism industry is a joint responsibility to be addressed by all businesses who must be accountable, show leadership, invest and collaborate to make Tourism for Tomorrow a reality.[4]

Louis D'Amore, Founder and President of the International Institute for Peace through Tourism (IIPT), had this to say:

International Tourism Arrivals in 2014 reached 1.13 billion – an increase of 51 million in just one year and representing a continued growth from a mere 25 million international arrivals in 1950. A further growth to 1.8 billion by 2030 is projected. Achieving this growth sustainably will present a major challenge when viewed in the context of the World Wildlife Fund 2014 Living Planet Report, which states that we are currently using the regenerative capacity of 1.5 Earths to provide the ecological services we use in one year. Unless we change course we will require the equivalent of two planets by 2030. A further examination of humanity's ecological footprint suggests that the very areas where the greatest growth in international tourism arrivals are projected are the areas most seriously exceeding their ecological capacity. Those regions and countries of the world which currently have a surplus of ecological capacity are generally the world's least developed countries and developing countries. The sustainable development of tourism will depend on directing most tourism growth to these regions and countries of the world, where it has the potential to generate employment, reduce poverty, contribute to sustainable socioeconomic, community and cultural development and protect the natural and cultural heritage. It will also depend on travel and tourism being a leading economic sector in contributing to the U.N. 10-Year Framework of Programmes on Sustainable Consumption and Production Patterns.[5]

The nature of the future growth of tourism

There is every indication that tourism is expected to grow in the future. However, the nature of this growth may be quite different from that in the past. According to most global forecasts, and information from leaders in the tourism industry, the future of the tourism industry will be one of change, vibrancy and growth. Travelers are demanding high-quality tourism experiences, variety, and flexibility in their tourism products, along with a clean and healthy environment. Positive tourism policy, strategic planning, and good management will be the hallmarks crucial to economic prosperity, sustainability and quality-of-life opportunities for most communities, destinations and countries of the world. A key to the prospective growth of tourism will be to ensure that careful planning, effective policies, and innovative and creative management take place.

As has been noted earlier in this book, the future success of managing sustainable tourism depends on governments, businesses, and local communities working together and following the same roadmap and blueprint for tourism development. The record is clear that often political objectives override wider sustainability issues such as safeguarding an area of major scenic and wildlife value or of historic significance. As noted, all the partners in the tourism industry must come together to endorse and implement good management practices with respect to future sustainability of tourism destinations.

This chapter will introduce selected major tourism issues developed by the author that are important to an enduring tourism industry for the future. Each section identifies and briefly discusses an overarching tourism issue of important concern to the future. Each year, usually in the month of August, the author develops a list of the "Ten Important World Tourism Issues for . . . the following year." These emerging issues that will matter in the future will be identified towards the end of Chapter 10.

Managing sustainable tourism responsibly

Sustainable tourism is part of an overall shift recognizing that orderly economic growth, combined with concerns for the environment and quality-of-life social values, will be the driving force for long-term progress in tourism development. As mentioned earlier in this book, we have a limited environment to work with, and much of the environment is already under siege from the many different industrial, technological, and unplanned tourism developments underway. To preserve these environmental resources, to impact positively on the social values of the community, and to add to the quality of life of local citizens worldwide, and at the same time elicit favorable economic benefits for tourism, is indeed a challenge. Sustainable tourism policy, planning, and management support social goals important to tourism and provide guidelines to give us direction as we move ahead. Without such guidance we might find tourism's future considerably less beneficial than we had hoped.

Better measures to educate tourism enterprises, small communities, and the traveling population about sustainable tourism must be continued as world populations and international travel increase. Respect for a destination's social, cultural, historical, natural and built resources today will be our legacy for future generations to sustain. More destinations will include sustainable tourism principles in their strategic plans. New policies on sustainable tourism will emerge as more and more host communities and travelers see the advantage of saving pristine destinations so their children and grandchildren will be able to enjoy the same places they did.

Research and education with respect to sustainable tourism is increasing quite rapidly. In the last five years there have been more books, research, and articles produced related to sustainable tourism than were available in the previous 25 years. There are more university courses and graduate programs in sustainable tourism today than was true over the past 25 years. While European, and a few non-European, universities have had programs on sustainable tourism education for many years, it is still a relatively new topic in many countries. For example, the first Master of Science Degree in Sustainable Tourism in the United States was started in 2010 at East Carolina University. Shortly thereafter, many additional programs have become available. This trend is also true worldwide in many nations, as their tourism educational programs include a component on sustainable tourism. In addition, there are large numbers of meetings, conferences and general assemblies taking place each year with sustainable tourism on their agendas.

While this book has given considerable importance to sustainable tourism, the significance of managing the cultural, natural, and social impacts of tourism cannot be overemphasized. Enhancing an understanding among nations and promoting a culture of peace will result in improved sustainable tourism development. We now know that sustainable destination management within the tourism industry can augment global society's outlook and contribute to protection of tourism resources for future generations. We have realized that science, education, and business practices are critical partners in managing sustainable tourism.

Safety and security in tourism

Concern for the safety and security of world travelers remains an extremely important issue for the travel and tourism industry. Providing safety and security in the travel industry will continue to be a major challenge for tourism policy, planning, and management. In brief, safety and security are vital elements in the provision of quality tourism. A tourism destination that is not considered to be safe and secure is not going to survive very long.

The first item on many security agendas is the universal issue of the relationship of tourism to terrorism – a factor in both safety and security. Over the years there has been considerable discussion about safety and security with respect to terrorism. While terrorism has existed throughout history, the terrorist attacks in the United States on September 11, 2001, became a rallying cry in terms of a need for national and international tourism policies to counteract the impact of terrorism on the tourism industry. The aftermath of this tragic event seemed to galvanize many nations to act together to design policies to thwart the actions of potential terrorists. Even though the 2001 event was many years ago, for the older, seasoned traveler, going through the onerous inspection systems at airports is a continued reminder of just how important safety and security is for the travel and tourism industry. The process of travel has become increasingly more complicated, whether in terms of traveling by air, obtaining a passport or visa, or knowing which destinations are safe. It is important that we have good tourism policies that protect the traveler but at the same time are not so overbearingly restrictive and time-consuming as to deter travel.

There is much turbulence, strife, and unrest throughout the world that has created concerns for the tourism industry. Over the last few years, the world has been troubled with many different global political problems, wars, and other kinds of turmoil that detract from travel. But terrorism appears to continue to be the most important single issue when it comes to safety and security. For example, on August 1, 2015 the U.S. Department of State issued 38 "travel warnings," suggesting a traveler carefully consider whether to go to a country with a travel warning. The Department also issued 5 "travel alerts" related to short-term events in a country that a traveler might want to avoid, like, for example, a health alert. At many world events today there is heightened awareness of the vulnerability of the global tourism industry to various challenges, from crime and civil disorder to terrorism. Data and research on safety and security in the tourism industry clearly support the old adage, "When peace prevails, tourism flourishes" – but unfortunately the present state of the world is not very "peaceful."

Measures to support security, once seen as an encumbrance to travel (and for many travelers, particularly business travelers, they remain irritants) are now endured, if not welcomed and demanded, by many tourists. Accordingly, safety and security is now not only a requirement for transporting travelers, but also part of a destination's responsibility to assure the visitor of a safe and sound vacation experience. While the issue of terrorism permeates the agenda for security, perceived crime at a destination is also of concern for many visitors as well.

The impact of the world's economy on tourism

What is happening with respect to the world economic situation has a major impact on the future of global travel. The global economic recession that took place in many countries in 2008–2009 put a heavy strain on travel, and for the first time in many years (since the terrorist attacks in 2001, which had a negative impact on world tourism) international tourist arrivals declined. In 2010 and 2011, while the world economy was still somewhat in jeopardy, global tourism increased slightly. By 2012 many of the world economies had bounced back, and tourism has had healthy increases ever since. The economic outlook for 2015 and 2016 is world growth of slightly over 3 percent. The economies of China and India still appear sound, although they are growing at a slower pace. Russia, Brazil, and much of South America, in general, are struggling. The severity of the Greek economic crisis has impacted heavily in Europe. In spite of economic difficulties in certain places in the world, overall the travel industry will likely grow between 4 and 5 percent.

Another factor of importance to the growth of tourism is what is happening with respect to population growth. There are 7.3 billion people in the world as of August 1, 2015. The five countries with the largest populations, which make up half of the world's total population, are China, India, the United States, Brazil and Indonesia. The economic growth in China, India, the United States and Indonesia basically looks favorable for the next couple of years. That should have a positive impact on travel growth. The situation in Brazil may suggest a weak economy in 2015–2016 but that should not deter the growth in the travel market.

The world today is a global village, and often what happens in one region of the world can have repercussions for other regions. One of the current volatile regions is the Middle East. It appears conditions in that region will not likely improve a great deal in the next couple of years and that will impact heavily on the economy within and outside the region. Factors such as wars, civil strife, the cost of passports and visas, airline and other transportation costs, government regulations, political relationships within a country and the problems of climate change, poverty, world disasters as well as issues of congestion at some destinations will have to be seriously considered. On the other hand, special events such as the Olympics, FIFA World Cup, World Fairs and Expositions, improved transportation, and population increases will have a positive impact on tourism. But, in the long run, without improvements in the world economy, the global travel market will be in jeopardy. Since the world economies are deeply intertwined, world policymakers will need to work together to avoid a downward spiral in the world economy.

Climate change impacts on tourism

Climate change and its direct or potential impact on tourism is one of the most controversial issues within the tourism industry, and elsewhere in other industries as well. Today there is excellent information on climate change and global warming. Two U.S. agencies that conduct research, produce scientific studies and release enormous amounts of information on climate change, are the National Aeronautics and Space Administration (NASA) and the National Oceanic and Atmospheric Administration (NOAA). According to a NASA Global Climate Change Report, 97 percent of climate scientists agree that climate warming trends over the past century are very likely due to human activities, and most of the leading scientific organizations worldwide have issued public statements endorsing this position.

NOAA's "State of the Climate in 2014 Report" confirms that 2014 was earth's warmest year on record. In 2014, the most essential indicators of earth's changing climate continued to reflect trends of a warming planet, with several markers – such as rising land and ocean temperature, sea levels and greenhouse gases – setting new records. As a result, sea level rises are taking place, which particularly threaten island nations and island destinations. The global temperature rise will have numerous impacts on the tourism industry. Some of the colder-climate countries may see increases in tourism due to warmer climates. Warming oceans will melt Arctic sea ice, causing numerous changes throughout the world. Decreased snow cover could impact drastically on the ski industry.

The tourism industry must address the climate change impacts as a part of a broad international agenda. The tourism industry, in connection with the transportation and accommodation sectors, is a major source of greenhouse gas emissions. The critical challenge is to develop a dynamic tourism policy plan now in order to thwart the negative impacts of climate change. Such a plan must be developed in conjunction with scientific organizations, business leaders, and government policymakers. Climate change is an issue with destinations, with the traveling public, with individual businesses and with energy-related tourism supply companies. In effect, climate change is already impacting destinations such as mountain regions, coastal destinations and others. With recent meetings and conferences taking place regarding climate change and tourism, strategies are beginning to be developed, especially with respect to island nations.

The tourism industry is exposed to numerous direct and indirect impacts from climate change. Climate change may lead to changes in biodiversity, thus affecting sustainable tourism. If climate change causes additional storms or hurricanes, coastal areas and islands will be threatened with short- and long-term damage. It could exacerbate wave and storm surge effects that occur with hurricanes, which could damage major tourism destinations. It is already clear that islands will remain vulnerable to the trend toward climate change, with drastic consequences for the flora and fauna and the wildlife in the oceans and inlets.

Tourism policy and strategic planning

Tourism policy is defined in the book *Tourism Policy and Planning* as "a progressive course of actions, guidelines, directives, principles, and procedures set in an ethical framework that is issues-focused and best represents the intent of a community (or nation) to effectively meet its planning, development, product, service, marketing, and sustainability goals and objectives for the future growth of tourism."[6] Tourism policy and strategic planning should usually start at the local level so that the community where tourism is taking place or the location of the destination involved and the stakeholders all have an opportunity to express their views. However, in some situations it is better to enunciate a national tourism policy so that guidelines are available to follow at all levels of government and industry. The point is that tourism policy and planning may take different avenues of approach in ultimately providing improvement in the quality of life of the local citizenry.

The global tourism industry will face many different issues over the coming years, and quite certainly, tourism policy and strategic planning will drive many of the dynamics of tourism well into the future. We can expect to see a greater global focus on the tourism industry's potential for quality growth. In tandem, sustainable benefits of tourism for local communities will continue to grow in priority and importance. There will be greater efforts toward partnerships of the private and public sectors in facilitating tourism, in combination with poverty alleviation, developing policies to combat negative impacts on tourism, and supporting the economic, sociocultural and environmental contributions of tourism for the benefit of world citizens.

There are many global tourism issues on the horizon today and there will be more for tomorrow that will require innovative policies and creative planning. For example, how does the tourism industry respond to a global economic slowdown? Are there new approaches to making destinations more safe and secure? What can the tourism industry do to improve global socioeconomic conditions? Will the ups and downs of fuel prices continue to disrupt the transportation of visitors? What can the industry do to maintain and improve sustainable tourism progress? Will we have available crisis-management plans to deal with natural and man-made disasters? Where is the new technology going to take us? Which countries will be the newly emerging tourism destinations? What are we going to do about climate change? Where is the leadership for global, national, and local tourism policies going to come from in the future? These are just a few of the world tourism questions we must find answers to if tourism is to grow quantitatively and qualitatively in the future.

Developing new tourism projects, maintaining present destinations, and improving travel-related facilities and services require comprehensive policies and detailed strategic plans that combine local needs, market competitiveness, and tourism sustainability. Those destinations, localities, and nations that prepare good policies and implement detailed strategic plans will reap the benefits for sustaining their tourism products in the future. When the policies and plans are multi-focused to include all aspects of tourism, the opportunities for future success will be greatly enhanced. Tourism policy for the future must link the planning function and political goals for tourism into a concrete set of guidelines to give us direction as we move ahead.

Use of new technology in the tourism industry

Utilizing electronic commerce (e-commerce) tools in tourism is at the threshold in terms of its impact on the tourism industry. The increase in travelers using e-commerce tools in planning their travel and vacations has grown dramatically over the past five years. Many people now use smartphones for checking weather, destinations, directions, making reservations, and for other travel-related reasons during trips. A destination without a website is unheard of in today's tourism marketplace. True, some websites are much better than others but there is no longer an excuse for a poor website, even for small properties and destinations. Websites have put large and small players on equal footing in many cases. For example, a bed and breakfast property with a good website can compete with the chain hotels, such as Marriott and Hilton.

As internet access continues to increase in many nations, so will online travel revenues. The number of internet users around the world is estimated to be over 3.5 billion in 2015. In other words, about half of the world's population has access to the internet. There is every reason to believe that the use of the internet will continue to grow by large percentages in the future.

Although the interactions between business and consumer, or destination and visitor, are becoming less personal, tourism still exists in what might be called the relationship economy. While the internet gives the power to the consumer, strategic advantages will be gained by those organizations who can effectively utilize technology to create and nurture relationships. As slow-movers catch up to fast-movers, new technological advances must be constantly pursued in order for any advantage to be maintained. The future will include increased use of content customization based on visitor research. A proactive e-commerce strategy is crucial for tourism businesses to enjoy sustained success.

It is obvious that the use of e-commerce tools for tourism will continue to grow and occupy a high-level placement in tourism policy, planning, management, and marketing discussions, now and in the future. Several current e-commerce tools equip tourism well for what surely will be a high-tech future for the tourism industry. Information is a critical marketing tool for tourism destinations, and providing it to the traveler most effectively provides a strategic advantage. Tourism is an experience – a combination of products and services – and the multimedia attributes of e-commerce can be effectively applied to tourism in cutting-edge ways to increase destination attractiveness.

Since a large part of tourism is marketing, tourism promoters who are technically savvy in interactive marketing will outpace their less skilled competitors. E-commerce tools not only connect consumers with suppliers but also create bridges among consumers and provide avenues for information exchange. Arguably, word-of-mouth travel accounts may be the best form of advertising for tourism businesses (if the experience of the traveler has been positive); however, today, through technology, there are many more ways to get the word-of-mouth experience to more people (especially through social media such as Facebook). Included in some of the social media tools being utilized for marketing are weblogs, podcasts, smartphones, internet, Global Positioning System, Travelytics, Facebook, Twitter, Pinterest, and many more. While tourism is still an industry where people-to-people contacts are extremely important – such as the pleasant person at the check-in counter or the concierge proving valuable information about a good restaurant – like in other industries, technology is replacing some of the "people jobs." We have just begun to open the pages of the book on technology applications with respect to tourism that will emerge in the future.

Barriers and obstacles to travel

Barriers and obstacles to travel affect not only the consumer, but also businesses looking to expand their service offerings in foreign countries. Common impediments include visa and passport requirements, travel allowance restrictions, duty-free allowances, travel delays and inconveniences, use of credit cards in international travel, increasing travel costs, foreign currency exchange, and other barriers and obstacles. In the past, for example, the U.S. had one of the worst records in terms of long delays for international travelers to obtain a visa to come to the country. More recently, the U.S. has expanded its visa waiver program and has also expedited the visa process. In addition, many international visitors complain about the length of time waiting to be processed through the immigration checkpoint at the airport. The U.S., however, has improved its customs checking process.

When fuel prices increase, the impact wreaks havoc on the travel and tourism sector. All forms of transportation, be it the automobile, airlines or other transportation modes, are immediately affected. In recent years, the volatile nature of alternations of prices in transportation makes it difficult to develop policies to alleviate the negative impact on the tourism industry. The mercurial and erratic price changes will likely continue, creating a need for the travel industry to find better ways to adjust.

In addition, the recent trend of airlines imposing numerous travel fees on travelers is both confusing to, and inconsiderate of, the traveling public. Such airline policies are inconsistent with the concept of "hospitality" and create a negative image of the airline, and make for an uncomfortable decision for passengers. Many tourists complain that the worst part of their vacation is the negative treatment by airlines.

Transformative impact of tourism on global socioeconomic progress

Until recently, there has not been a concerted focus by the travel and tourism industry on socioeconomic issues. Businesspeople in the tourism industry, like those in most other industries, seek, as their major goal, to obtain an economic gain by developing and marketing their tourism products. Sometimes, in doing so, there may be little interest by businesses in the impact their efforts may have on conserving the environment or improving the quality of life of the local citizens. The good news is that it appears that more businesses today are interested in concerns for the social-economic advantages of the local population. This is certainly the implied message from the World Travel and Tourism Council, as noted earlier in this chapter.

In addition, the United Nations (UN) and the World Tourism Organization (UNWTO) have emphasized the issues related to socioeconomic progress resulting from tourism development, especially with respect to the less developed countries (LDCs). This included a discussion of the issue of poverty alleviation through tourism as a principal goal of the UN. The UN recognized early on that the tourism industry could play a major role in helping to reduce poverty, notably in the LDCs. The UN challenged its specialized agency, the UNWTO, to take up the cause of poverty alleviation. While the LDCs have less than 5 percent of the world tourism market share, their growth is taking place at a much higher rate than that of the developed countries. Many of the undeveloped parts of the world offer beautiful natural assets, unique and interesting culture, large quantities of flora and fauna, and enormous opportunities for adventure travel.

The first case study in this book was about the ecotourism project on the Kalinago Indian Territory in the Commonwealth of Dominica and discussed the potential opportunity that ecotourism may provide for improving the quality of life in the territory. If the project is successful, and other individuals in the territory take advantage of the opportunity that ecotourism development can have on their economy, a major step toward helping the disadvantaged peoples of the territory may take place. The project has the potential to create additional small tourism-related businesses and provide new opportunities for agricultural and fish markets that are critical to economic growth in the territory.

Impact of disasters, health issues, and political disruptions on travel and tourism

Global health issues, natural disasters, and political disruptions are extremely critical and worrisome issues with respect to their potential impact on tourism. Visitors to destinations around the world have become interested in knowing more about health issues in countries they might consider visiting. For example, the Ebola scare in 2014 impacted tourism in a number of countries. Travelers often get special immunization shots or adjust their travel itineraries to avoid areas where there may be malaria or other health concerns. Ironically, travelers can be the ones responsible for spreading epidemics of certain diseases. A good source of information for avoiding areas with health issues is the website of the World Health Organization.

Earthquakes, tsunamis, floods, hurricanes, storms, mudslides, and other disasters will continue into the future and will impact heavily on tourism. Such disasters not only pose great problems for destinations, but may also cause airline disruptions and many other types of problems. Potential visitors avoid areas that have been impacted by disasters, which in turn means tourism as an economic development tool is negated.

Political disruptions have created unpredictable conditions in many countries throughout the world. The Middle East is in turmoil; parts of Africa are in continuous conflict; and the situation in the Ukraine has not improved. Currently there are more than 35 conflicts of one kind or another taking place on the planet. Many travelers would like to visit some of the affected destinations if they were more safe, peaceful, and secure.

Increased travel by emerging nations

The economy of China, while not quite as robust as it was in 2013–2014, continues to be strong and the Chinese are continuing to be the main growth source for international travel. Another country with large numbers of outbound travelers is India. The Indian economy has been improving over the past few years and that has created an opportunity for many in the country to travel internationally. Another largely populated country, Indonesia, has seen positive growth in their economy, which has stimulated opportunities for greater international travel.

2016 and beyond

2015 was a good year for travel growth and 2016 should be even better. The tourism industry is alive and well, with dynamic growth, new destinations coming into the marketplace, and greater opportunities for sustainable tourism to increase. If the issues cited in this chapter are well understood, and global leaders in the tourism industry make good decisions, the future growth of tourism will have a positive impact on improving the quality of life for citizens throughout the world. At the end of this chapter, the "Ten Important World Tourism Issues for 2016" have been produced.[7]

Conclusion

This book has emphasized that one key to quality growth in the tourism industry is to promote good management of sustainable tourism. Stakeholders in all aspects of tourism development and management should safeguard the natural and built environment and cultural heritage with a view to achieving sustainable economic growth that meets the needs and aspirations of present and future generations. The book has advocated that local populations where tourism takes place should have the opportunity to share in the economic, social, and cultural benefits generated by visitors. The world is cognizant of both the differences and similarities of peoples and cultures as we plan for the future of tourism. It has been noted that greater peace in the world will lead to quality tourism growth and benefits for everyone.

Ten important world tourism issues for 2016

1 Importance of maintaining a destination's sustainability regarding social, cultural, natural and built resources
2 Concerns for safety and security remains an important issue for the travel and tourism industry
3 Impact on the travel and tourism industry resulting from the global economic slowdown
4 Responding to increased interest in potential long-term consequences of climate change impacts on tourism
5 Necessity for increased local/regional/national leadership in tourism policy and strategic planning
6 Educating users about optimizing the application of new technologies in the tourism industry
7 Resolving barriers to travel: visas, fuel price increases, airline/transportation fees, and airline delays
8 Understanding the transformative effect that travel and tourism has on global socioeconomic progress
9 Effect on travel and tourism from natural/human-induced disasters, health issues, and political disruptions
10 Changes in tourism demand resulting from increased travel by emerging nations

"A guest never forgets the host who had treated him kindly."

Homer, *The Odyssey*, 9th century BCE

Sources of information: university discussions, conferences and seminars, tourism documents, internet, survey information, industry data, books, articles, and publications, utilization of a modified Delphi approach to gather certain research information, and comments from interested colleagues, students, and others. See also Chapter 12, "Future World Tourism Policy Issues," in *Tourism Policy and Planning* (2nd edition – Edgell and Swanson, 2013); "The Essence of Understanding Issues that Portent the Future of Global Tourism" (David L. Edgell, in Volume 11, Number 2, 2013 of the *Journal of Hospitality and Tourism*); and Chapter 10, "Future World Issues that will Impact on Managing Sustainable Tourism" (draft manuscript of the second edition of *Managing Sustainable Tourism: A Legacy for the Future*, August 1, 2015).

Case study 10: Sustainable tourism as a development strategy along coastlines[8]

"Serene silences and howling winds, turquoise hues and infuriated white caps, soft sand and rounded pebbles, warmth and cold, recreation and meditation, pain and happiness have guided our steps toward the beach, this unique place where the ever-changing natural elements and human emotions singularly connect."

Foreword to *The Last Beach* (2014)

Sustainable tourism should be an integral part of an economic development strategy in coastal areas. Coastal sustainable tourism development is a connatural composite topic that is sometimes controversial and often misunderstood. The key to balancing the equation of conserving the natural, built, and social environments on the one hand and adding economic value on the other is a well-planned and well-managed sustainable tourism program. Good sustainable tourism planning and management techniques promote the effective and efficient use of resources, enrich the economy of the local community, and improve the quality of life of the local citizens.

Sustainable tourism is arguably the fastest growing segment of contemporary tourism today. Its best definition incorporates two complementary tacks: the "natural environment" (ecotourism, geotourism, adventure tourism, agritourism, and rural tourism) and the built environment (history, heritage, culture, arts, and unique structures). There is an expected overlap in this confluence – both within the basic concept of sustainable tourism and a crossover in the various elements of the definition. The current research in this book stresses that positive sustainable tourism development is dependent on futuristic policies, strategic planning and new management philosophies. Such dependency should include a harmonious relationship among local communities, the private sector, not-for-profit organizations, academic institutions, and governments at all levels in developmental practices that protect natural, built, and cultural environments compatible with economic growth. This approach has major overtones for most coastlines in the world.

To ensure that sustainable tourism is a part of coastal strategies for the future, there must be efforts to inspire businesses and people to accept good practices, whether they choose to enhance the natural scenic beauty as it intermingles with flora and fauna or enrich the built environment. In that respect, a major challenge is to provide best practices to help guide the management process and provide future generations with the opportunity to enjoy and benefit from sustainable tourism. Sustainable tourism as an economic development strategy is dependent on all stakeholders understanding that in the longer term the natural and built environments are what visitors desire as a part of their tourism experience.

(Continued)

Case study (continued)

Measures of sustainable tourism

Several important elements make the sustainable tourism experience unique along the world's coastlines. For example, the shorelines of the coasts may offer scenic natural beauty, flora and fauna, and/or rich cultural and heritage resources. The surrounding land and water resources may provide visitors with such activities as swimming, sunbathing, surfing, fishing, scuba diving, snorkeling, boating, whale and dolphin watching, bird viewing, climbing, painting, photography, visiting historic communities, and numerous other recreational opportunities. Accordingly, it is critical for sustainable tourism development along coastlines to include:

- Good coastal management practices
- Clean air and water, healthy ecosystems
- Maintenance of a safe and secure recreational environment
- Beach restoration, including beach nourishment
- Sound policies for wildlife and habitat conservation
- Protection of the built environment: history, heritage, and culture
- Educational/awareness programs that promote good sustainable tourism practices

While discussions and controversy may arise over how these attributes can best be accomplished, the businesses, developers, tourists, local communities, not-for-profit entities, and educational institutions all have a stake in working toward a healthy, clean, safe, and well-managed coastal environment. If it is not protected now, the stakeholders will lose in the future. It is imperative that strategies be developed to sustain productivity, the economy, and social values of coastal areas and communities. The seven standards, as noted above, can serve as complementary measures for appraising *sustainable tourism as a development strategy along coastlines*.

Research by Edgell (2005) on "Sustainable Tourism Prescriptions for Success"[9] identifies an additional dimension of sustainable tourism development. These prescriptions include:

- Introduce good sustainable tourism management techniques early on in the planning and development stages of the tourism project.
- Acknowledge and utilize innovative methods for promotion and marketing of sustainable tourism during the developmental stage of the tourism project.
- Promote quality economic growth, environmental integrity, and sociocultural aspects of sustainable tourism development throughout the project.
- Include sustainable tourism early warning indicators in the project to identify emerging problems to allow timely corrective action and future prevention.

Idealistically, these principles would occur in the development and planning stages of a destination; although, when interacting with "mature" destinations, the above prescriptions with modifications are still applicable.

Goals and objectives of sustainable tourism management including coastlines

The goal along coastlines is to promote orderly economic growth as part of the management of sustainable tourism. The need is to balance the numbers of visitors with the capacities of the given environments, both natural and built, in a way that allows for the greatest interaction with the least destruction and disruption. There are many differences of opinion on how this can best be accomplished; however, there is general agreement that establishing a workable sustainable tourism policy and management philosophy is a good starting point.

Today's sustainable tourism practices, particularly in marine areas, offer immeasurable new advantages for developing quality destinations. Expanding interest in wildlife viewing has given rise to a sizable range of wildlife tourism products, from whale and dolphin watching on the oceans to a vast array of wildlife viewing of birds, bears, otters, wolves, deer, wild horses, and other fauna along the waterways and coastlines. Beautiful scenery, unique geological structures, vibrant flora, endless beaches, and historic sites have inspired outdoor activity, especially with the use of new photography technology and digital cameras. In such natural areas, tourism opportunities have grown immensely in the past few years. When recreational activities are added to this mix, such as surfing, canoeing, fishing, diving, and boating, it is easy to see why water-related tourism is so popular. The increase in cultural awareness is rising as many travelers seek to experience firsthand the "flavor" of the locale. As stated earlier in this case study, the composition of sustainable tourism incorporates the natural environment and the built environment – the history, heritage, culture, arts, and structure of the place.

Coastal tourism is an important area for application of the principles and practices of sustainable tourism. Research (Miller et al., 2002) shows that tourism along coastlines is a fast-growing segment of the travel industry and offers numerous opportunities to discuss some of the issues of sustainable tourism. They note that "some coastal tourism is organized for a special purpose such as ecotourism, adventure tourism, scientific tourism, and dive tourism. As with other human endeavors in the coastal zone associated with development, tourism is viewed positively by some for the opportunities it creates, while others condemn coastal tourism for its unacceptable consequences."[10]

Today, tourism is recognized as one of the fastest growing industries in the world. This rapid growth and its concurrent development practices put particular pressure on coastal sustainable tourism management, planning, and policy. The concern with respect to sustainable tourism is to acknowledge that tourism experiences may be positive, or in some circumstances negative, resulting in the need for good management principles and practices. The coastlines are excellent laboratories to study "sustainable tourism as a development strategy" and to convince those engaged in activities related thereto to better understand the major role sustainable tourism management plays in the overall strategies to maintain these important resources for the future.

(Continued)

Case study (continued)

The impact of tourism on coastlines

Orrin Pilkey and J. Andrew G. Cooper, in their book *The Last Beach* (2014), cite many of the mistakes made by developers along coastlines which compromise or destroy beach areas throughout the world. The book also notes the negative impact on beach properties from the potential impact of climate change and global warming. However, they do say,

> That is not to say that beach tourism is necessarily always damaging. Low-impact beach tourism exists; however, this tends to be the exception rather than the rule. There are cases where the influence of foreign visitors has been important in preventing damage. International surfing groups, such as Surfriders, and various conservation organizations have successfully campaigned to preserve some beaches from poorly planned development.[11]

Stanley Riggs et al. (2011), in the book *The Battle for North Carolina's Coast: Evolutionary History, Present Crisis and Vision for the Future*, note how poorly managed the coastline of the Outer Banks in North Carolina is. Riggs et al. note the recent trend of overbuilding and unlimited high-rise hotels and condominiums as having long-term detrimental impacts on the shorelines. Their point is that the development and management of a sustainable barrier island/estuarine system with a viable coastal economy that can function and survive means making changes in principles and practices currently taking place along the coast. Riggs et al. say that "to preserve the barrier island-based tourist and recreation economy, as well as the natural resources on which it is based, it is imperative that we start to work on viable, long-term management plans that include selective downsizing and adaptation to a dynamic and rapidly changing natural system."[12]

Stephen Page, writing in *Tourism Management* (2015), included an interesting study from a book written by Dr. Joanne Connell, of the Exeter University Business School, about "Repositioning a Resort to Address Mass Tourism Demand – Calvia, Mallorca." The study noted the negative aspects of coastal tourism in the Municipality of Calvia, beginning in the 1960s. Lack of planning early on and problems of managing an "ageing" tourist destination left the community deteriorating and in dire straits. However, the community leaders came together "to develop a philosophy, strategy and programme of actions for the tourism sector based on sustainable development." The objectives to improve sustainability of the destination included: limit growth, preserve nature, improve water and other infrastructure, encourage cycling, walking and public transport, improve quality of tourism, rehabilitate urban areas, conserve heritage, and improve quality of life. A significant spin-off to the Calvia initiative is the transferability of the concept of environmental management and improvement to similar resorts.[13]

The message from these three examples is clear. To avoid coastal erosion, aesthetic pollution, water pollution, air pollution, noise pollution, over-use of resources, poor development, and potential problems from climate change and global warming, it is necessary to have positive tourism policies, strategic planning and good management. Negative impacts and conflicts are most often due to ignorance of coastline environments and a lack of planning. It was also noted in the examples that sustainable tourism along coastline communities should also emphasize the benefit of nature tourism, cultural and heritage tourism, and responsible tourism.

Cultural tourism and the coastlines

When sustainable tourism along coastlines is discussed, often the culture of the area as a visitor attraction is ignored. The tendency is to emphasize all the water-related activities, thereby placing very little emphases on the cultural resources of the area. Yet most visitors to beach areas are looking for a variety of tourism products, and often the history, heritage, and culture of a seacoast offers unique opportunities for enjoying a wide range of experiences.

Recognized as a distinct subset within sustainable tourism, cultural tourism is one of the most important and fastest growing tourism trends. Also known as "cultural heritage" tourism, it is highlighted in this case study because its impact is often overlooked in research on coastal destinations. This type of tourism has been ascribed a variety of definitions. Culture tourism may be defined by its destination – such as museums, theaters, art galleries, historical sites, architectural treasures, and heritage or ethnic events. Alternatively, cultural tourism may be defined by the motivation of cultural tourists to seek an authentic experience with a unique heritage, social fabric, or place. Nonetheless, the foundation for cultural tourism is a community's cultural and heritage assets, which include built environments (museums, theaters, and art galleries, for example), historical sites, and natural environments, as well as cultural practices and collections.

All of these options for cultural tourism exist along coastlines throughout almost every country of the world. Unlimited numbers of communities along coastlines have multiple opportunities to enhance cultural tourism products or develop new ones. The predominance of festivals, heritage gatherings, historical re-enactments and plays, the variety of museums, and local events indigenous to the destination are a common denominator in many communities of the world. Visitors can partake in a vast array of experiences that afford them the opportunity to embrace the cultural ethnicity of a locale. Many destinations have made significant progress in this respect, but much more needs to be accomplished and implemented to ensure successful development through sustainable tourism along the coastlines.

Many global economies have been transitioning from their traditional developmental means to a more creative economy as international tourism is on the rise. Sustainable tourism factors are well into this movement and the recognition of cultural tourism as a means of diversifying coastal tourism is acting upon this trend. In addition to the economic opportunities, cultural tourism can produce social and community development benefits. These include conveying a sense of local heritage and cultural pride along a coastal region. While the trend toward more interest in cultural tourism is general in its application, certainly it is applicable to the world's coastlines. The tourist today is very active, with respect to both recreational activities along the coasts and interests in the cultural heritage

(Continued)

> ## Case study (continued)
>
> of the area. Every indication is that this phenomenon will continue into the future and will offer coastal communities many new alternatives beyond those traditional amenities along the coasts. One popular destination, the Spanish island of Mallorca, is expanding its tourism image away from the traditional summer holiday mass market towards the development of additional market niches through promoting the cultural attractions of numerous art galleries and museums, and off-season walking and hiking tours in the many beautiful villages and into the mountains. Sustainable tourism as a development strategy along coastlines should embrace the need to preserve nature, heritage, and cultural values, so that the community and visitor have a quality tourism experience.

Chapter summary

There are many issues that will impact on the future of managing sustainable tourism and the 10 which are included in this chapter represent a good sample of a few that have recently been identified. The tourism industry is growing so fast that many sustainable tourism advocates are concerned with the impact such growth will have on the natural and built environments. It is helpful to highlight the issues that need immediate attention.

This book includes quotations provided to the author from three international leaders of the tourism industry who understand the concerns for managing tourism based on sustainable tourism concepts. They represent organizations that have worked hard to get the message of sustainable tourism to their constituents. As individuals they can do little with respect to specific tourism projects, but as leaders they can provide the moral suasion to inspire the general tourism industry to be aware of and understand the need for good principles and practices in managing sustainable tourism.

Managing sustainable tourism is the first issue considered in that this issue permeates and relates to most of the other issues. Safety and security has been a major issue for many years and will continue to be of major importance. The world's economic situation will have a great deal to do with the future growth of tourism. That was particularly noted in the great recession of 2008–2009. Climate change and global warming are two subjects that are talked about frequently with respect to almost all industries but are of great concern to the tourism industry. It has been acknowledged that if the tourism industry does not have strong tourism policies and good planning the future may not be as favorable as we have hoped for. Few industries have been impacted more by new technology than the tourism industry. About the only guarantee is that more is coming. Barriers and obstacles to travel have been with us for a long time and must be constantly acted upon if tourism is to grow. If the tourism industry could somehow be transformed such that the less developed economies throughout the world would gain substantially from tourism development, we would see a decrease in poverty and an increase in the general quality of life of the world's citizens. The tourism industry will see many natural disasters, man-made disasters, health concerns and political disruptions in the future. The tourism industry must be prepared for these crises by disseminating critical information to the traveling public. Many of the "emerging nations" are contributing to the growth of tourism, and hopefully this trend will continue.

The case study with respect to sustainable tourism along coastlines reviews some of the principles and practices of sustainable tourism discussed throughout this book. Three books are mentioned that address sustainable problems that will impact on the tourism industry in the future. The good news is that even such crowded coasts as those of Mallorca can seek to improve efforts toward good sustainable tourism management.

Chapter review questions

1 How best do you think the tourism industry should manage the growth of tourism to avoid damaging the natural and built environments?
2 Do you think the current global leadership is moving in the right direction?
3 Review the "Ten Important World Tourism Issues for 2016" to see if you agree or disagree with them.
4 Based on your own experiences in visiting a coastal destination, what thoughts do you have to improve sustainable tourism along the coastlines?
5 When you visit a beach destination do you also seek out opportunities to appreciate nature and cultural activities?

Notes

1 World Tourism Organization (UNWTO) (2015) press release, April 15, 2015.
2 World Travel and Tourism Council (2015) "Economic Impact Analysis." www.wttc.org.
3 Edgell, Sr., D. L. (2015) Retrieved from email message sent from UNWTO to David Edgell on July 16, 2015.
4 Edgell, Sr., D. L. (2015) Retrieved from email message sent from WTTC to David Edgell on July 1, 2015.
5 Edgell, Sr., D. L. (2015) Retrieved from email message sent from IIPT to David Edgell on July 19, 2015.
6 Edgell, Sr., D. L. and Swanson, J. R. (2013) *Tourism Policy and Planning: Yesterday, Today, and Tomorrow* (2nd edition), London: Routledge, p. 10.
7 Edgell, Sr., D. L. (2015) "Ten Important World Tourism Issues for 2016," August 1, 2015.
8 Edgell, Sr., D. L. (2005), Case Study 10 based on the document "Sustainable Tourism as an Economic Development Strategy along Coastlines" submitted for The Gabriel Escarrer International Award for Tourism Studies, September 22, 2005.
9 The "Sustainable Tourism Prescriptions for Success" emanated from research conducted by David L. Edgell, Sr., first introduced in a study conducted for a North Carolina Sea Grant program, under the auspices of the National Oceanic and Atmospheric Administration, 2005.
10 Miller, M., Auyong, J., and Hadley, N. (2002) "Sustainable Coastal Tourism: Challenges for Management, Planning, and Education," September 16, 2002, retrieved from http://nsgl.gso.uri.edu/washu/washuw99003/1-Introduction_Miller.pdf.
11 Pilkey, O. and Cooper, J. A. G. (2014) *The Last Beach*, Durham, North Carolina: Duke University Press, p. 166.
12 Retrieved from http://www.businessnc.com/articles/2011-09/betting-on-a-shore-thing-category/?back=articles, August 3, 2015.
13 Page, S. (2015) *Tourism Management* (5th edition), London: Routledge, pp. 98–100.

Index

Abdullah II, King of Jordan 146
adventure tourism 27, 29, 62, 124, 171, 197, 224
Africa 34, 35; *see also* South Africa
agricultural industry: America and 118–19, 124; environment and 63
agritourism 117–18; Hawaii and 118; Napa Valley, California and 118, 124; Tuscany and 118; wine tours 118
airlines: branding and 186, 194; negative treatment by 224; travel fees and 224; *see also* aviation
Alaska: Arctic wolves, protection of 45–6; polar bears, need to preserve 46
Alligator River National Wildlife Refuge 86
alphabet, Phoenician 35
ambergris 189
Ambergris Caye, Belize 188–93; beach areas 193; history of Belize 189; La Isla Bonita 190; location 189; master plan for development 190–1; Mayan heritage and 190, 192; measuring sustainable tourism on 191–3; origins of name 189; rating of 192–3; San Pedro Town 190
American Society of Travel Agents (ASTA) 66–7; Castro and (1959) 104; *Ten Commandments of Ecotourism, The* 66–7, 91, 209–10; World Travel Congress (1985) 148
Amman Declaration on Peace through Tourism (2000) 145–6, 153
Andean Condors 170, 171, 174, 175
Andes Mountains 171, 174, 175
Antarctic Treaty 105
APEC *see* Asia-Pacific Economic Cooperation
Artemis (goddess) 38

Asia-Pacific Economic Cooperation (APEC) 6, 8, 72, 103; Code for Sustainable Tourism 9; membership 9; "Public/ Private Partnerships for Sustainable Tourism" 9; sustainable tourism and 9, 71; Tourism Charter 9; Tourism Working Group (TWG) 9
Associated Press 81, 83
ASTA *see* American Society of Travel Agents
astrologers 41–2
Athens 37
Audubon International 187; Sustainable Communities Program 200
Augustine, St. 137
Australia 68, 148, 186, 192
aviation: impact on environment 45, 62–3; Lindbergh and development of 45, 62; supersonic jets, Lindbergh's opposition to 45, 63; *see also* airlines

Bahamas, Ministry of Tourism 9, 10
Bald Head Island Conservancy 80, 200
Bald Head Island Natural Area 200
Bald Head Island, North Carolina 200, 212
Bald Head Woods Coastal Reserve 200
Bass Pro Shops 187
Bath, John Granville, 1st Earl of 49
Batista, Fulgencio, General 107
BCE *see* Before the Common Era
beach tourism: Blue Flag Campaign and 65–6, 91; global climate change and 88; sustainability and 90, 230
Beagle, HMS 43
Becken, S.: and Hay, J. 81; and Viner, D. 83
Before the Common Era (BCE) 34; cultural tourism 36; Olympic Games

and 36; peace through travel 149–50;
see also Herodotus (485–425 BCE)
Belize: Ambergris Caye 188–93; historical
background 189; location 189; Maya
ruins and 189; National Geographic
rating 192; pollution and 189; tourism,
economy and 189
Belize Barrier Reef 189, 190, 192, 193
Bensusen, Sally 15
Big Cedar Lodge, Missouri: Dogwood
Canyon Nature Park and 187; marketing
sustainable tourism 186–7; Ozark
Mountains and 186; Table Rock Lake
and 187; Top of the Rock golf course
and 187
bilateral tourism agreements 146–7
Bill and Melinda Gates Foundation 95
biodiversity, climate change and 221
Biodiversity Agreement 105
bird watching 118, 131, 171, 185; Andean
Condors 170, 171, 174, 175
Birkemeier, Bill 82
Black Bear Tour 124, 125
Black, Rosemary 103
Blair, Tony 149
Blue Flag Campaign 65–6, 91
Blueprint for New Tourism report (WTTC)
103
Bonsai, Philip 104–5
Boo, Elizabeth 133; Ecotourism: The
Potentials and Pitfalls 116
Borlaug, Norman 94
Brandenburger, Adam M. and Nalebuff,
Barry J. 123; Co-opetition 123
branding 162, 165, 167, 176, 186, 194;
Canada and 165, 186; Costa Rica and
186; Dominica and 186; slogans 186,
194; United Airlines and 186, 194
Brazil, economic growth 220
Breton, Raymond 25
Bricker, K. et al. 212; Sustainable Tourism
and the Millennium Development
Goals 103
Britain, Dominica and 25–6
British Columbia, Canada 181
British Empire, emancipation of slaves
(1834) 26
British Virgin Islands 164, 165
Brundtland Commission 65

Brundtland, Gro Harlem 65
Brundtland Report (1987) 62, 64, 65,
90, 142
built tourism environment 62, 197, 227;
management of 204; warning sign,
sustainability and 204–5
Bureau of Ocean Energy Management
200
Byzantine Empire 39

California 118, 124
Calvia, Mallorca 230
Cambyses, King of Persia 37
Canada: branding, Canada, Keep
Exploring 165, 186; British Columbia,
tourism planning and 181; "Code of
Ethics and Guidelines for Sustainable
Tourism" (1992) 67–8; Cuba, tourism
and 105, 108; Gwaii Haanas National
Park Reserve 186; Haida Heritage Site
186; Hotel and Restaurant Association
181; National Parks Act (1930) 67;
National Round Table on the
Environment and the Economy 68;
national tourism vision 133; Nature
and Outdoor Tourism Ontario 129;
Parks Canada 133; sustainable tourism
and 91, 133, 148; sustainable tourism,
strategic planning and 165; Tourism
Industry Association of Canada 68;
Tourism is Your Business: Marketing
Management 181
Canadian Tourism Commission 165;
Corporate Plan Summary (2015–19)
161, 165
Cape Hatteras National Seashore
Recreation Area 86
Cape Town Declaration on Responsible
Tourism 16
Cape Town, South Africa: conference
(2002) 16; Responsible Tourism Policy
16–17, 180, 193
Cape Verde, Republic of 201
Caribbean Islands 21–2; Anguilla 23;
French colonies in 25; Greater Antilles
24; Guadeloupe 21, 25; Lesser Antilles
22; marketing 29; Martinique 21, 25;
ratings in National Geographic Traveler
23; Saint Kitts and Nevis 23; Saint

Vincent and the Grenadines 23, 164, 166; *see also* Ambergris Caye, Belize; Belize; Belize Barrier Reef; Dominica, Commonwealth of; Kalinago Ecotourism Project

Caribbean Sea 24–5

Caribbean Tourism Organization (CTO) 6, 8, 9–10, 72, 103; conferences 10; report (2015) 23; sustainable tourism and 71; tourism authorities and 9–10; tourism statistics 23; tourism to Belize 189; tourist arrival statistics 108; vision and purpose 9

Carnival Cruise Ships 105

Carolina 47–8; Bath, County of 49; Bath, Town of 49; Charles Town (Charleston) 47, 48, 52; colony of 52; division into North and South 52; Lords Proprietors of 47, 49, 52, 55; New Bern established 55; South Carolina 47, 48, 52, 207; Tuscarora War 52; Yamasee War 52; *see also* Lawson, John; North Carolina; North Carolina Outer Banks

carrying capacity 62, 72, 85, 90, 199, 212; definition 199; environmental impact assessment (EIA) and 180, 193

Carson, Rachel, *Silent Spring* 63, 91

cartography 40

Casas, Batolomé de las 106

Castro, Fidel 104, 105, 107

Castro, Raul 107

CE (Common Era) 24, 34

Ceballos-Lascuráin, Héctor 13, 42, 44, 208

CEC *see* Commission for Environmental Cooperation

Center for Responsible Travel 17, 103; report (2015) 132

Center for Sustainable Destinations 103, 191

Charles, Eugenia 26

Charles I, King 52

Charles II , King 47, 52

China: economy of 220, 225; Manzi province, horoscopes and 41–2; Marco Polo's journey to 39–40

Citizen's Advisory Committee on Environmental Quality 46

City of Cape Town *see* Cape Town, South Africa

Cleary, Kristin, *Native American Wisdom* 34

Clemens, Samuel (Mark Twain) 138

climate change: beach tourism and 88; biodiversity and 221; coastal areas and 86, 201, 230; droughts 82; economic impact of 83; floods 82; forest fires 82; global warming and 81, 212, 216, 221; greenhouse gas emissions and 221; human activities and 221; hurricanes and 81, 82, 83, 85, 221; IPCC and 83; islands and 201; Kyoto Protocol 105; NASA Global Climate Change Report 220–1; NOAA, "State of the Climate in 2014 Report" 221; North Carolina Outer Banks and 80–4; sea levels, rise in 81, 221; sustainable tourism and 12, 201; tourism industry and 80–3, 88–9, 90, 201–2, 220–1; tsunamis 82

Clinton, Bill 17–18, 148

Club of Rome, *Limits to Growth, The* report 63

clustering 123–4, 134

coastal erosion, North Carolina and 81, 83, 86, 87

coastlines: Calvia initiative 230; climate change and 230; cultural tourism and 231–2; economic growth and 229; flora and fauna 229; goals and objectives of management 229; growth of coastal tourism 229; impact of tourism on 230–1; measures/standards of sustainable tourism 228; sustainable tourism as a development strategy 227–2; wildlife viewing and 229

Cold War 140, 152

Columbia Charter (1988) 142, 144–5

Columbus, Christopher 40; Cuba and 105–6; Tainos, cruel treatment of 106; voyages of 24–5

Commission for Environmental Cooperation (CEC) 71–2

Common Era (CE) 24, 34

community-based tourism (CBT) 99–100; case study 100; definition 99–100

competition/competitiveness 4; sustainability and 181, 183; *see also* coopetition

Condor Lodge Ecotourism Project, Peru 170–6; Andean Condors and 171, 174; Andes mountain range 174; Antilla (village) and 174; Apurimac River Canyon and 174; defining ecotourism in relationship to 172–3; environmental impact and 175; evaluation as an ecotourism destination 175–6; flora and fauna of the area 174; languages spoken 174; location of 174–5; marketing campaign, need for 175–6; Quechua language and 174; Sierra region and 174; sustainability and 172, 175; TIES principles and 173, 177; topography of the area 174

Connell, Joanne 230

conservation 12, 13, 14, 17, 26, 72, 209–10; Cape Town and 180; Carson, Rachel and 63; Cuba and 105; IUCN and 45, 63, 209; Lindbergh and 45–6, 62, 63; Morris and 187; nature tourism and 116, 117; of resources 16, 69, 158, 161; see also Nature Conservancy

Contentnea Creek, North Carolina 212; description of 210; development potential 211; economic development, ecotourism and 211; ecotourism and 206–7, 211; Grifton community 210–11; heritage tourism and 207–8; mapping and analysis of 210

Coolidge, John Calvin 44

cooperation, at local level 4

Cooperative Research Centre for Sustainable Tourism 65

coopetition: concept of 4, 134, 182; definition 123; management of sustainable tourism and 202–3; partnerships and 202–3, 212; strategy for managing sustainable tourism 202; sustainable rural tourism development and 123–4; sustainable tourism management and 202–3

Coronado, Francisco Vásquez de 127, 131

Costa Rica: branding 186; ecotourism destination 66; mission statement 163; vision statement 163

Covington, R. et al. 88

Cromwell, Oliver 47, 52

CTO see Caribbean Tourism Organization

Cuba 104–11; American automobiles and 109; Batista dictatorship 107; British occupation of Havana 106; building restoration, need for 105; Canadian tourists and 105; Castro, Fidel and 104–5, 107; Columbus and 105–6; conservation/environmental policy 105; cruise ships and 105; culture 109; economic decline 105; economics of tourism 108; European tourists and 105; Helms-Burton Act (1996) 107; independence and 107; international environmental agreements and 105; literacy rate 109; Mesoamerican tribes and 106; Old Havana 105; rebellions 107; Spanish colonization of 106; sustainable tourism and 108–9, 111; Tainos 106; tourism and 104–5; tourism arrivals (2014) 108; trade embargo, U.S. and 107; UNESCO sites and 109–11; United States and 106–7; U.S. citizens and 104–5, 107; U.S. relations with 107–8; USSR and 105

Cuban Revolution (1953–59) 104, 107

Cuban-American relations 105

cultural heritage: definition 78; groups of buildings 78; monuments 78; sites 78; UNESCO and 78

cultural and heritage tourism 17–18; NTHP and 76–7

cultural tourism 17–18, 19, 74, 76; benefits of 231; coastlines and 231–2; definition 17, 18, 36, 76, 77; Greeks, eight century BCE and 36; Herodotus and 36–9; NTHP and 17, 76–7; UNESCO World Heritage program and 76; United States and 17–18; see also heritage tourism

cuneiform writing, invention of 34

Curtis, Charles 127

Cusco (Cuzco), Peru 171, 174, 175; Inca heritage and 171; UNESCO World Heritage Site 171

Daily Reflector 83

D'Amore, Louis 137, 139, 152, 217

Darwin, Charles 46; Beagle, HMS and 43; circumnavigation of the globe 43; ecotourism and 42–4; finches,

study of 43; Galapagos Islands and 43; Humboldt's book and 43; *On the Origin of Species* 43, 57; study of bird life 43; *Voyage of the Beagle, The* 43, 57
Descartes, René 33
desert travel: Marco Polo and 40–1; mirages and 40–1
destinations: advantages of good planning 161; brand image and 162; criteria for rating 74; good tourism planning and 161; planning goals 165; sustainability surveys 74
destinology 175
DiCaprio, Leonardo 122, 134
diplomatic relations, Vienna Convention on 147
Dixson, Bob 122
Dogwood Canyon Nature Park 187
Dominica, Commonwealth of: advertising and 23; African slaves, importation of 25, 26; airports/air service 23; anthem 22; Antillean Creole language 22; Arawaks 24; beaches and 22; Boiling Lake (hot spring) 22; branding 186; Britain and 25–6; Calibishie area 22; capital city, Roseau *21*, 22; Caribs 20, 24; carnival-festival celebrations 22; case study 19–29; Catholic religion and 22; Ciboney 24; climate 22; coastal waters, fish life and 22; Columbus and 25; diversification, need for 29; Dominican Creole 22; ecotourism and 14, 23–4, 26–7; Ecotourism Lodge *13*; France and 25–6; French language 22; geothermal-volcanic activity 22; history and heritage of 24–6; hot spring 22; hurricanes and 22; independence and 26; Kalinago Territory (reservation) 20; Kalinagos 19, 20, 22, 24, 25; Kokoy native language 22; languages spoken 22; Leeward Island English-Creole 22; location of 21; map of *21*; Morne Trois Pitons National Park 27; "motto" for 22; national bird 22; nature island of the Caribbean 20–2; nature tourism and 23; niche markets and 29; population of 22; rating in *National*

Geographic Traveler 23; "Real Mas, The" 22; rivers, number of 22; Roseau (capital city) *21*, 22; Sisserou parrot 22; size of 22; Spanish explorers and 25; tourism statistics 23–4; tropical rainforests 22; UNESCO World Heritage Site 27; Waitikubuli, meaning of 25; word-of-mouth advertising 23
Dominican Republic 108
Dubrovnik, Croatia 17

e-commerce, tourism and 222–3
Earhart, Amelia 44, 79
Earth Council, *Agenda 21 for the Travel and Tourism Industry* 70–1
Earth Summit (1992) 65
East Carolina University: Center for Geographic Information Science 210; Center for Sustainability, Natural Resources, and the Built Environment 84, 86, 198, 205; Master of Science in Sustainable Tourism program 84, 205, 218; *Pledge to Travel Green* 205–6, 212
Ebola scare (2014) 225
ecological capacity 217
ecological footprint 217
economic benefits 11, 18, 158, 216; *see also* employment
Economic Research Associates, rural tourism study (1989) 119–21
ecotourism 13–14, *19*, 72, 208–10; ASTA guidelines 66–7, 209; authenticity and 173; benefits of 206; Darwin, Charles and 42–4; definitions 13–14, 26, 42, 44, 71–2, 172–3, 208–9; destinology and 175; education and 173; International Year of Ecotourism (2002) 74; Lindblad Expeditions and 117; Nature Conservancy and 209; Peru and 171–2; principles of 66–7; *Ten Commandments of Ecotourism, The* (ASTA) 66–7; TIES ecotourism principles 14, 26, 173, 208–9; UNEP and 98; World Conservation Union definition 209; *see also* Bald Head Island (BHI), North Carolina; Condor Lodge Ecotourism Project, Peru; Contentnea Creek, North Carolina; Costa Rica; Dominica, Commonwealth of; Kalinago

Ecotourism Project; Maho Bay Resorts; San Blas Islands, Panama

Ecotourism Lodge, Kalinago Territory, Dominica *13*, 20, 27, *28*; Kalinagos and 20, 27

Ecuador, Galapagos Islands 43

Edgell, David L., Snr 167, 172, 196–7; Ambergris Caye tourism and 188, 191; Contentnea Creek 206, 210; *Coopetition: Global Tourism beyond the Millennium* 123, 182, 202; coopetition and 123, 203; definition of sustainable tourism 78; *et al.* 82, 183; and Haenisch, R. 123, 182, 202; international governmental organizations and 6; *International Tourism Policy* 11, 94, 139, 149; and McCormick, Carolyn E. 79; *Managing Sustainable Tourism: A Legacy for the Future* 12, 61, 78, 90; planning and management 158, 181; ratings, *National Geographic* and 192; rural environments 99; rural tourism articles 123; strategic marketing plan *184*; "Strategic Marketing Planning for the Tourism Industry" 167; sustainability of tourism 126; sustainable tourism guidelines 203–4; "Sustainable Tourism Prescriptions for Success" 228; and Swanson, Jason R. 19, 101, 138, 140, 144; *Tourism Policy: The Next Millennium* 99; *Tourism Policy and Planning: Yesterday, Today, and Tomorrow* 19, 82, 101, 138, 140, 144, 221; "Travel and Tourism, the Language of Peace" 148; *Worldly Travelers, The* 196

educational institutions, tourism courses and 10, 84, 205, 218

Edwards, R. *et al.*, "Connecting Communities to the Tourism Supply Chain" 100

Egypt 17; Bubastis city 38; early visitors to 35; festivals/religious gatherings and 37–8; Herodotus' journey to 37; Nile River 37, 38; Persian King Cambyses and 37; pyramids and 17, 35, 37, 38, 171

Egyptian culture, Herodotus and 35, 36, 37–8

Egyptians: boat-building and 35; travel and 35

Eisenhower, Dwight David 151, 152, 154

Eisenhower, Mary Jean 151

Eliot, T.S. 170

employment: in Cuba 108; ecotourism projects and 172; LDCs, tourism and 97; poverty alleviation and 100, 101; tourism and 5, 99, 100–1, 108, 145, 215, 216; women, tourism employment and 97, 100, 101

environment: American travelers and 74; Blue Flag Campaign 65, 66; Brundtland Commission and 65; Brundtland Report (1987) 62, 64, 65; impact of aviation on 45, 62–3; international agreements 105; pesticides/chemicals, impact of 63; "red flags" in 1960s 63; UN conference (1972) 63; UN conference (2002) 65, 67

environmental impact assessment (EIA) 180, 193

Environmental Modification 105

Environmental Protection Agency 63

Environmental Protection Award (1978) 64

Europe: Blue Flag Campaign 65; Cuban tourism and 105; sustainable tourism and 68

European Commission 8, 128

Exeter University Business School 230

experiential tourism: Baby Boomers generation and 131; case study 127–33; component of sustainable travel 132–3; definitions 129–30; Kansas Tallgrass Prairie National Preserve 130–2; marketing 131–2; Millennials (Generation Y) 131; objectives of 129–30

FEE *see* Foundation for Environmental Education

FEEE *see* Foundation for Environmental Education in Europe

FERMATA 129

Fiji, Republic of 201

Flint Hills Discovery Center 127, 128, 134; LEED Gold certification and 127

Flint Hills, Kansas 134; *Experiential Tourism Strategy for the Kansas Flint*

Hills 129; flora and fauna 130, 131;
Kansa tribe 130; Native American
cultural history 130, 131; native
grasslands 127–9; Nature Conservancy
and 128; Osage tribe 130
Flint Hills Legacy Conservation
Area 128
Fort Raleigh National Historic Site 86
Foundation for Environmental Education
in Europe (FEEE) 65–6
Foundation for Environmental Education
(FEE) 66; Blue Flag Campaign 66
France: Blue Flag Campaign (1985) 65;
Dominica and 25–6
Frangialli, Francesco, General 81
Frost, Robert 115

Galapagos Islands, Darwin and 43
Gandhi, Mahatma 94, 148
Gates, Bill 95
Genghis Khan 41
geotourism 14–16, *19*, 132; charter
principles 15–16; definitions 14–15, 39,
77; National Geographic Geotourism
Charter 15–16; target marketing and
184–5; TIA and 15, 74, 131–2
Global Code of Ethics for Tourism 7, 15
global conflicts 147, 150, 225
Global Partnership for Sustainable
Tourism 103
Global Peace Parks Program 153
Global Sustainable Tourism Council 103
Global Travel and Tourism Summit 103
global warming 81, 212, 216, 221; *see
also* climate change
Gobi Desert 40–1
Goeldner, Charles R., and Ritchie, J.R.
Brent 81, 90, 123, 160, 162, 172–3, 176;
competitiveness and sustainability 181;
market segmentation and 185;
partnerships 203; target marketing
185; *Tourism: Principles, Practices,
Philosophies* 3, 12, 123, 185, 203
golf, Top of the Rock golf course 187
Graffenried, Christoph von 55, 56, 207,
208
grasslands 128–9; European Commission
and 128; Flint Hills and 128–9;
mismanagement of water and 128

Greece: ancient Greek travelers 36;
Athens 37; conflict, city-states and 150;
cultural tourism and 36; economic crisis
and 220; Olympic Games and 36;
Olympic Truce and 150; Phoenician Star
(North Star) and 35; sporting events
and 36; travel difficulties and 150; *see
also* Herodotus
Greene, Maurice 179
Greensburg, Kansas 122; LEED Platinum
certification and 122; Master Plan
goals 122; sustainability and 134
Greensburg (TV series) 122
Griffin, Tony and Boele, Nicolette,
"Alternative Paths to Sustainable
Tourism" 70

The Hague Declaration on Tourism (1989)
143–4
Halicarnassus 37
Hall, C. Michael *et al.*, *Safety and Security
in Tourism* 102
Hamilton, Sam 83
Harvard University Business School,
Institute for Strategy and Competitive-
ness 124
Hawaii, agritourism and 118
Head, John, *Global Legal Regimes to
Protect the World's Grasslands* 128
Heath, Sir Robert 52
Helsinki Accords (1975) 140–1, 146, 152
heritage tourism 17; Contentnea Creek
207–8; definition 76; NTHP and 76–7;
see also cultural tourism
Herodotus (485–425 BCE) 17, 36–9;
Athens, visit to 37; birthplace,
Halicarnassus 37; Bubastis, celebrations
at 38; Egypt, journey to 37; Egyptian
culture and 35, 36; the "Father of
History" 37; *Histories, The* 35, 36, 37,
38, 39; Nile River and 37, 38; Olympic
Games, peace and 150; oral presenta-
tions and 36; peace through travel and
149–50; Persian Empire and 37;
Phoenicians and 35; translation
difficulties and 39
Hickel, Walter J. 46
Homer, *Odyssey, The* 36, 226
Homo erectus 33

Homo neanderthalensis 33
Homo sapiens 33
Honey, M. and Gilpin, R. 173
Hoover, Herbert 127
horoscopes 41–2
Hose, Thomas 14
Hudson, M. 208
human migration 33; the Americas and
    24; Dominica and 24
Humboldt, Alexander von 42, 46;
    *Personal Narrative of a Journey to the
    Equinoctial Regions of the New
    Continent* 42–3
Hussein, King of Jordan 146

IATC *see* Inter-American Travel Congress
IIPT *see* International Institute for Peace
    through Tourism
India: economic growth 220; National
    Rural Employment Guarantee Act 94;
    tourism and 225
indigenous peoples: Arawaks 24; Caribs
    20, 24; Ciboney 24, 106; Embera
    people 28–9; Guanajatabeys 106; Incas
    171, 174; Kuna people 28; Maori
    people 200–1; Masai tribe 45; Maya
    189, 190; Mesoamerican tribes 106;
    Tainos 106; *see also* Kalinagos; Native
    Americans
Inskeep, Edward 126; *National and
    Regional Tourism Planning* 157–8, 159,
    176, 188
Inter-American Bank 10
Inter-American Travel Congress (IATC)
    (1997) 8–9, 73; "Sustaining Tourism by
    Managing Its Natural and Heritage
    Resources" 8–9
Inter-American Travel Congress of the
    Organization of American States 8–9
Inter-Parliamentary Union (IPU) 143
Intergovernmental Panel on Climate
    Change (IPCC) 83
International Centre for Responsible
    Tourism 17
international conferences: Amman
    Declaration on Peace through Tourism
    (2000) 145–6; Columbia Charter (1988)
    142, 144–5; Conference on Security and
    Cooperation in Europe (1975) 140–1;

The Hague Declaration on Tourism
    (1989) 143–4; Helsinki Accords (1975)
    140–1, 152; IIPT and 152–3; Manila
    Declaration on World Tourism (1980)
    141–2; peace through tourism and
    140–6; Tourism Bill of Rights and
    Tourist Code (1985) 143
International Congress of Official Tourist
    Travel Associations 6
International Council of Cruise Lines
    75, 103
International Council on Monuments and
    Sites (ICOMOS) 15, 198
International Federation of Tour
    Operators 75, 103
*International Handbook on Tourism and
    Peace* 139
International Hotel and Restaurant
    Association 75, 103
International Institute for Peace through
    Tourism (IIPT) 8, 10, 103, 139–40, 144,
    152–3, 217; *Credo of the Peaceful
    Traveler* 153; mission statement 10;
    philosophy of 10; world peace summits
    145; World Symposium (2015) 137
International Labor Organization 8
international organizations, sustainable
    tourism policies and 5–10
International Society for
    Ecotourism 103
international tourism 5–6, 11; arrivals
    (2014) 5
International Union for Conservation of
    Nature (IUCN) 45, 63, 209
International Year of Ecotourism
    (2002) 74
IPCC *see* Intergovernmental Panel on
    Climate Change
Ireland, Newgrange 17
IUCN *see* International Union for
    Conservation of Nature

Jamaica Social Investment Fund 99–100
Jefferson, Thomas 106–7
John Paul II, Pope (Saint) 138, 148, 151
Jordan, Kingdom of 146
Journal of Sustainable Tourism 68
*Journal of Tourism and Peace
    Research* 138

Kalinago Ecotourism Project 20, 27–9, 224; "Aywasi" Echo Lodges 27; benefits of 27, 29; ecotourism lodge *13, 28*; Kalinago Chief's support for 20, 27; marketing of ecotourism lodges 29; precedent for 28–9; sustainable development and 29

Kalinago Territory 20

Kalinagos 19, 22, 24, 25, 27; ecotourism lodge and 20, 27; handicraft production 27

Kansas: experiential tourism and 129–30; *Experiential Tourism Strategy for the Kansas Flint Hills* 129; Flint Hills Discovery Center 127; Flint Hills of Kansas 127–9; Greensburg 122, 134

Kansas Tallgrass Prairie National Preserve 126, 128–32, 134; experiential tourism 130–1; marketing experiential tourism 131–2

Kennedy, John F. 107, 151

Kenya 45

Khrushchev, Nikita 152

Kiribati, Republic of 201

Klagenfurt University, Austria, Centre for Peace Research and Peace Education 139

Konchellah, Jilin ole "John" 45

Kotler, P. *et al.*: market segmentation 185; *Marketing for Hospitality and Tourism* 180, 193; marketing plan 188

Kublai Khan 41; Marco Polo and 40, 41; sustainable environment and 41; Yan dynasty and 40

Kyoto Protocol 105

Lane, Bernard 115, 116

languages: in Dominica 22; Native Americans and 55; in Peru 174; UNWTO official languages 7

Lawson, John 47–56; "Account of the Indians of North Carolina, An" 53–5; beasts of Carolina 51; birds of Carolina 51; Carolina, exploration of 48–9, 52, 207; Catechna Village and 207; climate of Carolina 51; *Dictionary of North Carolina Biography* 47; fish of Carolina 51; flora, fauna, native cultures of North Carolina 49–51; founder of Bath, North Carolina 49; indigenous people and 48, 50, 51; insects of Carolina 51; natural history of Carolina 50–1; North Carolina, writings on 47, 49–51, 207; Pamlico River and 48, 49, 207; plant specimens, collection of 56; Royal Society lectures and 47; settlers, recruitment of 55; Sewee Indians and 50; Surveyor General position 49, 55; torture and killing of 56, 208; Tuscarora Indians and 48, 56, 207–8

LDCs *see* least developed countries

Leadership in Energy and Environmental Design (LEED) 122, 127

least developed countries (LDCs): ecological capacity and 217; poverty alleviation, tourism and 224; safety/security and 102; socioeconomic issues 224; tourism and 97, 102, 111, 224; travel advisory lists and 102

Leeds Metropolitan University 22, 72, 74, 191

Leonidas, King of Sparta 38

Lindbergh, Charles Augustus 62; Alaskan wildlife, protection of 45–6; Citizen's Advisory committee on Environmental Quality and 46; conservation issues and 45–6, 62, 63; environment, impact of aviation on 45, 62–3; environmental issues and 63, 91; Masai tribe and 45; medals awarded to 45; Nature Conservancy and 46, 63; Philippines, indigenous people and 46; Pulitzer Prize and 45; responsible tourism and 44–6; *Spirit of St. Louis* (monoplane) 44; *Spirit of St. Louis, The* (book) 45; supersonic jets, opposition to 45, 63; transatlantic flight 44; U.S. Army-Air Force and 44–5; U.S. commercial aviation and 45; *We* 44; World War II and 44–5; World Wildlife Fund and 45, 63

Lindblad Expeditions 117, 133

Living Planet Report (2014) (WWF) 217

Long, Patrick 121

McCool, S. 173

McDonough, Megan Eileen, "Discovering Dominica" 20

Machu Picchu, Peru 171
Magellan, Ferdinand 40
Maho Bay Resorts 64–5, 66, 75–6, 91;
    development process 64–5;
    Environmental Protection Award
    (1978) 64, 208; recycled materials used
    in 65; sale of 65
Maldives, Republic of 201
Mallorca 230, 232, 233
Malta, Republic of, mission statement
    164
Manila Declaration on World Tourism
    (1980) 141–2, 143
Mansfeld, Y. and Pizam, A., *Tourism
    Security and Safety* 102
Maori people 200–1
Marco Polo *see* Polo, Marco
maritime forests: Bald Head Woods
    Coastal Reserve 200; North Carolina
    Outer Banks 80
market segmentation 184–6;
    segmentation criteria 185, 194
marketing 179–88; carrying capacity and
    180; customer research and 183;
    environmental impact assessment (EIA)
    and 180, 193; goals, sustainable
    tourism policy and 179–80; packaging
    182; partnership 182; people 182–3;
    place 182; planning 183; positioning
    182; price 182; product 182;
    programming 182; promotion 182;
    "rifle approach" to 184, 185; "shotgun
    approach" to 184; social media and 29,
    183, 223; strategic market planning
    183–4; strategic marketing plan *184*,
    187–8; sustainable tourism marketing,
    ten "P's" of 181–3, 193–4; sustainable
    tourism products and 179–88; target
    marketing 184–6; target marketing
    and 184–6; tourism policy and 179–80
Mauro, Fra, map of the world and 40
Maya: Ambergris Caye and 190; ruins in
    Belize 189
Maya Route, The (*La Ruta Maya*) 189
Medieval Period: Age of Discovery 39;
    cultural/geotourism and 39–42;
    Renaissance and 39; travels of Marco
    Polo 39–42
Mediterranean region 35

Memphis, USS 44
Mexico 190
Micronesia, Federated States of 201
Middle East region 33, 34, 37; the *Cradle
    of Civilization* 34; evolution of modern
    travel and 34; the *Fertile Crescent* 34;
    volatile conditions in 220, 225
Milesmedia 205
Miller, Marc L. 229
Minnesota, Village of Smokey Hills 120
mission statements 163–4, 176
Missouri: Big Cedar Lodge 186–7; Dog-
    wood Canyon Nature Park 187; Top of
    the Rock golf course 187
Mitchell, J. and Ashley, C. 99
money: invention of 34; Sumerians
    and 34
Mongol Empire, Kublai Khan and 40
Moore, James 47, 48
Morris, John L. 187
Morrison, Alastair: market segmentation
    criteria 185; *Marketing and Managing
    Tourism Destinations* 181, 185, 194
Mosselaer, Ferry Van de, and Duim, René
    Van der 98, 99
Moufakkir, O. and Kelly, I., *Tourism,
    Progress and Peace* 138
Mulcahy, K. 210

Napa Valley, California 118, 124
National Aeronautics and Space Adminis-
    tration (NASA) 220
National Geographic: Center for Sustain-
    able Destinations 14, 103, 191; Center
    for Sustainable Tourism Initiative 22;
    Sustainabilty Tourism Initiative 79;
    Sustainable Tourism Initiative 73, 74
National Geographic Geotourism Charter
    15–16
National Geographic (magazine) 131
National Geographic Society 15, 91
National Geographic Traveler 15, 22–3,
    91; destinations, sustainability survey
    74; Dominica's rating 23; geotourism
    and 132; geotourism study,
    sponsorship of 73–4, 131–132; North
    Carolina Outer Banks' rating 79;
    ratings criteria 22–3, 192; "Reef and
    Islands of Belize" 192

National Oceanic and Atmospheric
  Administration (NOAA) 216, 220, 221
National Park Service (U.S.) 130, 132
National Park Trust (U.S.) 130
National Parks Act (1930) (Canada) 67
*National Policy Study on Rural Tourism
  and Small Business Development*
  (1989) 119–21
National Rural Tourism Foundation
  (NRTF) 121–2
National Scenic Byway program 120–1
National Tourism Policy Act (1981) 120
National Travel and Tourism Strategy
  (U.S.) 132
National Trust for Historic Preservation
  (NTHP) 17, 76–7
Native Americans 48, 53–5, 127, 130;
  alcohol and 54; Arapaho proverbs 19,
  34; Choctaw tribe 34; Christianity and
  55; customs 53–5; dwellings/wigwams
  53; governance 54–5; Iroquois tribe 34;
  Kansa tribe 127, 130; languages and
  54–5; naming customs 53; Osage tribe
  130; prisoners of war, treatment of 54,
  56; Sewee Indians 50; sustainability
  and 34; Tuscarora tribe 48, 54, 55, 56,
  207–8; Tuscarora War 52, 55, 56;
  white/European settlers and 54–5, 207;
  Yamasee War 52
natural capital 181
natural environment 63, 197, 227;
  management of 204; strategic
  planning and 158; warning signs,
  sustainability and 204–5
naturalists 42–3
Nature Conservancy 46, 63, 103; Flint
  Hills project and 128
Nature and Outdoor Tourism
  Ontario 129
nature tourism 23, 27, 29, 72;
  development guidelines 116–17
New York Times 46, 64
New Zealand: eco-efficiency of
  sustainable tourism 68–9; Maori
  people and 200–1; sustainable tourism
  and 68–9, 148, 186, 200–1; Tourism
  Sustainability: A Discussion Paper 68–9
New Zealand Tourism Strategy (2015) 163
Newgrange, Ireland 17

niche markets 29, 169, 184, 199, 204, 232;
  see also adventure tourism; bird
  watching; ecotourism; market segmen-
  tation; nature tourism; special interest
  tourism
Noorda, Ray 202
North America, key natural and cultural
  assets 72
North American Free Trade Agreement 6,
  71, 72
North Carolina 47, 48, 49, 52; Bath
  County 49; Bath town 49; Black Bear
  Tour 124, 125; Climate Action Plan
  Advisory Group (CAPAG) 84, 85; flora,
  fauna, native cultures of 49–51;
  Lawson's writings on 47, 49–51; Rural
  Economic Development Center 210;
  Significant Natural Heritage Areas 200;
  Small Towns Economic Prosperity Grant
  210; *see also* Bald Head Island;
  Contentnea Creek; North Carolina
  Outer Banks; Pocosin Lakes National
  Wildlife Refuge
North Carolina Coastal Reserve 80
North Carolina Outer Banks: aerial
  reconnaissance of 85; Alligator River
  National Wildlife Refuge 86;
  attractions and 86; barrier islands and
  83, 85, 86, 87, 89; beach tourism,
  sustainability and 90; beachfront real
  estate, climate change and 88; Cape
  Hatteras National Seashore Recreation
  Area 86; carrying capacity and 85; case
  study of 79–90; climate 80; Climate
  Action Plan Advisory Group (CAPAG)
  and 84, 85; climate change, Atlantic
  Ocean coastline and 86; climate
  change, impact of 80–4, 86–9; climate
  change, strategic plan guidelines 89;
  climate change, tourism and 83–4, 85;
  coastal erosion and 81, 83, 86, 87, 88;
  coastal wetlands and 83, 87; dynamic
  nature of 82, 83, 85, 86, 87; economy,
  tourism and 86; fish, climate change
  and 83, 87; flora and fauna, diversity
  of 83–4; Fort Raleigh National Historic
  Site 86; future sustainability of 84;
  Hatteras Island 79–80; infrastructure,
  effects of 87; invasive species and 83;

Kill Devil Hills 80; Kitty Hawk (town) 80; "Lost Colony" area 80; maritime forests 80; *National Geographic Traveler* rating 79; Ocracoke Island 80; overbuilding and 230; Pea Island Wildlife Refuge 86; pirates and 80; policy guidelines, need for 88; pollution and 85; public health, climate change and 87; real estate, climate change and 86, 87, 88; real estate development and 83; research bodies and 82, 84, 85, 86; research, main areas of 84; Roanoke Island 80, 84; sea levels, rise in 81, 82, 83, 85–6, 89; sustainability of tourism, implications for 86–8; tourism, climate change and 83–4; tourism as economic driver 83; tourism issues, understanding 84–6; wildlife habitats, climate change and 83, 87, 88; Wright Brothers National Memorial 80, 86
North Star/Phoenician Star 35, 57
NRTF *see* National Rural Tourism Foundation
NTHP *see* National Trust for Historic Preservation

OAS *see* Organization of American States
Obama, Barack 107
Oceanic Foundation, The 63
OECD *see* Organization for Economic Co-operation and Development
O'Gorman, Kevin D., *Origins of Hospitality and Tourism, The* 35
Olympic Games 36, 150
Olympic Truce 150, 155
Organization of American States (OAS) 6, 8–9, 71, 103; *Sustainable Tourism Development Policy and Planning Guide* 73
Organization for Economic Co-operation and Development (OECD) 6, 8, 72, 103; rural tourism principles and 117; sustainable tourism and 8; sustainable tourism in rural areas 70; Tourism Committee of 8; "Tourism Policy and International Tourism in OECD Countries" 70

Our Common Future (1987) *see* Brundtland Report (1987)
Outer Banks of North Carolina *see* North Carolina Outer Banks
Oxford Economics 5, 7, 215

Pacific Asia Travel Association (PATA) 6, 9, 68; 40th Annual Conference (1991) 68; Code for Environmentally Responsible Tourism 68; Code for Sustainable Tourism 9
Page, Stephen 230; *Tourism Management* 230
Palau, Republic of 201
Panama, Republic of: Chagres National Park 28; Embera indigenous communities 28–9; San Blas Islands 28–9; sustainable tourism and 28–9
parks: Canada and 67, 133; Chagres National Park 28; Dogwood Canyon Nature Park 187; Gwaii Haanas National Park Reserve 186; legislation (U.S.) 130, 132; management guidelines 116–17; Morne Trois Pitons National Park 27
Parks Canada 133
PATA *see* Pacific Asia Travel Association
Pea Island National Wildlife Refuge 86
peace through tourism 8, 137, 138–9, 219; Amman Declaration on Peace through Tourism (2000) 145–6; in ancient times 149–50; case study 148–55; Columbia Charter (1988) 142; Conference on Security and Cooperation in Europe 140–1; global leaders and 150–1; The Hague Declaration on Tourism (1989) 143–4; Helsinki Accords (1975) 140–1, 152; international conferences and 140–6, 152–3; international organizations advocating 139–40; literature on peace and tourism 138–9; Manila Declaration on World Tourism (1980) 141–2; sustainable tourism and 147–8; Tourism Bill of Rights and Tourist Code (1985) 143; twentieth-century landmark policies on 152; *see also* International Institute for Peace through Tourism

Peace through Tourism World
Symposium 137
People to People International (PTPI)
151; Cavaliere per la Pace (Knight of
Peace Award) 151; Student Ambassa-
dor Programs 151
Persian Empire 37, 38
Peru: Antilla village 174; biodiversity and
171; Condor Lodge Ecotourism Project
170–6; Cusco (Cuzco) 171, 174, 175;
ecotourism and 171–2; Incas 171, 174;
indigenous peoples 171; Lima 171;
Machu Picchu 171; sustainability and
171–2; tourism and 170–1; UNESCO
World Heritage Site 171
pesticides/chemicals, environment
and 63
Pew Research Center report (2015) 104
Philippines 46
Phoenicians 35, 57
Pilkey, Orrin and Cooper, J. Andre, Last
Beach, The 227, 230
pirates 37, 80, 150
Pocosin Lakes National Wildlife Refuge
124–5
political disruptions, tourism and 225; see
also global conflicts
Pollard, Justin, Wonders of the Ancient
World 35
pollution 204, 230; Belize and 189; North
Carolina Outer Banks and 85
Polo, Marco (1254–1324) 39–42;
astrologers and 41–2; desert travel,
descriptions of 40–1; Gobi Desert,
crossing of 40–1; horoscopes and 41–2;
journey from Venice to China 39–40;
Kublai Khan and 40, 41; Travels of
Marco Polo, The 40, 42
Porter, Michael 124; Cluster Mapping
Project 124; Competitiveness in Rural
US Regions: Learning and Research
Agenda 124
poverty: conflicts and 154; decline of
global GDP and 155
poverty alleviation 94–5; pro-poor
tourism, MDGs and 98–9; sustainable
tourism and 12; tourism and 96–7, 224;
tourism policy and 94, 111; "Tourism
and Poverty Alleviation" report

(UNWTO) 96; United Nations and 94,
95–6, 153; UNWTO and 96–7, 153–4
prehistoric monuments 17
prehistoric period, travel and 33
pro-poor tourism (PPT): direct effects
from tourism to the poor 99; dynamic
effects on the economy 99; Millennium
Development Goals and 98–9;
secondary effects from tourism to the
poor 99
PTPI see People to People International
Putnam, George P. 44

Raleigh, Sir Walter 79
Randall, Clarence B., International Travel
report (1958) 154
recycled materials, Maho Bay Resorts
and 65
regional organizations 8, 71, 103
responsible tourism 16–17, 19; City of
Cape Town policy 180; definition 16,
44; Lindbergh and 44–6
Responsible Tourism in Destinations
Conference (2002) 16
Rifai, Taleb 137, 216
Riggs, Stanley et al. 230
Royal Society 47
rural environments: community-based
tourism and 99; planning for sustainable tourism 125–6; sustainable tourism
tour (Black Bear Tour) 124–5
rural tourism 70, 115–16, 133; adventure
tourism 124; agritourism and 117–18,
124; Black Bear Tour, North Carolina
124; clusters/cluster mapping and
123–4; coopetition and 123–4;
definition 115; international
development principles and practices
116–17; OECD report and 117; rural
populations and 116; rural tourism,
national policy study 119–21; special
interest themes 124; sustainable
tourism tour and 124–5; Tallgrass
Prairie Preserve, Kansas 126; Training
Guide for Rural Tourism Development
126; United States and 118–22, 134

safety and security, tourism and 12,
101–2, 139, 143, 219

Saint Vincent and the Grenadines 23, 164, 166
Salazar, Ken 128
Santayana, George 157
Scowsill, David 137, 216
Selengut, Stanley 64–5, 91
Seneca, Lucius Annaeus 60
Seven Wonders of the World 171
Seven Years' War 25
Seychelles, Republic of 201
slavery 25, 26
Smith Island Land Trust 200
Snider, Anthony 80
social media, marketing and 29, 183, 223
South Africa 16–17; see also Cape Town, South Africa
South America: Condor Lodge Ecotourism Project 170–6; Darwin and 43; Galapagos Islands 43; human migration to 24; Humboldt's writings and 42–3
space tourism 10
Spain: colonization of Cuba 106; see also Columbus, Christopher
Spanish-American War (1898) 107
Sparta 38
special interest tourism 115, 117, 124, 131, 171
Stevens, John 49
Stonehenge, England 17
strategic planning 4, 176; branding 162, 165, 167; Canadian tourism plan summary (2015–19) 161, 165; definition 159; external environmental scan in 169–70; goal-oriented tourism planning 164; institutional elements of 159; master plans 160, 162; mission statement and 158, 163–4, 176; planning goals 164–5; planning objectives 165–6; planning process 160–2; planning process, internal analysis 167–9; planning strategies 166; planning tactics 166; protection of natural environment and 158; SMART analysis 167, 177; strategic tourism plan implementation 166–7; sustainable tourism and 157–60; SWOT analysis 167, 177; vision statement and 158, 162–3, 176

Sumerians 34
sustainability: competitiveness and 181; concept of 125, 199; Greenburg, Kansas and 122, 134; Native American cultures and 34; natural capital and 181; Peru and 171–2; of tourism 126; tourism and 216; warning signs 204–5
sustainable development: strategic tourist plan implementation 166–7; World Summit on Sustainable Development (2002) 16, 98
sustainable environment: concepts and philosophies, development of 62–3; Kublai Khan's palace and 41; Marco Polo's description of 41
sustainable resource management 69
Sustainable Tourism Certification Network of the Americas 103
sustainable tourism 4, 19; academic research on 72; Agenda 21 for the Travel and Tourism Industry 70–1; alternative paths to (1990s) 70–1; ASTA guidelines 66–7; Australia and 68, 148; authenticity and 173; benefits of 18, 61; best practices for managing 63–5; branding and 162, 165; built environment and 62, 197, 227; Canada and 91, 133, 148; carrying capacity of the environment 62, 180, 199; challenges 12; climate change and 12, 201, 221; coastlines and 227–32; components 19, 227; cooperation, need for 4; Cuba and 108–9; customer research, marketing and 183; definitions 12–13, 71, 78, 96, 97–8, 198, 227; development, global partnerships and 102–3, 104; development, MDGs and 102–3; as a development strategy along coastlines 227–32; eco-efficiency 68–9; economic benefits and 158, 179; education and 173; environmental impact assessment (EIA) steps 180; environmental responsibility and 200; the essence of 61–2; experiential tourism as component of 132–3; a foundation for 18–19; future success of 217–18; guidelines and strategies 73–4, 203–4; issues impacting on the ability

to manage 201–2; land planning and 200; leadership in the cause of 216–17; long-term planning and 181; management, issues impacting on 201–2; management perspective and 198–9; management practices 205–6; managing in the new millennium 211–12; Manila Declaration on World Tourism (1980) 141–2; MDGs, development partnerships and 102–3; misconception about 198; mission statement 163–4; natural environment and 62, 197, 227; New Zealand and 68–9, 148, 186, 200–1; 1980s, development 65–6; 1990s, development 66–8; 1990s, new directions 68–70; 1990s, other paths to 70–1; 1990s, regional approach 71–3; PATA code 68; peace through tourism and 147–8; philosophic approach to 11; philosophies and concepts, development of 62–3; planning goals and 164–5; planning objectives 165–6; planning strategies 166; planning tactics 166; principles for 69, 228; principles and practices 197–8; public-private partnerships and 103; responsible management of 218–19; special concepts in managing 199–200; strategic goals and 158; strategic (master) plans and 160; strategic planning and 157–60; strategic planning, external environmental scan 169–70; strategic planning process 160–2, 167–9; strategic tourism plan implementation 167; strategies and guidelines 203–4; trends in 200–1; twenty-first century, guidelines for 73–4; twenty-first century, new concepts 74–7; understanding 11–12; UNEP definition of 97–8, 198; UNESCO, impact of 77–8; UNWTO concept of 208; UNWTO definition of 96; UNWTO/UNEP conceptual definition 199; vision statement, development of 162–4

Sustainable Tourism Certification Network of the Americas (STCNA) 103

Sustainable Tourism Cooperative Research Centre 162–3

Symko, Christina and Harris, Rob, "Making Paradise Last: Maho Bay Resorts" 64

Tallgrass Prairie National Preserve: experiential tourism 130–2; Kansas 126, 128–9, 130–2; marketing experiential tourism 131–2

Tallgrass Prairie National Preserve Act (1996) 128

target marketing 184–6

Teach, Edward (Blackbeard) 80

technology: impact on tourism 5; marketing, social media and 29, 183, 223; tourism and 10, 222–3

Tennessee Tourism Strategic Plan 188

Teresa of Calcutta, Mother 94

terrorism: September 11 attacks 143, 219; tourism and 143, 219

The International Ecotourism Society (TIES) 13–14, 26, 173, 206; principles of ecotourism 14, 26, 177; report (2002) 75

Thoreau, David, Walden 45

Thurot, Jean-Maurice, Economia 104

TIA see Travel Industry Association of America

TIES see The International Ecotourism Society

Tomos, R. and Elgegren, J. 171

Top of the Rock golf course 187

tourism 3, 197; advertising and 223; carrying capacity and 72, 90; climate change and 80–3, 88–9, 90, 201–2, 220–1; community participation and 72; community-based 99–100; concept of sustainability and 4; definition of 3; diversification and 72; dynamic growth, sustainability and 12; e-commerce and 222–3; Ebola scare (2014) 225; economic benefits of 11, 158, 216; economic growth and 158; economic impact of 86; elements of 4; emerging nations and 225; employment in, MDGs and 100–1; employment of women and 101; factors affecting 4; future growth of 217–18; future of 225–6; global economic recession and 220; global importance of 5; "Global Report on Women in Tourism 2010" 101; health issues and 224–5; international perspective 5–6; least developed countries (LDCs) and 97, 102, 111; local communities and 88; Millennium Development Goals (MDGs) and 100–1; natural disasters, impact of 225; nature conservation promoters and 72; non-economic benefits of 11; peace and 138–9; peace and (case study) 148–55; political disruptions and 225; population growth and 220; poverty alleviation and 96–7, 111–12; rural areas, impact in 99; safety and security 101–2, 219; security incidents and 102; social media and 223; sustainability elements in the study of 4; technology and 5, 10, 222–3; in the twenty-first century 94; weather conditions and 81; world economy and 5, 6, 148, 155, 220; world GDP and 216; world tourism issues for 2016 226

Tourism Bill of Rights and Tourist Code (1985) 143

Tourism Charter, APEC and 9

Tourism Concern 69

Tourism Industry Association of Canada 68; Code of Ethics for Tourists 133

tourism policy: bilateral tourism agreements 146–7; definition 221; Global Code of Ethics for Tourism 7, 15; global tourism issues and 222; strategic planning and 221–2

Tourism Policy and Export Promotion Act (1992) 121

tourists: Baby Boomers generation (U.S.) 131; Canada, Code of Ethics for Tourists 133; code of behavior and 143; Google and 88; international tourist arrivals 5, 215, 216, 217, 220; Internet and 88; Millennials (Generation Y) (U.S.) 131; recreational visits (U.S.) 132; safety and security of 12, 101–2, 139, 143; "10 Ways to Care" 205–6; travel alerts and 102; travel warnings and 102; weather and 88, 202

Tourtellot, Jonathan 15, 132

travel: alerts 102, 219; in antiquity 34–6; barriers and obstacles to 223–4; Egyptians and 35; evolution of modern travel 34; fees, airlines and 224; fuel price increases and 223–4; Herodotus and 35, 36, 37–8; the language of peace and sustainability (case study) 148–55; Phoenicians and 35; prehistoric period 33; restrictions 104, 105, 107, 108; right to 210; Sumerians and 34; trade routes mapped by Phoenicians 35; warnings 102, 219

Travel Industry Association of America (TIA) 15, 131–2; *Geotourism: The New Trend in Travel* 15, 74, 131–2; sponsorship of geotourism study 74

Tuscany, Italy, agritourism and 118

Twain, Mark, *Innocents Abroad, The* 138

UN Educational, Scientific and Cultural Organization *see* UNESCO

UN Environment Programme (UNEP) 8, 9, 75, 112; definition of sustainable tourism 97–98, 198; ecotourism and 98; "green economy" 97; "Industry as a Partner for Sustainable Development" 75; *Making Tourism More Sustainable* (UNWTO/UNEP) 198; 10-year Framework of Programmes on Sustainable Consumption and Production Patterns 217; "Tourism: Investing in Energy and Resource Efficiency" (2008) 97; tourism sustainability and 97–8

UN Millennium Development Goals (MDGs) 7, 95–6; employment in tourism industry and 100–1; global partnerships, tourism industry and 102–3; *Millennium Development Goals Report, The* (2011) 95–6; safety and security and 101–2; sustainable tourism development and 102–3; targets 96; tourism and 153–4

UN (United Nations) 6; Commission on Sustainable Development (1999) 71; Conference on Environment and Development (1992) 67, 142; Conference on Environment and Development (2002) 65; Conference on the Human Environment (1972) 63;

Declaration of Program of Action on a Culture of Peace 146; International Year for the Culture of Peace (2000) 146; International Year of Ecotourism (2002) 74; International Year of Peace (1986) 152; International Year of Peace (1988) 144; "Life of Dignity for All, A" (2013) 96; Millennium Summit (2000) 95, 98, 153; poverty, alleviation of 95–6; World Commission on Environment and Development 62, 64, 65; World Summit on Sustainable Development (2002) 16, 98

UN Women, "Global Report on Women in Tourism 2010" 101

UN World Tourism Organization (UNWTO) 5, 6–7, 70, 72, 81, 137, 139; *Agenda 21 for the Travel and Tourism Industry* 70–1; authenticity of host communities and 173; conferences 10; definition of sustainable tourism 96, 198; first General Assembly meeting of 6; General Assembly 7; *Global Code of Ethics for Tourism* 7, 15; global tourism policy and 152; *Making Tourism More Sustainable* (UNWTO/UNEP) 198; Manila Declaration (1980) and 142; membership 7, 96, 152; official languages of 7; partnerships 203; peace through tourism 8; poverty alleviation and 96–7, 153–4; pro-poor tourism (PPT) concept and 98; socioeconomic issues and 224; *Sustainable Tourism Development Guide for Local Planners* 70; sustainable tourism, management/partnerships and 203; Tourism Bill of Rights and Tourist Code (1985) 143; tourism growth, sustainability and 216; "Tourism and Poverty Alleviation" report 96, 154; tourist arrivals data 215; UN MDGs and 96

UNESCO 17; Cuba's sustainability 109–11; impact on sustainable tourism 77–8; World Heritage program 76

UNESCO World Heritage Sites 17, 78; Alejandro de Humboldt National Park 110; Archaeological Landscape of the First Coffee Plantations in the South-East of Cuba 109; in Cuba 109–11; Cusco (Cuzco), Peru 171; Desembarco Del Granma National Park 110–11; Dubrovnik, Croatia 17; Historic Centre of Camaguey 109; Morne Trois Pitons National Park 27; Old Havana and its Fortification System 110; San Pedro de la Roca Castle, Santiago de Cuba 110; Trinidad and the Valley de los Ingenios 110; Urban Historic Centre of Cienfuegos 110; Vinales Valley 110

Union of Soviet Socialist Republics (USSR) 105, 152

United Airlines, slogan 186, 194

United Kingdom: "Beyond the Green Horizon: Principles for Sustainable Tourism" 69; Tourism Concern 69

United States: agricultural industry 118–19, 124; Cuba and 104–5, 107–8; cultural tourism and 17–18; Department of the Interior 86; Environmental Protection Agency, establishment of 63; Green Building Council LEED Platinum certification 122; Greensburg, Kansas 122; Helms-Burton Act (1996) 107; National Park Trust 130; National Parks Service 130; National Scenic Byway program 120–1; National Tourism Policy Act (1981) 119, 120; National Travel and Tourism Strategy (2012) 132; native grasslands 126, 128; rural communities 118, 119, 120, 123; rural tourism 118–22, 123, 134; September 11 attacks 143, 219; Spanish-American War (1898) 107; Tourism Policy and Export Promotion Act (1992) 121; trade embargo, Cuba and 107; travel alerts and warnings 102; travel restrictions, Cuba and 105, 107–8; USTTA, rural tourism study 119–21

United States Agency for International Development 103

United States Fish and Wildlife Service 83, 124

United States Green Building Council, LEED certification and 122, 127

United States Travel and Tourism Administration (USTTA) 119; rural tourism

articles (Edgell) 123; rural tourism study 119–21
United States Virgin Islands 64–5, 75–6
University of Colorado, Center for Sustainable Tourism 72
University of North Carolina Coastal Studies Institute 84
University of the West Indies 10
UNWTO see UN World Tourism Organization
Urias, D. and Russo, A. 173
U.S. Corps of Engineers, Field Research Facility 84, 85
USACE Engineer Research and Development Center 82
USAIRWAYS Magazine 20
USSR see Union of Soviet Socialist Republics
USTTA see United States Travel and Tourism Administration

Vatican City 109
Venice, Republic of 39
Vienna Convention on Diplomatic Relations 147
Village of Smokey Hills, Minnesota 120
Virgin Islands: British 164, 165; United States 64, 75, 91
vision statements 158, 162–3, 176

Weaver, David and Lawton, Laura, Sustainable Tourism: A Critical Analysis 65
White House Conference on Travel and Tourism 17–18
White, John 79–80
Whitman, Walt 127

wildlife 80, 86, 124–5, 229; habitats, climate change and 83, 87, 88; see also bird watching; Black Bear Tour; United States Fish and Wildlife Service; wildlife refuges; World Wildlife Fund
wildlife refuges: Alligator River National Wildlife Refuge 86; Pea Island Wildlife Refuge 86; Pocosin Lakes National Wildlife Refuge 124–5
World Conservation Union 103, 171, 209
world economy: absence of peace and 154–5; tourism and 5, 6, 148, 155, 220
World Heritage Sites see UNESCO World Heritage Sites
World Summit on Sustainable Development (2002) 16, 98
World Tourism Organization see UN World Tourism Organization (UNWTO)
World Travel and Tourism Council (WTTC) 5, 6, 7–8, 70, 71, 103, 137; Agenda 21 for the Travel and Tourism Industry 70–1; Asia Regional Summit (2013) 148–9; Blueprint for New Tourism report 103; employment, tourism industry and 100–1; membership 7; research and 7; tourism and peace 8, 139; tourism research and 215; Tourism for Tomorrow 217; tourism, world GDP and 216; UNWTO and 7
World War II 45, 151
World Wide Fund for Nature 69, 103
World Wildlife Fund 45, 63, 116, 217
Wright Brothers National Memorial 80, 86
Wright, Orville and Wilbur 80
Wright, P. 172
WTTC see World Travel and Tourism Council